THE SOVIET CONCEPT OF 'LIMITED SOVEREIGNTY' FROM LENIN TO GORBACHEV: THE BREZHNEV DOCTRINE

The Soviet Concept of 'Limited Sovereignty' from Lenin to Gorbachev

The Brezhnev Doctrine

Robert A. Jones
Senior Lecturer and Course Leader
Department of Public Sector Administration and Law
Sheffield City Polytechnic

MACMILLAN

First published 1990

Published by
THE MACMILLAN PRESS LTD
Houndmills, Basingstoke, Hampshire RG21 2XS
and London
Companies and representatives
throughout the world

Printed in Hong Kong

British Library Cataloguing in Publication Data
Jones, Robert A.
The Soviet concept of 'limited
sovereignty' from Lenin to Gorbachev.
1. Soviet Union. Foreign relations, 1917–
1982
I. Title
327.47
ISBN 0–333–43326–2

Contents

v

List of Figures

A note on Transliteration

The US Library of Congress system of transliteration has been used for Russian names and words. Exceptions to this are conventional usages in English (e.g. Zinoviev, not Zinov'ev) and the names of authors of Soviet works published in English, since the Soviets use a different system of transliteration (e.g. Korolyòv, not Korolev): in these cases, the names are given as they appear in the works cited.

R.A.J.

1 Introduction

Until the emergence of the Peoples Democracies after the Second World War, the Soviet view of the concept of sovereignty had been shaped primarily by the USSR's experiences as a weak and insecure socialist country in a world of hostile bourgeois states and also by communist attempts to foment rebellion against imperialism in Asia and Africa. In one sense, therefore, the principle served the Soviets as a legal barrier standing 'in the path of Imperial expansion'[1] and in another as an offensive propaganda weapon, a 'slogan in national-liberation struggles in the East'[2] and in other zones of the capitalist camp. That a posture of respect for sovereignty could serve Soviet foreign policy interests was explicitly recognised by leading Soviet theoreticians in the interwar period, even by those who could acknowledge the principle's bourgeois genealogy,[3] or who could pejoratively dismiss reverence for this 'legal dogma' as a form of 'juridic fetishism'.[4] By the late 1930s, sovereignty had been elevated in Soviet doctrine to paramount status as the cardinal principle governing relations between states,[5] a position which was stridently affirmed in the early postwar period by Vyshinskiĭ,[6] Zhdanov,[7] Koretskiĭ[8] and many other Soviet statesmen and theoreticians.

In this work, however, I intend to examine Soviet attitudes towards sovereignty in a context in which the relationship between this principle and the aims of Soviet policy has been considerably less harmonious – within the Soviet bloc.[9] From the Soviet standpoint, international relations within the bloc differ from, say, the prewar situation in Eastern Europe in two fundamental respects: firstly (as a result of the West's *de facto* acceptance of Soviet determination to fill the power vacuum left in the region by the demise of Nazi Germany), the Kremlin now has the power to override the sovereignties of the bloc states without serious risk of a war with the West. Western acceptance of the 'rules of the game' which confirm Eastern Europe as a Soviet sphere of interest has been repeatedly reaffirmed in the postwar era.[10] It seems reasonable to argue, therefore, that Soviet behaviour in postwar Eastern Europe, an international arena in which the USSR possesses an unassailable preponderance of military power, constitutes one of the principal tests of the Soviet Union's entitlement to the status of a 'consistent champion of international sovereignty'[11] and of the related assertion that respect for sovereignty constitutes an inviolable principle of Soviet foreign policy.[12]

Secondly, it soon became apparent after the Hitler war that the occupied states of East and Central Europe were being forcibly transformed into socialist regimes which, with minor modifications due to variations in local conditions, were miniature models of the Soviet system. Although there was some variation in both the timing and pattern of sovietisation in Eastern Europe,[13] by 1948 Bulgaria, Romania, Hungary, Poland, East Germany and Czechoslovakia had all effectively been subjected to the Soviet policy of 'duplication'[14] – the creation of nominally independent Soviet Marxist-Leninist regimes as an alternative, or possibly prelude, to the incorporation of the states of Eastern Europe into the Soviet Federation. The assimilation of independent states into the Soviet sphere through the imposition of structural uniformity buttressed by Soviet armed force did not represent an entirely new departure in Soviet foreign policy: it had been applied for a short period, for example, by Soviet Russia (the 'RSFSR') to the independent Republics of the Ukraine, Belorussia, Armenia, Azerbaizan and Georgia prior to the enforced amalgamation of these territories into the USSR[15] and to Outer Mongolia, the Soviet regime's innermost satellite, following a Soviet invasion of this area in 1921.[16] However, prior to 1945, *de facto* annexation had been the principal Soviet method of integrating independent states into the Soviet sphere, as demonstrated by the fate of the majority of territories which had seceded from Russia after the Bolshevik Revolution.[17]

The key features of the bloc states' forced march towards Soviet socialism were the formation of bogus coalition governments; the imposition of new constitutions which, with the exception of the East German, bore an unmistakable resemblance to the Soviet 'Stalin' constitution of 1936;[18] the creation of agencies of government closely modelled on Soviet institutions; the adoption of economic programmes based on Soviet doctrines (e.g. centralised economic planning, rapid industrialisation and the collectivisation of agriculture); and (most significantly) the assumption of power by East European communist leaders, who had returned from refuge in the Soviet Union in the baggage train of the Red Army. Following the emergence of a coherent and authoritative Soviet theory of 'Peoples Democracy' in 1948,[19] Soviet pronouncements on the future pattern of political development in Eastern Europe clearly indicated that, although these fledgeling regimes were at a lower stage of development than the USSR, they were following a trail already blazed by the world's first socialist country. The East European communist parties were entrusted with an historic mission 'to lead their peoples towards socialism', guided by Soviet experience.[20] Again with the exception of East Germany (which, although viewed as 'democratic', was also officially described as still primarily bourgeois in character) these regimes were entitled 'Peoples Democracies' or 'Peoples Republics' in order to underline their status as progressive regimes of a 'mixed' character moving rapidly towards socialism.[21]

Although the Peoples Democracies were said by Soviet theorists to be at an intermediate stage of development between the 'bourgeois state and the socialist state, between capitalism and socialism',[22] it was also made clear that this situation was not immutable, since the principal tasks of the East European communist parties (the dominant force in the coalitions) were to direct and accelerate this transmutation. Soviet theoreticians acknowledged that the circumstances in which these regimes emerged differed from the experience of the Soviet state: nevertheless, Peoples Democracy was viewed as 'a form of proletarian dictatorship'.[23] Mankovskiĭ, for example, a leading Soviet legal specialist, argued that the Peoples Democracies embodied the three essential aspects of the dictatorship of the proletariat (they used state power to suppress exploiters; they sought to complete the divorce between the proletariat and the bourgeoisie and were struggling to build a socialist society through the liquidation of classes) and therefore could justifiably be regarded as socialist even though socialism had not yet triumphed completely in these countries.[24] The socialist credentials of these new regimes was also stressed by Vyshinskiĭ at the United Nations, who referred to them as 'states of the period of transition, charged with the task of developing the countries of Eastern Europe along the socialist path'.[25]

Eastern Europe's Marxist theoreticians were, therefore, confronted with a novel problem concerning the relevance of the principle of sovereignty to an exclusively socialist interstate subsystem, since the precedents for socialist international relations prior to the emergence of the Peoples Democracies hardly provided a convincing legacy of experience (Soviet theorists acknowledged that international relations within Eastern Europe were of a 'new type'[26]). By scraping the barrel of history, it is possible to identify four prior examples of 'horizontal' (i.e. international) relationships between 'sovereign' socialist entities. Firstly, we might cite Soviet Russia's tenuous relations with the ephemeral Hungarian and Bavarian Soviet Republics in 1919 (the Hungarian Soviet endured for 133 days and the Bavarian for 9). Soviet Russia's communications with these revolutionary mayflies amounted only to exchanges of fraternal greetings, Soviet promises of military aid (which could not be given because of the adverse military situation in the Ukraine) and tactical advice from Lenin and other Bolsheviks.[27] Secondly, it might be argued that relations between Soviet Russia and the independent Soviet Republics which were established in territories which once formed part of the Tsarist empire prior to the formation of the USSR also provide a precursory example of 'socialist international relations', albeit of a highly distinctive kind. Although these republics possessed the formal trappings of sovereign states and were formally free to enter into relations with other countries (and indeed actually did so[28]), they were subjected to increasingly strict control by the Moscow communist party prior to their enforced amalgamation with the RSFSR (a modern work on 'Socialist Internationalism' relegates discussion of these relations to a brief footnote).[29] A third possible example of socialist international relations prior to the Second World War was the Soviet regime's relations with the Mongolian People's Republic set up in 1921. The *de facto* status of the Mongolian Republic, however, has been somewhere between that of a constituent Republic of the Soviet Federation and an East European Peoples Democracy: the bilateral relations between the Soviet state and Mongolia prior to 1945, as Konstantinov has acknowledged, 'were not fully developed and internationally recognised, nor were they given legal force in international treaties'[30] (although the Mongolian Republic may nevertheless have served as a model for the Peoples Democracies of Eastern Europe[31]).

Fourthly, we may cite the relations between the constituent Republics of the highly centralised Soviet Federation. Sanakoyev, a prolific Soviet commentator on international affairs, denies that there is a direct analogy between the Soviet Union's internal relations and socialist international relations. Nevertheless, he acknowledges that the experience gained in the development of the Soviet Federation played a significant role in the formation of socialist principles of international relations after the Second World War. However, Sanakoyev and other Soviet commentators qualify this assertion by arguing that the Soviet Union, as a united, multinational state, exemplifies a form of relations between nations and peoples rather than between fully sovereign states[32] (although as a result of an amendment to the Soviet constitution in 1944, the 16 Republics comprising the Soviet Federation were formally transformed into externally sovereign entities with the right to establish foreign Ministries and to engage in diplomatic relations with 'other' countries).[33] The wider relevance of the Soviet experience of federalism has been an insistent theme in Soviet international relations theory: the Soviet federal model has been held up as the solution to nationality problems within states and as the ideal framework for the eventual merger of socialist countries.[34]

These highly dubious examples of 'socialist international relations' could not plausibly have been said to have provided a substantial foundation for the development of international relations within the socialist camp. Contemporary Soviet theoreticians recognise the significance of these examples (and in fact cite other influences, such as the relations between the Soviet Union and the communist regions of China from the late 1920s and relations with the Spanish Republic during the Spanish Civil War[35]) but also acknowledge that 'socialist international relations' prior to 1945 differed in quality, scope and content from the 'new type' of international relations – between fully sovereign states – which came into being only with the advent of the Peoples Democracies in Europe and Asia.[36]

But the problem of 'socialist inter-state relations' was not only novel: it is highly probable that the founders of Marxism would have regarded it as absurd. Thus although astonishingly little was written by Marx and Engels about the nature of the socialist society of the future, in their meagre and fragmentary writings on this subject they nevertheless emphasised that the coming revolution was a world revolution and that transnational class-cleavages were already undermining the *raison d'être* of state frontiers.[37] The progenitors of the Soviet Union's official creed brushed aside the whole question of relations between socialist states by assuming that, in the global political order which would come into being after the demise of capitalism, mankind would no longer be fragmented by the bonds of national sentiment or trammelled by state boundaries or other obsolete trappings of the capitalist superstructure: the horizons of Marx's and Engels's thinking were premised on the assumption that vertical conflicts between classes were of far greater historical significance than horizontal antagonism between states and that the basic unit of the international system, the state, was a phenomenon of capitalism and therefore soon to be relegated to history's museum of antiquities along with the spinning wheel and the bronze axe.[38] In Marx and Engels' causal schema, the preconditions for revolution on a world scale had already been brought into being as a result of the universal tendencies inherent in the capitalist mode of production, which were manifested in the formation of a world market (since 'the need of a constantly expanding market for its products chases the bourgeoisie over the whole surface of the globe. It must nestle everywhere, settle everywhere, establish connections everywhere'[39]); in the tendency of capitalism to reproduce itself in more or less the same form wherever it appeared – i.e. the homifience of capitalism;[40] its destructive and regenerative functions – i.e. the annihilation of pre-capitalist societies and the 'laying of the material foundations of Western society';[41] in the homogenising effect which uniformity in the mode of production had upon conditions of life in all parts of the world;[42] in the inexorable spread of capitalism to non-European zones[43] and in the emergence of class-struggle on a world-scale.[44] The capitalist mode of production, despite its European origins, was, therefore, perceived by Marx and Engels as a global phenomenon with global consequences. Furthermore, since capitalism was viewed as the rock upon which existing configurations of power in the world were built, Marx and Engels regarded it as inconceivable that the system of inter-state relations could survive the demise of the capitalist system.

Marx acknowledged that, during the transitional phase between the overthrow of capitalism and the advent of communism, it was likely that the state would survive in the form of a revolutionary proletarian dictatorship which, like any other form of dictatorship, would be an instrument used by one class to oppress another[45] (he did not predict the length of the transition period). And as Berki[46] and Kubálková and Cruickshank[47] have pointed out, Marx's conception of the future communist society is so unclear as to be open to a number of possible interpretations. Berki, for example, has argued that close textual analysis of Marx's work supports the conclusion that Marx envisaged the existence of horizontal antagonisms (and therefore of a form of international relations) even in a post-revolutionary world.[48] Kubálková and Cruickshank have discerned in Marx's writings an attitudinal shift from an 'early vision of men in an undivided world, which undoubtedly runs throughout his work and imparts a moral climax to his theories, to the gradual and reluctant, acknowledgement of the existence of some horizontal divisions even after the communist revolution'.[49] Nevertheless, the universalist tenor of Marx's work, buttressed by his assumption that 'national differences and antagonisms between peoples are daily more and more vanishing',[50] by his assertion that there was nothing immutable about international relations, which was simply 'an expression of a given division of labour',[51] and by his stated belief that the state would be abolished or transcended (in Engels's phrase it would 'wither away'),[52] has provided the theoretical underpinning for the dominant interpretation of Marx's vision of post-revolutionary society – i.e. that it would take the form of a global community (or, in a term endorsed by Engels, a 'World Republic'[53]), rather than a collection of separate, antagonistic units. The assumption that relations between states were epiphenomena of the capitalist system and therefore that global revolution would herald the end of international relations, has generally been regarded as a central tenet of classical Marxism.[54]

The paradigm of an imminent global revolution leading inexorably to a stateless world communist society which can be traced back to Marx and (especially) Engels was enthusiastically embraced by Marx and Engels's Bolshevik epigones, who freely used such terms as the 'World Soviet Republic',[55] 'World Federative Republic of Soviets',[56] 'International Soviet Socialist Republic',[57] 'World Soviet Socialist Republic'[58] or 'International Union of the Proletariat'[59] to signify a transitional stage preceding the advent of world communism. The Russian Revolution was thus viewed by the founders of Soviet socialism as merely the first skirmish in a global armageddon between the classes which would culminate in proletarian revolution on a world scale. It was, furthermore, taken for granted by the Bolsheviks that the fragmentation and disintegration of the world capitalist system would, *pari passu*, render 'international relations' obsolete as Marx and Engels had predicted. Trotsky's professed intention, when appointed Commissar for Foreign Affairs in 1917, merely to issue a few revolutionary proclamations and then shut up shop[60] is now regarded as a classical example of revolutionary chiliasm on a collision course with political reality. However, as Trotsky himself peevishly noted in his autobiography, Lenin was also wedded to the belief in the imminence of world revolution and therefore was also initially sceptical about the prospect of revolutionaries having to engage in so bourgeois an activity as foreign relations.[61] True to the predictions made by Engels about the course of the coming revolution (in the 'Principles of Communism' Engels had argued that the revolution would take place 'simultaneously in all civilised countries, that is, at least in England, America, France and Germany'[62]), Lenin assumed that the overthrow of the capitalist world would result from an international 'chain reaction' or 'domino' effect rather than via a protracted and unrelated series of national revolutions. He reflected in 1921 that, before the October revolution, and for some time after, the Bolsheviks were convinced that a revolution in Russia could not be sustained without corresponding revolutionary outbreaks (occurring 'immediately or at least very quickly') in the most advanced capitalist countries.[63] The revolutionary struggle was deemed by Lenin and the Bolsheviks to have its own expansionary dynamic, with the energy from proletarian victory in one country flowing as ineluctably as lava into the others, engulfing state frontiers in the process. It is perhaps little wonder, therefore, that in the heady first days of the Bolshevik revolution, the idea that revolutionaries would have to engage in 'diplomacy' could be dismissed as an absurd hypothesis.

Faced with the stubborn refusal of history to arrive on time and in the right places (i.e. with the failure of the revolutionary struggle in Germany, France, Britain and the United States), Lenin was forced to accept that the militarily weak and vulnerable Soviet regime would have to engage in diplomatic intercourse with capitalist states if it was to survive the menace of capitalist encirclement. However, Soviet diplomacy was regarded by him as a purely temporary expedient, pending the extension of the international revolution to the heartlands of capitalism. He regarded it as inconceivable that the Soviet regime and the capitalist world order could coexist for any length of time.[64] Furthermore, this tactical decision, dictated by the pressure of events, in no way compromised Lenin's belief that the notion of relations between fully sovereign socialist states was a contradiction in terms. Rather, he proclaimed that the aim of socialism was not only to end the division of mankind into tiny states, or to end the separation of nations, by merely drawing nations closer together ('*sblizhenie*'), but rather to integrate them ('*sliianie*').[65] He was also to reject the notion of a United States of Europe in favour of the more embracive (though still unsatisfactory) idea of a 'United States of the World', until complete communist victory brought about the final demise of the state:[66] in his view, the global revolution would result in the formation of a 'single world cooperative', operated by the world proletariat on the basis of a single plan.[67] In the 'Preliminary Draft Theses on the National and Colonial Questions' he argued that Federation of the Soviet type constituted a transitional framework leading to the complete unity of the workers of the various nations,[68] a view which was given institutional expression in the Soviet Constitution of 1923, which was said to mark a decisive step towards the 'union of all countries in the World Soviet Socialist Republic'.[69]

Given the universalist assumptions of classical Marxism-Leninism, it is hardly surprising that the creation of an 'International Soviet Republic as a transitional stage to the complete abolition of the state'[70] was the primary aim of the Comintern in 1920 or that Soviet leaders after Lenin could continue to entertain the prospect of a stateless world society, albeit as a distant goal and one which did not obtrude onto the 'operational' plane of foreign policy; even Stalin (hardly an earnest contributor to the 'withering away of the state'), could, at the 18th party congress, speak of the 'disappearance of the state' under communism (once capitalist encirclement is liquidated and replaced by socialist encirclement).[71] The prospect of the demise of the state, and with it of international relations, was also to be resurrected by Khrushchev in 1959, who asserted that the triumph of communism on a world scale would lead to the disappearance of state borders[72] (by way of illustration, Khrushchev gave the example of the declining significance of the boundaries between the Soviet Republics). Nor, therefore, should it be regarded as surprising that, over a decade before the emergence of the Peoples Democracies, a Soviet lawyer could openly admit that sovereignty was not 'in the least a socialist principle'.[73]

However, in the context of Eastern Europe after the War, Soviet and East European communists not only did not abandon the sovereignty concept on the grounds that it was inconsistent with Marxist-Leninist doctrine: on the contrary, they were insistent that mutual respect for state sovereignty was a central feature of international relations within the socialist camp. Soviet affirmations of the sovereignty principle within the context of socialist international relations took several principal forms in the early postwar years: firstly, through attempts to invest the principle with doctrinal legitimacy by cleansing it of its bourgeois associations and by providing it with a theoretical basis in Marxism-Leninism; secondly, through polemical assaults on contemporary Western prognoses concerning the obsolescence of sovereignty; thirdly, through implacable hostility to any suggestion that participation in international organisations involved any limitation upon sovereignty: fourthly, through attempts to insulate the socialist camp from Western penetration (which, in Soviet doctrine, constituted a dire threat to the sovereignty of the

Peoples Democracies); fifthly, the principle was given legal force in the matrix of bilateral treaties signed between the Soviet Union and the Peoples Democracies in this period; sixthly, through 'echo diplomacy' – i.e. the leaders of the Peoples Democracies reiterated Soviet statements concerning the pristine quality of state sovereignty within the camp of socialism; seventhly (and perhaps most fundamentally) in the role claimed by the Soviet Union in the restoration and defence of the sovereignties of the states of Eastern Europe.

Far from withering away, state sovereignty was said by Soviet theoreticians to be reaching the full flower of its development within the socialist camp, which was said to provide the natural soil for this process of efflorescence. The emergence of the Peoples Democracies and the reorientation of the foreign policies of the states of Eastern Europe convincingly testified to the fact that 'sovereignty and democracy, just as sovereignty and socialism, are mutually enriching'.[74] Soviet affirmations of the principle of state sovereignty were said to derive not from considerations of *realpolitik* or tactical expediency but from the very nature of the Soviet system.[75] Soviet attempts to bestow a Marxist pedigree upon the principle of sovereignty also involved a repudiation of the idea that bourgeois regimes could ever be sovereign in the true sense, since it was deemed inconceivable that an attribute as laudable as sovereignty could be the common property of socialist and bourgeois states. The difference between the bogus sovereignty of bourgeois states and the genuine sovereignty of socialist countries was said to be the difference between form and content.[76] Soviet theoreticians insisted that only in a socialist regime is sovereignty invested with real meaning, since a country in which the proletariat were under the yoke of the bourgeoisie could not properly be described as fully sovereign[77] (this theory had been espoused by Pashukanis in the interwar period, when he had argued that, only in the Soviet state, 'where power belongs to the workers, does sovereignty . . . exist'[78]). In capitalist states, sovereignty was simply a mask to disguise the class supremacy of the bourgeoisie. The sovereignty of socialist states, on the other hand, was a genuine 'peoples sovereignty' which was said to account for the non-aggressive nature of Soviet foreign policy, since in the USSR there were 'no classes or groups interested in foreign expansion or the pursuit of aggressive policies'.[79] The Soviet state, therefore, had no territorial designs on other countries.

Nor did Soviet writers concede that their assertion of an umbilical relationship between sovereignty and socialism represented a departure from orthodox Marxist doctrine: indeed, it was insisted that the principle of sovereignty was a fundamental aspect of the Marxist theory of the state.[80] The socialist character of the sovereignty principle derived from the fact that the behaviour of communists was guided by the principle of proletarian internationalism, a concept which Soviet theorists derive from the 'Communist Manifesto'. Thus the assertion by Marx that the workers 'had no country' has been interpreted as meaning that the proletariat had first to acquire political supremacy by becoming the ruling class within a state before it could be said to possess a country of its own. It was for this reason that the communist parties, guided by the principle of proletarian internationalism, were the most resolute champions of the sovereignty of their nations.[81] The clearest example of this was said to be the 'new, higher type of patriotism' which existed in the Soviet Union.[82] Therefore, within the camp of socialism sovereignty was reaching the apogee of its development. Even the slightest departure by Soviet theorists from the new orthodoxy concerning the inviolability of the sovereignty principle was likely to incur the wrath of their colleagues. Thus in 1948 I. D. Levin was castigated by his fellow legal theoretician Korovin for reiterating (in a major work on the subject) the classical Marxist orthodoxy that sovereignty was a transitory phenomenon and would eventually die out.[83] Other Soviet scholars were criticised by Vyshinskiĭ for failing to define the term sovereignty with sufficient rigour.[84]

The argument that only socialist states are (or ever can be) fully sovereign represents a considerable shift from the view of Ratner mentioned above and from the tenets of classical Marxism. Nevertheless, insistence upon the organic connection between sovereignty and socialism has been a central theme of Soviet international relations literature in the postwar period and constitutes a central pillar of the Brezhnev Doctrine of 'limited' socialist sovereignty (a contemporary Soviet scholar could affirm that Marx emphasised the necessity of respect for sovereignty in international relations).[85] Instead of being relegated to the museum of antiquities, the sovereignty principle was refurbished, anointed with doctrinal legitimacy and set in place as a central feature of international relations between socialist countries.

Secondly, the Soviet Union's 'zealous guardian' role in relation to the principle of national sovereignty was demonstrated by means of polemical asaults on the 'cosmopolitan' ideas concerning the obsolescence of sovereignty emanating from the West (pejoratively termed 'mondialism' by the Soviets). The targets of these polemics were both academic scholars – dismissed by Zhdanov in this context as 'bourgeois intellectual cranks and pacifists'[86] – and prominent Western statesmen, such as Eden and Bevin, who had advocated a supranationalist solution to the danger of international conflict and who wished to provide the UN with real teeth.[87] Thus Frantsev dubbed Cobban, Kohn, Hertz and Toynbee as pedlars of theories of limited national sovereignty for suggesting that the age of nation-states was drawing to a close.[88] Terms such as 'regionalism', 'continentalism' and 'universalism' were simply a 'cloak to cover the expansionist and aggressive policies of Imperialist powers' and were at odds with the principle of national sovereignty.[89] According to Chizhov, Western academic sociologists, economists and jurists were intensifying their propaganda for a world government by suggesting that in order to prevent a world war, it was necessary to renounce national sovereignty.[90] The philosopher Aleksandrov attacked the English author Compton for suggesting that the advent of nuclear weapons necessitated a move towards world government: thus 'under the guise of internationalism and the prospect of a third world war, bourgeois scholars have launched a drive for world government which is really a drive for imperial expansion and world mastery'.[91] Proposals by American jurists to strengthen the UN were simply cosmopolitan formulas for undermining the sovereignties of states and demonstrated that American legal doctrine was serving the American drive for world supremacy.[92] Korovin argued that 'instead of putting into practice the progressive principles of equality and self-determination, . . . the post-war official doctrine and international practice [of the West] is, conversely, towards maximum limitation and liquidation of the idea of sovereignty'.[93] Elsewhere he strongly objected to a statement by Eden in the British parliament that, as a result of the invention of the atomic bomb, there was no other way of protecting the world from atomic energy than 'a rejection of our present conception of sovereignty' and to a speech by Foreign Secretary Bevin in the same parliamentary debate, in which he had advocated that the UN should be invested with the power to make 'world laws' which would be binding on governments.[94] Korovin regarded such statements as blatant pieces of supranationalist kiteflying and dubbed Eden and Bevin 'the gravediggers of sovereignty'.[95]

Soviet participation in the formation and early development of the various organisations of the United Nations also brought the Soviet

Union's obsessive zeal in defence of the sovereignty principle to the fore. At the General Assembly, Vyshinskiĭ assailed Western statesmen for seeking to transform the UN into a supranational organisation by espousing 'false and reactionary theories based on the view that international cooperation necessitated the negation of state sovereignty'.[96] Similarly, Koretskiĭ, the Soviet representative to the International Law Commission in 1949, attacked the Commission's 'Draft Declaration on the Rights and Duties of States' on the grounds that 'in the draft declaration the true sense of sovereign equality had been distorted and deprived of meaning' because it had omitted reference to the word sovereignty and had referred only to the 'independence' of states, which was a dilution of the meaning of sovereignty.[97] Koretskiĭ argued that this glaring omission reflected a general trend in the General Assembly and other organs of the UN away from commitment to this principle. Koretskiĭ pointed out that the principle of sovereign equality was a cornerstone of the UN and was included in its Charter: at San Francisco the representatives had insisted upon the retention of the word 'sovereign', stating that 'the important principle was not merely the equality of members but the sovereign equality of nations. That qualification was vital for the protection of their political independence and territorial sovereignty. For states, in order to be equal, they must be sovereign and in order to be sovereign they must be equal'.[98] The draft declaration, therefore, did not protect states from 'intervention in purely domestic matters by international organisations or groups of states'.[99]

The danger to the sovereignties of the European countries posed by the Anglo-American military and economic blocs was also an insistent theme of Soviet statesmen and commentators in this period. Thus the 'Benelux', the Franco-Italian Customs Union, the Western Union, the Organisation for Economic Cooperation and the North Atlantic Pact are each 'landmarks on the road to complete liquidation of the sovereignties of the Western European peoples',[100] developments made possible by 'the treachery of the ruling plutocratic oligarchies and their right-socialist helpers, serving the interests of American monopolies striving for the political and economic enslavement of the peoples of the world'.[101] NATO – 'the supreme embodiment of the Anglo-American war machine' – was said to be the latest achievement of these groups in their aim to liquidate the sovereignties of their countries.[102] Moreover, in their struggle against the Marshall Plan, the communist parties of East Europe were 'courageously defending the national independence and sovereignty of their countries'.[103] The American contempt for sovereignty was also demonstrated by the development of new bourgeois doctrines of intervention, as manifested in the transformation of the Monroe Doctrine into an aggressive theory justifying American expansion.[104]

As a principle governing relations between socialist states, sovereignty was also given legal force in the matrix of bilateral treaties signed between the Soviet Union and the Peoples Democracies in this period. Each of these treaties of mutual assistance (which were signed not only between the USSR and the Peoples Democracies but also between the Peoples Democracies themselves) enjoined the signatory states to base their mutual relations upon strict respect for the principle of sovereignty and non-interference. Mutual assistance treaties were signed by the Soviet Union with Czechoslovakia (December 1943), Yugoslavia and Poland (April 1945), Hungary and Romania (February 1948) and Bulgaria (March 1948). Eastern Germany was not given 'full sovereignty' until 1954 and therefore was left out of the European treaty system. The treaties were applauded by Soviet commentators as shining examples of the Soviet Union's profound respect for the sovereignty of all peoples and states[105] and as tangible expressions of the new and higher form of international relations which was emerging between sovereign states within the socialist camp.[106] Zhdanov cited these treaties as proof of his assertion that treaties with the USSR were mutually advantageous and 'never contain anything that encroaches on the national independence and sovereignty of the contracting parties'.[107]

East Europeans were left in no doubt as to whom they should be grateful for the gift of sovereignty. As early examples of Soviet bloc 'echo diplomacy' we can cite Dragoĭcheva's declaration that, thanks to the Soviet Union, Bulgaria is 'an independent sovereign state, able to develop its economy and culture in accordance with its own wishes';[108] or Gheorghiu-Dej's assertion that Romanian-Soviet collaboration had played 'a decisive role in securing Romanian national sovereignty'.[109] The principle of sovereignty was also assigned a central place in Soviet conceptualisations of the 'new type' of international relations emerging within the socialist camp.[110] Soviet commentators insisted that the Soviet Union's role as a champion of sovereignty was not confined to the socialist camp: thus outside this sanctuary of genuine sovereignty and independence, the very existence of smaller powers was under threat from the USA and Britain, which were said to have entered a new phase of aggression and expansion. Therefore, the USSR was a 'resolute champion of the independence and sovereignty of Greece, Korea, Indonesia and all countries menaced by imperialist aggression'.[111]

These ideas hinged upon the assumption of superordinate roles for the Soviet Union in relation to the socialist camp: firstly, system boundary roles: 'boundary spanning' – responsibility for the camp's relations with the West: 'boundary maintenance' – defence of the camp against Western aggression; 'boundary extension' – responsibility for promoting the growth of the camp; and 'boundary definition' – responsibility for defining the criteria for camp membership; secondly, leadership roles within the system: responsibility for the direction, coordination and supervision of member states. Each of these roles had implications for the sovereignty of the states within the camp. The Soviet Union's rapid transformation of Eastern Europe into a tightly coupled, closed system was based on an unequal and unidirectional form of 'coupling', in which influence was expected to flow from the Soviet Union to the bloc states but not vice versa: thus the bloc states were required to synchronise their foreign and domestic policies with those of the Soviet Union. The socialist camp was not, however, a closed system for the Soviet Union, which, through its 'system boundary' roles, was free to develop outside contacts.

The Soviet conception of sovereignty in relation to the camp of socialism in the early post-war years can be summarised as follows:

1. the Peoples Democracies were fully sovereign and independent states;
2. the Soviet Union had restored the sovereignties of the East European countries by destroying Nazism;
3. the Soviet Union was the sentinel and guarantor of the sovereignties of the East European states, through its power to ward off imperialist aggression;
4. the communist parties of Eastern Europe were the most zealous defenders of the sovereignty of their countries;
5. the world was split into two antagonistic camps, the imperialist camp (the enemy of genuine 'peoples sovereignty') and the socialist camp: in effect, the camp of socialism constituted a form of 'bloc sovereignty', zealously defended by the USSR;
6. the Peoples Democracies were genuinely sovereign (i.e. sovereign in content as well as in form), in that they were forms of proletarian dictatorship. Conversely, the sovereignty of capitalist states was a juridic camouflage for the class supremacy of the bourgeoisie;
7. the bourgeoisie of Western Europe were eagerly participating in

the liquidation of the sovereignty of their countries, in two ways: firstly, through the 'sale' of their countries to the American monopolies; secondly, through their commitment to cosmopolitan plans for European Union;

8. the USA and Britain were striving for Anglo-Saxon hegemony over the world and therefore constituted a threat to the sovereignties of smaller powers: the imperialists were using military, political and economic instruments to undermine and liquidate the sovereignties of other states;

9. the Soviet Union rejected *carte blanche* Western theories concerning the 'obsolescence' of sovereignty and repudiated any suggestion that participation in international organisations necessitated the restriction of state sovereignty;

10. new forms of international relations were developing within the socialist camp, based on genuine respect for sovereignty and guided by the principle of proletarian internationalism.

Two basic themes underlie these ideas: firstly, the indissoluble link between sovereignty and socialism: the sovereignty of the East European states depended upon maintenance of communist party rule, socialist construction on the Soviet model and close alliance with, and support for, the Soviet Union; secondly, the need for ideological vigilance against the internal and external enemies of socialism: externally, there was the constant danger of 'Western penetration and infiltration'.[112] Lenin had once scoffed at the Western bourgeoisie's mortal fear of 'ideological infections' emanating from the weak and vulnerable Soviet state:[113] in the postwar era, the Soviets have exhibited a similar concern about Eastern Europe's vulnerability to 'ideological infections' emanating from the West. Internally, the danger came from the counter-revolutionary aspirations of residual bourgeois-nationalist elements and deviations from the Soviet model. Despite the triumphalist tone of Soviet writing on Eastern Europe in the early postwar period, the possibility of capitalist restoration in the region was recognised by Kuusinen in 1948: thus he argued that if a country at the intermediate stage of development does not rapidly 'move toward socialism, it will revert back to capitalism':[114] in particular, he argued, the 'tenacity' of capitalism's roots in peasant economies could not be underestimated. Although the replacement of capitalism by socialism was inevitable 'as a result of the operation of the inexorable laws of social development', this process was not 'spontaneous or automatic', since it depended upon the guiding role of the communist parties and upon close cooperation of the Peoples Democracies with the Soviet Union.[115] In the terminology of modern Soviet commentators, therefore, the success of socialism depended upon a combination of 'objective' and 'subjective' factors. These ideas continue to form the core of the Soviet doctrine of 'socialist' sovereignty (with the exception that in the early postwar years the Kremlin had no need to add nullifying riders concerning the ability of the East European states to exercise their sovereign rights).

This study traces the Soviet Union's response to challenges to its conceptualisation of 'socialist' sovereignty and seeks to shed light upon several key aspects of Soviet foreign policy: firstly, upon the Soviet Union's essentially dualistic, or 'bi-axial' perspective on international relations. The Soviet doctrine of sovereignty has traditionally rested upon two axes: upon 'legal-positivist' conceptions, derived from Western political thought and enshrined in the general principles of international law; and upon the verticalist notion of 'proletarian internationalism', based upon Soviet interpretations of classical Marxist-Leninist doctrine: the 'legal positivist' axis reflects the Soviet Union's obsessive concern about interference in its internal affairs; the 'proletarian internationalism' axis hinges on the necessity for a 'class approach' to foreign policy and is central to the Soviet self-image as a 'special' type of state. The conceptual framework from which the Soviet doctrine of sovereignty has largely derived, therefore, is comprised of a matrix of vertical and horizontal concepts. This study will seek to explore the interplay between these conflicting perspectives in Soviet theory. The possibility that, in the Gorbachev era of 'new thinking', the Soviet doctrine of sovereignty may be developing a 'third axis' will also be examined.

Secondly, a study of the development of the Soviet Union's 'bi-axial' approach to sovereignty should shed some light upon the dynamics of doctrinal change in Soviet foreign policy – upon the factors which are likely to precipitate shifts in doctrine and upon the relationship between 'doctrine' and 'policy' (even though these connections may be so complex and problematic as to defy the possibility of conclusive answers). For example, in the postwar era the CPSU has been forced to respond to fundamental shifts in its relationships with other communist parties, both within and outside its 'power zone' in Eastern Europe. Soviet loss of control over other parties has not occurred uniformly, but has reflected the increasingly heterogeneous nature of the international communist movement.

The Soviets have responded to this increase in environmental complexity by tailoring their doctrines of socialist international relations
to suit different 'audiences'. Soviet pronouncements on sovereignty
meant for audiences outside the USSR's, 'power zone' in Eastern
Europe have blurred perceptions of Soviet toleration thresholds
within it. A related issue concerns the degree of continuity in Soviet
doctrine: to what extent, for example, have post-war Soviet theories
of sovereignty departed from the pre-war bedrock of ideas? Has
there really been an 'evolution' in Soviet theory, or has the rise of the
'Mezhdunarodniki'[116] (international relations specialists performing
the functions of research and ideological spokesmanship) simply
enabled the Soviets to expound these ideas with more accomplished
sophistry than hitherto?

Disputes about sovereignty have constituted a kind of weather
vane of the state of socialist international relations: these disputes
first arose during the Soviet-Yugoslav split in the late 1940s and have,
in different forms and with varying degrees of intensity, bedevilled
the CPSU's relations with both ruling and non-ruling communist
parties ever since. Thus the sovereignty issue has been central to the
debates within the communist movement about the meaning and
implications of 'proletarian internationalism'; the relationship between national and international interests; the role of the CPSU;
'models of socialism'; and the bases of collaboration between parties.
A reference to the 'sovereignty of parties' in a Soviet compendium on
'Socialist Internationalism' (published in the late 1970s) provided a
telling insight into the force of 'horizontal' cleavages over vertical
proletarian solidarity within the international communist
movement.[117] In the era of 'new thinking', there is evidence that the
Soviets have embarked upon a fundamental re-evaluation of old
doctrinal orthodoxies concerning the character of socialist international relations (and, by definition, of the USSR's relations with
other socialist states). A broader aim of the work is to explore the
factors which have served to shape the Soviet Union's changing
conceptualisations of socialist international relations.

Thirdly, the study will provide examples of the use of verbal
strategies in international relations. Franck and Weisband have
described the role played by enunciated concepts and doctrines in
international relations as a form of 'word politics'.[118] Mlynář has
commented on the disparity between Soviet public pronouncements
(which conform to, and foster, the Soviet Union's self-image) and the
crude power language used by Soviet leaders in their meetings with

their Czech counterparts following the invasion of Czechoslovakia in 1968.[119] Incongruities between the official doctrines and the actual policies of states are readily discernible: this study, however, will also seek to examine the functions served by the sovereignty principle as a 'verbal strategy' in Soviet foreign policy.

2 The Genealogy of the Soviet Conception of Sovereignty

DEFINITIONS OF SOVEREIGNTY IN WESTERN AND SOVIET THOUGHT

Surveys of the genealogy of the sovereignty principle have generally exposed the vagueness and inconsistency with which the term has been used.[1] The fact that sovereignty is a laudatory political word as well as a legal concept has doubtless contributed greatly to this confusion. Nevertheless, it may still be possible to identify a common core of meaning amid the 'quagmire'[2] of definitions. Both Western and Soviet writers agree that a seminal contribution to the development of the concept was made by Bodin in 1576, although, in keeping with the Soviet penchant for attributing laudible inventions and discoveries to Russian figures, the Soviets have also acknowledged the contribution to sovereign statehood made by fifteenth- and sixteenth-century Tsars, such as Ivan the Great and Ivan the Terrible.[3] In Bodin's theory, sovereignty is 'the absolute and perpetual power of the state' – i.e. the supreme power of the state within a specific territory. Bodin recognised that this supreme power was limited by divine law and by obligations to, and agreements with, other states.[4] Bodin's conception, therefore, identifies the two central elements in modern definitions: i.e. the internal aspect of sovereignty – meaning 'supremacy', 'exclusive competence' or 'domestic jurisdiction'; and the external aspect – meaning political and juridic independence, or autonomy, from any other authority (although it was Grotius who explicitly recognised the international implications of the principle[5]).

Both Western and Soviet definitions hinge on two essential attributes of sovereign statehood: the notion of supremacy within a territory (the internal aspect) and independence in the international arena (the external aspect).[6] Sovereignty means, therefore, the ability of a state to determine its domestic and foreign policies (including the right to choose its form of government) free from subordination to any other authority: when a state claims 'respect for sovereignty' it means that it accepts the obligation not to interfere in the internal affairs of other states and respects their independence. The external aspect has also been referred to as the notion of 'relative sovereignty' – meaning that sovereignty in the international arena is not unlimited, since the state is subject to international law and is expected to respect the sovereignties of other states. However, although in this sense no sovereign state has 'absolute sovereignty', it is nevertheless independent of any other power. The notion of 'absolute sovereignty' is also rejected in Soviet theory, since 'no state is free to do as it pleases'.[7] Korovin reminded a Western critic in 1947 that the Soviet Union has never favoured the notion of 'absolute sovereignty'.[8] The contemporary Soviet legal specialist Chernichenko notes that international law does not bestow sovereignty upon states and therefore cannot bestow 'domestic jurisdiction'.[9]

On the level of bald, one-sentence definitions, Western and Soviet conceptions of sovereignty are often remarkably similar. Western scholars would find nothing odd in the following Soviet definitions, chosen more or less at random: 'independence of a state authority from all other authorities, both inside and outside the state's boundaries (Vyshinskiĭ, 1948[10]); 'the right of states to freely decide their internal and external affairs, without interfering in the internal affairs of other states and without breaching the generally accepted norms of international law' (*Juridical Dictionary*, 1956[11]); 'the supreme right of the people (nation or national minority) to shape its own destiny, its freedom to choose the social system, form of government and its leaders' (Konstantinov, 1978[12]); 'complete legislative, executive judicial authority of the state within its territory, the authority not being subordinate to the authority of other states in the sphere of international relations' (*Dictionary of International Law*, 1982[13]). The succinct definitions by leading Soviet theoreticians (e.g. Dorogin, Traĭnin, I. D. Levin, Modzhorian, Durdenevskiĭ, Lazarev, Lepeshkin and Tunkin) cited by Ushakov in his book on sovereignty could be fitted without incongruity into Western lexicons.[14]

It is in the interpretation of the two central concepts of 'supremacy' and 'independence' that the difference between Western and Soviet definitions of sovereignty resides. The Soviet perspective on sovereignty also incorporates 'rider definitions' deriving from the Soviet Union's 'class approach' to international affairs: like other political concepts, sovereignty has been filtered through the prism of Soviet Marxist-Leninist doctrine. Shevtsov asserts that sovereignty (in both its internal and external aspects) 'is socially determined and is assessed from a concrete class standpoint'.[15] Ushakov criticises bourgeois jurists for regarding sovereignty as a 'formal-legal', as distinct from a 'political legal' concept.[16] Both Western and Soviet perspectives on sovereignty embrace the notion that the formal independence of a state may disguise a situation of actual dependence: Aspaturian distinguishes between 'client', 'vassal' and 'fictional' states at the dependency end of the independence-dependence continuum.[17] Schwarzenberger has also developed a sovereignty continuum ranging from absolute independence to absolute dependence.[18] The existence of 'vassal states'[19] and 'paper sovereignties' is also acknowledged in Soviet theory, although inferior sovereignties of this kind are regarded as impossible within the socialist camp. At the time of the formation of the 'Peoples Democracies', a major Soviet textbook on international law argued that Soviet (i.e. 'genuine') sovereignty was manifested in the USSR's 'complete political and economic independence from the capitalist world'.[20]

Similarly, the Soviet conception of 'supremacy' is informed by the doctrine of 'popular sovereignty', which hinges on the notion of proletarian supremacy. For example, according to Traĭnin, ' "supremacy" within the capitalist world is supremacy of the bourgeois class'.[21] Similarly, Konstantinov argues that 'in the present historical situation of transition from capitalism to socialism [sovereignty] is primarily the right of people to build socialism and communism'.[22] In

The 'Internal' Aspect

rule of the proletariat	**bourgeois supremacy**
socialist states	all capitalist states

The 'External' Aspect

independence	**dependence**
all states within the socialist camp	weaker capitalist states
powerful capitalist states	

Figure 2.1 The Soviet class perspective on the 'internal' and 'external' aspects of sovereignty

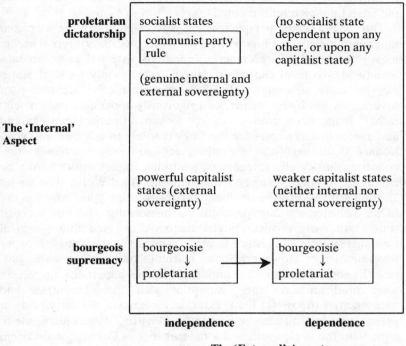

Figure 2.2 The Soviet class approach to sovereignty

an analysis of the Soviet-Czechoslovak declaration in 1969, Kozhev-nikov and Blishchenko argued that the 'class approach' to sovereignty included a duty to defend working-class power and the revolutionary socialist gains of working people.[23] Chkhikvadze asserts that whereas sovereignty in a socialist state 'rests on a firm political sovereignty of the working people', in imperialist states 'sovereignty serves as a juridical and political form of monopoly rule'.[24] In the postwar period, Soviet commentators have, in accordance with their 'bi-axial' approach to international relations, demonstrated an ability to shift deftly from conventional to 'rider' definitions to suit prevailing Soviet policy requirements.

The Soviet class perspective on sovereignty can be depicted diagrammatically (see Figure 2.1); if sovereignty in its internal aspect means 'proletarian supremacy', and in its external aspect means 'independence from capitalism', then logically only socialist states can be truly sovereign. However, this restrictive definition of sovereignty has by no means been rigorously applied by the Soviets; rather, it has been used selectively to suit different situations and audiences. For example, for the Soviets solely to advance an exclusionary definition (which would place non-socialist 'newly free' countries outside the category of sovereign states) would hardly be conducive to good Soviet relations with the Third World. The Soviet Union's strident posture of champion of sovereignty has required use of an inclusionary definition, embracing socialist and non-socialist states. An early postwar Soviet textbook asserted that powerful capitalist states could reduce weaker countries to the status of 'paper sovereignties'.[25] However, Soviet warnings that smaller states outside the socialist camp were imperilled by US imperialist aggression were predicated on the assumption that these countries had sovereignties to lose (at least 'externally'); even in the early postwar period, the dualistic class approach (see Figure 2.2) was too crude to cope with the complexities of a heterogeneous international system containing a diversity of state forms.[26] Nevertheless, the notion that capitalism is a menace to, and socialism a safe haven for, genuine sovereignty has been a major component of the postwar Soviet theory of sovereignty.

POSITIVE AND NEGATIVE SOVIET ORIENTATIONS TOWARDS SOVEREIGNTY BEFORE THE SECOND WORLD WAR

In addressing themselves to the question of the role and significance of sovereignty within a socialist interstate subsystem, Soviet theoreticians were not exactly confronted with a *tabula rasa*. In the period from the Bolshevik Revolution to the end of the Second World War, the Soviets had been forced by circumstances to devote considerable attention to the subject of sovereignty. Broadly speaking, the Soviet theory of sovereignty in the interwar period developed in response to three situational factors, none of which had been anticipated by the Bolsheviks prior to the Revolution. Firstly (following the failure of the 'world revolution'), the need for the regime to enter into relations with other states and to develop attitudes to the rules and values of the international system: the Soviet regime needed to formulate theoretical positions with regard to the central issues of international law and the conduct of states. As a 'state actor' in the international system, the regime sought to develop standpoints on sovereignty which were congruent with its foreign policy objectives. Secondly, the survival of powerful nationalist and separatist sentiments within the territories which had formerly been part of the Tsarist empire also forced the Bolsheviks to tackle the urgent and complex issues of national relations, self-determination and federalism: the issue of sovereignty, therefore, also assumed central importance in relation to the structure of the Soviet multinational state. The third factor was the internationalist ideology of the Bolsheviks which encouraged, even necessitated, the development of transnational political relationships between communist parties. The dominant role played by the Soviet party in the Comintern, an organisation transcending state frontiers, raised questions concerning the compatibility of the proletariat's national and international loyalties (see Chapter 5).

The extent to which postwar Soviet theorists drew upon these prewar notions, which were developed in circumstances where the Soviet regime was an isolated socialist state (and the centre of the world communist movement) provides insights into patterns and continuities in Soviet thought: the theoretical antecedents of the postwar Soviet conceptualisation of sovereignty within the socialist camp can each be traced to a prewar bedrock: far from precipitating a sharp break in Soviet theory, the advent of the Peoples Democracies and the emergence of 'socialist international relations' resulted, in large measure, in the adaptation and transposition of prewar Soviet doctrines to suit the USSR's post-isolation environment. For example, the notion that 'socialist international relations' are characterised by harmony, peace and cooperation can be traced back to prewar theories concerning the relationship between the socioeconomic bases of states and their foreign policies; the theory of two mutually antagonistic camps (deriving largely from Stalin) was developed when the Soviet Union was an isolated socialist state; the doctrine of 'peaceful coexistence' has its genealogy in Bolshevik 'realpolitik';[27] the idea of the convergence of socialist states bears a striking resemblance to the Bolshevik theory of the merger of nationalities;[28]

the idea that socialist states infuse generally recognised principles of international law (including sovereignty) with a qualitatively superior content was developed by Pashukanis in the 1930s;[29] similarly, postwar theories concerning intervention and 'limited sovereignty'[30] can also be traced back to prewar Soviet formulations.

The similarity between pre- and postwar Soviet conceptions of sovereignty can be attributed to several factors: firstly, to the continuity in the objectives of Soviet foreign policy: changes in the USSR's external environment did not result in a qualitative change in Soviet core objectives; secondly, to the fact that Soviet theorists in the pre- and postwar eras approached their subject matter from the same frame of reference: the standpoint of Marxist-Leninist doctrine, which, in some degree, imposed a 'tunnel vision' upon these commentators by forcing them into specific ways of seeing (the 'iron frame' effect of Marxist-Leninist doctrine); and thirdly, to the fact that some of the theorists associated with early postwar Soviet conceptions of the 'new type' of international relations, for example Korovin and Kozhevnikov, had written prolifically in the prewar era. There are however, some differences, stemming largely from the increasing complexity of the Soviet Union's postwar international environment.

The evolution of Soviet attitudes towards sovereignty in the interwar period not only provides insights into the relationship between enunciated theoretical positions and policy (a test of the common Western assumption that Soviet legal theory serves Soviet policy[31]) but also of the eclectic nature of Soviet international relations doctrine. Soviet writers such as Stuchka, Korovin and Pashukanis showed a familiarity with Western literature on international law and with Western definitions of sovereignty.[32] However, they also sought to reinterpret these notions in ways which accorded with the Soviet Union's current situation as an isolated socialist regime in a period of 'capitalist encirclement'. In the values which gave shape and texture to the contemporary Soviet theory of sovereignty it is possible to discern the influence of both Western and Soviet Marxist-Leninist frames of reference.

The claim that, from the earliest days, the Soviet state has been a consistent defender of the principle of state sovereignty has petrified into dogma in Soviet international relations literature. However, Soviet professions of support for the sovereignty principle have by no means been as unwavering as Soviet theorists now so trenchantly claim. Indeed, Soviet pronouncements on sovereignty have spanned the spectrum of attitudes, ranging from outright rejection to unqualified support. The shifts in the Soviet conception of sovereignty can be plotted by examining changing approaches to the concept in Soviet legal literature. Verger's textbook on international law (1922) took a 'rejectionist' line,[33] whereas Korovin in 1924 adopted a more ambivalent posture.[34] As Vishniak has observed, until the 1930s Soviet lexicographical references to sovereignty were disparaging in tone: he notes the difference in the references to sovereignty in the 1930 and 1943 editions of the *Short Soviet Encyclopaedia* (the latter edited by Vyshinskiĭ).[35] In 1930 a Soviet theorist could remind his readers that Marxists marched under the flag of proletarian solidarity rather than sovereignty.[36] Other commentators conceded that this 'bourgeois' principle could have an instrumental value to the Soviet state.[37]

The transition from the attitude of rejection, to cynical acceptance and then to one of obsessive reverence for the sovereignty principle coincided with the transformation of the Soviet Union's role within the international system: 'pariah' states pursuing revolutionary goals are likely to reject explicitly the fundamental values of the system. By the mid-1930s, the Soviet Union had sought and gained entry into the international community of states and 'verticalist' rhetoric was no longer congruent with its foreign policy objectives. The Soviet Union was admitted to the League of Nations in 1934 (becoming a permanent member of the League's council) and sought to improve its relations with Britain and France (with whom it signed a defence treaty in 1935). In this year, Molotov defined the USSR's relations with other states as being based on 'cooperation and competition'.[38] The conciliatory posture of the Soviet Union in this phase – prompted by the looming danger from Germany and Japan – was articulated in an article by Radek in the American journal *Foreign Affairs* in 1934, which emphasised the uniquely pacific nature of Soviet foreign policy.[39] In 1935, Korovin, writing for a Western audience, argued that 'the Soviet state as a juridic conception, as a sovereign, as a subject of law, is in no way to be distinguished from the conception generally accepted in international law' and asserted that the Soviet government, had 'at all times and in all places' defended the principle of strict non-interference.[40] In a *Pravda* interview with a Western correspondent (5 March 1936) Stalin denied that the Soviet regime had ever planned to export revolution to the West.

By the late 1930s, Soviet doctrine on international law had shed most of its 'revolutionary' aspects, and reflected legal positivist thought, in keeping with the Soviet Union's defensive posture towards the outside world. Its offensive actions (against Poland, Finland and the Baltic states) were said by the Soviets to be in complete conformity with international law. Thus as Ginsbergs has shown, its annexation of Eastern Poland was justified on several legal grounds – 'debellatio' (the Polish state had ceased to exist and therefore Soviet treaties with Poland were invalid); 'derelictio' – the Polish government had abandoned the area; 'pre-emptive self-defence' (against the possibility of German aggression); 'humanitarian' (protection of minorities and of Poles against Germans); and 'self-determination' for Ukrainian and Belorussian minorities.[41] The Soviets also explained their attack upon Finland as a legitimate act of self-defence – even though, in anticipation of victory, they had emplaced a communist 'democratic government of Finland' headed by Kuusinen at Terijoki on the Soviet-Finnish border: the Soviets stated that they had acceded to the request of this 'government' for Soviet military aid.[42] Regardless of the spuriousness of these claims to legality – the attack upon Finland led to the Soviet Union's expulsion from the League of Nations – the fact that they were made at all demonstrated the Soviet regime's *formal* acceptance of the prevailing norms of international law (the Soviets also held 'plebiscites' in Eastern Poland and the Baltic states). Aleksandrov's *Political Dictionary* in 1940 defined sovereignty in conventional 'legal positivist' terms as 'political independence not limited in any way by any other authority'.[43]

Pipes has argued that the emergence of the Soviet Union between 1917 and 1923 was 'a compromise between doctrine and reality',[44] in that it manifested both the Bolshevik desire for centralisation and a recognition of the survival of nationalism. In reality, it was a very uneven compromise, in that centralisation was the predominant value underlying the Soviet 'federalist' solutions to the national problem (i.e. in this case, the Bolsheviks, through the application of power, possessed the ability to 'adjust' reality to their procrustian doctrines of centralisation by effectively crushing secessionist movements in the Soviet borderlands). Similarly, the Soviet Union's posture towards the outside world also resulted from an asymmetrical 'compromise' between doctrine and reality: however, in its relations with the capitalist world, it was Soviet doctrine that had to be adjusted to the 'reality' of a hostile international environment.

A classification of Soviet orientations towards sovereignty in the interwar period

Shifts in the Soviet attitude towards sovereignty in the interwar period justify an attempt at classification. Perhaps the simplest classificatory scheme would be based on the distinction between 'positive' and 'negative' Soviet orientations. However, within each of these categories, several subdivisions can be identified. The typology below builds upon two variables: firstly, upon the value assigned to sovereignty in Soviet pronouncements. Negative evaluations derived from perceptions of sovereignty as an obstacle to the realisation of Soviet goals, whereas positive evaluations signalled its use for defensive or offensive purposes; secondly, upon Soviet postures towards the prevailing norms and values of the international system. In this category, we can distinguish between 'verticalist' (class-based) and 'horizontalist' (state-centric) postures: both 'verticalist' and 'horizontalist' arguments were used by the Soviets in support of offensive and defensive foreign policy strategies in this period. An (admittedly crude) matrix of Soviet postures towards sovereignty can be constructed by charting the resulting permutations, as shown in

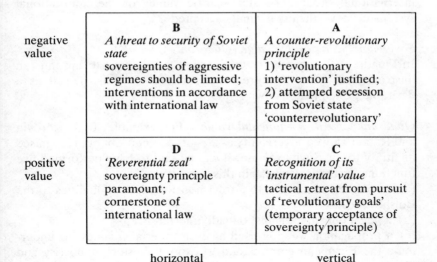

	B	A
negative value	*A threat to security of Soviet state* sovereignties of aggressive regimes should be limited; interventions in accordance with international law	*A counter-revolutionary principle* 1) 'revolutionary intervention' justified; 2) attempted secession from Soviet state 'counterrevolutionary'
positive value	**D** *'Reverential zeal'* sovereignty principle paramount; cornerstone of international law	**C** *Recognition of its 'instrumental' value* tactical retreat from pursuit of 'revolutionary goals' (temporary acceptance of sovereignty principle)
	horizontal	vertical

Figure 2.3   Soviet attitudes towards sovereignty in the interwar period

Figure 2.3. This matrix enables us to unravel the various strands of both 'positive' and 'negative' Soviet attitudes towards sovereignty in the interwar period, as shown below.

Sovereignty as a negative value (Quadrants A and B)

Quadrant A: Sovereignty as a counter-revolutionary principle.
(1) An obstacle to world revolution: vertical (class) cleavages are assumed to be paramount over horizontal (inter-state) divisions; that is, the values of the existing international system are rejected. Rejection was expressed in starkest form during the period of 'revolutionary optimism' (1917–20), although it has resurfaced in various forms in support of later Soviet offensive strategies.
(2) An obstacle to the consolidation of the Soviet multinational state (secessionist demands of nationalities within the Soviet sphere are deemed 'counter-revolutionary').

Quadrant B: A threat to the security of the Soviet state. The sovereignty of aggressive regimes (cf. the European fascist powers) has to be limited, in the interests of international peace. In this quadrant, the principle of sovereignty is viewed as secondary (and in some instances, antithetical) to the paramount value of maintaining international order. The state-centric values of the international system are nevertheless formally accepted.

Sovereignty as a positive value (Quadrants C and D)
In Quadrant C sovereignty is regarded as a means to an end (an 'instrumental' value), whereas in Quadrant D it is viewed as a desirable principle in its own right.

Quadrant C: An instrumental value.   For example, both Korovin and Ratner viewed sovereignty as a bourgeois concept but recognised its utility to the Soviet regime. It can be said to have performed five functions for the Bolsheviks in this period:
(a) a 'magnet' function – to attract non-Russian nationalities to the Bolshevik cause;
(b) a 'legal bulwark' against outside interference;
(c) a propaganda weapon used against imperialist states, to undermine the European empires and to expose Western hypocrisy and 'double standards';
(d) a 'masking' function – to conceal to the outside world the extent to which the sovereignty of the Union republics was limited;

(e) an 'emollient' function – to reassure nations incorporated into the Soviet multinational state that they continued to enjoy full sovereignty.

Quadrant D: 'Reverential zeal'. From the mid-1930s, sovereignty became elevated to an exalted place in Soviet international relations doctrine: the explicit cynicism of Korovin and Ratner was supplanted by obsessive reiteration of the paramountcy of sovereignty in international affairs.

However, the Soviets have never had a 'pure' doctrine of sovereignty based exclusively on any one of these orientations: for example, even in the 'rejectionist' phase immediately after the Revolution, the Bolsheviks signed international treaties in which the principle was enshrined and called upon other states to respect the sovereignty of the regime. Similarly, even in the phase of full formal acceptance, the Soviets have reserved the right to depart from their reverential attitude, by arguing that aggressive regimes forfeit the protection afforded by the sovereignty principle. For example, in his famous 'peace is indivisible' speech delivered at the League of Nations in 1936, Litvinov argued that pleas of sovereignty should not constitute 'an obstacle to the performance of international obligations'.[45] In the postwar era, the Soviets were also to argue that aggressive regimes (cf. Franco's Spain), whose existence constituted a danger to international peace, should not be able to shelter behind the principle.[46] It would be more accurate, therefore, to speak of concurrent strains (of shifting importance) in the Soviet conception of sovereignty rather than of chronologically distinct phases.

BOLSHEVIK DOCTRINES OF 'REVOLUTIONARY INTERVENTION'

Respect for the principle of state sovereignty did not accord with Bolshevik ambitions for world proletarian revolution, as exemplified by the doctrine of 'revolution from without' and by statements favouring 'red intervention' made by Zinoviev, Bukharin, Lenin, Trotsky, Tukhachevskiĭ and others. The doctrine had first been applied by the Soviets when they had rendered aid to the Finnish, Lithuanian, Latvian and Estonian parties in order to establish Soviet regimes in these areas in 1918.[47] However, it was to be expressed in its clearest form in relation to Bolshevik efforts to establish a Soviet regime in Poland in 1919–20. At this time there was no internationally agreed border between Poland and Russia, but even if there had been, the revolutionary pronouncements of these leaders indicated that it would have presented no obstacle to a westward push of the Red Army.

In relation to the Russo-Polish War, Zinoviev proclaimed that any effort by the Red Army to extend the Revolution beyond the borders of Soviet Russia by military force – at bayonet point – was justified. As head of the Comintern, he was not content to wait until the contradictions within each capitalist country had worked themselves out and was determined to give history a push by rendering military assistance to revolutionary forces in Europe, thereby hastening the inevitable demise of the capitalist order. Zinoviev's espousal of the 'domino' theory of revolution was expressed in his assertions that 'the light from the revolution is setting the world on fire' and that 'if tomorrow the proletarian revolution is victorious in Berlin, we shall unite with proletarian Berlin against bourgeois Paris and imperialist London. If tomorrow in Paris or Rome the workers should seize power, we will unite with proletarian Rome against bourgeoise Vienna or with the workers of Paris against Ebert's Berlin'.[48] He predicted that communism would triumph within Europe within a year. As the Red Army advanced into Poland in 1920, Zinoviev asserted that 'old Europe was hurtling towards the proletarian revolution'[49] and that a successful military advance westward by the Soviets would have meant 'a tremendous advance of the international proletarian revolution', since the fate of the Revolution literally depended upon the Red Army's every advance.[50] In Zinoviev's doctrine of revolutionary aid, state frontiers were of no greater significance as a defensive barrier than matchwood in a forest fire (Marx had, in 1863, entertained the possibility that the insurrection in Poland would result in the 'lava' of revolution flowing from East to West[51]).

Zinoviev's doctrine of revolutionary intervention was closely connected to his vision of the Comintern's role as the future government of a global Soviet Republic (which, like the Comintern and the Soviet state, would have been organised on the basis of 'democratic centralism'). Zinoviev's directives to the Kun regime indicated that he regarded the Comintern as a power over and above that of a foreign government (despite the fact that the International was dominated by Russians and that Zinoviev had asserted that ideological leadership would, temporarily, have to belong to the Bolshevik party).[52] Zinoviev's eagerness to extend the revolution westwards at the point of Soviet bayonets accorded with a reference to Moscow (made at the second Comintern congress) as the 'combat headquarters of the world proletariat'.[53] The ambivalence in the Soviet attitude towards sovereignty was already apparent, in that in addition to the calls for revolutionary war, made when Soviet forces were nearing Warsaw, an appeal of the second Comintern Congress also denounced intervention against Soviet Russia (Soviet Russia also stated that it unequivocally recognised the 'independence and sovereignty of the Polish Republic'[54]).

The distinction between 'revolutionary' and 'reactionary' intervention meant that the actions of the Soviet state were to be judged by qualitatively different standards from other states. In particular, 'red intervention' was justified on the internationalist grounds that the advance of the revolution would benefit all mankind and was therefore fundamentally different from the selfish and predatory interventions of capitalist states. Moreover, international revolutionary war waged across state boundaries was regarded by the Bolsheviks as an historical inevitability. In *The A.B.C. of Communism*, Bukharin and Preobrazhenskiĭ had asserted that 'the proletariat as a state must fight with bourgeois states . . . not for the seizure of other's goods, but for the victory of communism, for the dictatorship of the working class'.[55] The doctrine of revolutionary intervention was also espoused at the Bolsheviks' 8th party congress in 1919, when a resolution asserted that the Red Army was not only a defensive instrument, but could also be used to 'render decisive support' to the proletariat of imperialist states.[56]

Despite Lenin's stated opposition to 'pushing' revolutions,[57] he also favoured an attempt to spread the revolution westward by military force in 1919, in an effort to link Soviet power with the revolutionary struggle in Germany. Lenin was not opposed to war as such and believed that revolutionary war was inevitable in order to sweep away the capitalist world order. In 1921, he had argued that 'revolutionary wars' – for example, wars waged against capitalists in defence of the oppressed classes, wars in defence of nations oppressed by imperialists and in defence of the socialist revolution against foreign invaders – were justified.[58] His opposition to a revolutionary war at that juncture was based on tactical considerations. Lenin's assertion of the legitimacy of international revolutionary warfare ('a genuine revolutionary war at this point would be a war conducted by a socialist republic against the bourgeois countries, with the aim of ... overthrowing the bourgeoisie')[59] and his assumption of an inextricable link between the revolutionary struggles waged against capitalism in all parts of the world is hardly compatible with belief in the inviolability of the sovereignty principle.

At the 4th Comintern Congress in 1922, Bukharin had advocated that the 'right of red intervention' be laid down in the Comintern programme.[60] Bukharin based his plea on a literal interpretation of the statement in the 'Communist Manifesto' that the workers would conquer the whole world, which could only be done with bayonets.[61] Trotsky had stated at the Comintern's foundation congress that the soldiers of the Red Army were 'acting not only as troops defending the Russian Socialist Republic, but also as the Red Army of the 3rd International'.[62] At the 8th party congress, he described the epoch as 'the beginning of civil war of the proletariat against all bourgeois states and armies'.[63] Exhortations made at the Comintern Congresses for the Red Army to render decisive help to the proletariats of the world in their struggles against capitalism should not be dismissed as vainglorious rhetoric, since the Red Army's decisive assistance was indeed given to Belorussia in 1919, Armenia, Azerbaizan, Bukhara and Khiva in 1920 and Georgia and Mongolia in 1921. The help rendered to these territories was said to be in response to requests for assistance from revolutionary committees, a rationale which was later used to justify Soviet interventions in postwar Eastern Europe. Thus the independence of the border zones (territories of the Russian empire which took advantage of Article 18 of the 'Declaration of Rights of the Peoples of Russia' issued by the Bolsheviks in 1917, which affirmed the right of the peoples to self-determination, including the right of secession and the right to form independent states) was brought to an end by Soviet invasions launched in response to 'appeals for fraternal assistance' by beleaguered communists.[64]

Soviet military actions were launched despite the fact that Soviet Russia had signed non-aggression treaties with the seceded Republics and had recognised their right to independence. The RSFSR also launched an abortive military campaign against Finland and had sought to render military assistance to the Kun regime in 1919. General Tukhachevskiĭ (an enthusiastic exponent of the doctrine of 'revolution from without') had advocated the creation of an 'international general staff' in order to coordinate the international revolutionary war against world capitalism.[65] Tukhachevskiĭ was to write later that victory in the Russo-Polish war would have been the link between the October Revolution and the impending revolution in Western Europe.[66] Despite the warnings of the Moscow Poles (e.g. Radek and Marchlewski) that the Polish people would not welcome the Red Army, after repulsing Pilsudski's drive into the Ukraine the Bolsheviks nevertheless established a transitional government of Polish workers in Bialystok in July 1920.[67]

Stalin also developed a theory of revolutionary aid, based on his notion of the 'ebb and flow' of revolutionary situations. At the 14th party conference in 1925, he argued that the Soviet Union was compelled to create a military force capable of providing aid to the proletariats of other countries. Moreover, even when the proletariat had attained power it would be difficult for the workers to retain it and therefore it would be necessary for the Soviets to provide assistance. He noted that neighbouring states (such as Latvia and Estonia) might soon succeed in overthrowing the bourgeoisie and that therefore 'if war begins, we shall not sit on our hands . . . We shall be the last to come out, but will do so in order to throw the decisive weight into the balance, to tip the scales.' He warned that if the imperialist states did attack the Soviet Union, the Soviet regime would seek to 'set free the revolutionary lion in every country'.[68] Stalin's reactive, 'balance-tipping' theory of revolutionary intervention was less heroic than the proactive, hortatory call for global revolutionary warfare made by Zinoviev, Bukharin or Tukhachevskiĭ. Nevertheless, it assumed a role for the Red army in consolidating proletarian power outside the Soviet state. Moreover, the distinction between 'revolutionary extension' and 'revolutionary consolidation' may, in fluid and complex conditions, be very fine.

Elaborate theoretical justifications for 'revolutionary intervention' were also developed by some Soviet jurists in the 1920s, notably by Korovin and Pashukanis, both of whom categorised Intervention as a projection of the class struggle across state boundaries: therefore any specific intervention had to be judged by whether it served to turn the wheel of history forwards or backwards. In this period, there was no officially codified Soviet theory of International Law and therefore Soviet legal scholars were relatively free to advance their own theories and to debate with rival schools (a freedom which was soon to disappear). Although Korovin and Pashukanis were critical of each other's ideas, they both sought to apply Marxist class analysis to International Law. Pashukanis' creative theorising made him the premier scholar in this field until 1937 (when he was denounced, arrested and eventually shot). In the early 1920s, Korovin formulated a theory of an 'International Law of the Transition Period' and was a prolific writer on international legal topics until the early 1960s – even furnishing a justification for the Soviet intervention in Hungary in 1956. Although the 'Brezhnev Doctrine' derives from a confluence of many strands of Soviet thought, Korovin's contributions give him as good a claim as any to the dubious title of the 'father' of the Soviet theory of 'limited sovereignty'.

The Marxist premise concerning the 'superstructural' nature of law forced Korovin to reject the possibility that the emergence of the Soviet regime had made no difference to international law. He regarded it as inconceivable that there could be a single system of international law applicable to both bourgeois and socialist states. Korovin's emphasis on the 'class character' of international law reflected the current official conception that the world was split into two irreconcilable camps, an idea given expression in section 1 of the 1924 constitution of the USSR.[69] Despite the absence of a common international law, the two camps could, according to Korovin, cooperate on the basis of mutual self-interest, in certain narrowly defined fields, such as technical cooperation and trade.

Korovin's attitude towards sovereignty and intervention exemplified his belief that established legal principles and practices were to be judged on the basis of their utility to the Soviet regime. Approaches to intervention had to be appraised on the basis of the situation and 'international experience' of the Soviet Republic,[70] without hindrance from 'juridic fetishism' and legal dogmas, such as the notion of sovereignty.[71] The Soviet Union stood in the role of 'champion of the doctrine of "classical sovereignty" ', in as much as formally it served as a legal armour, protecting it from capitalist aggression.[72] In the period of 'bourgeois encirclement', every restriction of sovereignty of the USSR was a victory of the capitalist world over the land of socialism.[73]

Korovin argued that 'stern denunciation by workers' Russia . . . of the class interventionary campaign of the Entente does not constitute a repudiation of Intervention as a method of class struggle, but rather a repudiation and condemnation of a particular intervention'.[74] Following an analysis the four interventions against the Soviet state, he described these interventions as a 'manifestation of the class struggle on an international scale' and as such – with the exception of treaty relations, which were to the mutual advantage of both systems in the transitional epoch – was 'the usual form of interaction between two opposing forces in the international arena'.[75] In his view, 'intervention, despite its notorious reputation, has the potential to be a great instrument of progress, a surgical instrument, to ease the birth labours of the new world'. In the hands of the Entente powers, it was profoundly regressive, an absurd attempt to stop the wheel of history and hold back the growth and advance of social power – an attempt to stifle its struggle for life.[76] As an illustration of 'surgical intervention', Korovin gave the example of the support rendered by the Red Army to countries on the Baltic region and in the Caucasus in order to establish socialism.

In his essay on 'International Law' written for the *Encyclopaedia of State and Law* Pashukanis had asserted that international law was based on a system of compromises between two irreconcilable and antagonistic systems – capitalism and socialism, which would endure until the complete victory of the socialist system. Pashukanis rejected Korovin's contention that the Soviet state had altered the form of international law, since he observed that it was applying many of the forms which had been developed by bourgeois states, for example in relation to trade treaties and immunity.[77] He also distinguished between the 'form' and 'content' of international law, by arguing that, although bourgeois and socialist law may resemble each other in form, their content was qualitatively different, in that bourgeois forms practised by the Soviet state had been injected with a special socialist content.[78] Pashukanis' theory amounted to an assertion that the Soviet Union could take whatever principles of bourgeois law it found beneficial to its interests and reject the rest: he explicitly acknowledged that the role of law should be to serve policy. Pashukanis was attacked for his 'similar in form, different in content' theory on the grounds that it could subject the Soviet Union to the bourgeois system of international law.[79]

In his entry on 'Intervention' in the *Encyclopaedia of State and Law*, Pashukanis distinguished between Soviet and all other forms of intervention: Soviet intervention was said to have a progressive character never before seen in history, whereas interventions by bourgeois states were motivated by the desire for exploitation and territorial aggrandisement.[80] He defined 'intervention' as 'imperious ['*vlast'noe*'] interference by one state in the internal affairs of another state, or in its mutual relations with a third state' and described it as 'one of the forms of class-struggle'.[81] He went on to argue that

however, in as much as the struggle occurs between the exploiting classes – the bourgeoisie and the landlords – and in as much as state power remains located in their hands, and in as much as Intervention derives from class motives, it is utilised for purposes of territorial seizure, with the aim of extending the influence of the interventionary states. This is probably the case even with revolutionary classes, as was true of the French bourgeoisie at the end of the 18th and the beginning of the 19th century. The liberating campaigns of the French revolutionary armies led immediately to the aggressive policies of Napoleon 1.

He gave examples of 'class interventions' against proletarian revolutions – Bismark against the Paris Commune, and against the proletarian revolution in Russia – and argued that 'only the proletariat as a class, not at all interested in exploitation, is capable of fighting for broad class aims, emancipation from all national egoism, and consequently, only a proletarian state is capable of revolutionary intervention in its pure form'.[82] The notion that the legitimacy of intervention was to be judged by its degree of 'revolutionary purity' provided the Soviets with a doctrine which categorised all interventions against the Soviet state as deriving from selfish motives but yet which legitimised all Soviet interventions, on the grounds that these were historically unique examples of international altruism.

The theory that socialist military intervention is legitimate providing that it serves the interests of socialism (as defined by the Soviets) constitutes a cardinal assumption of the Brezhnev Doctrine of limited sovereignty. The theory cannot, however, be regarded as a recent invention – a novel *ex post facto* – rationalisation for Soviet military intervention in Czechoslovakia, because it merely represents a reorientation and refabrication of the theory of legitimate socialist intervention formulated by Bolshevik leaders and theoreticians in the early years of the Soviet regime: the most obvious difference between the old and new versions of this theory is that Soviet 'surgical interventions' are no longer aimed at serving the obstetric function of 'easing the birth pains of the new world' but rather at aborting the birth of Prague Springs, Polish Summers and similar threats to Soviet hegemony. Whatever else the original theory of 'surgical intervention' was designed to serve, it was not meant as an aid to the preservation of the status quo in Eastern Europe, or as an ideological rationale for the pursuit of Soviet state interests. It is ironic, however, that medical analogies continue to play a role in contemporary rationalisations for Soviet intervention – whereas the early version viewed it as a midwife of revolution, the modern conception, as articulated in the Brezhnev Doctrine, regards Soviet intervention (disguised as 'fraternal mutual aid') as assistance to 'healthy forces' endangered by the malignant disease of capitalism.

Unlike Korovin and Pashukanis, however, contemporary Soviet theorists deny that the Soviet Union is capable of interventionary behaviour. Indeed, the Soviets were to become embarrassed by these hortatory references to intervention: in the mid-1930s, Korovin asserted that 'the USSR is in principle opposed to all intervention and has never proposed to propagate socialism in other countries by means of Soviet bayonets, since it considers the exportation of revolution nonsense'[83] (in the 1930s both Korovin and Pashukanis were forced to repudiate their early theories of international law, which were out of kilter with the positivist trend in Soviet legal theory).[84] Similarly, in the modern Soviet version of Tukhachevskiĭ's book, *The March to the Vistula*, Chapter 3, entitled 'Revolutions From Without' was omitted altogether:[85] the current doctrine cites Lenin's record as an opponent of the idea of 'pushing' revolutions and 'armed missionary undertakings', but ignores his statements in favour of extending the revolution by force.[86]

'NATIONAL SELF-DETERMINATION' IN BOLSHEVIK THEORY AND PRACTICE

Bolshevik attitudes to the principle of self-determination of nations also provide insights into Soviet conceptualisations of sovereignty in the interwar period. The policies of Lenin and Stalin towards national self-determination derived from 'realist' considerations of power and tactical advantage, since they favoured the objectives of state centralisation and the integration of nationalities. However, for tactical reasons, based on their recognition of the temporary significance of national sentiment, they were prepared to countenance the formal right of secession of the Union Republics, within the framework of a federal or confederal state.[87] Kamenev's reference (made at a Ukrainian party congress) to the self-determination slogan as 'a weapon of the bourgeois counter-revolution against Soviet Russia' exemplified the essentially hostile attitude of the Bolsheviks towards the principle.[88] This ambivalence was to be manifested in the incongruity between the formally sovereign status of the Union Republics and their actual subordination to Moscow.

Aspaturian[89] identifies four aims of the national self-determination policy of Lenin prior to the Revolution: firstly, to attract non-Russian nationalities, by convincing them that the Bolsheviks were not 'Great Russian chauvinists'; secondly, to weaken the 'bourgeois nationalist' movements; thirdly, to exacerbate nationality problems within the Empire; and fourthly, to foster cooperation between the Great Russians and other nationalities which would endure after the Revolution. The right of nations to self-determination had been contained in the 'Programme of the Russian Social Democratic Workers' Party' in 1903, to which Lenin contributed. Before the Bolshevik Revolution, Lenin regarded the demand for national independence as progressive, but not socialist, since it was at odds with the internationalist doctrine of the Bolsheviks: as 'the party of the proletariat the Social Democratic party seeks to foster the self-determination of the proletariat in each nationality rather than that of peoples or nations. We must unswervingly work for the *closest* unity of the proletariat of all nationalities'.[90] Lenin was opposed to federalism as a policy to deal with the national question on the grounds that it would foster the survival of national divisions. His espousal of the right of nations to self determination was a tactical ploy, used to incite the non-Russian nationalities within the Tsarist empire and the peoples of Asia to revolt against their colonial masters. Lenin's opposition to federalism prior to the Bolshevik revolution accorded with his conception of the organisation of the party – i.e. that it must be based on the principle of democratic centralism, the most extreme form of centralisation: nor did Lenin believe that the nations should be free to develop their own cultural or education policies.[91]

Nevertheless, at the 8th party congress in March 1918 Lenin opposed the 'leftist' position on the national question advanced by Bukharin and Piatakov (who had proffered the slogan 'down with frontiers'[92]), in favour of a commitment to self-determination of nationalities.[93] At the congress, Piatakov had pointed out that 'self-determination' made no sense in the light of policies of economic centralisation being vigorously pursued by the Bolsheviks: Lenin's response was to stress the voluntariness of economic union. He argued that, although Piatakov's declaration that internationalists should not want 'nations' but rather a union of proletarians was 'splendid', this would not come about immediately.[94] Lenin's duels with Piatakov on the national question are frequently cited by modern Soviet scholars as evidence of his commitment to self-determination.[95] He argued that 'just as mankind can arrive at the abolition of classes only through a transitional period of dictatorship by the oppressed class, it can achieve the inevitable integration of nations only through a transitional period of the complete emancipation of all oppressed nations – i.e. their freedom to separate'.[96] However, as Urban has argued, Lenin's theoretical works support the conclusion that by self-determination of nations he meant the self-determination of the proletariat.[97] Lenin argued that no Marxist could deny 'that the interests of socialism are of higher value than the right of nations to self-determination'[98] and that the demand for self-determination had to be subordinated to the revolutionary struggle against the bourgeoisie.[99]

The 'Declaration of the Rights of the Peoples of Russia' (signed by Lenin and Stalin (then the People's Commissar for Nationalities) on 2 November 1917 recognised the equality and sovereignty of the peoples of Russia, including the right to form an independent state and to secede.[100] The constitution of the RFSFR described the Republic as a 'free union of free nations'.[101] As a result of the centrifugal forces unleashed by the declaration, Lenin acceded to the independence of the Ukraine (March 1918) and Belorussia (January 1919), and of Azerbaizan, Armenia and Georgia in 1920–1. Some of these Republics had exercised their sovereignty by engaging in diplomatic and military relations with major Western powers.[102] Several territories declared their independence from the RSFSR in 1918 (Lithuania, December 1917; Transcaucasia, February 1918; Estonia, May 1918; and Latvia, November 1918). However, the RSFSR did not recognise their independence until December 1918 and refused to recognise Georgia as an independent state until 1920, despite the fact that it had declared its independence in February 1918.[103]

Two months after the Declaration of the Rights of the Peoples of Russia, the Bolsheviks issued another declaration which seriously qualified the commitment of the RSFSR to the principle of self-determination. Thus the 'Declaration of the Rights of Toiling People' of 1918 gave the right of self-determination only to 'toiling and exploited people' and not to nationalities as a whole.[104] When the first constitution of the USSR had been drafted, Stalin had emphasised that federation was a transitional stage on the road to a World Soviet Socialist Republic.[105] Stalin was further to qualify Bolshevik support for the principle of self-determination by subordinating it to a higher principle – the right of the working class to its own dictatorship. In 1920, Stalin argued that the detachment of the border regions from Russia was against the interests of these regions and of Russia itself: the seceded regions would inevitably become enslaved by imperialism. Therefore the demand for secession was 'counter-revolutionary'.[106]

Declarations of the independence of the Soviet republics served a useful propaganda function (both internally and externally), but in practice this 'independence' was vitiated by the subordination of the local communist party organisations to the Russian party. All Lenin's pronouncements on self-determination must be considered in the light of his refusal to grant even a modicum of autonomy to the national communist parties (for example, although Lenin accepted the right of the Ukraine to self-determination, he adamantly opposed any suggestion of autonomy for the Ukrainian communist party[107]). Lenin refused to brook the idea of national communist parties for the national republics (except in the Ukraine and elsewhere, where it was made necessary by the terms of the Brest-Litovsk treaty), but even here the 'independent' parties were strictly subordinated to the Moscow Bolsheviks. The 8th congress endorsed the principle of the centralisation of the party, even in areas (such as the Ukraine, Belorussia and Latvia) where independent Soviet Republics had been established.

The Bolsheviks utilised the self-determination slogan during the civil war in the border lands occupied by White forces, but pursued centralist policies in the areas under their own control (as soon as the Bolsheviks regained control of the Ukraine, they reversed their commitment to the Ukrainian right of secession[108]). The practice of the Bolsheviks, as distinct from their formal commitment to self-determination, was to dispatch the Red Army in order to return seceded territories to Moscow's control. The signing of treaties between Soviet Russia and the Soviet Republics of Azerbaizan, the Ukraine and Belorussia and Georgia between 1920 and 1921 served to maintain these Republics' formal gloss of independence. However, from the autumn of 1918 they were subordinated to Soviet Russia by means of various centralisation measures: for example, through military, economic and administrative integration of the Ukraine with the RSFSR.[109] Even before foreign policy was formally transferred from the national republics to the RSFSR in 1922, Moscow had assumed control of the Republics' external relations. However, to admit to a policy of centralism would have laid the Bolsheviks open to the charge of 'Great Russian chauvinism' and would have complicated the reintegration process. Therefore, despite their opposition to federalism, they accepted it as a temporary solution in order to forestall further secessions and to provide a constitutional camouflage for the integration of the seceded independent border republics into the Soviet state (resulting in the Treaty of Union of Soviet Russia, the Ukraine, Belorussia and the Transcaucasian Federation (Azerbaizan, Armenia and Georgia) in December 1922.

At the 10th congress of the party in 1921, anti-separatist resolutions were the order of the day and the right of nations to self-determination was virtually abandoned. In his report to the 10th All-Russian Congress of Soviets in December 1922, Stalin contrasted the tendency towards the disintegration of capitalist multinational states with the ever closer unity of nationalities in the Soviet Federation.[110] In a speech delivered at the 12th party congress in April 1923, Stalin argued that 'it should be remembered that besides the right of nations to self-determination there is also the right of the working class to consolidate its power, and to this the right of self-determination is subordinate . . . [thus] in 1920 in order to defend working-class power we were forced to march on Warsaw',[111] a view he was to reiterate at the 14th conference in 1925, when he argued that the Soviet Union was compelled to create a military force capable of providing aid to the proletariats of other countries.[112]

The ambivalence and inconsistency of the Bolsheviks with regard to the sovereignty of the independent republics within the former Tsarist territories can be understood in relation to the tactical advantages of a non-centralist posture: the Bolsheviks were centralists to their bones, but allowed temporary secessions where it would have been difficult or impossible to retain direct control (indeed, at the time of the Revolution, some of the nationalities were already separated from Russia): they formally adopted federalist solutions, while at the same time rigorously pursuing a policy of centralisation. Prior to the Bolshevik revolution, Lenin utilised national sentiment as a weapon to weaken the Tsarist state: after the Revolution, it had exhausted its utility, but was too powerful to be openly repudiated. The Bolsheviks agreed in principle to self-determination but condemned separatist movements as 'counter-revolutionary'. Although the right of secession was proclaimed in various documents of this period there were provisions which made independence and the right of secession mere constitutional fictions. (Article 4 of the 1924 Constitution granted the right of secession to the Republics.) Article 17 of the 1936 (Stalin) constitution retained the right of secession, even though Stalin argued that no Republic would wish to exercise that right.[113]

The legal scholars Alymov and Studenikin emphasised that Soviet federalism was based on democratic centralism: Soviet federalism was said to be the basis of the future World Soviet republic[114] and an example to the world of the correct solution to nationality problems. Soviet commentators in the postwar period have also frequently pointed to the salutary example of the Soviet federal solution to the nationality problem.[115]

LINKS BETWEEN PRE- AND POSTWAR SOVIET ATTITUDES TOWARDS SOVEREIGNTY

The links between prewar and postwar Soviet theories of sovereignty which derive from the Soviet Union's external relations and its policies on the 'national question', are readily apparent: these include:

1. the use of voluntarist terminology (the right to independence and to secede from the Soviet federation) as a cover for Soviet control. The Peoples Democracies possess the formal right to withdraw from the Warsaw Pact;
2. recognition of the value of the sovereignty concept as a juridic defence against interference by other states;
3. use of the sovereignty principle as a slogan to weaken the Soviet Union's enemies and attract support to the regime;
4. recognition of the bourgeois genealogy of the concept, which provides the Soviets with a doctrinal justification for discarding respect for sovereignty whenever it is incongruent with Soviet interests;
5. the distinction between 'reactionary' and 'progressive' intervention, which provides a theoretical rationale for Soviet aggression (disguised as 'fraternal mutual aid').

Each of these functions of sovereignty was to be employed by the Soviets as integral elements of their policy towards Eastern Europe in the postwar era.

3 Sovereignty and Stalin's Policy towards Eastern Europe

STALIN'S POLICY OPTIONS IN EASTERN EUROPE

Within the region of Eastern Europe in the early postwar years, Stalin had the ability to consign the concept of sovereignty to the dust-heap of history by incorporating the states occupied by Soviet troops into the USSR. In the interwar period the Soviet Union had been forced by the prevailing balance of power to limit its policy objectives in the region to the pursuit of limited and conventional security interests. Any 'aspirational' ambitions which Soviet policy makers might have entertained about the possibility of a dramatic westward shift of the USSR's boundaries would have been dismissed as fanciful in the sobering light of political and military realities: the outcome of the Second World War opened up an array of policy options for the Soviets which would have previously been deemed impracticable. There is some evidence which suggests that Stalin was not unmindful of one tantalisingly attractive policy option – the prospect of wholesale territorial expansion in Eastern Europe – which had been brought within the bounds of possibility by the outcome of the War.

Despite Soviet attempts to transform Eastern Europe into a closed system, Soviet policy towards Eastern Europe in the postwar period was inextricably linked to the Soviet Union's assessments of its power balance with the West. As Garthoff has shown, by the late 1940s the Soviets had developed a rich vocabulary of terms relating to force and power in international relations.[1] In the early postwar years, Soviet statesmen and theorists espoused favourable and optimistic assessments of the balance of forces between the capitalist and socialist systems.[2] According to the Cominform Declaration (1947) the Second World War had brought about 'fundamental changes in the international situation', characterised by 'a new disposition of the basic political forces operating in the world arena': the forces of imperialism were weakening (as a result of the worsening crisis of capitalism) whereas those of socialism were growing stronger under

Soviet leadership.[3] In 1947, Varga, the head of the Soviet Institute of World Economics and World Politics, was criticised by other Soviet theorists for arguing that postwar capitalism had entered a phase of temporary stabilisation:[4] in the Zhdanovite orthodoxy of 'struggle between two systems', capitalism was in the throes of a new crisis, forcing the big imperialist powers to become even more aggressive and expansionist.[5] Nevertheless, the outlook for capitalism was judged to be bleak, since the imperialist camp was decaying and riven with antagonism.[6] Although we should acknowledge the possibility that these assessments may have served primarily propagandistic functions, it is undeniable that the Second World War had brought about an 'upswing' in Soviet power on the European continent.

In the interwar period, Stalin had formulated a 'power disequilibrium' model of the international system based on the notion of the 'ebb and flow' of 'revolutionary situations'[7] (by the 'flow of the revolutionary tide' Stalin meant in practice an accretion of Soviet power relative to the West). Stalin's ebb and flow theory is not a conventional balance of power model, since it focuses upon the structural characteristics of the capitalist and socialist systems and therefore incorporates a broader range of factors than military capability. His basic conception of the two systems was of the organic decay of capitalism (drawn out by temporary stabilisations) and of the organic growth of socialism (slowed down by temporary setbacks). Capitalist societies were regarded as crisis-prone and riven with antagonistic contradictions: the capitalist camp was being weakened within by economic crises and inter-state rivalries, and by the growing strength of progressive forces (these included anticolonial movements and the enlightened sections of the working class in capitalist states). Stalin acknowledged that revolutionary progress did not flow in a straight line, in a 'continuous upsurge', but rather followed a 'zig zag course of advances and retreats': thus the revolutionary tide had flowed in 1905 and then ebbed: the tide came again in 1917. 1925 was a temporary period of ebb, and therefore the Soviet Union had to guard itself against the interventionist plans of the big capitalist powers.[8] In 1927 he asserted that a new revolutionary upswing in Europe had begun, as a result of capitalism's deepening crisis.[9] At the 16th party congress in 1930, he reaffirmed that the 1927–30 period marked a turning point, in favour of the socialist camp, due in large measure to the decay of industry and agriculture in the West.[10] Arguably, Soviet perceptions of 'upswings' are likely to lead to phases of expansion and 'downswings' to phases of consolidation in Soviet policy.[11]

At the close of the Second World War, the 'upswing' in Soviet power may have encouraged Stalin seriously to consider the possibility of incorporating both the vanquished and the liberated countries of Eastern Europe into the Soviet Union, through the creation of a Moscow-dominated socialist confederation. Lenin's 'aspirational' goal had been that of world proletarian revolution (which he regarded as a 'core' value, having priority over Russian territorial interests), although following the sobering experiences of the Bolsheviks in the international arena between 1917 and 1920, he dismissed hopes that this goal would soon be achieved as madness.[12] Under Stalin's rule, however, the 'aspirational' objective was drained of revolutionary content and was directed towards the consolidation and expansion of the Soviet regime. The amalgamation of countries on or near the western borders of the Soviet state into a single unit (albeit confederal in form) would not have represented an abrupt departure in Stalin's thought, for he had advocated a confederal solution to the 'nationality problem' in Eastern Europe as early as 1920. In a critical reply to Lenin's 'Theses on the National and Colonial Question' adopted by the second Comintern congress, Stalin had suggested that the future Soviet Germany, Poland, Hungary and Finland be incorporated into a confederal union with Soviet Russia.[13]

Lenin had rejected the proposal made by Stalin in 1922 to incorporate the Ukraine, Belorussia, Azerbaizan, Georgia and Armenia into the RSFSR by changing their status from 'independent' to 'autonomous' republics on the grounds that it would have been tantamount to the re-creation of a Russian state and would damage the Soviet image as a champion of self-determination in the East.[14] Instead, he favoured the creation of a new federation, comprising the RSFSR and the other Republics.[15] Lenin and Stalin recognised the inherent dangers to state unity which genuine federalism would have created: their commitment to democratic centralism meant that their differences in approach to the question of federalism and of self-determination were superficial, and derived from considerations of expediency rather than from significant divergences of opinion concerning the degree of genuine autonomy to be granted to the Soviet Republics.

The USSR, established in December 1922, had been deliberately designed so that other territories, once sovietised, could be added on to it and therefore in its potential for expansion it was a manifestation of the global revolutionary vision of the Bolsheviks. At the 10th All-Russian Congress of Soviets in 1922 Stalin had argued that the amalgamation of the Soviet Republics into a single confederal state was made inevitable by three factors: economic circumstances, foreign dangers and the intrinsically international nature of Soviet power.[16] However, the 'open ended' federal principle upon which the Soviet state was founded lent itself not only to the millenarian revolutionary objectives of Lenin, but also to the pursuit of the more conventional and historically familiar state-centred foreign policy goals of territorial expansion *per se*. Stalin was not averse to the ploy of harnessing the internationalist principles of Lenin to the Russo-centric 'core' objectives which were the driving force of his foreign policy. The amendments made to the Soviet Union's constitution in February 1944 (although no doubt designed partly to bestow a veneer of legality upon the Soviet annexation of the Baltic states, Western Belorussia and the Western Ukraine, and also to give the Soviet Union extra seats in international councils) also provided a framework for future territorial expansion.[17] The constitutional amendments contained provisions which enabled the Union Republics to establish the trappings of statehood (they were formally declared to be internally and externally sovereign with the right to establish foreign ministries, defence organisations, etc.) and which enabled other states to join voluntarily – or, more plausibly, be joined involuntarily on to the USSR. From this standpoint, these constitutional amendments, which bestowed upon the Soviet Union a double or 'concurrent'[18] sovereignty, and which were said to constitute a 'new stage in the sovereignty of the Union Republics'[19] might plausibly have been viewed as the prelude to a Soviet annexationist policy in Eastern Europe. The Union Republics were declared to be states which had voluntarily relinquished certain diplomatic functions to the Union, although these powers were said to be recoverable at any time[20] (the right of withdrawal was, however, limited by various all-Union constitutional provisions which nullified the ability of the Republics to exercise these rights). Furthermore, although the right to secede was guaranteed in the Constitution, there were no provisions for ascertaining whether or not the citizens of a particular Republic wished to avail themselves of this right.[21] A further juridic obstacle to secession was that, according to article 6 of the Constitution, it was the Union, not the Union Republics which owned the land. But the key factor which ensured that the right of secession would never be exercised was the fact that Moscow maintained strict control over the communist organisations in the Union Republics.

The Soviets asserted that the 1944 amendments had led to a strengthening of the sovereignties of the Union republics, without in any way resulting in a weakening of the unity of the USSR. As Korovin argued: 'in the USSR, continuous strengthening of the sovereignties of the Union republics . . . will not only not lead to national discord or a weakening of the internal unity of the Union but, (conversely), will secure the growth of brotherly cooperation of the peoples of the USSR.'[22] Moreover, the strengthening of the sovereignty of the Union would serve to consolidate the sovereignties of the Union Republics, because the USSR would be in a stronger position to defend the Republics from attacks from outside.[23]

Although the USSR was officially said to be a voluntary union (so that countries were free both to enter and to withdraw) the element of 'voluntariness' in practice was limited indeed. Even prior to their enforced amalgamation with the RSFSR in 1922, the Soviet Republics were ruled from Moscow and therefore were not in a position to enter the USSR 'voluntarily'. The manner by which the Baltic Republics (annexed in 1940) entered the Union was hardly a convincing testimony to the voluntariness of entry. The 'voluntariness' of withdrawal from the Union was also open to question. In 1920 Stalin had argued that, although the non-Russian nations within the Soviet domain possessed the inalienable right to secede from Russia, the demand for secession at that point was 'counter-revolutionary' because 'it would undermine the revolutionary might of central Russia' and because 'the seceded border regions would unquestionably fall into imperialist bondage'.[24] Stalin argued that Georgia, Armenia, Poland and Finland had retained only the appearance of independence, whereas in reality they were the 'complete vassals of the entente'.[25]

SATELLITISATION: ALTERNATIVE OR PRELUDE TO ANNEXATION?

Regardless of whether the 1944 amendments were in part designed to pave the way for the incorporation of Eastern Europe into the Soviet Federation, it is significant that the Soviets were espousing a notion of 'double' or 'concurrent' sovereignty which was founded on the idea of symbiosis – as distinct from a tension – between the sovereignty of the Soviet Federation and the sovereignties of the Union Republics.[26] This notion might be termed the *matryoshchka* doctrine of sovereignty, in that it assumes that an amalgam of sovereignties can be contained within a larger sovereign unit (although the analogy is not quite apt, since the Federation is said to be an integral union in which the component units are said to be organically and indissolubly inter-connected): before the end of the Second World War, therefore, the Soviets had already developed the theoretical and constitutional framework for the transmutation of the East European countries into 'fully sovereign' Union Republics of the USSR. Two years after the introduction of these constitutional amendments, Stalin announced in an 'electoral address' in Moscow that the Soviet Federation provided the basis for the future union of nations.[27]

Evidence that Stalin was contemplating a policy of wholesale annexation in Eastern Europe is provided by Djilas, who was present at a meeting presided over by Stalin in the Kremlin in 1948, at which various federal and confederal schemes for reforging the boundaries of Eastern Europe were discussed.[28] According to Djilas, who based his judgement on 'Stalin's stated position and on vague allusions by Soviet diplomats at the time',[29] Stalin was considering the idea of joining the countries of Eastern Europe on to the Soviet Union – 'the Ukraine with Hungary and Romania, Belorussia with Poland and Czechoslovakia, while the Balkan states were to be joined with Russia'.[30] In this period, the prospect of the amalgamation of the Eastern European countries into the Soviet Federation was seriously, indeed enthusiastically, entertained by several prominent East European communists and therefore Stalin's electoral address cannot be dismissed as a rhetorical flight of fancy. For example, a Soviet policy of annexation in Eastern Europe would have received the enthusiastic support of Gheorghiu-Dej[31] of Romania and Eduard Kardelj of Yugoslavia: when the Soviet break with Yugoslavia came out into the open, the Soviet Central Committee informed its Yugoslav counterpart that, in 1945, Kardelj had suggested to the Soviet Ambassador in Belgrade that Yugoslavia should be incorporated into the Soviet Union.[32] Whatever the truth of this particular allegation, prominent members of East Europe's communist parties were eager to gain favour with Stalin by pandering to (and seeking to anticipate) his every whim: so closely were the Peoples Democracies bound to Moscow in the early postwar years, the establishment of these regimes might reasonably have been interpreted as a decisive stage in the transmutation of the states of Eastern Europe into Soviet

Republics. The policy of 'duplication' served not only to draw these countries more closely into the Soviet orbit, but also removed some of the main obstacles to complete political union of the Soviet Union and the East European states (e.g. opposition groups, outlets for public dissent, disparities in political and economic structures, etc.).

Why then, did Stalin exercise 'forbearance' and forgo a policy of outright annexation? Despite its claim to be inherently incapable of acts of annexation, the Soviet Union had by no means resisted entirely opportunities for territorial aggrandisement as a result of the Second World War. For example, although a signatory to the Atlantic Charter, which prohibited states from pursuing policies of territorial aggrandisement as a war aim, the USSR annexed part of Eastern Prussia (including the capital city of Konigsberg) and the Czechoslovak area of Ruthenia at the end of the Second World War. The acquisition of territory as a war aim was not, therefore, alien to Soviet foreign policy as Soviet spokesmen have consistently claimed. The reasons for Stalin's decision to restore formal sovereignty to both vanquished and liberated countries of Eastern Europe must, there-fore, be sought elsewhere.

The maintenance of the formal sovereignty of the East European states held several possible attractions for the USSR. One obvious advantage of maintaining the fiction that the East European countries were fully sovereign states was that it helped to mask (albeit not very effectively) the extent of Soviet interference in the area. A policy of wholesale annexation in Eastern Europe might have weakened the appeal of Soviet communism in the colonial world (and in parts of Western Europe) by raising awkward questions concerning the Soviet Union's entitlement to the status of a valiant and selfless champion of self-determination. The cutting edge of the sword of sovereignty wielded by the Soviets in their propaganda campaigns against West-ern colonialism would undoubtedly have been dulled (regardless of the constitutional camouflage with which an annexationist policy would have been disguised). It is doubtful, however, if concern about the Soviet Union's 'world image' was the primary factor in staying Stalin's hand. Stalin and his successors in the Kremlin have demons-trated a preparedness to forgo the diplomatic asset of a favourable 'world image' in pursuit of Soviet 'core' objectives in Eastern Europe.

A Soviet annexationist policy would have increased the prospect of armageddon between the USSR and the West: the Western response to perceived Soviet expansionary drives in Greece, Turkey and Iran, coupled with Soviet behaviour in Eastern Europe, was an indication of the worsening state of relations between the Western allies and the Soviet Union.[33] Although the Western powers had grudgingly acquiesced in the integration of the states of Eastern Europe into the Soviet sphere, formal incorporation of Eastern Europe into the USSR would have been a different matter. The formation of a protective belt of compliant East European states also had the effect of insulating the Soviet regime from direct Western influence, and provided it with a deep defensive barrier against military attack from the West. The removal of this 'cordon sanitaire', through a westward shift of the Soviet Union's borders, would have inflamed the already widespread Western fear that Stalin was poised to overrun the whole of Europe.

Stalin's decision not to annex the occupied states of Eastern Europe was also probably influenced by the well-founded belief that the incorporation of, say, Poland, Hungary, Romania, East Germany and Czechoslovakia would, sooner or later, have created grave internal problems for the USSR. Given that Hitler had so inflamed national feelings in the region, the sovereignty slogan was popular with East Europeans and the Soviets were quick to realise its political appeal – to the extent of utilising 'horizontal' antagonisms in Eastern Europe (for example, the traditional hostility between Romanians and Hungarians, and Polish anti-German feeling) in order to foster Soviet goals. The East European communist parties used territorial disputes with neighbours (Romania with Bulgaria over Dobruja, Hungary with Romania over Transylvania and with Czechoslovakia over Teschen) in order to bolster their standing as 'patriots' and thus improve their domestic popularity.[34] The emergence of 'nationalist' tendencies within the East European communist parties was evidence of the continuing importance of ethnic sentiment within the region. Annexation of these countries would have been of a different order of magnitude from that of the Baltic states in 1940: nationalist resistance in these mini-states could be crushed easily. Furthermore, Latvia, Lithuania and Estonia had previously been part of the Tsarist Empire. Several of the bloc states had never comprised part of Russian Imperial territory and therefore the Soviet claim on these countries was decidedly weak. Stalin may have calculated that the incorporation of Eastern Europe would have been too great an ethnic mouthful – although fear of 'territorial indigestion' had not deterred the Soviets from annexing areas inhabited by non-Russian nationalities in the 1920s.

The analysis has so far been based on the assumption that Stalin regarded the prospect of a Soviet annexation of Eastern Europe as intrinsically desirable and that he was dissuaded from pursuing this objective by the pressure of events and the fear of nationalist revolts which an annexationist policy might have provoked. However, Stalin's behaviour towards the People's Democracies could, perhaps, be plausibly interpreted as evidence of an awareness on his part of the possible dangers which might have resulted from the incorporation of Eastern Europe into the Soviet Federation. Thus, in addition to the policy of 'duplication', Stalin also rigidly enforced a policy of insulation in relation to the Peoples Democracies – by ensuring that contacts between the peoples of Eastern Europe and the Soviet Union were kept to a minimum. Deutscher[35] argues that this policy was rooted in Stalin's paranoid fear that contact between the Western-oriented peoples of Eastern Europe (and in particular the Czechs, East Germans, Poles and Hungarians) and the Soviet population might infect Soviet citizens with subversive ideas.

Therefore, Stalin may have perceived the countries of Eastern Europe as the equivalent of a Trojan horse, which could have jeopardised the survival of the USSR's totalitarian bureaucratic structures from within. In addition to the policy of sealing off Eastern Europe from Western influence, Stalin also erected 'iron curtains' within the region: the desire to avoid the transference of cultural (especially political) values from the westward-looking states of Eastern Europe into the Soviet Union might thus have been the mainspring behind Stalin's policy of *divide et impera*, as manifested in his preference for bilateral contacts within the bloc. The multilateral agencies created by Stalin in this period – the Cominform and the CMEA – were little more than paper organisations: the Cominform was never invested with real power and withered away: nor was it a 'universal' communist organisation like the Comintern, since only two non-ruling parties (the Italian and French) were invited to its founding conference in 1947);[36] the CMEA came to life only after the traumas of 1956. Far from encouraging formal integration of the states of Eastern Europe through the medium of supranational agencies (which he would have been able to tightly control) Stalin took steps to prevent the development of multilateral links within the region: he brought to an end the Tito–Dimitrov plan for a Balkan Federation, which would have united Yugoslavia and Bulgaria (and possibly Romania and Albania) – even though this plan had initially received his imprimatur (at a meeting in Blad in July–August 1947, Dimitrov and Tito discussed the formation of a Balkan Union, based initially on a customs union, which could also have included Hungary, Czechoslovakia and perhaps even Poland). By January 1948, all federal and confederal plans or customs unions were being denounced by the Soviets.[37]

Brzezinski[38] has pointed out that an 'ideological' explanation for Stalin's decision not to annex these states might also be advanced, in that it could be argued that the countries of Eastern Europe were at a lower stage of socioeconomic development than the Soviet Union and therefore were unready for a merger with the world's first socialist society. This theory accords with Khrushchev's conception of the process by which the unification of socialist countries would be achieved – i.e. that the entry of socialist states into communism would be 'simultaneous' and would result from a process of 'convergence' or 'levelling up' of the less developed countries to the status of the most advanced.[39] However, the theory of 'simultaneous entry into communism' entered the corpus of Soviet doctrine only in the late 1950s, underpinning Khrushchev's drive for integration within the socialist camp. Far from inhibiting the process of unification, the theory has been used by Soviet theorists as an *ex post facto* rationalisation for the slow progress of socialist integration and as a method of reassuring the states of Eastern Europe that functional collaboration with the USSR will not impose unacceptable political and economic costs on the participating states and that full integration will not occur for a long time.[40] As Brzezinski[41] has noted, the 'unreadiness' argument is hardly credible as an explanation of why Stalin baulked at a policy of wholesale annexation in Eastern Europe, since the Soviet Federation itself was formed out of the most diverse kind of socioeconomic formation. Furthermore, even a cursory analysis of Stalin's foreign policy actions demonstrated that he would hardly have been troubled by doctrinal subtleties of this kind: for example, he had ignored this theoretical taboo when the Baltic states had been incorporated into the USSR.

It is of course possible that Stalin intended to annex the Peoples Democracies at some future date, when circumstances were more propitious – e.g. following an American military withdrawal from Europe. This does not, of course, mean that Stalin would have worked out a finely detailed blueprint for expansion. However, the entry of China into the socialist camp in 1949 and Tito's refusal to accept the subordinate role assigned to him by Stalin made the emergence of a socialist interstate subsystem inevitable. The existence of a phalanx of nominally independent, but in reality subordinate, socialist states was in any case not without its advantages for the USSR. For example, the Peoples Democracies provided the Soviet Union with an enthusiastic chorus of support for Soviet actions in the international arena: the Soviet Union had endeavoured to obtain seats in the UN for each of the constituent republics of the Soviet Federation, although only Belorussia and the Ukraine were given membership. However, the Peoples Democracies complemented the Soviet Union's existing instruments of diplomacy by their unwavering support for Soviet foreign policy positions (including the propaganda battles with Tito).

At the time there were substantial advantages in indirect rule, in that it offered fewer dangers and more practical benefits than wholesale territorial expansion. In relation to an earlier period in Soviet history, Ulam has noted that the failure of Soviet attempts at expansion was possibly a 'blessing in disguise for the future of communism in Soviet Russia'.[42] Ulam is referring to Soviet Russia's rout in the Soviet-Polish war of 1920, which ended Soviet plans for the transformation of Poland into a communist state: a Soviet conquest of Poland might well have provoked a wholehearted military thrust against the still vulnerable Soviet regime by the allies and therefore the defeat may well have contributed to the survival of the Bolshevik state. By the same token, and again with the benefit of hindsight, it might be argued that, far from 'missing the boat' by not annexing the states of Eastern Europe in the early postwar years, Stalin avoided a policy which, sooner or later, would have proved disastrous for the Soviet regime.

It also seems unlikely that Stalin could have foreseen the emergence of the centrifugal forces within the bloc which presented major challenges to Soviet hegemony within a few years of his death. Jamgotch[43] attributes this 'blind spot' to the nature of Marxist-Leninist ideology, which in his view provides no useful insight into the significance of national cleavages within a socialist regional system. However, the sheer weight of Soviet power in the region in this period may have nullified any anxieties the Soviets may have entertained about the prospects of maintaining Eastern Europe in a position of strict subordination. Indeed, a major reason why the Soviets could give unqualified verbal support to the sovereignty principle within Eastern Europe was precisely because of the pervasive nature of Soviet control. As will be seen, Soviet theoreticians have been driven to qualify their hitherto 'unqualified' affirmations of the sovereignty principle (by, for example, making disparaging references to 'unlimited sovereignty' as a standard of bourgeois law,[44] an 'anarchic argument', a 'false slogan'[45] and an example of 'mendacious phraseology'[46]) when the Peoples Democracies begin to behave like sovereign states in their relations with the USSR. At such times and particularly during Soviet crises of control in Eastern Europe, the Soviets have sought to divest the sovereignty principle of its generally accepted meaning, by reminding states within the bloc that relations between socialist states must ultimately rest upon the paramount Marxist-Leninist value of 'proletarian internationalism'.

Stalin's preference for a policy of 'indirect rule' (the control of Eastern Europe through the medium of dependent satraps, propped up where necessary by Soviet force) raises the central issue of whether the Peoples Democracies deserved to be recognised as sovereign states at all (an issue which Durbrow, the head of the US State Department's East European Affairs Division, sought to raise in this period).[47] Regardless of semantic differences between East and West over the meaning of sovereignty, the East European regimes were grudgingly accepted as sovereign states by the West: they took their places at the UN and were recognised even by the Western states which had volubly denounced the manner of their creation and which denounced their 'sovereignty' as merely the juridic camouflage for Soviet dominance. The 'Stimson doctrine' (non-recognition of puppet regimes such as Manchukuo) was not applied to Eastern Europe by the US.

ASYMMETRICAL POWER RELATIONSHIPS WITHIN INTERNATIONAL SUBSYSTEMS

History provides many examples of 'asymmetrical' or hegemonial relationships within international systems. The most commonly used description of the Peoples Democracies in the West has been the term 'satellites';[48] but other terms – such as 'buffer states', 'penetrated political systems',[49] 'vassal states', 'fictional states', 'client states',[50] 'dependent states'[51] and 'derivative regimes'[52] have also been used. Each of these terms implies a disparity between the formally sovereign status of a regime and its *de facto* subordination to the will of a more powerful state. Evaluation of the status of the East European regimes was made difficult by the fact that the concept of 'Peoples Democracy' was virtually unknown prior to the formation of the 'new democracies' in Eastern Europe. A distinctive feature of relations between the Soviet Union and the Peoples Democracies was the significance of interparty (as distinct from interstate) connections. Since the Soviet party claimed to be the leading party in the international communist movement, the subordination of the East European regimes could be justified on the grounds of the paramount need for ideological solidarity. Vali has argued that 'party to party subordination' was the key element in the 'fictive and delusive' attribution of independence to the East European satellites.[53] Each of these subordinate parties exercised a pervasive control over the institutions of their countries, and therefore *de facto* Soviet dominance within the bloc was assured – a form of proprietorial rights exercised through 'indirect rule'.

The Western legal scholar Korowicz distinguishes between 'legal-factual' and 'factual-political' satellitisation, the difference being that 'legal-factual' satellitisation is based on treaties which formally subordinate the satellite to the hegemonial power, whereas 'factual-political' satellites are formally independent.[54] Korowicz notes that contemporary international law disregards the 'factual-political' type of satellitisation, because it does not fall within the ambit of juridical problems (i.e. a factually dependent state is regarded as fully sovereign in international law).[55] However, the distinction is regarded as significant, because factual-political satellitisation may allow the satellite to enter into foreign relations, which may at some point lead to an enlargement of its independence. Given that the history of the Soviet regime had been a movement towards internal centralisation and – where possible – outward expansion (regardless of any formal commitments to the sovereignty and self-determination principles) the prospects for the enlargement of the independence of the Peoples Democracies in the early postwar years could hardly have looked very promising. For example, the transmutation of the governments of Peoples Democracy from coalitions into 'proletarian dictatorships' did not augur well for the independence of these regimes. Similarly, if the East European countries were perceived as performing the function of 'buffer states' between the Soviet Union and the West, previous Soviet behaviour suggested that even the nominal independence of these states would be short lived: in 1920, the Bolsheviks had created the 'Far Eastern Republic' as a buffer against Japanese aggression, but within two years it had been absorbed into Soviet Russia.

Nevertheless, with the benefit of hindsight it is possible to discern both centripetal and centrifugal forces acting upon the relations between the Soviet Union and the Peoples Democracies in this period. Although the East European states were clearly situated towards the 'dependence' end of the 'dependence-independence' continuum, like all international relationships, intra-bloc relations were essentially dynamic. Aspaturian[56] distinguishes between 'fictional', 'vassal' and 'client' states: a 'fictional' state possesses some of the formal attributes of statehood but 'remains a legal and political component of another state or subject of international law' (and, in particular, has no separate legal system);[57] 'vassalage' is synonymous with the status of 'puppet' or 'satellite' regimes; the broadest of Aspaturian's three categories is that of 'clientage': 'client states' possess all of the formal attributes of independent statehood. Unlike a 'vassal', a 'client state' possesses, in large measure, control over its internal affairs and its government is not imposed by the larger state. However, the foreign policies of clients will be conditioned by the requirements and sensitivities of the larger state. He discerned signs that some of the states of Eastern Europe were already moving from 'vassalage' to 'clientage'.[58]

The description of the Soviet bloc as an imperial or colonial system (a charge made by Tito in 1948) also implies restrictions on the sovereignty of the bloc states. 'Imperialism' generally implies international domination. The object of this domination, in contemporary theories of imperialism (derived largely from Lenin), is economic exploitation. More recently, Western scholars have sought to utilise 'dependency theory' in order to make sense of the asymmetrical relationships between the Soviet Union and the Peoples Democracies. This strain of the modern theory of imperialism seeks to explain how Western capitalist states (the 'centre') have maintained their exploitative relationships over formally independent 'Third World' countries (the 'periphery'). However, its central propositions – the assumption of inequality between the capitalist powers and the underdeveloped states; the notion that the economies of the dependent states have been deliberately malstructured by the capitalist powers in their own interest; the idea of cultural as well as political penetration of the dependent states; that relationships between the capitalist powers and the 'Third World' are essentially exploitative and based upon unequal commercial relationships; that formal sovereignty of the underdeveloped states is simply a cover for a complex web of dependence; and that the elites in the 'periphery' have a vested interest in maintaining their countries in a state of subjection[59] – seem highly pertinent to the relationships between the Soviet Union and the Peoples Democracies.

In modern dependency theory, the elites in the periphery are also viewed as politically dependent upon the centre. The Kremlin's 'duplication' policy was founded on a contrived symbiosis between the East European and Soviet parties. Other Soviet policies (e.g. the redirection of the pattern of East European trade; the restructuring of the economies of the bloc states; the imposition of Soviet political and legal structures and of Soviet (Russian) cultural values upon these states; and of the outflow of resources from the 'periphery' to the 'centre') fit the model of 'dependence' outlined above, despite the fact that a key element of 'dependency' theory is that capitalism is the driving force of 'centre-periphery' relationships. Soviet economic exploitation of the bloc states in the Stalin period is well documented and one study has estimated that the outflow of resources from Eastern Europe to the Soviet Union in this period was roughly equal to the inflow of resources from the US under the Marshall Plan.[60] Contemporary writers have noted that Eastern Europe is now an economic liability to the Soviet Union and therefore that the economic exploitation motive central to the dependency model no longer 'fits'.[61] However, even in the Stalin years, there were differences between Soviet hegemony in Eastern Europe and the 'centre-periphery' model outlined above. For example, the Soviet Union's primary motive in establishing its *gleichschaltung* in Eastern Europe was probably the search for security on her Western borders. Moreover, in dependency theory, capitalist domination of the Third World is not assumed to necessitate the imposition of 'duplicative' regime structures within the periphery. Similarly, in dependency theory, the organisational nexus of centre-periphery relations is the transnational corporation rather than interstate or interparty relationships. In Eastern Europe, the local populations tended to regard themselves as culturally superior to the hegemonial power.

The asymmetrical power relationships between the Soviet Union and the bloc states were made possible by the *de facto* delineation of Eastern Europe as a Soviet 'zone of influence' or sphere of interest. Vazquez defines a 'zone of influence' as a 'space tacitly or expressly reserved to the hegemony of one state'.[62] Kaufman see three principal elements in a 'sphere of interest': firstly, a power declares its interest in attaining a status of dominance; secondly, this status is recognised by major outside powers; thirdly, regimes within the sphere accept (acquiesce or resign themselves to) their dependent conditions.[63] Others have made the distinction, following Lord Curzon, between a 'sphere of interest' and a 'sphere of influence', with the former referring to the fact that a state may have an interest in an area, but may not seek to become the dominant influence, although Curzon acknowledged that the tendency was for 'the weaker to crystallise into the harder shape', with spheres of interest becoming spheres of influence, culminating in complete incorporation.[64]

Roosevelt, Secretary of State Hull and the Joint Chiefs of Staff explicitly opposed the principle of spheres of interest during the War.[65] At Yalta it was agreed that the states of Eastern Europe should have democratic, representative governments. However, Soviet and American interpretations of the concept of 'democratic, representative government' were poles apart (an example of the semantic cross purposes which were later to pervade the Helsinki accords). Moreover, Churchill's percentage formula for deciding spheres of preponderance in Eastern Europe (accepted by Stalin in his meeting with Churchill in Moscow in October 1944) provided formal Western acceptance of the region as a Soviet sphere of interest:[66] however, the formula principle (e.g. that the Soviets would have a 75 per cent influence in Bulgaria and the others 25 per cent) was a mathematical synonym for traditional spheres of interest terminology, such as 'taking the lead'. Eastern Europe has never been a 'sphere of interest' in the literal sense in the postwar era: rather, it has been in Rusk's words, a 'sphere of domination'.[67] The Soviets blame the US and Britain for the division of Europe and argue that Stalin rejected Churchill's proposals for the division of Europe on the basis of spheres of interest.[68] Western misunderstandings concerning the postwar division of Europe, as Lowenthal argues, derived from a failure to comprehend the nature of Soviet Marxism-Leninism, which is an ideology of dominance:[69] the Soviets could not tolerate non-communist 'friendly governments' within their sphere, any more than they could tolerate a non-communist opposition within their domestic system.

4 Early Postwar Soviet Theories of Socialist International Relations

THE ROLE OF THE SOVIET UNION WITHIN THE SOCIALIST CAMP

The Soviet decision to pursue a 'duplicative', as distinct from an annexationist, policy in postwar Eastern Europe presented Soviet theoreticians with several interrelated theoretical problems: firstly, what was to be the role of the Soviet Union within the camp of socialism? Would it, for example, renounce its position as the fount and centre of the international communist movement now that the socialist revolution had been extended to other states? The second question concerned the nature of the 'new type' of international relations which were said to be burgeoning within the camp: in what ways did international relations between socialist states differ from relations between bourgeois states? Thirdly, what were the essential characteristics of the 'new democracies' in Eastern Europe? Fourthly, since the Soviet Union and the Peoples Democracies comprised a 'camp', what was to be the posture of this collective socialist entity towards the capitalist world? The issue of sovereignty was central to each of these questions: thus the Soviet solution to the problem of defining the essential nature of 'socialist' international relations hinged on an assumption of a harmonious – indeed, symbiotic – relationship between sovereignty and socialism.

The formulation of sophisticated answers to these questions was hindered by the intellectually inhibiting conditions in which Soviet theorists worked: firstly, there was the problem of achieving synchronicity between theory and Soviet policy (the danger of 'lags and leads'). Soviet theorists could be criticised for failing to anticipate shifts in Soviet policy leading to the enunciation of 'new orthodoxies'. For example, the views of leading economist Varga on the state of capitalism (in 1946 he argued that it had entered a period of temporary stabilisation) and on the nature of the 'new democracies' (he regarded them as progressive, but not socialist, regimes) were soon to be askew with new orthodoxies.[1] Similarly, theorists could be penalised for prematurely espousing future orthodoxies: e.g. the international legal specialists Korovin and Kozhevnikov were penalised for tentatively advancing the notion of 'socialist international law' years before it became official Soviet doctrine.[2] Secondly, the development of Soviet theories concerning contemporary international issues was impeded by the dearth of scholarship in this field: as a discipline, International Relations did not begin to develop in the Soviet Union until after the 20th party congress in 1956.[3] Thirdly, Soviet legal scholars in this period acknowledged that the function of their work was to serve Soviet policy: this primarily meant policy advocacy (exposition and justification) rather than research as an aid to policy formulation.[4]

These constraints did not mean, however, that Soviet doctrine in this period was rigid and inflexible: as De George has argued, 'the Soviet pattern of thought is both dogmatic and unchanging in certain basic presuppositions and flexible and changing in large elements of its superstructure'.[5] Indeed, Soviet theorists were required to adapt theory to new circumstances and conditions: theoretical reformulations leading to the enunciation of 'new orthodoxies' were underway in a number of key policy areas: e.g. the discussion concerning capitalist crises and cycles; the nature of 'Peoples Democracy'; international legal relations within the socialist camp; and Marxism, and the problem of linguistics, a discussion initiated by Stalin.[6] However, despite Stalin's forays into the realm of doctrine, he made no first-hand contribution to postwar theoretical discussions concerning Eastern Europe.

'Slav solidarity'

Soviet expositions of the relationship between the Soviet Union and Eastern Europe were clearest in their references to the special role of the USSR. There were two phases in Soviet attempts to reconcile the USSR's primacy in Eastern Europe with the claim that the Peoples Democracies were fully sovereign states: the first phase lasted roughly until the classification of the Peoples Democracies as socialist states. In this period, Soviet commentators espoused 'slavic realm' or 'slav solidarity' theories as means of justifying the Soviet Union's special role in the region: for example, although Leonidov rejected Western assertions that the Soviet Union was pursuing a 'pan-Slavic' policy, he nevertheless argued that the Second World War brought about a 'new phase in Slav history', in which the Slav nations would strengthen their ties with the Soviet Union (he assured his readers that the Soviet Union had no intention of imposing its own social system upon other Slav states).[7] East European communists also incorporated 'pan-Slavic' elements into their expositions of Soviet-East European relations. For example, Gomulka argued in the first number of the Cominform journal in 1947 that 'alliance with the USSR is the keystone . . . and Slav solidarity is the second bulwark of our foreign policy'.[8]

There were several reasons, however, why 'Slav solidarity' was an unsatisfactory basis for Soviet regional hegemony: firstly, it could strike no chord with Romanians, Hungarians or East Germans; secondly, it would have been incongruent with the Soviet self-image as a special type of state, founded upon universalist socialist principles (indeed, the term 'USSR' was deliberately chosen to avoid identification with specific national groupings); thirdly, it would have impeded the possibility of the future expansion of the Soviet Union into non-Slavic areas of Europe; fourthly, the Soviets already had a serviceable doctrine which bestowed upon the USSR a unique 'vanguard role' in the international system: 'proletarian internationalism'.

In the second phase, Soviet paramountcy was justified by reference to the USSR's position as 'head of the socialist camp'.[9] As Zhdanov asserted: 'History has placed the USSR at the head of the progressive development of mankind, culture and the civilisation of nations.'[10] The positive attitude of the USSR towards other socialist states was said to be no cynical policy option, but rather the natural outcome of the regime's socialist character (a position following from the Marxist–Leninist postulate of the relationship between base and superstructure).[11] An analysis of Soviet commentaries on Eastern Europe in this period elicits four special roles claimed by the Soviet Union in the region, each deriving from the advanced level of development of the world's first socialist state.

1) *A vanguard or 'standard bearer' role*

The Soviet Union was said to be blazing a trail for other socialist states to follow. Farberov and other Soviet commentators proudly stressed the extent to which the experience of state construction in the USSR was being utilised in the Peoples Democracies.[12] Thus the Soviet Union was a state of a new type, showing 'all peoples the road to communism'.[13] A *Pravda* editorial in 1949 declared that 'the experience of the building of communism accumulated under the leadership of Lenin and Stalin is now at the service of the workers of the Peoples Democracies'.[14] Because the Peoples Democracies were following the same path of development as the Soviet Union, they could benefit from Soviet experience and tutelage. As Gheorghiu-Dej of Romania put it: 'the rich experience of socialist construction acquired by the Soviet people is our guiding star.'[15] For Gottwald, mastery of Soviet experience was an essential requirement for socialist construction in Czechoslovakia,[16] a principle of development reiterated through the bloc.[17]

2) A pedagogic role

The trailblazing, paragon role of the Soviet Union did not mean that the Kremlin was content merely to set an example of correct Marxist-Leninist practice to fledgeling socialist regimes: it took on an active pedagogic role in instructing the Peoples Democracies in the techniques of socialist construction, using the 'reliable compass of Lenin-Stalin teaching'.[18] The Peoples Democracies were required to learn from Soviet experience in all spheres.[19] In an article entitled 'A Treasure Store of Experience', N. Leonidov wrote a glowing account of the Soviet Union's selfless actions in helping the Peoples Democracies along the 'tried and tested' road to socialism: he also noted that delegations from the Peoples Democracies were visiting the Soviet Union to study the 'great example'.[20] The teacher–pupil relationship was justified on the grounds of the Soviet state's unique, 'world-historic' experience of socialist construction and of the ideological leadership of Stalin, the 'teacher and guide of all working people'.[21]

3) A 'chaperon' or 'defender' role

The Soviet 'chaperon role' sought to protect the new democracies from two principal dangers:

a) *the external danger* from the aggression of the advanced capitalist states (whether in the form of direct military aggression or economic subversion). By vanquishing fascism and thereby creating the conditions for the emergence of the Peoples Democracies, the USSR could claim to be the 'parent' of the Peoples Democracies and could claim parental rights. As Frantsev put it: 'People in the new democracies understand that only thanks to the Soviet army were the countries liberated . . . they are aware that, without the help and support of the Soviet Union, they would not be able to construct socialism.'[22] Only the Soviet state possessed the military capacity to defend the Peoples Democracies against

Western aggression: 'only the constant support and assistance of the Soviet Union guaranteed the Peoples Democracies the preservation of their national sovereignty . . . and the possibility of their successful evolution towards socialism.'[23] Indeed, the very existence of small and vulnerable states in the international system depended upon the preparedness of the USSR to come to their defence. Only the might of the Soviet Union prevented the forces of world imperialism from 'strangling the Peoples Democracies in their cradles'.[24] In Soviet publications and in the Cominform journal, East European communist leaders gratefully acknowledged the Soviet Union's defensor role: in Dimitrov's words, without 'the Soviet Union there would be no . . . independence for the peoples of South Eastern Europe'.[25]

b) *the danger from within*   The Soviets delivered stern warnings about the danger from 'national nihilism' and the 'anti-patriotic ideology of "bourgeois cosmopolitanism" '.[26] Thus although the bourgeoisie had been defeated in the Peoples Democracies, nationalism was said to be 'the main danger to the successful construction of the new state system and to the advance of the [Peoples Democracies] towards socialism'.[27] This danger could only be averted by faithful adherence to proletarian internationalism: in practice this meant support for the Soviet Union, because 'the attitude to the Soviet Union is the keystone of genuine proletarian internationalism for all Communists, for all genuine patriots'.[28]

4) *An 'economic benefactor' role*

The 'selfless help' of the Soviet Union towards the Peoples Democracies was, according to Soviet commentators, playing a crucial role in the process of economic reconstruction in Eastern Europe.[29] Soviet economic assistance was said to have a positive character, unadulterated by ulterior motives. The 'fraternal assistance' rendered by the Soviet Union to the Peoples Democracies in the Stalinist period followed, according to contemporary Soviet commentators, from the regime's fidelity to the principle of proletarian internationalism. Soviet journals were full of articles extolling the 'disinterested aid' rendered by the world's first socialist state to the Peoples Democracies.[30] Western economic assistance, by contrast, was motivated by the desire to exploit and dominate the recipient state. As Leonidov asserted: 'unlike the enthralling Marshall Plan agreements, the Soviet Union is assisting the industrialisation of the Peoples

Democracies quite disinterestedly and with full respect for their national sovereignty.'[31] Exuberantly fanciful descriptions of Soviet-East European relations in this period hardly squared with the observations of Tito (who accused the Soviet Union of wishing to turn the formerly independent states of Eastern Europe into 'mere colonies in the heart of Europe')[32] or with Western analyses.[33]

Each of these four self-assigned roles served to limit the sovereignties of the East European states. For example, the 'vanguard' and 'pedagogic' roles set the parameters of development for the Peoples Democracies: the single legitimate path of development was the one already traversed by the world's first socialist state. In the immediate postwar period, East European communist leaders denied that the new regimes would replicate the Soviet form.[34] However, this 'particularist' position was soon abandoned in favour of the ortho-doxy that the Soviet road was the only correct path towards socialism – crystallised in Gottwald's slogan: 'the Soviet Union – our model'. The 'chaperon' role gave the Soviet Union the right not only to defend the welfare of its wards but also to define that welfare (and to correct any wayward behaviour – such as the desire to follow the pied piper of Marshall Aid). A 'chaperon' is well placed to define the threats and to identify the enemies against which the ward must be defended. It also provided a justification for the stationing of Soviet troops in Eastern Europe. The 'economic benefactor' role – meaning in practice the redirection of East European trade and economic sovietisation – served to bind the bloc states closer to Moscow.

The 'Touchstone doctrine'

Despite Soviet claims that relations within the bloc were based on equality, and on a rejection of the 'big power hegemony' exercised by the USA in its domain, the Peoples Democracies were placed in a position of inferiority and subordination to the Soviet Union from the beginning of the Soviet *gleichschaltung*. In his article extolling the Soviet Union's 'aid' policy to the Peoples Democracies, Leonidov declared that, because of the Soviet Union's special position within the international communist movement, the USSR had a right to expect unwavering support from the peoples of Eastern Europe. He even quoted with reverential zeal Stalin's definition of 'international-ism' – i.e. 'an internationalist is one who is prepared unreservedly, unhesitatingly and unconditionally to defend the USSR'.[35] Leonidov's reminder that communists abroad had a duty to support the prevailing Soviet conception of doctrinal orthodoxy in international affairs was a bald, but nevertheless faithful, restatement of the Soviet 'touchstone' doctrine, which had been formulated in the period when the Soviet regime had been the beleaguered citadel of world socialism and when, therefore, the aspirations of communists throughout the world could plausibly seem to depend upon the survival of the world's first socialist state. In these circumstances, it is perhaps little wonder that the fates of the Soviet Union and of world socialism could appear inextricable, or that Stalin's definition of 'internationalism' could gain general acceptance within the international communist movement. However, Leonidov clearly indicated that the emergence of the Peoples Democracies made no difference to the validity of Stalin's conception of 'internationalism'.

The 'touchstone' doctrine proved to be too valuable for the Kremlin to discard after the emergence of other socialist states (other potential 'touchstones'): East Europe's leaders publicly reiterated the prewar slogan that fidelity to the USSR was the touchstone of genuine internationalism.[36] By 1948, however, the validity of the Soviet claim to ideological infallibility (and of its corollary – that there was only one road to socialism) was being challenged from within Eastern Europe. Yugoslavia's references to Soviet foreign policy as 'unsocialist', 'imperialist' and 'hegemonistic', combined with Tito's explicit rejection of the USSR's claim to a leading role within the international communist movement, constituted a serious blow to the Kremlin's ambition to retain its status as the directing centre of world socialism. The Soviet response to Tito's refusal to follow the Kremlin's line – anti-Tito diatribes, unilateral repudiation of the Soviet-Yugoslav mutual assistance treaty, ostracism (as exemplified by the expulsion of Yugoslavia from the Cominform in 1948) and threats from Stalin's 'little finger' – all failed to bring Yugoslavia back into line.

The shift in the primary focus of loyalty of international communists from the movement *per se* to the Soviet state represented a reversal of the means–end chain: however, although the touchstone doctrine was to lose much of its power in the postwar era, in some respects, it was to assume even greater prominence in Soviet thought, as a direct result of challenges by both ruling and non-ruling parties to the Soviet Union's claim to a special position within the world communist movement. The doctrine was frequently employed by the Soviets as a means of condemning developments in the Peoples

Democracies which deviate from the path of socialist orthodoxy as defined by the USSR. Since this theory bestows upon Moscow the exclusive right to pronounce upon the correctness or otherwise of the domestic and foreign policies pursued by the Peoples Democracies (and also to take the necessary measures to reverse dangerous departures from the Soviet road to socialism) the touchstone doctrine can be said to bear a remarkable resemblance to the Brezhnev Doctrine of limited sovereignty. Indeed, Lendvai has characterised the doctrine as an 'updated and broadened version' of the touchstone theory.[37] Again, it might be viewed as another example of the Soviet tendency to refashion old doctrines by extrapolating organisational principles formulated in the period when the Soviet Union was the only socialist state onto the 'horizontal' interstate socialist system of the present era. Originally, the touchstone doctrine owed its force to the fact that – in theory at least, if not in Stalinist practice – it was viewed by the international communist movement as a 'vertical' concept: loyalty to particular state interests was subordinated to the higher international interest as represented (temporarily) by the Soviet Union.

'PEOPLES DEMOCRACY': A NOVITIATE STAGE OF SOCIALIST DEVELOPMENT

The Soviet assumption of special roles in relation to the socialist camp hinged upon a definition of Peoples Democracy which would justify the subordinate and dependent status of the East European regimes. The notion of a 'Popular Democratic state' as expounded by Soviet theorists crystallised into an authoritative form around mid-1948. Prior to this, there was no unanimity of view among Soviet commentators concerning the nature and characteristics of this new state form.[38] The genealogy of this notion in Soviet thought has been traced back to three principal sources: firstly, to Soviet categorisations of its satellites in the prewar period; thus in the first years of Bolshevik rule, it was used to characterise the regimes installed in parts of Russia by Soviet military force in which local communist party organisations had to rely on the peasantry in the absence of an industrial working class in those areas:[39] the nominally independent Peoples Republics of Bukhara, Khiva and the Far East were soon absorbed into the Soviet Federation. The Soviet Union's Asian satellites, Outer Mongolia and Tannu Tuva, were described as 'bourgeois democratic republics of the new type' in the 1930s.[40] Secondly, to the relationships which communist parties developed with non-communist groups before the Second World War, owing to circumstances unfavourable to the establishment of a 'pure' form of proletarian dictatorship – i.e. the idea of coalitions against fascism, in which communist parties would assume the leading role. The idea of a 'united front' against fascism had first been tried in France in 1934 and was officially adopted by the Comintern a year later at its 7th congress. Following an article in *Pravda* in May 1934 – which stated that it was permissible for communists to forge alliances with socialist groups, the French, Italian and Spanish communists all signed pacts with socialist parties. As Claudin has noted, the idea of a 'Peoples Front' – i.e. of collaboration between communist and bourgeois parties – was a novel one for the Comintern.[41] Indeed, the very notion of collaboration with bourgeois parties ran counter to the Leninist principles of organisational and doctrinal purity upon which the Comintern had been founded. Nevertheless, the concept of the 'Peoples Front', from a communist standpoint, did not embrace the notion of an equality of influence between the coalition partners: rather, it was viewed as a temporary marriage of convenience in which the communists would assume the dominant role. The term 'Peoples Democracy' first appeared in an editorial in the Comintern journal in October 1936.[42] Thirdly, Schwartz has noted that the ideas in Mao Tse Tung's work on *New Democracy* (1940) bear a striking resemblance to early Soviet conceptualisations of 'Peoples Democracy'.[43]

The development of the Soviet theory of 'Peoples Democracy' illustrates the conflict in Soviet objectives towards Eastern Europe in the early postwar years. As Rosa[44] has pointed out, this lack of a coherent theory of Peoples Democracy probably derived from expediency: on the one hand, it benefited the Soviets to stress the differences in developmental patterns of the Soviet Union and the East European states (in order to allay East European fears of enforced Sovietisation and Russification) and on the other the Soviets felt it necessary to assume ideological leadership within the region by formulating an explanatory theory of 'Peoples Democracy' which squared with Marxism-Leninism, Ross Johnson has noted the significance of both 'instrumental' motivations (e.g. to correspond with the popular mood for change, but to avoid the unpopularity that overt Sovietisation would have engendered) and 'ideological' responses (which would serve to justify the communist parties' assumption of leadership – and the Soviet Party's leading role within the socialist camp).[45] The development of the Soviet theory of Peoples Democracy exemplifies the links between ideology and 'action' in Soviet policy and the relationships between Soviet ideological formulations and Soviet foreign policy goals: the orthodoxy which emerged in 1948 – espoused not only by Soviet commentators, but also by East European communist party leaders – justified the integration of the states of Eastern Europe into the Soviet sphere. By 1947, the notion of 'gradualism' as a theory of the development was being supplanted by formulations which emphasised the rapid transition of Eastern Europe towards Soviet socialism.[46]

The problem of the nature of the East European regimes stimulated a lively debate amongst Soviet theoreticians. Skilling[47] has divided the process of deliberation about the character of the Peoples Democracies into four phases: an initial phase, which corresponded to the formation of National Front governments; secondly, 'reconsideration'; thirdly, 'statements of the new doctrine'; and fourthly, 'comprehensive theoretical formulations'. The first interpretation, advanced for example by Varga,[48] stressed that they were unique or 'special' democracies, not socialist regimes; they were not 'proletarian dictatorships, or socialist economies: rather they were states of a 'mixed' character. Ross Johnson[49] has argued that the pre-1948 conceptualisation had six principal elements: uniqueness; they were products of national democratic (not socialist) revolutions; the existing state form had not been destroyed (as in the Soviet Union); their economies were still of a 'mixed' type; they had mixed class systems, even though the communist parties played a key role; they were moving towards entry onto the socialist road, in accordance with their national peculiarities.

From 1947, economists and constitutional lawyers, notably Lazutkin, Mankovskiĭ and Farberov,[50] challenged the 'non-socialist' conception of Peoples Democracy. In this phase, emphasis was placed upon the dominant role played by the East European communist parties in smashing the bourgeois state (a Bolshevik idea) and in intensifying the class struggle.[51] The theory which was to gain official approval can, in large measure, be traced to the work of the young Soviet legal scholar Naum Farberov. Farberov stressed the similarity of the developmental patterns of the Soviet and East European states and argued that 'Peoples Democracy is a form of the dictatorship of the proletariat'.[52] The watershed in the development of an authoritative line on 'Peoples Democracy', according to Rosa,[53] was the

Cominform resolution on the situation in the Communist party of Yugoslavia on 29 June 1948, which emphasised that Peoples Democracy depended upon Soviet experience, and that it was based on the rule of the communist parties, intensification of the class struggle and progress towards communism. The emergence of the new line coincided with attacks upon Tito, Gomulka and others who were said to be opposing the correct line of socialist development. In the resolution, the new orthodoxy, which stressed that the Soviet system was the only permissible model of socialist construction, was clearly enunciated. Skilling dates the statement of the new doctrine to a speech by Dimitrov in December 1948.[54] Detailed theoretical expositions of the new line by Farberov,[55] Mankovskiĭ – who referred to the Peoples Democracies as 'states of the Paris Commune type'[56] – and others appeared in Soviet journals the following year.

The later phases stressed the similarities between Soviet development and the construction of socialism in Eastern Europe and also emphasised the role of the Soviet Union in guiding the Peoples Democracies towards socialism: thus 'the path to socialism of the Peoples Democracies is a variation of the general path of socialism . . . and . . . is based on the experience of socialist construction in the USSR'.[57] The East European communist parties were modelled on the Bolshevik party, and in particular were based on the hierarchical principle of 'democratic centralism':[58] they had 'cast off the tutelage of foreign capital';[59] all of them pursued a 'progressive nationality policy'.[60] The immature nature of the Peoples Democracies was exemplified by the survival of bourgeois democratic institutions (such as multi-party systems) and an unrestricted franchise (the Bolsheviks had refused suffrage to certain groups) and by the fact that socialism had not yet triumphed in all economic spheres within these states.[61] The relevance of the Soviet model for the Peoples Democracies was a recurring theme of these articles: this theme also figured prominently in analyses of 'Peoples Democracy' by theoreticians within the bloc states. For example, in the Polish legal journal *Państwo i Prawo* in 1949, Stanislaw Ehrlich argued that it was essential for the Peoples Democracies to maintain a close collaboration with the Soviet Union and to learn from Soviet experience.[62] Yugoslavia was no longer categorised as a 'Peoples Democracy' or even a member of the socialist camp.

The Soviet theory of 'Peoples Democracy', therefore, evolved from a position where this state form was viewed as a type of bourgeois (progressive) regime into the 1948 orthodoxy that it was an

embryonic form of socialist state. The essential difference between
the Soviet state and the 'popular democratic' form of government was
between entelechy and potentiality: although the Peoples Democracies were not fully developed 'proletarian dictatorships', they nevertheless fulfilled the functions of proletarian dictatorship and were
rapidly moving towards a 'pure' form of working-class power, guided
by the benificent hand of the Soviet Union.

In Soviet theory, the notion of the 'dictatorship of the proletariat'
is attributed to Marx and Engels. Draper[63] has identified eleven
references to 'dictatorship of the proletariat' in the corpus of Marx
and Engels, although none of these works contains detailed descriptions of the governmental apparatus through which the working class
would exercise power. In 'The Civil War in France', Marx referred to
the Paris Commune as a government of the working class. Draper
notes that a primary emphasis of Marx's laudatory description of the
Commune is upon its democratic and non-elitist character – e.g. the
mass franchise, participation of the people in governmental decision-
making, election of judges and other public officials, public control of
the police, etc.[64] In his introduction to the 'The Civil War in France'
Engels referred to the Paris Commune as the 'dictatorship of the
proletariat', implying that proletarian dictatorship was synonymous
with rule of the working class over the bourgeoisie. The proletarian
dictatorship envisaged by Marx and Engels was to be based on the
principle of majoritarian democracy. The regimes imposed on the
countries of Eastern Europe by the Soviets after the Second World
War, therefore, bore little resemblance to the transitional state form
postulated by Marx and Engels: in practice, these regimes were based
on the dictatorship of a small revolutionary elite nominally acting on
behalf of the proletariat – but in reality subordinate to the CPSU –
and therefore owed more to the ideas of Lenin and Stalin than to
either Marx or Engels. Tucker, however, has argued that, because
Marx and Engels cite the Paris Commune as an example of proletarian dictatorship, they must have accepted that the 'dictatorship'
would use violence against the proletariat's class enemies.[65]

Lenin had criticised Kautsky for stating that Marx spoke of the
dictatorship of the proletariat not as a form of government but as a
condition inherent in majoritarian democracy, a condition which
rendered revolutionary violence unnecessary.[66] He also attacked
Kautsky for asserting that Marx viewed the Commune as a democratic political order based on the mass franchise (i.e. the bourgeoisie
had not been deprived of their voting rights).[67] Furthermore, Lenin

ridiculed Kautsky's statement that a class could not govern and referred to him as a 'parliamentary cretin'.[68] One of the central features of the Paris Commune, according to Lenin, was that it had 'abolished parliamentarism'.[69] Lenin went on to assert that it would be possible for a whole class to rule without the need for the representative machinery of parliamentary government – i.e. that the proletariat could rule directly. Thus if the Paris Commune was left out of the account, the Soviet regime was the first in the world to engage the exploited masses in the work of government.[70] However, despite Lenin's insistence that it would be possible for a whole class to govern, in his report on the party programme delivered at the 8th party congress in 1919, he admitted that the Soviets, which (theoretically) were organs of government by workers, were in fact organs of government *for* workers by the advanced stratum of the proletariat.[71] He also ruefully admitted that the stratum of workers who were actually governing was unbelievably minute.[72]

In 'Left-Wing Communism, an Infantile Disorder', Lenin attacked the authors of a pamphlet entitled 'The Split in the Communist Party of Germany' (The Spartacus League) for posing the question 'who is to exercise (the dictatorship of the proletariat): the communist party or the proletarian class?' He asserted that the mere presentation of the problem 'dictatorship of the proletariat' or 'dictatorship of the class' indicated confused thinking, since classes were led by political parties.[73] Repudiation of the 'party principle and of party discipline' would lead only to 'petty bourgeois diffuseness and instability' and therefore the 'strictest centralisation and discipline'[74] were required within the party. The 'slightest relaxation of the party's iron discipline'[75] would strengthen the power of the bourgeoisie against the proletariat. Lenin's conception of the 'dictatorship of the proletariat' – the notion of rule by a hierarchically organised and disciplined group on behalf of the working class which was not yet 'ready' to rule directly – bears a much closer resemblance to the form of power installed by the Soviets in Eastern Europe after the War than to the 'Paris Commune' form envisaged by Marx and Engels.

SOVIET CONCEPTUALISATIONS OF 'INTERNATIONAL RELATIONS OF A NEW TYPE'

The 'new type' of international relations of socialism were said to have a number of fundamental characteristics which differentiated them from bourgeois or bourgeois-socialist relations: they were 'a new, higher type of mutual relations between peoples free from the power of capital';[76] they were inherently harmonious; they were influenced by internationalist imperatives (the notion of proletarian internationalism had not yet developed into a comprehensive theory of socialist international relations, but nevertheless served as a justification for the touchstone doctrine and as a doctrinal counter to the 'bestial ideology of bourgeois nationalism');[77] they were non-exploitative; they were based on 'fraternal mutual aid' (given freely and not motivated by expectations of gain); and were based on genuine mutual respect for sovereignty.

The 'harmonic' conception of socialist international relations was clearly based in the 'second image' conception of foreign policy – i.e. the idea that the nature of a regime in large measure determines the nature of its foreign policy. The 'second image' perspective enabled Soviet commentators to establish a qualitative and fundamental distinction between the foreign policies of bourgeois and capitalist states. This stark contrast had been articulated by Korovin in 1946: 'it is indisputable that any state of the imperialist type can follow the road of unbridled nationalism. It is also indisputable that there is another type of state (Soviet socialist) the social nature of which excludes entirely the possibility of following such a path'.[78] The nature of the Soviet system not only prevented the USSR from behaving aggressively in the international arena, but also impelled it to defend the sovereign independence of smaller states against the rapacious and predatory ambitions of imperialist powers. Because the Soviet Union was a 'truly democratic' state, its foreign policy was in harmony with the interests of all people throughout the world. As an article in *Novoe vremia* put it: 'because of its nature as a socialist state, where there are no capitalist monopolies, no private ownership of the means of production and no exploiting classes, the Soviet Union has never experienced the desire to violate the sovereignty of any other country.' Therefore, there never could be Soviet expansion, messianism or penetration.[79] In contrast to capitalist international relations, relations between socialist countries were based on principles which strengthened world peace. These new relations were said to offer a glaring contrast to the imperialist policy of economically and politically enslaving weaker nations, of exploiting the raw material resources of backward countries.[80] Capitalist states were constantly trampling upon the sovereign rights of other countries, if not always with guns and bayonets then with the marionette's strings of finance and other veiled forms of dependence. The harmonic conception was also espoused by East Europe's communist leaders in this period. Poland's Berman affirmed that the Peoples Democracies were guided 'not only by their own national interests, but also by the common interests of their sister nations. They have eliminated forever the strife . . . which previously divided them'.[81] According to Gheorghiu-Dej, Romanian foreign policy was of a 'new type', no longer of vassal Romania.[82]

After the Second World War Soviet and East European communists brought to the peoples of Eastern Europe the glad tidings that at last their countries had been freed from the bondage of foreign capitalist exploitation, since economic and political relations between countries within the socialist camp were qualitatively superior to capitalist economic relations.[83] Soviet economic assistance was said to have a positive character, in that it was proffered with no ulterior motive and was guided by proletarian internationalism. Western economic penetration was judged to be undesirable and unnecessary, in that the development of closer economic links between the socialist countries of Eastern Europe offered an attractive alternative to the lure of American dollars: thus 'without subjecting themselves to foreign loans and without sacrificing one iota of their sovereignty, [the countries of Eastern Europe] are able to successfully develop their economies'.[84] Economic collaboration between the Soviet Union and the Peoples Democracies represented a 'new, higher type of mutual relations between peoples', in which foreign trade was developed 'on the basis of complete equal rights and mutual advantage'.[85]

RELATIONS WITH THE WEST

The nature of relations between the East European states and the capitalist world also flowed from the 'second image' perspective. The Zhdanovite 'struggle between two camps' doctrine was based on four central assumptions: firstly, relations between the capitalist and socialist worlds were based on irreconcilable antagonism. Secondly, the socialist system was inherently superior to the capitalist system in all areas of development. For example, there were two lines of economic development in Europe, capitalist and socialist: the former was crisis prone and unable to attain prewar levels of wealth: by contrast, the socialist camp was said to have attained these levels by

1948.[86] Thirdly, the socialist system was advancing, whereas the capitalist system was in an advanced and dangerous state of decay. Fourthly, the peoples within the 'zone of peace' had to guard against imperialist aggression and penetration.

Progressive regimes had to be vigilant against ensnarement by foreign loans and other forms of capitalist economic enthralment: the levers of economic pressure were said to figure prominently in the strategy of Western capitalism towards progressive regimes. Stalin's 'quarantine' policy was most tellingly manifested in his refusal to allow the Peoples Democracies to take advantage of Marshall Aid, despite the fact that the communist leaderships in Czechoslovakia, Poland and Hungary were initially eager to participate in the US recovery plan for Europe. In the words of the Soviet legal specialist Chizhov: 'socialist countries do not subject themselves to the pernicious influence of American capital'.[87] Thus the purpose of the Marshall Plan was to bring the countries of Eastern Europe under the sway of American imperialism and therefore opposition to the Plan reflected 'the noble desire to defend their independence and sovereignty from the filthy clutches of the transatlantic claimants to world hegemony.'[88] Participation in the Marshall Plan was said to imply the virtual destruction of the national independence and sovereignty of the states of Eastern Europe.[89] Attacks upon the Marshall Plan were key elements in the declaration issued at the founding conference of the Cominform in 1947. The Declaration stated that 'the Truman-Marshall Plan is only a constituent part of the European sub-section of the general plan of global expansion pursued by the US', a plan which also included attempts to enslave Eastern and Latin American countries.[90] Gottwald, the head of the Czechoslovak communist party, accepted an invitation to attend the Paris conference convened to discuss the Plan, but, as a result of Soviet pressure withdrew and from then on became openly hostile towards it. The Poles and Hungarians also initially expressed an interest, but then reversed course. Amongst the European Peoples Democracies, only Yugoslavia and Bulgaria attacked the Plan from the outset. As the Soviet commentator Marinin argued; 'in their struggle against the Marshall Plan, the communist parties are the courageous defenders of the national sovereignty and independence of their countries'.[91]

The component elements of the 'new type of international relations' as expounded in Soviet theory in this period were to form the ideological underpinning of Soviet control strategies within the bloc –

e.g. the special roles of the Soviet Union; the Soviet Union as the most advanced socialist state; proletarian internationalism as a doctrinal talisman against the evils of bourgeois nationalism and as a rationale for fealty to Moscow; the beneficent character of socialist international economic collaboration; genuine mutual respect for the sovereignty of other states; and opposition to Western penetration. Far from withering away in the era of 'polycentrism', the 'touchstone' doctrine has frequently been invoked by the Soviets and pro-Moscow East European communist leaderships. However, the credibility of the doctrine was to become increasingly difficult to maintain. Soviet schisms with China, Yugoslavia, Albania, Romania and non-ruling parties in Western Europe have exposed the inadequacy of doctrinal contrivances of this kind (even the Soviet Union's most loyal allies were to question some of the central assumptions of the Soviet model of inter-socialist relations).

5 Marxist–Leninist Doctrine and the Soviet Theory of Sovereignty

To argue that sovereignty is not a Marxist concept *per se* does not mean that the usages given to the sovereignty concept in Soviet thought do not bear the imprint of classical doctrinal orthodoxies: Soviet Marxism's putative founding fathers (Marx, Engels and Lenin) made several indirect – and, in some respects, ironic – contributions to the development of official Soviet attitudes towards the sovereignty concept, although the influence of Lenin (and, in particular, Stalin's Russo-centric brand of 'Leninism') is far more salient than that of Marx or Engels. Soviet theoretical approaches to the subject of international relations have generally been based on the adaptation and transposition of the 'vertical' notions of 'classical' Marxism – e.g. the primacy of the class struggle, the need for international proletarian solidarity in the fight against capitalism, the inherently exploitative and aggressive nature of the capitalist system and the inevitability of socialism's victory over capitalism – onto the horizontal plane of the modern state system. It would hardly be an exaggeration to argue, however, that Soviet perceptions of the pattern and structure of the resulting conceptual matrix (whether the vertical or horizontal planes are given priority in Soviet thought) have been functionally related to the requirements of Soviet foreign policy.

Consideration of the sovereignty concept from the standpoint of the official ideology has an instrumental value for Soviet foreign policy in two principal ways: firstly, it serves to weaken the potency of the 'legal positivist' definition whenever respect for sovereignty is perceived as detrimental to Soviet interests; secondly, by defining sovereignty by reference to the paramount values of Marxism-Leninism, the Soviets provide an ideological rationale for the Soviet Union's assumption of special responsibilities within the international communist movement.

It is possible to identify at least four elements of the postwar Soviet theory of sovereignty which have been extrapolated from classical Marxist doctrine.

1 THE PRIMACY OF THE INTERNATIONAL CLASS STRUGGLE

The orthodox view that communism is an international creed and that class differences are of greater historical significance than cleavages born of national sentiment – an idea which can be traced back to the 'Communist Manifesto' – has provided the Kremlin with a doctrinal justification for subordinating the sovereignty concept to the higher value of 'proletarian internationalism' whenever the former has conflicted with Soviet interests. The platform of the first Comintern congress (drafted by Bukharin) stated that 'the International, which subordinates so-called national interests to the interests of the international revolution will embody the mutual aid of the proletariat of the different countries'.[1] For Lenin, 'proletarian internationalism' required: 'that proletarian struggle in one country be subordinate to the world-wide class struggle' and that 'any nation which achieved victory over its own bourgeoisie should be willing to make great sacrifices in order to defeat international capitalism'.[2] These statements meant that the obligations of proletarian solidarity transcended state frontiers and were assertions of the primacy of the vertical class struggle over 'horizontal' antagonisms deriving from national sentiment and 'bourgeois patriotism'.

Soviet adaptation of the 'internationalist' perspectives of Marx and Engels on to the horizontal plane of international relations is exemplified by Soviet responses to crises of control in Eastern Europe. The major shift in Soviet usage of this classical perspective is that it is now used to consolidate Soviet hegemony within the region rather than to foster the goals of global revolution. Soviet military aid in postwar Europe, for example, has been rendered not to the proletariats of Western capitalist countries struggling to slough off the yoke of capitalism, but rather to socialist states offending against prevailing doctrinal orthodoxies. The Soviet invasion of Hungary was thus said to have been a worthy example of the Soviet Union's fulfilment of its international duty of proletarian solidarity with the beleaguered Hungarian proletariat.[3] In the aftermath of the invasion of Czechoslovakia, Sanakoyev noted that Lenin asked, ' "which should be put first, the right of nations to self-determination or socialism?" Lenin asked and right there replied, "socialism should".'[4]

The theory that the general interests of world socialism must take precedence over the interests of each socialist state has been a major theme of Soviet strictures towards Eastern Europe in the postwar era. A major disruptive factor within the international communist movement, however, has been that the Kremlin has refused to accept the self-abnegative implications of such strictures and has tended to equate the 'general' interest with the diplomatic and security requirements of the USSR (in particular its compelling security needs within Eastern Europe')[5]. The Marxist conception of 'internationalism' was thus transmuted from a revolutionary principle (articulated to signal the shift in the focus of proletarian loyalty from the nation to the international working class) into a controlling instrument. The 'internationalist' prescriptions of Marx and Engels were aimed at hastening the demise of the 'horizontal' division of the world: conversely, the Soviet Marxist definition has been employed in order to maintain 'horizontal' divisions in forms which accord with prevailing Soviet conceptions of the USSR's interests. 'Proletarian internationalism' not only guides socialist states but also constrains them and thus establishes a crucial divide between tolerable and intolerable behaviour. A primary cause of conflict within the Soviet bloc, however, has been that this 'divide' has vague and shifting boundaries. Ideological disputes between the Soviets and other parties (ruling and non-ruling) over the relationship between 'national and international interests' have shown that the definition of 'internationalism' is no longer an exclusively Soviet prerogative.

Until the Gorbachev era, the assumption of the primary significance of the 'class struggle and the alignment of class forces' in the international arena was the central premise of the Soviet Union's essentially manichean postwar world view. For example, in 1972, in assailing Western 'multipolarity' hypotheses, Shakhnazarov contended that 'there is no multipolar world, just as there is no world of two or three superpowers. There is a world of two main social poles, socialism and capitalism.'[6] With the advent of polycentric communism, the 'two social systems' world view became increasingly askew with reality: there is now abundant evidence that the diverse strands of the communist movement are not attracted to a common pole by the 'force field' of proletarian solidarity.

As Lynch has shown, Soviet commentaries on international relations in the 1980s tend to focus on states rather than upon class factors.[7] Several possible reasons can be adduced for this shift of emphasis; firstly, the Soviets have been forced to concede that class alignments are not necessarily the main determinants of the foreign policies of socialist states. In the early 1970s, the Soviets attributed the Chinese pursuit of 'Great Han Chauvinism' to the failure to give due regard to the class factor.[8] For Shakhnazarov in the early 1970s retreat from the 'class orientation' was 'the biggest sin of the Peking leaders';[9] secondly, pluralist pressures emanating from both ruling and non-ruling parties, fearful of the 'solidarist' implications of the Soviet conception of global dualism; thirdly, Soviet analysts now recognise that the 'global polarisation' approach is a poor device for comprehending and explaining the complexities of an increasingly heterogeneous international system. As Kirshin has argued, 'world politics' now includes relations between various political forces in the world arena – classes, nations, states, military and political coalitions, ideas, doctrines and theories;[10] fourthly, the Soviets have become disillusioned with the revolutionary potential of the 'newly free' countries and of the proletariat of the advanced capitalist states.

Nevertheless, in the Gorbachev era of 'new thinking', the 'class approach' has been supplemented, transmuted and (perhaps temporarily) downgraded rather than abandoned: although Soviet commentators on international affairs now tend to eschew hortatory references to the 'class struggle', it is also clear that the notion of the struggle between two opposing socioeconomic systems has not been discarded. Shakhnazarov, in 1988, described the 'struggle between two socio-economic systems' as 'a constant' in the Soviet theory of world development, but argued that it was not the only concept – 'not at this stage of history anyway'.[11] Moreover, since a cardinal assumption of Soviet theory is that the capitalist and socialist systems have different class bases, it would be difficult for the Soviets to discard the notion of inter-systemic class cleavages and rivalries. According to Antonovich (pro-rector of the Soviet Academy of Social Sciences attached to the CPSU central committee), *perestroika* rules out neither rivalry nor class confrontation between capitalism and socialism: rather, in the nuclear age, it rules out attempts to end this confrontation by military means.[12] Similarly, Plimak has argued that, in order to avoid the danger of nuclear catastrophe, the class struggle now has to take more 'civilised' forms.[13] Although contemporary Soviet commentators castigate the USA for an 'egoistic class approach' to world political problems, and advocate the primacy of 'universal human interests' over 'class interests', their ideas continue to be predicated on a 'two systems' world view: thus, far from renouncing the pursuit of proletarian class interests, Zagladin argues that these interests are best fostered through the pursuit of 'universal human interests' (indeed, he perceives these interests as being essentially one and the same).[14] Nor has Gorbachev eschewed reference to the relationship between class and foreign policy: in his speech to the CPSU central committee in November 1987 (*Pravda*, 3 November 1987), he referred to the 'class basis' of the proletariat's peaceful coexistence policy.

2   LENINIST DOCTRINES OF UNITY AND DISCIPLINE

Soviet attitudes to socialist international relations reflect Lenin's insistence upon the need for unity and discipline within the communist movement. The authoritarian stamp of Lenin's approach to organisational questions has been characterised by Hammond as: 1) fear of spontaneity – 'his distrust of the spontaneous tendencies of the proletariat and doubt that the proletariat would automatically bring about the revolution'; 2) vanguardism – 'his conviction that, for this reason, the worker must be led and objective revolutionary development pushed by a vanguard of politically conscious leaders'; 3) elitism – 'the idea that the vanguard should consist of a small, carefully-selected party of the most conscientious professional revolutionaries'; 4) party monopoly – Lenin's insistence that the party should have no competitors.[15] The principles of monolithic unity and democratic centralism have played a major role in shaping the authoritarian character of the Soviet political system: analogical reasoning is hardly necessary to establish connections between the principles of 'monolithism' and 'democratic centralism' and the need for unity and discipline within the international communist movement.

Despite the fact that the notion of a socialist interstate system forms no part of his thought, Lenin's approach to organisational issues readily lends itself to transposition onto the broader canvas of international relations. Lenin firmly set his ideas on organisational issues within an international framework and insisted that the imperatives of revolutionary discipline governing the structure and operation of the Bolshevik party had a wider relevance. They were to be applied to both foreign communist parties and to the Third International. His conception of 'revolutionary discipline' knew no geographical boundaries and applied just as much to the British and French communist parties as to the Bolshevik party itself: at the first Comintern congress, he had argued that 'a key task confronting the West European comrades is to explain to the people the nature, importance and necessity of the Soviet system'.[16] At the second congress, he attacked the British communist Ramsay for declaring that the decision concerning affiliation to the Labour party should be left to the British. Lenin replied that there would be no point in having an International or a congress if 'every little group were to say "let us decide the issue" '.[17] The 'Bolshevisation' of the world's communist parties (the application of the Russian model, regardless of differences in local conditions) was, for Lenin, a prerequisite for the success of the coming world proletarian revolution. At the fourth congress, he insisted that foreign parties must study 'the organisation, structure, practice and content of revolutionary work' (meaning the Bolshevik experience). He went on to say that if foreign communists did study these lessons, there were excellent prospects of world revolution:[18] however, even in Lenin's time (and despite the authority deriving from their success), the Bolsheviks found it difficult to maintain unity.[19]

At the second congress, Lenin played a major role in ensuring that the organisational principles governing the operation of the Bolshevik party were rigorously applied to the Third International: the 21 conditions for membership (19 drafted by Lenin) emphasised that the organisation was to be highly centralised and that decisions of the Executive Committee were to be obeyed by all member parties on pain of expulsion. Lenin's insistence upon 'iron discipline' and upon the need for communist parties to avoid the danger of 'dilution' through association with social-democratic groups was justified on the grounds that the aim of non-communist elements was to 'sabotage the proletarian revolution';[20] article 12 of the 'conditions' declared that parties belonging to the International must be based on the principle of democratic centralism: thus 'the communist party will be able to fulfil its duty only if its organisation is as centralised as possible, if iron discipline prevails':[21] article 16 stated that the decisions of Communist congresses were binding on all member parties; article 21 stated that members of the party who rejected in principle the conditions and theses put forward by the Communist International were to be expelled forthwith. At the 8th party congress, Lenin had expressed satisfaction that the revolutionary movement abroad was assuming the Soviet form – which justified his belief that the Soviet government was the 'world form of proletarian dictatorship'.[22] At the second Comintern congress, Zinoviev stressed the need for communist organisations to be built upon the foundations of 'iron proletarian centralism'.[23] The Bolshevik insistence upon a small, highly centralised and disciplined revolutionary organisation did not derive from

Marx: indeed, Marx vigorously opposed the form of organisational elitism adopted by the Bolsheviks.[24] 'Democratic centralism' and 'monolithism' should, therefore, with greater accuracy, be described as Leninist rather than Marxist ideas.

The Third International was a highly disciplined world organisation with its headquarters in Russia. However, the fact that leadership of the organisation had passed to the Bolsheviks was viewed by Lenin as a temporary by-product of the Revolution. The Bolsheviks, according to Lenin, had marched in advance of other sections of the world proletariat not because they wanted or deserved to, but because of the 'softness of the Russian bourgeoisie'.[25] Formally, the Soviet party was granted no special status within the organisation and Lenin would have repudiated any attempt to elevate Moscow into an immutable 'Vatican' of world socialism. Lenin had affirmed in 1919 that leadership of the international communist movement had passed to Russia only for a 'short time'[26] and elsewhere had alerted other members of the Bolshevik party to the dangers of 'Great Russian Chauvinism'. Other leading Bolsheviks at this time also made it clear that they expected the headquarters of the Comintern to be transferred to a Western European capital once the revolution had spread westwards. Zinoviev had predicted that the whole world would become communist within two or three years – Western Europe (excluding perhaps England) in one year and the US and Asia within two years of proletarian victory in Europe.[27] However, Lenin's internationalist conception of the International was soon to be replaced by Stalin's Russo-centric interpretation of its functions: Bolshevik in organisational form and Russian in goal orientations.[28]

The transformation of the Third International into an instrument of Soviet foreign policy (the process of 'goal displacement', whereby the organisation was harnessed to particular national, as distinct from international, goals) was given a theoretical underpinning in the theory of 'socialism in one country'. The assertion by Klara Zetkin at the fourth Comintern congress that every strengthening of Soviet Russia means the weakening of the world bourgeoisie'[29] and that all communists throughout the world must struggle to defend and support the Soviet regime was posited on the assumption that proletarian revolution 'must triumph internationally as world revolution'.[30] Support for the Soviet regime, therefore, was a means to an end: in the literature on organisation theory, 'goal displacement' of the means–end reversal kind has been attributed to several factors: for example, to environmental pressures which push the organisation off course, so that it pursues survival goals rather than aspirational goals; to over-ambitious goal-setting (official goals are pitched too high for available resources and are therefore unattainable); to changes in personnel responsible for goal-setting; and to the pursuit of 'intangible' and imprecise goals. Each of these has some relevance to goal transformation processes within the Third International.

The change in the organisation's orientation was evident in the character of the resolutions passed at the 4th and 6th congresses.[31] The 6th congress programme, under the heading 'Duties of the International Proletariat to the Soviet Union', declared that in the event of an attack by the imperialist states upon the Soviet Union, the international proletariat had a duty to fight on the side of the world's first socialist state.[32] In the early years of the International, Moscow had been regarded by the Bolsheviks as 'the combat headquarters of the world proletariat'[33] and the Red Army owed formal allegiance to the International, not to the Soviet state *per se*. The accession of Stalin, particularly the defeat of Trotsky, who derided the idea of 'socialism in one country', meant that the revolutionary purposes which the International had been designed to serve were set aside in favour of Soviet state interests. However, the International did not entirely discard the rhetoric of the global revolutionary struggle: rather, it assumed a harmony between the interests of the world proletariat and Soviet state interests. At the 6th congress the Soviet Union was lauded as the main force in the emancipation of the world proletariat, a role predicated on the assumption that what was good for the Soviet Union was good for the communist movement: the subsequent history of international communism is studded with attempts by the CPSU to retain this fusion principle virtually intact.

The principles of party monopoly and elitism were also transposed by the Soviets (albeit with limited success) onto the horizontal plane of socialist international relations. The Soviet attitude towards communist international organisation and towards socialist international relations has borne the heavy imprint of Stalin's Russo-centric interpretation of Lenin's organisational obsessions. For example, the Soviet claim to a special status within the international movement seems strikingly reminiscent of the concept of the leading role of the party within the domestic system. Indeed, all four of the characteristics of Leninist authoritarianism identified by Hammond – fear of spontaneity, vanguardism, elitism and party monopoly – have been reflected in Soviet attitudes to the role of the CPSU in the international communist movement in general and within the Soviet bloc in particular. In 1956 a secret CPSU directive issued to both ruling and non-ruling parties stated that the 'CPSU considers it remains the directing party among the communist organisations of the world. Each communist party is judged in the light of the . . . relations which it has with the CPSU, for the interests of the CPSU are closely tied in with those of other states and parties.'[34] However, this directive was issued prior to the explosions of 1956, and before the Soviet-Chinese schism – i.e. before the Soviet Union was forced by circumstances to reassess the theory of its 'leading role'. By the end of 1960, following open Chinese criticism of the character and direction of the Soviet Union's foreign policy, the CPSU formally abandoned its claim to the status of the 'directing party'. In 1962, a major Soviet work on Marxism-Leninism denied that the CPSU claimed a leading role.[35] Nevertheless, it qualified this denial by stating that the Soviet Union and the CPSU are still charged with a 'special responsibility for the development of the world socialist system'.[36] Soviet techniques of deviation control within the movement have extended beyond polemics and have also included exclusionary tactics (attempts at collective ostracism of renegade parties); interference in the internal affairs of other parties; and material rewards for loyalty to the Soviet line.[37]

The Soviets deny that there is now an 'international or organisational centre' of the international communist movement. The CPSU also formally regards the imposition of the will of one party on another as inadmissible and acknowledges the equality and independence of other parties. Nevertheless, it can be demonstrated that the CPSU has assigned to itself unique roles within the movement. Firstly, the 'unifying force' role, deriving from the Soviet obsession with ideological cohesion – affirmation of the need for unity, close cooperation and coordination (unity is not assumed to occur spontaneously, even though parties are 'objectively united by their class struggle' and by their common goals, ideology and organisational principles[38]). The role of the CPSU in convening interparty meetings, conferences and symposia demonstrates that it does not regard itself as just another party. Secondly, the role of 'guardian of ideological orthodoxy': prior to Gorbachev's accession, this was manifested in attacks upon a diverse range of deviations from correct Marxist-Leninist principles by other parties (for example, in Soviet diatribes against parties which repudiate the movement's 'revolutionary patrimony' in favour of a 'new internationalism',[39] or 'ideological pluralism'). A dim view has been taken of socialist states which stress sovereignty rather than internationalism, since 'words about sovereignty and independence' can 'become a screen which covers an actual deviation from the Marxist-Leninist principles that govern relations between socialist countries'.[40] Thirdly, a pedagogic role: the Soviet Union's unrivalled experience of socialist construction has been used to justify the CPSU's claim to speak with an authoritative voice concerning the universally valid laws governing the development of the world socialist system (and the strategy and tactics to be followed by non-ruling parties).[41] Fourthly, the authority stemming from the Soviet Union's powerful and progressive role in the international system – i.e. in the 'restructuring' of international relations and in the peaceful settlement of international conflicts (thus Soviet peace initiatives have forced the USA along the road to detente[42]). Gorbachev has called for more sophisticated interparty relations and has explicitly repudiated the idea that any party is omniscient: however, he also made a favourable reference to the Comintern in November 1987.[43] Under his leadership, the CPSU has downgraded but not abandoned its aim of fostering international communist solidarity.

3 'POPULAR SOVEREIGNTY'

Soviet theoreticians have sought to claim for socialism exclusive rights over the sovereignty principle by postulating a direct relationship between 'external' or international sovereignty (i.e. the independence of a state from, and its equality with, any other state) and the location of internal sovereignty (i.e. domestic political supremacy or, from the Soviet Marxist standpoint, class-rule).[44] According to the theory of sovereignty which flows from these terminological assumptions, bourgeois states can never be truly sovereign because, in a class society, the will of the people is over-ridden by the interests of the bourgeois minority. As Lenin had stated: 'no bourgeois republic, however democratic, was ever anything other than a machine for oppressing the workers by capital, an instrument of bourgeois dictatorship',[45] and elsewhere he had described the state as 'a machine by which one class maintains its rule over another'.[46] As Korovin was to argue in 1947:

Soviet sovereignty is the first example of genuine popular

sovereignty, in that the Soviet state has no antagonistic classes and is completely united. In addition to being a genuine popular sovereignty, Soviet sovereignty also achieves genuine national sovereignty, in that it is sovereignty of both the state and of its constituent nations. Conversely, bourgeois sovereignty is a disguise for class supremacy by the bourgeoisie of the most powerful nation.[47]

The foreign policies of bourgeois states, therefore, could not reflect the will of the majority, nor were they in harmony with the true interests of working people. Korovin's association of popular sovereignty with proletarian dictatorship and monolithicity implies that only socialist states based on the Soviet model are sovereign in the true sense: Western countries are on this definition excluded from the category of sovereign states. The distinction between the 'form' and 'content' of sovereignty was also made by I. D. Levin, who argued that sovereignty in a bourgeois state was the class dictatorship of the bourgeoisie and therefore was not a genuine peoples sovereignty.[48] Ushakov was later to argue that, because small countries in the West are dominated by 'foreign capital and its hirelings', 'formal sovereignty is a cover for economic vassalage'.[49] According to Tunkin in 1959, imperialism transformed state sovereignty into an insignificant and empty shell.[50] Definitions of sovereignty in specialist Soviet dictionaries also contrast the 'fictional' sovereignty of bourgeois states (a camouflage for bourgeois class supremacy and foreign domination) with the genuine popular sovereignty embodied in socialist states.[51] In the Soviet conception, therefore, sovereignty has more than merely a 'formal-juridic' character.[52] The principle of 'popular sovereignty' has been included in each of the Soviet Constitutions.[53]

The Soviet equation of genuine or popular sovereignty with proletarian supremacy (in the monolithic form associated with the rule of the communist parties of the Soviet Union and of Eastern Europe) has also served as the basis of the Soviet distinction between 'bourgeois' patriotism and 'genuine' (proletarian) patriotism. Bourgeois patriotism was said to reflect the narrow class interests and aggressive policies of capitalist states and the willingness of the bourgeoisie to betray their countries (as they had done by supporting the Marshall Plan): in the first Cominform journal it was asserted that: 'the bourgeoisie of Europe have definitely taken the path of betrayal of the national interests and rejection of the sovereignty of their countries . . . the working class, headed by the communist parties, is the most consistent leader of all the patriotic and democratic forces who defend the sovereignty and independence of their country'.[54] With the liquidation of the exploiting classes in the USSR, the Soviet regime was said to have attained 'unprecedented moral and political unity, finding clearest expression in Soviet patriotism'.[55] Nationalism, according to Frantsev, was the 'ideology and policy of the exploiting classes': by contrast, proletarian internationalism was a powerful weapon of all workers in their struggle against all forms of class and national oppression.[56] The charge of 'chauvinism' and 'bourgeois nationalism' was levelled against 'nationalist' elements within the communist parties of Eastern Europe in the 1940s (when so-called 'national' communists were replaced by 'Muscovites'). From the earliest period of the Soviet *gleichschaltung*, there was recognition in Moscow of the possibility of latent opposition to Soviet hegemony. The Kremlin's definition of 'proletarian internationalism', allied to its dualistic theory of patriotism, meant that the Soviet Union was the ultimate arbiter of the national interests of the Peoples Democracies.

The Soviet theory of popular sovereignty has provided the USSR with a blanket ideological justification for interfering in the affairs of other states, without thereby compromising formal professions of support for the sovereignty principle. In patrolling the borders of the Soviet bloc, the Soviet Union defended the 'popular sovereignty' of socialist states from internal and external enemies. Moreover, it was made plain from the beginning of the establishment of the Peoples Democracies that the genuine representatives of the people, in whom genuine sovereignty resided, were the local communist parties (the revolutionary vanguard of the proletariat). Therefore, any threat to communist rule was, *ipso facto*, a threat to the genuine sovereignty of the people. Soviet military interventions in Eastern Europe have been explained by reference to the theory of popular sovereignty: in defending the 'socialist gains' of Hungary and Czechoslovakia, the Soviet Union was acting to protect the 'genuine sovereignty' of these countries against internal and external counter-revolutionary forces seeking to turn the sovereignty of these countries into an empty notion. In November 1956, Korovin argued that 'it is well known that many bourgeois constitutions appeal to the "will of the people", but can there really be any "sovereignty of the people" in a society that is based on the exploitation of some people by others and which is divided into classes with opposing interests?'[57] In relation to the events in Czechoslovakia in 1968, Tunkin argued that socialist sovereignty was popular both in form and substance, because socialist states acted in the interests of the people.[58]

In this sense, the Soviet conception of sovereignty may be likened to a distorting mirror which inverts surface appearances: what may look like a *prima facie* case of aggression (e.g. a military attack upon another socialist state) is said to be a defensive, altruistic action undertaken out of respect for the sovereignty principle. The distinction between genuine (i.e. socialist or popular) sovereignty and bogus (or bourgeois) sovereignty leads logically to the view that interference in the internal affairs of capitalist states by communist regimes does not constitute a violation of sovereignty at all: rather, communist attempts to foment or support revolutionary struggles abroad can, on this logic, be categorised as attempts to assist the proletariat of foreign lands to achieve 'genuine' (i.e. 'popular') sovereignty through the establishment of proletarian dictatorship. Similarly, a defensive measure by the legally elected government of a liberal-democratic state (only 'formally sovereign') aimed at resisting communist subversion must be viewed as a counter-revolutionary act designed to prevent the working class from achieving political power (from supplanting the bogus sovereignty of the bourgeoisie with the genuine 'popular' sovereignty of the proletariat).

4 'BASE AND SUPERSTRUCTURE' IN SOVIET INTERNATIONAL RELATIONS THEORY

The Marxist assumption that legal, political and cultural phenomena are aspects of a society's superstructure and are determined by its economic base leads logically to the view that legal and political relations within a socialist community (if necessary at all) would differ from bourgeois legal and political forms.[59] Although both Marx and Engels acknowledged the possibility of a 'kickback' effect – of the superstructure influencing the base – and acknowledged that superstructural phenomena or 'surface reflections' could not be entirely explained by reference to economic conditions, they nevertheless assumed that economic factors exerted a decisive influence upon the character and pattern of domestic and international politics. As Marx asserted in his famous letter to Annenkov: 'Is not the whole inner organisation of nations, are all their international relations anything else than the expression of a particular division of labour?

And must not these change when the division of labour changes?'[60] The relationship between base and superstructure, one of the most confusing and problematic of Marx's theories, has been used by Soviet theorists as a fundamental premise in their explanations of the qualitative differences between the foreign policies of socialist and bourgeois states.

The assumption of a functional relationship between the internal structure of a state and its foreign policy is by no means an exclusively Marxist idea. Waltz,[61] for example, identifies three images of international relations which provide contrasting explanations of the nature and causes of war: the first image is based on the assumption that causes of war must be attributed to the nature of man, an idea embraced by Confucius, St Augustine, Spinoza and by some modern behavioural scientists. The second image involves the identification of 'internal defects' within states. Waltz has noted that this image comes in a rich variety of forms, both Marxist and non-Marxist: it can be traced, for example, to the writings of Kant, Adam Smith, J. S. Mill, Cobden and Bright, J. A. Hobson and twentieth-century pacifists. However, Waltz notes that it is in Marxist thought that the 'second image' has been most fully developed. Marxist analysis is thus based on the assumption that capitalist states are controlled by the bourgeoisie in their own interests and that war is the 'external manifestation of the class struggle'.[62] In the Marxist variant of the second image, it is assumed that war and international conflict are products of the capitalist mode of production and therefore that abolition of capitalism will, *ipso facto*, mean abolition of war.

Lenin was to apply this mode of reasoning in his analysis of the First World War and of modern imperialism: he characterised the War as an 'Imperialist war' which had its roots in the exploitative and predatory nature of capitalism.[63] The Leninist brand of the 'second image' (i.e. that war and imperialism are coeval with capitalism and that imperialism is a superstructural aspect of monopoly capitalism) has constituted a central premise of Soviet theoretical works on the subject of international relations. War and violence are attributed to the existence of capitalism: the state as such is not regarded as intrinsically aggressive and warlike, since the internal structure of socialist regimes is such that (according to 'mainstream' Soviet theory) the very possibility of conflict between them is precluded – although the bitter dispute with China has forced Soviet scholars to admit the possibility of a war between socialist countries[64] – a possibility at variance with Marx's own version of the 'second image'.

The third image identified by Waltz – i.e. that war is a product of the structure of the international system – also has its variant in Soviet Marxist thought, in that the structure of the international system, and in particular the division of the world into 'camps', is viewed largely as an outcome of the balance of forces in the world between capitalism and socialism[65] – i.e. the superstructures of capitalist and socialist societies are projected onto the horizontal plane, so that the international system is represented as essentially 'hybrid' in nature. Waltz argues that in the 'third image', world government is viewed as the remedy for world war.[66] Until the era of 'new thinking', the Soviets consistently argued that 'world government' was impossible as long as capitalism existed, since only 'the victory of communism on a world-wide scale will provide the necessary material and intellectual preconditions for the merging of nations'.[67] However, in 1988, Shakhnazarov advocated the formation of a 'world government' of sovereign states (not a world state) as an answer to common global problems.[68]

Although both Marx and Engels rejected the simplistic notions of a unidirectional causal relationship between base and superstructure, it is nevertheless possible to discern significant differences in their views on this issue. Neither developed a fully coherent and internally consistent view of the base-superstructure problem. As has frequently been noted, Marx's categorisation of the elements which comprise the 'base' and the 'superstructure' is not always consistent: in the 'Grundrisse' for example, Marx assigns 'legal relations' to the base, whereas in the 'Contribution to Political Economy', law is viewed as a superstructural phenomenon. Similarly, Engels never succeeded in fully clarifying his own thoughts on the subject.[69] Rader has argued that Marx advanced a sophisticated conception of the relationship, based on the notion of interpenetration and overlap between the two categories, whereas Engels perceived the relationship in terms of an interaction between two discrete categories of phenomena.[70] The crucial difference between Marx and Engels's interpretation of these interrelationships according to Rader is that the character of the elements comprising the base and superstructure in Marx's scheme is modified as a result of the interaction, whereas Engels's more simplistic model assumes no such alteration.[71] In his letter to Bloch, Engels repudiated the idea that the 'economic factor' was the only determining one and sought to counteract mechanistic interpretations of the relationship between superstructure and base.[72] However, he never entirely freed himself from a determinist view of the base-superstructure relationship and came perilously close to the 'uni-directional' model he derided in his later writings. As Rader has noted, Marx put forward an 'organic totality model' of base-superstructure relationships, based on the conception of an inter-penetration between productive forces and superstructural phe-nomena, whereas Engels advanced a less complicated (but perhaps ultimately more problematical) interaction model.[73]

The 'second image' perspective has three principle implications for 'socialist international relations': firstly, it leads logically to the view that, since socialist states have similar socioeconomic structures, 'socialist' international relations exhibit different characteristics from relations between bourgeois states. In particular, this simplified version of the base-superstructure model forms the basis of the 'harmonic' conception of socialist international relations – i.e. that relations between socialist states are based on fraternal mutual assistance and that conflict, war and exploitation cannot occur amongst states which are genuinely socialist. Secondly, that 'genuine' (i.e. proletarian) national and international interests are fully com-patible and exist in an organic harmony; thirdly, since bourgeois states' foreign policies are shaped and directed by the expansionary dynamic of the capitalist mode of production, socialist countries must be constantly vigilant against open and covert attacks upon their sovereignties by the forces of imperialism.

The implications of the base-superstructure relationship for inter-national relationships is a theme examined in many Soviet works. Soviet legal specialists acknowledge that Marx's writings on this subject constitute a seminal contribution to the theory of internation-al law.[74] In 1947, Krylov asserted that 'law, in Marxist doctrine, is a superstructure founded on an economic base . . . reflecting the will of the dominant class in the state'[75] He defined international law as a 'juridic superstructure edificed upon the world economy, represent-ing the cooperation between the dominant classes of the different states and their international communications'.[76] Much later, Tunkin argued that the general character of international law 'as a category of the superstructure is determined by the economic structure of a society', but is also influenced 'by other parts of the superstructure, (politics, national law, philosophy, morals etc)'. However, although he acknowledges that base-superstructure relationships involve a 'complicated interplay of varying phenomena', he nevertheless main-tained that state policies were determined 'basically by the economic conditions of the ruling class in the given state'.[77] Similarly, Gubin views 'the social and class nature of international relations and international law' as determined by the means of production dominant in the given epoch.[78] The assumption that analysis of international relations must be approached from a class perspective – that foreign policy has a 'class character' and that international law is a manifestation of the will of the ruling classes – has formed the dominant premise of Soviet explanations of foreign policy behaviour. In 1969, Gantman argued that the laws of the class struggle indelibly 'stamp the foreign policy of a state'.[79] The nature of a regime (e.g. whether it is a dictatorship of the bourgeoisie or of the proletariat) therefore determined whether or not it was capable of violating the sovereignty of other states.

In 1975, the assumption of a crude unidirectional relationship between base and superstructure was rejected by Sanakoyev, who acknowledged the possibility of an international 'kickback effect' between the foreign and domestic policies of states. He qualified his assertions that the policy of a state – external and internal– pertains to the political superstructure and is 'determined by economic conditions prevailing in a class state and the nature of a given socioeconomic system'[80] and that 'the economic factor exerts a decisive influence on the shaping of a policy' by stating that 'this does not mean that superstructural factors play a passive role in working out the home and foreign policies. In determining the closest interconnection and interaction between the economic base and superstructure Engels stressed that political, legal, philosophical, religious, artistic and other developments are based on economic progress. He wrote: "but all these react upon one another and also upon the economic basis" '.[81]

In contemporary Soviet thought, the mechanical dependency model of base-superstructure relationships tends to be rejected in favour of an appreciation of the significance of the superstructure as 'an active factor in history', so that it is 'only in the final analysis that the economy determines the social superstructure'.[82] In contemporary Soviet academic literature, it is possible to find sophisticated appraisals which go beyond mechanical dependency. As Lynch has shown, Soviet International Relations specialists tend to assign greater weight to political and 'subjective', rather than to economic and 'objective' elements in their analyses.[83] This shift away from classical perspectives may well be due to the fact that, in an increasingly heterogeneous international environment, the base-superstructure model is a crude and unreliable analytical device. Can it, for example, explain the 'anti-Soviet' policies pursued by certain other socialist states? Krasin acknowledges that the connection between the basis and superstructural elements in the developing countries is 'looser' than it is in the developed capitalist countries, because the 'basis structures there are themselves unstable', which allows a freer scope for the political superstructure.[84] It is also now acknowledged by some Soviet theorists that elements of the political superstructure in a socialist state may precipitate a reversion back to capitalism and that even socialist states may suffer from 'antagonistic contradictions'.[85]

This chapter has sought to identify the strands in the Soviet doctrine of sovereignty which derive from the Soviet Union's official ideology: it has shown that, despite pronouncements on sovereignty which reiterate 'legal positivist' arguments, 'verticalist' interpretations of the concept have played a central role in Soviet thought. For example,

1. the 'class approach' to international relations has provided Soviet commentators with an alternative set of value premises to the generally accepted principles of international law: both 'class-based' and 'legal-positivist' value systems have been incorporated into the Soviet doctrine of sovereignty
2. Leninist authoritarianism and the Soviet conception of socialist international relations: the need for 'unity and discipline' has been a constant theme of Soviet strictures towards other communist parties (both ruling and non-ruling) in the postwar era
3. the doctrine of 'popular sovereignty' establishes the crucial link between sovereignty and socialism
4. the base-superstructure paradigm has constituted the conceptual foundation of the Soviet Union's dualistic approach to international affairs. Even though its weakness as an analytical tool is now widely recognised by Soviet theorists, it has been modified rather than abandoned, since it is the central postulate of the Soviet conceptualisation of 'socialist international relations'.

6 The Ideological Dimension

Analysis of the role and significance of the ideological dimension in Soviet foreign policy is a precondition of any serious inquiry into the Soviet Union's relations with the Peoples Democracies. Several specific reasons can be advanced in support of this view: firstly, the significance which the Soviets themselves have attached to ideology as a determinant of foreign policy (a guiding and directing force of state behaviour[1]) and to 'ideological warfare'[2] as a fundamental feature of the international system;[3] secondly, Soviet assertions that the nature and dynamics of contemporary international relations are explicable only by reference to the 'Marxist-Leninist science of international relations', which, according to Zagladin, is a 'reliable compass', enabling socialist states to identify and assess the 'character, alignment and balance of forces acting in the world';[4] thirdly, the fact that the CPSU's relations with other ruling and non-ruling communist parties have frequently been marred by 'ideological' disputes (even though some Western analysts perceive disputes between socialist states as being broadly explicable in terms of 'conventional' interstate conflicts, it is significant that the adversaries have felt it necessary to couch their arguments in the language of ideology);[5] fourthly, the history of postwar Eastern Europe is, as Vali has argued, the history of two competing ideologies: Marxism-Leninism and nationalism and therefore the ideological dimension in the relations between the Soviet Union and the bloc states cannot be ignored.[6] Similarly, Taras characterises the history of Peoples Poland as 'a protracted and profound ideological crisis': the same might be said of the history of postwar Eastern Europe as a whole.[7] Since the Soviet regime is founded upon Marxist-Leninist ideology, a 'crisis of ideology' is also a crisis of the system itself.[8] Fifthly, the Soviet Union's justifications of its duty to render 'fraternal military aid' to other socialist states have been based upon arguments which derive from Marxism-Leninism. We might also cite the use by the Soviets of Marxist-Leninist terminology as a coded power language during crises with the bloc.

The Soviets have been dismissive of Western 'convergence' theories, which hinge on the assumption of the declining significance of ideology. In the early 1970s, Shakhnazarov described 'de-ideologisation' as 'a major anti-socialist subversion'.[9] This is not to say that the Soviets have always been consistent with regard to the role of the ideological factor in international relations: for example, from the early 1970s to the beginning of the 1980s (an assertive phase in Soviet foreign policy) the tendency in Soviet commentaries was to emphasise the inevitability and growing importance of ideological warfare between two opposing systems:[10] however, after the culmination of this phase, commentaries began to appear which criticised statesmen in the West for seeking to 'ideologise' their domestic and foreign policies and increasingly 'to subordinate foreign policy to commandments of an ideological nature':[11] these attempts were said to be linked to attempts to 'soften up socialism' by waging 'psychological warfare' (the Soviet term for Western criticisms of the socialist camp[12]). The main implication of Gromyko's assertion that the Soviet Union was against the transplantation of ideological differences into the international relations sphere[13] seemed to be that only socialist countries had a right to engage in 'ideological warfare' and that Western statesmen ought to be more accommodating in their dealings with the Kremlin: statements such as these do not imply that 'ideology' ought to be abandoned, or deny the close relationship between ideology and foreign policy.[14] Although the evidence cited above derives from the pre-Gorbachev era, the 'new thinking' is said to be firmly based upon a 'principled Leninist stand'.[15] Gorbachev has called for the removal of the 'ideological cutting edge' from interstate relations,[16] but has also repeatedly insisted that his reform programme derives from a creative application of Leninist principles.

THE TRIPLE FUSION OF IDEOLOGY, POWER AND NATIONAL INTEREST

The debate in the West about the relationship between Soviet foreign policy and ideology has centred on two interrelated questions: firstly, upon the functions performed by Soviet Marxist-Leninist ideology – is it the main determinant of Soviet policy in the international arena, or is it primarily an *ex post facto* rationalisation for Soviet actions and policy orientations? This distinction has stimulated a lively controversy amongst Western scholars[17] and has been expressed in various forms: for example, Adomeit distinguishes between *antreibsideologie* – ideology as a motivating force or 'action guide' and *rechtfertigungsideologie* – ideology as a legitimising factor.[18] Comey distinguishes between 'ideology stressing analysis' (which views Marxism-Leninism as the 'key to the explanation of Soviet foreign policy') and *realpolitik* analysis, which identifies the pursuit of national interest as the mainspring of Soviet foreign policy, with Marxist-Leninist terminology serving an 'authenticating' function – a cover for the pursuit of Soviet state interests:[19] on the basis of this assumption, a strong element of continuity has been observed between Tsarist and Soviet foreign policies: Soviet expansionist tendencies are thus interpreted as a manifestation of Great Russian imperialism and of 'objective factors of geopolitics and imperial management'[20] rather than of internationalist imperatives.[21] Comey[22] and Carew-Hunt,[23] however, note that some Soviet policy decisions can only be understood by reference to ideological motivations (in both cases their arguments hinge upon the premise of fusion between ideology and national interest in Soviet policy): Comey cites the Sovietisation of postwar Eastern Europe and the collectivisation of Soviet agriculture as examples of the influence of ideology upon Soviet policy formation.[24]

The tendency in Western scholarship is now to reject the 'either-or' premise upon which this debate is pivoted: various authors have sought to make sense of Soviet foreign policy by utilising a 'fusion' model.[25] In the fusion model, 'national interest', 'power' and 'ideology' are viewed as being inextricably intertwined or synthesised:[26] this alloy of ideology and national interest is regarded as serving both motivating and legitimising functions in Soviet policy. Adomeit speaks of the ideology being supplemented rather than supplanted by Russian state power.[27] Similarly, Lowenthal argues that Stalin tackled the dilemma of 'ideology' or 'national interest' by making the paramountcy of Soviet state interests integral to the ideology.[28] In previous chapters we have observed how Soviet patriotism and Soviet policy objectives are said to harmonise with, and indeed enhance, the interests of the world community: therefore, any success for the Soviet Union, any accretion of its power, is regarded by the Soviets as a success for all mankind.

The triple fusion of ideology, power and national interest in Soviet foreign policy derives from the earliest days of the Soviet regime and is a phenomenon of 'goal fusion' rather than of 'goal displacement' of the means-end reversal kind. During the period when the Soviet Union was an isolated socialist state, a variant of this fusion model found almost universal acceptance within the international communist movement, since the future of world socialism was viewed as hinging upon the survival of the Soviet state. Bromke attributes this fusion to the fact that Marxism-Leninism is now embedded in the Russian nationalist tradition[29] and argues that the process of fusion was already under way in Lenin's time (for example, Lenin accepted the terms of the Brest-Litovsk treaty) although it was under Stalin that it was fully developed. Regardless of the relative merits of these models ('ideology versus national interest' or 'triple fusion') as frameworks of analysis, two intractable problems remain. The first is definitional: neither the term 'ideology' nor 'national interest' have generally agreed and unambiguous meanings; the second is methodological: even if we could agree on terminology, we are still faced with the task of ascertaining the extent to which 'ideological' factors influence Soviet foreign policy: for example, it would obviously be naive to take policy-makers' statements concerning their motivations at face value (regardless of whether they claim to be acting in accordance with the 'national interest' or with Marxist-Leninist principles). We therefore must rely on inferences concerning the causal connection between belief and behaviour.

Marx himself made a notable contribution to the semantic confusion surrounding the meaning of the term 'ideology': as Seliger has noted Marx used *ideologie*, *ideen*, *anschaungen* and *doktrinen* interchangeably[30] Taras points out that for Marx 'ideology signified a philosophy, a political programme, a form of social consciousness, a set of norms and values, a political theory legitimising a particular social order, a "spirit of the age", and a scientific discipline'.[31] Both Western and Soviet commentators have subsequently added to this confusion.[32] Nevertheless, the term is not used in an entirely arbitrary manner: the core of meaning in most modern definitions is that 'ideology' signifies a belief system oriented towards action.[33] For the Soviet philosopher Krasin, Marxism differs from all other ideologies, in that it is free of myths: conversely, 'exploiter class' ideologies need myths in order to obscure reality (he defines 'ideology' as 'a system of views, convictions and ideals expressing the interests of a definite class'[34]). The assumption of the inseparable connection, or 'unity', between theory and policy has been an insistent theme of Soviet writings on ideology: it is said to be a mutually interacting or 'dialectical' relationship, in that theory and policy are assumed to exert influence upon each other.[35]

Many Western definitions break down the concept into two component categories: firstly, 'fundamental principles',[36] 'foundations' or 'core beliefs'; secondly, the application of these principles – referred to by various authors as the 'operative ideology'[37] or the 'action programme'.[38] Brzezinski defines modern revolutionary ideology as 'essentially an action programme derived from certain doctrinal assumptions about the nature of reality'.[39] In Brzezinski's schema, therefore, the key relationship is between 'doctrine' (the core beliefs, or foundations of the ideology, which include fundamental beliefs concerning the nature of capitalism and socialism) and the 'action programme'.[40] Taras, following Zaslasky, also distinguishes between 'doctrine' and 'ideology', with the former referring to fundamental principles (Marxism or Marxism-Leninism) and the latter to the application of these principles.[41]

Taras seeks to solve this problem of conceptual imprecision by adopting a 'gradational' approach to ideology, which places ideological phenomena along a continuum of goals, ranging from 'long term' to 'immediate'.[42] Krasin argues that in structure ideology is like a ladder in that 'it has a gradation of steps or ideological platforms, some of which are organically fused with policy'.[43] The 'gradational' or 'ladder' approach seems similar to Frankel's distinction between 'aspirational' and 'operational' foreign policy interests,[44] or to Perrow's distinction between 'official' and 'operative' organisational goals.[45] The 'gradational' approach might be illustrated by reference to Carew-Hunt's postulate of a causal connection between Soviet ideology and foreign policy behaviour. Carew-Hunt has stressed the importance of Marxist-Leninist ideology as a key to the understanding of Soviet actions in the international arena and sees no contradiction between commitment to fundamental principles and *realpolitik*, since it is necessary to translate principles into action.[46] The key question is whether or not in the process, principles become distorted, or washed out.

We are then faced with the problem of putting flesh on the bone. The formulation of a set of categories is a fairly easy task: filling these categories is a much more formidable undertaking. How, for example, do we decide which aspects of Soviet policy form part of the 'fundamental principles' and which belong to the 'operative' ideology? Secondly, we need to define the nature of the influence which belief exerts upon action: Bialer views Soviet ideology as 'tendencies and patterns of thought and belief' rather than as a set of rigid dogmas that directly dictates Soviet actions.[47] De George offers a similar analysis, and uses it to explain change and continuity in Soviet foreign policy: he postulates a high degree of continuity in Soviet thought patterns, but considerable flexibility with regard to specific Soviet policies.[48]

THE FUNCTIONS OF SOVIET IDEOLOGY

The significance of these distinctions will become clearer as we seek to ascertain which aspects of the ideology are subject to revision and which (if any) are sacrosanct. We should, however, remember that the relative importance of the various functions of ideology in Soviet policy is no static phenomenon. Various possible (not necessarily distinct) functions of Soviet ideology have been suggested, viz.:

1 'Legitimation'

This means justifying or 'authenticating' the regime and its policies, as distinct from influencing policy formation. The 'incantation of slogans' may serve as a camouflage for pragmatic and self-serving pursuit of Soviet national interests.[49] With regard to Soviet control of Eastern Europe, two legitimising arguments have been employed in the postwar era: the security argument (protection against German 'revanchism' and imperialist aggression); and the 'ideological' rationale based upon the notion of international duty. These arguments are fused by the reasoning that the protection of the sovereignties and 'socialist gains' of the Peoples Democracies are closely related objectives which can only be achieved by the Soviet Union. Crises of control within the Soviet bloc have tended to result in renewed Soviet emphasis upon the ideological dimension in international relations: in particular ideological reasoning has been used to explain and justify Soviet interventions. Within the socialist camp, however, 'ideological' justifications of the Soviet Union's hegemonic position within the bloc have increasingly been challenged. Meyer has argued that 'self-legitimation'[50] can be regarded as an important function of the ideology, in that leaders within the bloc engage in a kind of 'collective monologue', which reinforces their own perception of a particular view of reality. It seems plausible to argue that ritually expressed affirmations of the 'touchstone doctrine' and of the importance of fraternal links between the bloc communist parties fall into the category of 'self-legitimation'. In a constant search for legitimacy, according to Meyer, Soviet doctrine became 'a rigid catechism chanted compulsively in ritual affirmations of loyalty and approval'.[51]

Shlapentokh distinguishes between 'institutional legitimation' – of the party, its organs and leader – and 'policy legitimation'.[52] This distinction could be extended to embrace the Kremlin's relations with Eastern Europe: thus we could also distinguish between legitimation of the Soviet-dominated regional system in Eastern Europe (systemic legitimation) and legitimation of specific Soviet policies. As Shlapentokh has argued, the Soviets make extensive use of negative comparisons (drawing unfavourable comparisons between the Soviet and Western systems) as a key part of the Soviet legitimation process.[53] On this basis he distinguishes between 'positive' (praise of the Soviet system) and 'negative' (exposure of the weaknesses of rival systems). A key policy legitimation role is now performed by specialist academic institutes in international affairs, which, in addition to their work in the field of policy-oriented research and analysis, also provide elaborate theoretical justifications for Soviet policy. Eran has identified 'ideological spokesmanship' as one of the primary functions of the *Mezhdunarodniki*[54] Unger has noted that, in the domestic context from the late 1960s, the function of 'agitation' (the dissemination of a few simple ideas to the many) has been supplemented by the 'propaganda' function (the dissemination of many, more complex, ideas to the few):[55] a similar trend towards more sophisticated explanations may be observed in the foreign policy field.

2 The 'masking function'

Ideological orthodoxies are reiterated, according to Comey, to divert attention from current realities.[56] Continual repetition of ideological slogans and phrases serves to disguise the incongruity between official interpretations and the real world. In Eastern Europe in the early postwar period, the Soviets employed 'masking' techniques (e.g. references to the paramount value of sovereignty within the socialist camp) to disguise blatantly unequal relationships between the Soviet Union and the Peoples Democracies. Constant references to 'socialist internationalism', 'fraternal mutual aid' and other definitive characteristics of socialist international relations may serve to mask the real nature of these relations. 'Mental fictions'[57] of this kind constitute a kind of doctrinal fig leaf used to camouflage ugly realities and distract attention from the fact that revolutionary objectives are far from being realised (or may have been abandoned altogether). In the postwar era, reiteration by the Soviets of the 'harmonic' conception of socialist international relations has constituted a good example of the 'masking function'.

3 A guide to analysis/action

The contribution of ideology to policy formation can be considered in relation to two aspects: firstly, as a guide to analysis and secondly as an action guide. These aspects are normally regarded as closely interrelated, since if ideology is a means of perceiving the world, it is likely to affect how policy makers behave. Brzezinski argues that ideology (which here he defines as the 'link between theory and action') conditions behaviour through the selection of policy alternatives.[58] The guide to analysis function of the ideology (referred to by Adomeit as the 'analytical' or 'cognitive' function[59] and by Kubálková and Cruickshank as the 'taxonomic, explanatory and predictive' functions[60]) provides the Soviets with a way of seeing, a cognitive map, with which to make sense of external phenomena. According to Krasin, the cognitive function 'helps one to find one's bearing in the surrounding social reality' and enables policy makers to categorise and compare events:[61] thus it provides a means of assessing the dynamics of power in the international arena (e.g. in relation to the 'correlation of forces', between capitalism and socialism). It has predictive capabilities, in that it can be used to explain both the underlying nature of world events and the mainsprings of the foreign policies of particular states.

Lowenthal cites the example of the formation of the Peoples Democracies as evidence of the influence of the ideology upon Soviet policy, since in his view the Soviets could have imposed their hegemony upon Eastern Europe without adopting the 'duplicative' approach[62] (however, it might be argued that 'duplication' was the best method of legitimating Soviet regional hegemony). Similarly, the fact that the Soviets have frequently 'deviated' from Marxist-Leninist orthodoxy by entering into agreements with non-socialist states does not necessarily invalidate the 'guide to action' hypothesis, since commitment to the doctrine does not rule out pragmatic and tactical policy shifts. Kubálková and Cruickshank rightly suggest that socialisation processes within the Soviet Union (and more specifically within the communist party) must condition the way Soviet policy-makers perceive the world.[63]

As a guide to analysis, Soviet ideology has both advantages and disadvantages for its users: its principle advantages are that it provides the Soviets with a comprehensive cognitive framework with which, as Ukraintsev argues, the complexities of the world can be comprehended, through the application of the analytical categories of Marxism-Leninism.[64] Conversely, it may serve to distort, rather than clarify perceptions: thus its categories and underlying assumptions are too crude to provide a sophisticated appreciation of the complex-ities of international politics; secondly, like any ideology Marxism-Leninism lays stress upon a particular set of variables, which are assumed to have central importance in any accurate assessment of the structure and dynamics of the system. However, a way of looking is also a way of not looking and therefore other significant factors (e.g. the power of nationalism) may be undervalued: Marxism-Leninism, therefore, might be viewed as a way of misinterpreting the world.

The development of international relations as a discipline in the Soviet Union is attributable in part to the Soviet elite's recognition after 1956 of the complexity of the international environment and of the inadequacy of existing policy-oriented research.[65] Specialist institutes now perform the role of 'think tanks' for the CPSU central committee policy machinery, by undertaking research which may serve as an input at the formative stage of policy (the fact that the heads of some of these institutes have close connections with members of the central committee is indicative of their potential influence). The cooption of the specialist research institutes into the policy machinery is a manifestation of what von Beyme has termed 'apparatus pluralism',[66] or the institutional differentiation of the Soviet foreign policy-making process (in organisation theory, en-vironmental heterogeneity is regarded as a primary cause of dif-ferentiation in organisational structures). Publications by members of these institutes are not necessarily precise guides to government policy, since scholars now have greater freedom – within limits – to develop individual positions.

4   Coded language

Esoteric language performs several functions within political systems: firstly, it serves as a signalling device, reaffirming the sender's commitment to the values and rules of the system: Marxism-Leninism serves as an outward sign of commitment to the ideals of the international communist movement. Secondly, it is a means of legitimising ideas, in that policy pronouncements are more likely to be understood and accepted by other initiates if they are coded in the language of official discourse. Thirdly, coded language may serve a 'conflict prophylaxis' function, in that conflicting views can be expressed in vague formulae and oblique terminology, which avoids explicit criticisms of the adversary, but the meaning of which is well understood by insiders: the Soviet insistence upon a 'harmonic' interpretation of intra-bloc relations has meant that tensions and disagreements between the Soviet Union and the Peoples Democracies have had to be couched (in public at least) in coded language. However, in private 'showdown' meetings (for example, during the Hungarian and Czechoslovak crises) Soviet leaders have resorted to the language of power rather than of ideology and have emphasised geopolitical and strategic, rather than 'ideological' considerations: the coded language used by Soviet commentators during the Polish crisis of 1980–1 was well understood by Poles on all sides and served as a reminder of political realities in the region.[67]

5 Socialisation

Socialisation serves to prepare citizens to accept the values of, and their own status within, a social system. Krasin assigns importance to the 'axiological function' in 'substantiating the values for which the given class carries on its struggle'.[68] The implantation of Marxist-Leninist political structures within the region of Eastern Europe after the war involved a massive (though largely unsuccessful) socialisation programme which had interstate, as well as intrastate dimensions. On the interstate level, the Soviets have placed a high priority upon the maintenance of a complex network of interparty and interstate contacts within the region: they have also sought to enmesh the career structures of the East European elites into the Soviet control system.[69] Soviet ideological offensives aimed at restoring unity to the international communist movement under Soviet leadership may also be regarded as attempts at 're-socialisation'.

CONTINUITY AND CHANGE IN SOVIET IDEOLOGY

A second issue of concern to Western scholars has been the causes and nature of ideological revision in Soviet policy: do policy shifts reflect fundamental alterations of Soviet core beliefs or are they primarily tactical (and easily reversible) adjustments? The Soviets themselves stress the need to 'creatively develop' Marxist-Leninist theory in the field of international relations.[70] However, this does not mean that all aspects of the ideology are necessarily open to revision: core doctrines may remain untouched, whereas peripheral doctrines may be adjusted or discarded altogether. Zimmerman has discerned changes in both the role of ideology and in core doctrines.[71] Similarly, Mitchell has argued that ideological revision in the 1970s may have reversed some of the basic principles of classical Marxism.[72] Lynch has observed that international relations specialists in the 1980s tend to eschew reference to Marxist-Leninist doctrine and show greater willingness to incorporate Western ideas in their theories.[73]

In the postwar era the Soviets have engaged in doctrinal reformulations in many policy spheres: partly, these transformations of doctrine have been stimulated by changes in environmental conditions. Shlapentokh perceives cyclical trends or 'oscillations'[74] in Soviet ideology, with changes developing as reactions to failures of existing ideologies: however, these changes are unlikely to occur smoothly, since drives for change will be resisted by conservative factions. It is the nature of these responses which are the interesting feature of Soviet doctrinal shifts: do they represent, for example, a change in the core ideology – i.e. abandonment or modification of fundamental principles – or merely tactical adjustments to new circumstances through reinterpretation of secondary prescriptive values? The development of the theory of 'Peoples Democracy' provides an example of theoretical innovation in response to new circumstances. Similarly, the twists and turns in the Soviet theory of 'socialist international law' can in large measure be explained by reference to changing Soviet policy requirements.[75]

Other examples include the attempts at the 'creative development' of Marxism-Leninism which took place under Khrushchev. Many of the putatively 'new' theories which emerged under Khrushchev were, as Achminov has observed, restatements of principles which had a long genealogy in Soviet thought.[76] Achminov nevertheless accepts that Khrushchev sought to make significant changes to the content of

Soviet ideology from 1956 (for example, his pronouncements on the possibility of separate roads to socialism, the principle of 'socialist internationalism', the 1960 reformulation of the doctrine of peaceful coexistence, the doctrine of the 'just war', of relations with the developing world, and the revision of the 'two camps' doctrine[77]). These adjustments constituted responses to new circumstances and situations. In large measure, therefore, Khrushchev's forays in the field of ideological revision constituted attempts to adapt the ideology to prevailing circumstances.

Prior to the advent of Gorbachev, shifts in Soviet doctrine in the postwar era have been mainly in the field of foreign relations: the theories of the 'all-peoples' state' and of 'developed socialism' being the major exceptions. Achminov identifies 16 modifications of doctrine in the Khrushchev period, only one of which was concerned with domestic policy.[78] Examples of doctrinal shifts in Soviet policy towards the bloc are the changes which resulted from the traumas of 1956 and 1968: the crises of control in these years resulted in Soviet integration drives and ideological offensives designed to bind the bloc states more closely into the Soviet sphere. The ideological underpinning for these offensives was the 'solidarist' doctrine of 'socialist internationalism', which stresses the primacy of 'international' over 'national' interests.

Ideological revision

The analysis below identifies three interrelated factors deemed central to Soviet processes of ideological change:

1. elite perceptions of environmental conditions (favourable or unfavourable) which activate and give direction to Soviet policy shifts
2. the corpus of Soviet doctrine (the reservoir of ideas from which 'new' streams of thought are likely to emerge)
3. elite commitment to the maintenance of party rule (serving the 'homeostatic' function of system preservation).

1 *Elite perceptions of environmental conditions*
The USSR's international environment is comprised of several interconnected subenvironments: e.g. relations with developed capitalist states; the Third World, the socialist community (principally the

Soviet bloc), the world socialist system, etc. The heterogeneity of the Soviet Union's external environment, and the multiple linkages between domestic and international events, make it difficult to identify the influence of external pressures upon policy. Soviet perceptions of favourable or unfavourable circumstances (threats or opportunities) in the USSR's environment may precipitate doctrinal shifts. Comey argues that threats to the regime are likely to lead to deviations from the ideology (e.g. Brest-Litovsk and the Molotov-Ribbentrop pact):[79] but this is also likely to occur when new opportunities present themselves, the difference being that unfavourable conditions are likely to lead to a Soviet policy of accommodation and favourable conditions to Soviet foreign policy assertiveness. Moore has argued that the most striking modification of Soviet doctrine in relation to international relations is the 'sharp toning down of revolutionary optimism', since it was necessary to go back to the 1920s to find a statement by a Soviet leader which expressed belief in imminent world revolution.[80] The abandonment of 'revolutionary optimism' can be attributed in large measure to the relative weakness of the Soviet Union in the international system. In the postwar period, favourable Soviet estimates of the balance of forces between the Soviet Union and the capitalist world have resulted in modifications of doctrine (for example in the immediate postwar period and in the 1970s[81]).

Carew-Hunt has argued that, whenever the Soviets feel in a 'tight corner', they are likely to react by intensifying ideological indoctrination and by emphasising 'first principles'.[82] The crises within Eastern Europe provide many examples of this Pavlovian response: thus the Hungarian, Czech and Polish crises all led to Soviet ideological offensives and renewed stress upon the paramount role of proletarian internationalism in socialist international relations: each challenge to Soviet hegemony within Eastern Europe has led the Kremlin to seek to accelerate intrabloc integration processes. Challenges to Soviet conceptions of ideological orthodoxy from the international communist movement have also resulted in modifications of Soviet ideological positions in order to prevent further divisions (notably the doctrine of the CPSU's leading role in the movement) – although more often the Soviet response to such challenges has been to launch ideological offensives with the aim of reaffirming orthodoxies. Processes of ideological revision in the Soviet Union may also be influenced by Soviet perceptions of developments in other socialist countries (particularly in Eastern Europe and China): the influence exerted by domestic developments within the bloc countries (for example, the Hungarian economic reforms of the 1970s) upon Soviet reform processes has been referred to by Gitelman as the process of 'stimulus diffusion'.[83] Similarly, Rozman has observed that Soviet discussions of developments within China also have a bearing upon the internal debate concerning the nature of, and possible solutions to, the problems confronting the Soviet Union.[84] Domestic problems and policy failures (in particular, economic stagnation) have encouraged some contemporary Soviet scholars to depart from the Leninist 'theory of crises' by entertaining the possibility of 'antagonistic contradictions' within socialism.[85]

Western analyses of Soviet perspectives on international relations in the 1980s have shown that there have been marked departures from the ideological orthodoxy, in the direction of less dogmatic appraisals of international problems. For example, Valkenier contends that Soviet views on processes of revolutionary change in the Third World tend to be pessimistic and couched in terms of pragmatism and national interest rather than ideology.[86] In the Gorbachev era, the rejection of old stereotypes has been applauded by Soviet commentators as a hallmark of the 'new thinking' on international affairs.[87] Although modern Soviet leaders are not regarded as 'thinkers' in the mould of the old Bolsheviks, leadership changes do impact upon ideology. Khrushchev, for example, ushered in a period of heady ideological innovation, whereas Brezhnev presided over a static period (again, with the exception of 'developed socialism'). Similarly, the choice of Gorbachev was itself a product of an ideological shift: Shlapentokh refers to the new ideology which emerged between 1982 and 1985 as the 'Andropov-Gorbachev' ideology, which developed as a reaction to the stagnation of the Brezhnev years and was stimulated by fear of economic decline.[88] Many of the ideas which have become associated with the 'new thinking' were percolating within the Soviet intellectual elite before the accession of Gorbachev.[89]

2   The corpus of Soviet doctrine

Soviet theorists do not start from scratch when developing theoretical responses to new circumstances: rather, they will be expected to build upon an existing framework of officially approved ideas and concepts. This framework will serve not only as a guide to analysis, but also as a constraint upon theoretical innovation. Continuity in Soviet thought derives in some measure from the assumptions and patterns of thought which are shared by the Soviet elite. Although there has been a considerable expansion of Soviet research and analysis in the field of international affairs in the postwar era, theoretical innovation has been constrained by the intellectually inhibiting conditions in which Soviet scholars work. 'New departures' in Soviet theory have in large measure represented the adaption of old ideas to new situations, or the reweaving of previously enunciated and approved principles. Therefore, shifts in doctrine are likely to have a genealogy rooted in Soviet Marxist-Leninist thought. Nevertheless, since the Stalin era, there has been a significant relaxation of intellectual controls which has allowed for genuine debates between academic specialists on fundamental social and political issues. Changes in intellectual controls over the degree of permissible innovation in the realm of theory are also conducive to shifts in doctrine, a phenomenon most strikingly exemplified by the 'new thinking' (see Chapter 12).

3   *Elite commitment to the maintenance of party rule*

Lowenthal has argued that the operative parts of Soviet ideology are those which serve to maintain and justify the rule of the CPSU.[90] 'Self-preservation of the regime' is the dominant value, to which all others are subordinate.[91] Similarly, Moore argues that the central objective of the policy of the Soviet leaders has been to maintain and increase their own power rather than to propagate a specific social order.[92] In the international sphere, ideology has provided a source of legitimacy for the Soviet Union's regional hegemony: therefore, specific doctrinal pronouncements can be adapted or abandoned, providing that the legitimacy of the system itself (and in particular the party's right to rule) is safeguarded and fostered. Ideological pronouncements will be adjusted and modified to suit the requirements of party monopoly and thereby legitimise the party's paramount position in society: specific doctrinal pronouncements can be modified or abandoned, providing that the right of the party to make these pronouncements remains unchallenged.[93] After the shocks of 1956, the CPSU's 'ideological authority' within the movement, i.e. 'the right to interpret ambiguous principles in a changing situation',[94] began slipping from its grasp.

Within the Soviet Union itself, the party has been able to sustain its legitimacy by maintaining strict control over authoritative pronouncements on ideological matters. However, the Soviet party has also utilised ideology to legitimise its assumption of special roles in relation to the Peoples Democracies. Wesson has argued that the

Soviets may well have abandoned Marxism after the Revolution – 'effectively if not overtly' – had it not been necessary to justify control over a multinational empire.[95] By the same token Marxism might also be regarded as a 'necessity' for Soviet control of Eastern Europe. The Soviets have been prepared to countenance many changes in the internal policies of the Peoples Democracies: however, they have not yet been prepared to abandon the principle of party control as it applies to the bloc states, since it is communist party rule which is the ultimate guarantee of Soviet control in Eastern Europe.

Many of the propositions considered above can be illustrated by reference to the Soviet theory of sovereignty. For example, the formal enunciation of 'legal-positivist' conceptions from the mid-1930s should not be regarded as evidence of the 'abandonment of ideology': 'fusion' theorists would explain that, in Soviet conceptions, protection of the Soviet state and protection of the interests of socialism are perfectly compatible. Despite the Soviet Union's zealous commitment to the (horizontal) legal positivist conception of this principle, it has continued to reserve the right to espouse a (vertical) conception deriving from Marxist-Leninist doctrine – i.e. a class approach to sovereignty: 'bi-axialism' therefore permits great flexibility in Soviet postures towards the sovereignty principle. Abandonment of the Marxist-Leninist interpretation would remove a rationale for Soviet interference in Eastern Europe and would undermine the Soviet conception of the proper relationship between 'national and international interests' within the socialist camp.

7 Challenges to Soviet Regional Hegemony in the 1950s and the Soviet Response

The principal Soviet objective towards Eastern Europe in the early postwar years was to ensure that the states within the region remained tightly coupled and subordinate to the USSR. With the benefit of hindsight, 'tight coupling' was based on several flawed assumptions, reflecting the classic psychology of an ascendant imperial power: firstly, that the principal geo-political fact of life in the region – overwhelming Soviet power – would provide a solid and durable foundation for Soviet hegemony; secondly, that the indigenous beneficiaries of Soviet dominance – the local communist parties – would continue to perform the role of reliable and effective transmission belts of Soviet policy; thirdly, that the principal ideological alternative to Marxism-Leninism in the region – nationalism – could be vitiated, or harnessed by the local communist parties; fourthly, that the Peoples Democracies could be effectively insulated from centrifugal pressures emanating from outside the bloc. As Larrabee has argued, Stalin's policy towards Eastern Europe was based on the pursuit of control rather than of stability.[1] The primacy of control objectives in Soviet strategy was itself a destabilising factor, since it exacerbated the 'inauthenticity' of the regimes: conversely, attempts by the regimes to narrow their legitimacy deficits tended to be at the expense of Soviet control.

THE FORMAL AND 'SUBMERGED' RULES OF THE SOVIET HEGEMONIAL SYSTEM

As in any other system of control, Soviet hegemony in Eastern Europe was founded on a network of rules. In the late 1940s, Soviet hegemony was so strong that the Soviets could formally bestow upon the bloc states the 'blank cheque' of formal sovereignty, without fear that it would be drawn. Therefore, there was a crucial difference between the formal rules of the system (e.g. respect for sovereignty and independence) and the actual or 'submerged' rules, manifested in the tenets of proletarian internationalism. The function of rules in international systems has been examined by Cohen[2] and others. They serve:

1. a 'boundary function'[3] delineating prohibited zones (geographical areas or activities): by defining what is out of bounds, they perform deviation control functions;
2. a 'signpost' function:[4] i.e. a guide to expected behaviour;
3. a 'tripwire' function,[5] alerting the controllers to rule-violations;
4. a remote control function: rules avoid repetition of routine orders;
5. a 'punishment legitimising' function: breakers of the rules can be penalised;
6. conflict prophylaxis: knowing the rules means that behaviour leading to conflict can be avoided.

Systems of control break down when the power of rules by which they are effectuated is eroded: for example:

a) the actual rules may be challenged from within;
b) the rulemaker may change the rules, without consulting those responsible for rule enforcement or observance;
c) the rules may be challenged from without;
d) the rules may no longer be enforced and may fall quietly into disuse;
e) there may be genuine confusion about the meaning of the rules;
f) new situations not covered by existing rules may arise.

The explosions of 1956 led the Soviets to expose the real rules of the system, even though the controlling functions of these rules were camouflaged in the language of the official ideology. Put bluntly, the crises of 1956 caused the Soviets to make clear that, between socialist states, the rules of international conduct deriving from general international law (in particular the rule of respect for sovereignty) were in practice subordinate to the 'socialist' rules of proletarian internationalism. In the previous chapter, we noted that shifts in Soviet doctrine are precipitated by events: the shifts in emphasis in the Soviet doctrine of socialist sovereignty from the 'horizontal' (legal positivist) axis to the 'vertical' (proletarian internationalist) axis derived from Soviet responses to the crisis of control within the bloc.

The 'equity effect'

The conciliatory approach to Yugoslavia pursued by Stalin's successors was to have a destabilising effect upon the political climate within the bloc. Tito's refusal to accept the premises upon which the Soviet conception of socialist international relations were based (in particular, the Soviet insistence upon a special status for the CPSU and of the universal applicability of the Soviet model) involved more than a loss of prestige for the Soviets. The price for reconciliation demanded by Tito was Soviet recognition of Yugoslavia's sovereignty. The Soviet-Yugoslav declarations of June 1955 and June 1956 explicitly affirmed that relations between the two countries were based upon respect for sovereignty. There could be no plausible reason why relations between other socialist states should differ qualitatively from Soviet-Yugoslav relations. This might be termed the 'equity effect' of Soviet disputes with communist parties outside the bloc. Ostracism (exclusion of Yugoslavia from the category of socialist states) had enabled Soviet theoreticians to avoid this question. However, this specious argument had not prevented Tito from sniping from the sidelines at the Soviet theory and practice of socialist international relations. Tito insisted that the statements on sovereignty wrung out of the Soviet leadership had a wider relevance. Moreover, the prescriptive neologism 'polycentrism', coined by Italian communist party leader Togliatti shortly after Khrushchev's speech to the 20th party congress, presaged further challenges to Soviet orthodoxies.

SOVIET RESPONSES TO THE CRISES IN POLAND AND HUNGARY

In the early 1950s, the harmonic conception of the bloc as a haven of peace and progress was assiduously fostered by Soviet publicists.[6] However, cracks in this implausible façade were already apparent. Stalin's successors in the Kremlin appear to have realised that there had to be changes within the bloc: the more overt forms of Soviet control were reduced (for example, the number of Soviet 'advisers') and the joint stock companies which functioned to syphon off resources to the Soviet Union were indigenised. The revival of the CMEA and the creation of the Warsaw Pact in 1954 and 1955 respectively – although still largely paper organisations – also heralded a movement towards a more 'conciliar' approach in Soviet strategy. The Soviet 'vanguard role' meant that what was good for the USSR was good for Eastern Europe. The East European communist party leaderships were encouraged by the Kremlin to introduce destalinisation measures: the 'new course' led to factional struggles within the local parties and raised popular expectations. Khrushchev was seeking a moderate and limited form of 'destalinisation' in socialist international relations, comparable to measures being applied domestically – i.e. the easing of the more overtly oppressive, and counter-productive, features of Stalinism without damaging Soviet regional hegemony. Events were to show, however, that it was far easier for Khrushchev to conduct an experiment in 'controlled reform' within the USSR – where the power of the CPSU was unchallenged – than outside it.

The spontaneous revolt of East German workers in June 1953 did not constitute a major challenge to Soviet hegemony. Rather, it reflected popular exasperation against the SED's policies: although local strike committees were established, there was no leading figure upon which the demonstrators could focus their support and the rising was easily crushed. Nevertheless, the episode contained lessons for the future: the rising was ended by Soviet troops (who evidently acted with some restraint) following a genuine request for military assistance from the SED leadership; similarly, the Soviets could not admit that workers had revolted against their communist leaders and therefore the disorders were attributed to internal and external subversion – to foreign hirelings, and 'gangs of fascist thugs and saboteurs', aided by Bonn revanchists.[7] Similarly, the Soviets were forced to rescue a local party from its own people (the ultimate reliance of local parties upon Moscow meant that the Soviets would be pulled in to 'domestic' crises within the bloc). The reaction of Western states was confined to verbal protest.[8]

The crises in Poland and Hungary in 1956 effectively destroyed many of the underlying assumptions of 'tight coupling'. It is not difficult to point to particular causes of the Polish and Hungarian crises of 1956: for example, the new leaders of the CPSU lacked Stalin's stature (or capacity to induce fear) and Khrushchev's 'secret speech' at the 20th party congress created a dangerous climate of anticipation within the bloc. The Soviet leadership was also divided, which meant that in some measure the Kremlin became preoccupied with its own internal problems and sent confusing signals to the region. However, it seems obvious that there were more fundamental underlying causes of the Polish and Hungarian challenges to Soviet authority in 1956 – e.g. what Brzezinski has termed 'domesticism':[9] the fact that some communist leaders in Eastern Europe became preoccupied with their own country's problems and therefore no longer viewed domestic problems from a purely 'internationalist' – i.e. Soviet – perspective.

The Polish crisis resulted from an explosive confluence of destabilising factors: Khrushchev's policies of destalinisation exacerbated the deep divisions within the Polish workers' party; the failure of economic reform; and the deep hostility of the Polish people towards the government.[10] In June, riots in Poznan were brutally crushed by the authorities. The Soviets demonstrated their anxiety by granting credits to bolster the tottering Polish economy. In July, Bulganin and Marshal Zhukov arrived in Warsaw to impress upon the leadership the need to exert control over the party. However, their demands were resisted and the 'national communist' Gomulka was allowed to rejoin the party in August. In October, Ochab, who had succeeded to the premiership with Soviet connivance after Gottwald's death, was informed by the Soviets (at a day's notice) that Khrushchev would head a delegation to the 8th party plenum. The purpose of the visit was to prevent Gomulka attaining power. Khrushchev threatened the Poles with military force and the possibility of armed confrontation seemed high. The reasons why Khrushchev stayed his hand seem clearer in the light of the Soviet invasions of Hungary and Czechoslovakia: firstly, Khrushchev's encounter with Gomulka may have convinced him that the Polish army and workers militias would resist Soviet intervention; secondly, despite the divisions within the Polish communist party, the Soviets were faced with a united front; thirdly, Gomulka, as his subsequent career demonstrated, was no 'liberal' and Khrushchev may have sensed that under his leadership the party would not lose its grip; fourthly, unlike Nagy, Gomulka did not get carried away by the popular anti-Soviet mood in the country.

On 30 October, the Soviets published a 'Declaration', which was meant to clarify the relationship between the Soviet Union and the Peoples Democracies.[11] The Declaration, which stated that relations between states should be based on 'peaceful coexistence', was, according to the Yugoslavia's Ambassador to Moscow, good enough to have been written by the Yugoslavs themselves.[12] In retrospect, the 'October Declaration' appears to have been a panic measure to soothe the seething unrest in Poland and Hungary. Indeed, Soviet pronouncements on the sovereignty of socialist states have often appeared to have been influenced as much by a desire to achieve mollifying euphony rather than clarity and, in relation to the bloc, are usually accompanied by nullifying qualifications and contradictions. The statement that relations within the community of socialist nations were founded on the principles of complete equality, respect for territorial integrity, state independence, sovereignty and non-interference in each other's internal affairs was followed by the potentially ominous rider that close fraternal cooperation and mutual assistance were also essential features of these relations.

For China and Yugoslavia, the statements on sovereignty contained in the Declaration could be taken almost literally (although not quite, because the CPSU expected to retain its position of leadership within the movement and to maintain a 'general line', corresponding to the Soviet conception of Marxist-Leninist rectitude). Indeed, Peking recognised that, although 'socialist countries are independent, sovereign states . . . they are united by the common ideal of socialism and the spirit of proletarian internationalism'.[13] For the Kremlin, recognition of the sovereignties (*de facto* and *de jure*) of China and Yugoslavia merely constituted formal acknowledgement of an existing situation. For the bloc states, other parts of the statement had greater import.

Soviet intervention in Hungary

The concept of 'intervention' has been extended to cover a very broad range of international actions, from various forms of non-military interference to full-scale invasion. Talleyrand supposedly concluded, after diligent study of the subject, that 'intervention' was synonymous with 'non-intervention'.[14] An English writer could similarly observe that intervention seemed to mean anything 'from a speech of Lord Palmerston's in the House of Commons to the partition of Poland'.[15] Rosenau defines interventionary phenomena as having two primary characteristics – they are 'convention breaking' and 'authority oriented': interventionary behaviour thus involves a sharp break with routine behaviours and is aimed at either changing or preserving political structures in the target state.[16] It is to be distinguished, therefore, from the persistent and continuing involvement of one state in the internal affairs of another.

From the mid-1930s, the Soviet attitude towards intervention has been based on the reiteration of the following themes: firstly, that, from the first days of its existence, non-intervention has been a fundamental principle of Soviet foreign policy;[17] secondly, that by its very nature, the Soviet regime is incapable of interfering in the internal affairs of other states; thirdly, that it has been a staunch opponent of intervention and has sought to outlaw such behaviour in the international arena[18] (prior to the explosions of 1956, the Soviets had repeatedly sought to add a definition of intervention to the UN Charter[19]); fourthly, as long as capitalism exists, socialist and other progressive regimes have to be constantly on their guard against the threat of intervention. Soviet references to sovereignty have frequently been counterpointed by diatribes against Western intervention.[20] The Soviet image as a staunch opponent of intervention made it inevitable that the Kremlin would seek to explain its actions in Eastern Europe in 1956 as consistent with respect for sovereignty. The CPSU's assumption of special duties within the international communist movement also made it likely that Soviet interventions would be disguised as 'fraternal mutual aid'. Little identifies two broad approaches to the analysis of intervention, a 'push' school associated with Morgenthau which explains intervention in terms of *realpolitik* (a state will intervene in another state's internal affairs in pursuit of its own national interest); and a 'pull' school in which the intervening state is drawn into the affairs of other states.[21] The push theory seems particularly suited to Soviet explanations of Imperialist intervention (capitalist states are assumed to be inherently expansionist). Pull theories necessitate identification of the 'impulsion force' emanating from a target state. In the case of a tightly-coupled hegemonial system based upon the policy of duplication, domestic crises within subordinate states are also crises for the hegemonial power: because the hegemon assumes special 'system maintenance roles', it is drawn into 'domestic' crises at an early stage.

Although many general and specific causes of the Hungarian explosion can be identified, three factors were crucial. The first was domestic: the deep hostility of the Hungarian population towards the regime was exacerbated by the ouster of Nagy in 1955, (supposedly for neglecting heavy industry). In 1953, Nagy had embarked on a 'new course', involving economic liberalisation and relaxation of police terror. The parlous state of the economy and splits in the communist party also fuelled popular unrest. The second sprang from developments within the Soviet Union: the Soviet leadership was divided at the time of the Hungarian crisis, roughly between Khrushchevite and anti-Khrushchevite factions. The combined effects of destalinisation, attempts to bring Yugoslavia back into the fold and

Soviet interference in the internicine struggles within the Hungarian communist party all served to further destabilise the Hungarian regime. The third factor was the upheaval in Poland, which encouraged belief in the possibility of change.

Following clashes between students, demonstrating in favour of Gomulka, and the Hungarian political police (AVH) in Budapest on 24 October, Gerö (then head of the Hungarian government) called in Soviet forces to help restore order. On the 22nd, the students had drafted a programme which included demands for free elections and withdrawal of Soviet troops. Soviet tanks were in action in Budapest from the outset of these disorders. Within a week, street protests were followed by a general uprising. However, although an announcement of the Hungarian government's appeal for Soviet military assistance was broadcast on Budapest radio on 23 October, Nagy, who had succeeded Hegedus as Prime Minister on that day, vehemently denied responsibility for it. At a mass meeting in Budapest on 31 October, Nagy denied the assertion by Rákosi and Gerö that he had called in Soviet troops and described himself as 'a fighter for Hungarian sovereignty'.[22]

The Soviet decision to crush this 'counter-revolutionary putsch' was probably precipitated by a combination of factors: firstly, the realisation that, far from being in control, the Hungarian party had lost its grip on the situation and therefore a 'Polish solution' was impossible. The declaration by Nagy indicating that 'one party government' was to be abolished was clearly unacceptable to the Soviets (and, for that matter, to Tito, Gomulka and other 'national communists'). The implications of the events in Hungary, which signalled the end of communist rule in the country, were obvious to the other ruling parties. No ruling party disassociated itself from the second (and decisive) military intervention commencing on 4 November. Despite their differences, the ruling parties would not share power with non-communist groups. Secondly, Nagy's declaration of Hungarian neutrality and his announcement that Hungary had withdrawn from the Warsaw Pact breached another cardinal Soviet principle: for the bloc states, membership of the socialist camp was compulsory. Thirdly, the West was distracted and divided by the Suez crisis (even though Khrushchev told the Yugoslav Ambassador on the 25 October that the West was seeking to destroy each socialist state in turn,[23] Washington signalled to Moscow that it would not react militarily).

Conventional justifications

The Soviets were to advance several justifications for the 'fraternal assistance' rendered to Hungary: initially, the main thrust of Soviet arguments was upon conventional explanations deriving from general international law, viz.:

The 'invitation' argument
According to this justification, far from being a unilateral Soviet decision, Soviet military action had been undertaken only after a request for help from the Hungarian government.[24] However, although Gerö made a request on the 23 October, and Kádár announced on 4 November that Soviet military aid had been called in to quell the counter-revolution, in neither case can the request be regarded as a collective decision by the members of the Hungarian government. Indeed, the 'invitation' argument backfired in the face of Nagy's vehement denials. Moreover, the request of Kádár's 'Hungarian Revolutionary Worker-Peasant Government' is hardly convincing, since this government was a product, rather than a cause, of Soviet military intervention.

Treaty obligations
A second (related) justification was that Soviet military assistance was rendered to Hungary in accordance with the terms of the 1948 Soviet-Hungarian mutual assistance treaty and the Warsaw Pact. However, both treaties were directed against external aggression by other states and neither mentions domestic conflicts as being a *casus foederis*.[25] The Soviet argument that the Hungarian uprising constituted 'external aggression' because it had been fomented by American imperialists and Horthyite fascists was hardly convincing. Moreover, both treaties specifically stated that the contracting parties would adhere to the principle of non-interference in their mutual relations. Nagy's speech to a mass rally in Budapest on 31 October, in which he stated that 'we stand on the principle of equality, national sovereignty and national equality'[26] was hardly a deviation from the formal basis of Soviet-Hungarian relations as outlined in the treaties. The October Declaration also affirmed these principles. Nagy's miscalculation was to interpret Soviet diplomatic vocabulary too literally, since the Soviet definition of 'aggression' could be stretched to cover any perceived threat to Soviet hegemony in Eastern Europe.

Ideological justifications

In addition to the 'invitation' and 'treaty' arguments, the Soviets also sought to provide an ideological rationale for their actions in Hungary. Doctrinal explanations complemented the reasoning that Soviet actions in Hungary conformed to the accepted conventions of interstate behaviour. Although the Soviets were to utilise the same doctrinal justifications in relation to the intervention in Czechoslovakia twelve years later, 'ideological legitimation' played a less significant role in the Hungarian case for several reasons. Firstly, in Hungary there was an armed rebellion, which provided the Soviets with a rich smokescreen of atrocity propaganda; secondly, the Soviets were able to bestow a measure of plausibility upon the 'invitation' argument by quickly producing Hungarian leaders who acknowledged that they had requested Soviet aid; thirdly, in 1956, the Soviets still enjoyed the support of the international communist movement (the Chinese, and reluctantly, the Yugoslavs, endorsed the intervention); fourthly, in November 1956, the Suez crisis deflected international attention away from events in Eastern Europe; fifthly, the Hungarian crisis developed suddenly, without the prolonged build up which characterised the Czech and Polish crises in 1968 and 1980–1 (dubbed 'creeping counter-revolutions' by the Soviets): in these cases, 'proletarian internationalism' rhetoric was extensively used by the Soviets as a pressure language as well as an *ex-post facto* rationale; sixthly, until the Hungarian uprising, the Soviets had not needed a fully developed 'limited sovereignty' doctrine and therefore the ideological rationale which emerged after the rebellion underwent a 'gestation period': by contrast, the 'originators' of the 'Brezhnev Doctrine' in 1968 had a ready-made ideological justification stemming from the Hungarian episode.

The 'Pomelov Doctrine'

In their references to the Hungarian events in the aftermath of the crisis, Soviet theoreticians developed a doctrine of 'limited sovereignty' which predated the 'Brezhnev Doctrine' by over a decade. The 1956/7 version emphasised the following features: firstly, the qualitatively higher content of socialist sovereignty (so that the sovereignty of socialist states could not be judged by the standards of bourgeois law);[27] secondly, the organic unity of the socialist camp, so that 'under socialism there are not and cannot be contradictions between the national interests of a socialist nation and the interests of international cooperation', or 'radical contradictions between individual and collective builders of socialism';[28] thirdly, the paramount importance of the guiding principle of 'proletarian internationalism', to which all other principles were subordinate.[29] It was proletarian internationalism which impelled socialist countries to 'firmly reject the nationalist interpretation of the sovereignty slogan';[30] fourthly, the principle of 'mutual assistance', deriving from fidelity to proletarian internationalism;[31] fifthly, that the Soviet Union's actions in defending Hungary's sovereignty in 1956 were in harmony with the interests of all countries: therefore, the Soviets had been inspired by international duty, not by national self-interest.[32]

The Soviet Foreign Minister Shepilov attributed the 'attempted putsch' in Hungary to the forces of international reaction, which had made use of nationalist elements and the shortcomings of the Hungarian leadership in order to detach Hungary from the socialist camp: in Shepilov's 'domino theory', the other socialist countries would have suffered the same fate in turn. Their sovereignties, therefore, depended upon the cohesion of the camp as a whole, and upon the readiness of socialist countries to render aid. By aiding the Hungarian people, the Soviet Union had fulfilled its international duty, not only to Hungary but to all socialist countries.[33] Korovin, an erstwhile exponent of 'revolutionary intervention', scorned the notion of 'absolute sovereignty' and declared that the Soviet Union would not permit the possibility of one or several countries using their sovereignty to curtail the rights of other states.[34] He also distinguished between the 'bourgeois democratic conception of sovereignty' (merely the formal recognition of certain rights) and 'peoples sovereignty', which existed only within the camp of socialism: thus the USSR had extended and enhanced the traditional concept of sovereignty by injecting it with a qualitatively higher content.[35] Korovin dismissed the view that sovereignty was a manifestation of 'unbridled nationalism' as 'profoundly fallacious'.[36]

In a major article in *Kommunist* in January 1957,[37] senior party theoretician Pomelov developed a comprehensive 'ideological' justification for the intervention, by drawing upon all of the major subcategories of proletarian internationalism. He argued that the help rendered to Hungary by the Soviet Union revealed the highly developed political maturity of communists, since they were guided by Marxist-Leninist theory: the 'Soviet Union has always fulfilled and will always fulfil its international duty' in the interests of the unity of the socialist community, 'in complete fidelity to the practice of proletarian internationalism'.[38] Pomelov affirmed the principles of 'sovereignty, equality and respect for territorial integrity in relations between socialist states', but pointed out that socialist states do not merely 'coexist'; they maintained their relations on the basis of 'selfless help and cooperation'.[39] Pomelov also distinguished between 'socialist patriotism' and 'nationalism': socialist patriotism, unlike nationalism, harmonised with internationalism, so that genuine struggle for the interests of one's homeland was possible only by pursuing the socialist path, in cooperation with other socialist states. In a further article in July, Pomelov attributed the Hungarian rebellion to 'revisionist, national opportunist and bourgeois ideology'.[40] Like Kovalev years later, Pomelov juxtaposed the 'invitation' argument with the justification of 'fraternal aid' deriving from proletarian internationalism. Pomelov's article was an implicit refutation of the October Declaration.

Soviet commentaries in this period emphasised several themes: the need for revolutionary vigilance against the machinations of imperialism and 'bourgeois nationalism';[41] that the basic direction of socialist development is common to all socialist countries;[42] the need to take account of the international dimension: as Berkov reminded his readers, 'the ideology of the proletariat is an internationalist ideology . . . expressing the fundamental national interests of all peoples';[43] the 'readiness of socialist countries to help one another' in resisting 'counter-revolution' had been shown by the aid rendered by the Soviet Union. Timofeev's precondition for fidelity to proletarian internationalism – i.e. that 'the attitude towards the socialist camp headed by the Soviet Union is the touchstone of loyalty to proletarian internationalism'[44] – showed that Stalin's definition of 'internationalism' had not been abandoned.

The argument that Soviet military action in Hungary had been a defensive measure aimed at preserving Hungary's 'socialist gains' found general support among ruling and non-ruling parties in 1956. Only the Polish and Yugoslav parties among the ruling parties dissented from this view. Tito condemned the first intervention, but publicly supported the second and decisive Soviet action on the grounds that it had been necessary to save socialism. Tito's avowal of the belief that the defence of socialism is an imperative requirement which has priority over the principle of non-intervention was tantamount to an expression of support for the doctrine of limited sovereignty: it was not the doctrine itself, but the interpretation of the circumstances in which the doctrine became operative which lay behind Tito's objection to the first intervention. On 11 November, Tito declared that the principles enunciated in the Soviet-Yugoslav declaration in 1956 were valid for all socialist countries.[45] In reply to Tito's rebuke, a *Pravda* editorial declared that there could be no merits in going it alone, 'since it cannot aid the building of a socialist society'.[46] In other words, the aim of 'socialist construction' was viewed by the Soviets as the predominant principle, of greater practical significance than state independence. The Chinese also gave the Soviets their full endorsement: Chou En-lai paid visits to the Soviet Union, Poland and Hungary and affirmed the Soviet Union's leading role within the movement (the Chinese and East Germans had sought to reaffirm the Soviet Union's leading role immediately prior to the Polish and Hungarian crises).[47] At the first Communist World conference held in Moscow in November 1957, Mao also supported the doctrine of Soviet leadership. In the immediate aftermath of the Hungarian crisis, an orchestrated campaign began in the Peoples Democracies on the theme of the 'leading role' of the CPSU in the international communist movement.

The Soviets seem to have conceded that changes would have to be made to bloc relationships. One example of this belated realisation was the Soviet attempt to 'legalise' the presence of Soviet military forces in the Peoples Democracies by concluding a series of bilateral treaties with the 'host' countries. The communiqué issued after the Polish-Soviet talks in November 1956 stated that the sovereignty of Poland was not affected by the presence of Soviet troops in the country. The treaties signed between the Soviet Union and Romania and Hungary were similar to the Polish treaty, although, unlike the latter, both contained provisions which allowed the host country the final say in questions relating to the stationing of Soviet troops.[48] In May 1958, following a request from Bucharest, Soviet forces were withdrawn from Romania. No such option, however, was allowed the GDR. The difference in these treaties reflected the growing complexity of intra-bloc relations: however, there were still 'ground rules' which all bloc members were expected to observe.

It must have been obvious to the Kremlin that more fundamental changes in the nature of bloc relations were required if further crises were to be avoided. The dilemma facing the Soviets was how to steer a course between the scylla of 'national communism' and the charybdis of brutal Stalinist coercion: a policy of complete respect for the sovereignty principle would have meant the certain loss of Soviet control over Eastern Europe: Stalinist contempt for the sovereignty of the Peoples Democracies would, sooner or later, lead to further explosions. The new course adopted by the Soviets was essentially a compromise solution: it meant assuming a somewhat less overbearing posture, while at the same time retaining effective control. The bloc communist parties were to be allowed greater latitude in fulfilling their communist programmes, providing these did not contradict the line laid down by the Kremlin. Stalin's ball and chain was to be replaced by a kind of 'open prison' in which obedience to Moscow was to be assured by a network of ground rules, reinforced by incentives and sanctions. These more sophisticated attempts at control were to prove less than satisfactory: where, for example, did the boundary lie, between 'orthodox' economic policies adapted to meet specific local conditions and 'revisionism'?

THE ENUNCIATION OF 'SOLIDARIST' CONCEPTS

In the aftermath of the autumn crises, the Soviets pursued an ideological offensive, aimed at restoring unity to the socialist camp under Soviet leadership. As early as 6 November 1956, party ideologue Suslov had outlined the 'universal laws' of socialist construction (e.g. communist party rule, defence of socialist gains, the struggle with capitalism). The need to improve links between ruling parties was also recognised: until early 1957, the International Department of the Soviet Foreign Ministry had been responsible for relations with both ruling and non-ruling parties. The Department (headed by Boris Ponomarev since the early 50s) had been established after the dissolution of the Comintern in 1943. Ponomarev had headed the Cominform's Soviet Office. In 1957 a 'Department for Liaison with Communist and Workers Parties of the Socialist Countries' was established, under Andropov who had been Soviet Ambassador to Hungary since 1954. The obsession with ideological cohesion was manifested in Soviet 'conference mongering' activities, and in Soviet polemics against Yugoslavia. On 6 March 1957, *Pravda* published an editorial from the Romanian *Scînteia* which attacked Yugoslav foreign affairs minister Popović for suggesting that relations between socialist countries should be based on 'coexistence'. It reaffirmed the Soviet Union's leading role and of the validity of the 'general laws of socialist construction'.[49]

The Soviets soon acknowledged that the October Declaration had been an inadequate exposition of relations within the camp of socialism. At the 1957 conference of 64 parties in Moscow, they sought to redefine the character of relations within the world communist movement, by achieving three objectives: firstly, to obtain general agreement on the special role of the CPSU; secondly, to restore unity and to persuade the Conference to acknowledge the existence of a 'general line'; thirdly, to reconcile recent pronouncements on sovereignty with the concept of 'proletarian internationalism'. As a result, in large measure, of China's conciliatory mood, the Conference was a qualified success for the CPSU. Despite the fact that Tito refused to sign the Conference declaration, or acknowledge the division of the world into 'camps', the Soviets had reason to be pleased with the outcome. Mao supported the doctrine of Soviet leadership and the Moscow Declaration affirmed the CPSU's role as the vanguard of the world communist movement. Although the Declaration stated that all the Marxist-Leninist parties 'are independent and have equal rights', the significance of this aspect of the document was nullified by the rider that each party was responsible to the international communist movement.[50] This terminological balancing act continued with the Document's references to socialist interstate relations: the statement qualified its assertion that 'the socialist countries base their relations on the principle of sovereignty' by stating that this did not exhaustively define these relations.[51]

The onslaught on 'revisionism' and 'national communism'

Emphasis was also placed upon the 'revisionist' danger (not least in certain non-ruling parties) and upon the need for vigilance against imperialist subversions.[52] Despite some opposition at the 1957 Conference, it was finally agreed at a conference in Prague in 1958 that a new theoretical journal, *Problems of Peace and Socialism* (in English *The World Marxist Review*), would be established, as a theoretical forum and as a contribution to the restoration of ideological uniformity. It was edited by Rumiantsev, the former editor of *Kommunist*. In 1958, the Soviet Academy of Sciences and the new journal both held conferences on the theme of the struggle against revisionism. Another conference was held on this theme in Moscow in 1959.[53] 'Revisionism' was identified as the main danger confronting the communist movement, and was exemplified by 'statements against the historic necessity for the dictatorship of the proletariat . . . and of the principle of proletarian internationalism'.[54] Although 'national peculiarities' were recognised, the basic direction of socialist development' was viewed as common to all countries. Moreover, a 'correct understanding' of the Soviet Union's place in the movement was essential.[55] In Pomelov's words, the road to socialism was illuminated by the ideas of Marxism-Leninism, not by so-called 'national communism'.[56] 'National communism' was bluntly dismissed by Berkov as 'nonsense'.[57] Shevliagin accused 'national communists' in the Peoples Democracies and revisionists in the communist parties of capitalist states of seeking to break ties with the CPSU.[58]

In the aftermath of the Hungarian crisis, the Soviet theory of 'socialist international relations' was reformulated on the basis of the following assumptions: firstly, the qualitatively superior nature of socialist international relations; secondly, harmony, deriving from an absence of 'antagonistic contradictions' between and within socialist countries; thirdly, the 'drawing together' of socialist countries, resulting from objective processes of development: fourthly, mutual fraternal aid, given disinterestedly and not deriving from motives of self-interest; fifthly, the beneficent role of the Soviet Union within the camp. The enunciation of these concepts showed that, far from causing a 'retreat from ideology', bloc crises are more likely to precipitate a shift in Soviet theory towards concepts putatively derived from Marxist-Leninism. These doctrinal reformulations exposed the weakness of Soviet theorising in this period. As Zimmerman has argued, prior to 1956, Soviet scholars avoided the study of 'International Relations'.[59] Although the journal *International Affairs* had been established in 1955, it seemed mainly geared towards propaganda rather than serious analysis. Neither Stalin nor Khrushchev felt the need for specialist advice in this field.[60] After 1956, new foreign policy research institutions were formed. The Institute of the World Economy and International Relations (IMEMO) was re-established after the 20th party congress, reflecting Soviet acknowledgement of the need for more sophisticated responses to international problems: its journal resumed publication the following year. Nevertheless, Soviet scholarship in this field remained stultified by intellectual controls. The tendency to produce works by 'authors' collectives' (under nominated editors) ensured conformity with current official doctrine.

'Socialist Internationalism'

Central to this renewed attempt to define the character of socialist international relations was the concept of 'socialist internationalism'.[61] This notion, which rapidly gained currency in Soviet theory, was said to be the fundamental principle defining the character of relations between socialist states. 'Socialist internationalism' is viewed as the third and highest stage of proletarian internationalism, the others being the periods between the advent of Marxism and the Bolshevik revolution and between the Bolshevik revolution and emergence of the Peoples Democracies (in Soviet theory 'proletarian internationalism' is the basic principle governing relations between all elements of the international communist movement[62]). Proletarian internationalism was said to have arisen out of the realistion on the part of the working classes that there was a vital need for international solidarity in the struggle against world capitalism.[63] The term 'proletarian internationalism' was also broadened to encompass relations between communist and 'progressive' (non-socialist) forces in the Third World.[64]

The principle of 'socialist internationalism' has not been definitively enunciated, although the following elements are frequently cited: comradely mutual assistance; international solidarity and cohesion in accordance with Marxist-Leninist principles;[65] non-antagonistic fusion of internationalism and patriotism;[66] cooperation on the basis of mutual advantage; non-interference in the internal affairs of other states; voluntariness in international affairs; genuine (as distinct from merely formal) respect for sovereignty.[67] An imperative requirement of socialist internationalism was the need to strengthen and consolidate the socialist camp: fraternal mutual support was 'an objective law of the world socialist system'.[68] The principle of 'socialist internationalism' was to be affirmed in the statement of the meeting of the representatives of the communist and workers parties in 1960, where it was described as an 'inviolable law' of socialist international relations.[69] The principle has received affirmation in the CMEA charter (1962) and in the Soviet and the Bulgarian constitutions: it was given renewed emphasis in Soviet commentaries following the invasion of Czechoslovakia. For the Soviets it serves a hortatory function as a slogan of unity and a 'masking' or cosmetic function (to disguise the absence of such unity within the socialist camp).

The Soviet theory of socialist internationalism denies that there can be conflict between the national interests of socialist states and the interests of the socialist camp. The biological analogy favoured by Soviet theorists in their descriptions of the unity of national and international interests in this period was based on the assumption that socialist states were subsystems of a global socialist system, whose purpose they served: therefore, providing the state apparatus was in the hands of 'healthy forces', domestic and foreign policies would combine harmoniously with those of other socialist states and with the higher interests of the socialist community. The harmonic conception of socialist international relations derived from a mechanical application of the 'second image' perspective: the common class bases of socialist states ensured common aims and interests.[70]

Socialist international law

Socialist internationalism was soon to be elevated by the Soviets into a principle of international law (indeed, the 'guiding principle' of the 'new international law' developing between socialist countries[71]): it was not only a moral-political principle, but represented a new, higher stage in the development of international law.[72] Socialist internationalism was said by Shurshalov to be the basis of collaboration between socialist states.[73] Soviet writers insist that equality and non-interference, although component elements of socialist internationalism, are not the whole story. Rather, although socialist states observe generally recognised principles and rules, the legal principles which derived from proletarian internationalism are of a much higher type.[74]

Several Soviet legal specialists in the late 1940s and early 1950s, for example, Kozhevnikov, Korovin and Generalov,[75] had mooted the possibility of a nascent 'socialist international law' within the socialist camp. These suggestions were reinforced by a 1951 textbook edited by Korovin, which argued that the international legal norms and practices developing between anti-imperialist states formed the basis of an international law for the whole world.[76] However, the conception of an emerging socialist international law was attacked by other Soviet lawyers, who regarded it as a deviation from the official Soviet line that there was a common body of international law binding on all states: the dominant view in this period was that socialist states, unlike capitalist states, were genuinely committed to the observance of the general principles of international law. American legal doctrine on the other hand, served imperialist expansion.[77]

Prior to 1956, before the emergence of 'separate roads to communism' and before the USSR began to lose its grip both in Eastern Europe and in the wider international communist movement, the Soviets did not need to utilise the concept of socialist international law as a complementary means of maintaining bloc cohesion. Rather, in view of the widespread international criticism that the Peoples Democracies were little more than Soviet colonies, it served Soviet interests better to affirm that relations within the socialist camp were based on general international law. Before the Soviet Union began to experience serious crises of authority within the bloc, Soviet legal specialists jettisoned the notion of a distinctively socialist international law and moved to Tunkin's position (which he was later to abandon) that a common set of international legal principles applied to all states.[78] Although, a year after Stalin's death, Korovin reaffirmed his belief that the emergence of the Peoples Democracies had brought into being a new international law, coexisting alongside general international law, the dominant view in Soviet legal theory between 1948 and 1956 was that there was one international law for the whole world.[79]

The doctrine that international law within the socialist camp was of a qualitatively distinctive type came back in vogue, it seems plausible to argue, largely as a result of the traumatic developments of 1956. Following the 20th party congress and the Polish and Hungarian crises, the theory that a higher type of international law was in the making within the socialist camp emerged as the new orthodoxy in Soviet legal scholarship. A specific impetus to the re-emergence of the notion was Khrushchev's speech at the Polish Embassy in Moscow in 1957, which referred to the development of distinctively socialist forms of collaboration between the Soviet Union and the Peoples Democracies.[80] Tunkin, who had earlier dismissed the notion of a socialist international law, was, by 1958, affirming that 'we are witnessing the birth of a new international law . . . socialist international law'.[81] With the emergence of the new international relations, principles and rules had arisen which were of 'a much higher type compared with general international law', since they were socialist international principles and rules.[82]

Korovin identified three aspects of the new international relations as it applied to international law: firstly, in the application of generally accepted democratic principles (he gave the example of sovereignty, which in capitalist states, merely had a 'formal declarative character'[83]); secondly, it was demonstrated by scrupulous observance of international treaty obligations.[84] These legal relations were the 'birth of socialist international law, the international law of future humanity liberated from capitalist slavery';[85] thirdly, Korovin also argued that relations between socialist states and countries which had thrown off the colonial yoke were also influenced by these principles.[86] The functions of the new theory were exemplified in Usenko's definition of 'mutual assistance' as a socialist principle of international law, meaning 'the legal right to receive assistance from, and a corresponding legal duty to render assistance to, other socialist states' (as an example of 'mutual assistance', he cited the military aid rendered to Hungary by the USSR in 1956).[87]

Although, in these conceptualisations, socialist legal principles were regarded as already in existence, it was not argued that socialist international law had supplanted general international legal norms and principles: rather, the new law comprised an additional body of principles existing alongside general international law (binding on all states whatever their socioeconomic character): according to Usenko, the most important principles of contemporary international law 'apply equally to both socialist and capitalist states. But they only contain a *minimum* of requirements, the fulfilment of which must secure peaceful coexistence ... while the principles of socialist internationalism not only guarantee fulfilment of these requirements but go further ...'[88] The two were not viewed as antithetical, since in addition to applying socialist international legal principles in their mutual relations, socialist states also observed the general democratic principles of international law: furthermore, socialist international legal principles were said to have a salutory effect upon the character of general international law.[89] The new legal principles were regarded as harbingers of the general international law of the future. They were the fundamental principle of 'socialist internationalism' and the subordinate principles of sovereignty, equality and non-interference.[90] The transformation of international law was viewed as an aspect of the transformation of the international system itself, through the advance of socialism. The 'purist' doctrine of the future obsolescence of the state was therefore replaced by a form of conceptual hybridisation, in which the notion of world socialist victory was superimposed onto the existing framework of international relations. It was a further example of the Soviet abandonment of the 'millennarian' doctrine of a stateless world society in favour of the more realistic prognosis of a socialist international community organised into a 'horizontal' system of states.

The Soviet concept of the 'socialist commonwealth'

This concept was also rooted in the assumption that socialist states had joined together in a cooperative alliance in which the individual interests of each state and the interests of the commonwealth were harmoniously combined. Unlike the bogus and foredoomed commonwealths established by the decaying Imperial powers in this period, which were dismissed by Soviet theoreticians as cynical devices to maintain newly independent countries in the grip of Western economic exploitation, the 'socialist commonwealth' was said to be a genuine mutual benefit association, founded on the progressive socialist principles of mutual assistance and 'fraternal aid'. But did the members have the right to refuse proffered aid or to opt out of the association? Although these questions, in the form they are here presented, would have been dismissed by Soviet writers as absurd hypotheses, Soviet expositions of the nature of the 'socialist commonwealth' clearly indicated that it was viewed as a monolithic union and that each member state was duty bound to foster the cohesion of the socialist camp. Membership of the socialist commonwealth, therefore, was compulsory, despite explicit Soviet references to the 'voluntariness' of relationships between socialist states. As Sanakoyev put it in 1958: 'the world camp of socialism is a monolithic commonwealth of free and sovereign states with common interests and purposes, in which there is not and cannot be antagonism.'[91]

The 'catch 22' was that no socialist state, if truly socialist, would wish to withdraw from so palpably beneficial a union: therefore, withdrawal from the camp of socialism was unthinkable, since a policy of building socialism in isolation was judged to be not only harmful and theoretically untenable, but also dangerous to the socialist community, since imperialist states continually sought to exploit its weakest links. Hence any attempt to opt out of the community of socialist states could automatically be condemned as a perfidious sell-out to the forces of reaction. The actual composition of the 'socialist camp' in Soviet definitions has been subject to some variation, as a result of the Soviet Union's quarrels with other socialist states.

'Socialist patriotism'

In order to ensure that the constituent elements took adequate cognisance of the interests of the whole, the Soviets advanced the notion of 'socialist patriotism', the antithesis of reactionary bourgeois patriotism, in that it transcended the selfish interests of particular nation states.[92] The use made by Soviet theoreticians of the notion of 'socialist patriotism' is an example of the Soviet penchant for refurbishing 'reactionary' ideas and harnessing them to Soviet policy needs. The Soviet response to manifestations of national patriotism in Eastern Europe was not to denounce patriotism *per se*, but rather, to replace the reactionary 'national patriotism' with a distinctively socialist brand of national loyalty. Although the idea of socialist patriotism is attributed by Soviet writers to Marx and Lenin, the term 'social patriotism' seems first to have been used by Rosa Luxemburg, an implacable critic of the 'national patriotism' which divided workers into warring groups.[93] Marx and Engels had declared that the workers had no country. This declaration is interpreted by Soviet theoreticians as meaning that the working class owed no allegiance to a state dominated by the bourgeoisie, and not that workers could never have a country of their own.[94] The distinction between 'genuine' and 'false' (reactionary) patriotism in Soviet conceptualisations depends upon the location of internal sovereignty and is thus allied to the Soviet theory of 'popular sovereignty'. Moreover, the 'genuine' patriotism of the working class (best exemplified by Soviet patriotism) was in harmony with the interests of all working people throughout the world: genuine patriotism, therefore, involved the fusion of national and international loyalties. It was a patriotism devoid of the reactionary sting of nationalism and infused with a progressive socialist content.

After the Bolshevik Revolution, the notion of patriotic loyalty is said to have acquired a new strand of meaning, in that it became synonymous with the loyalty which the workers of all lands owed to the world's only socialist state. To betray one's country was not treason, if this action served revolutionary goals. With the emergence of other socialist states after the Second World War, Soviet theorists extended the idea of 'socialist patriotism' to encompass the notion of a polyvalent patriotism. Perhaps the most striking and, in the circumstances, enlightening, exposition of this polyvalent theory of patriotism was given by Khrushchev during his visit to Hungary in 1958, when he stated that, although the Soviet delegation came to Hungary as representatives of the Soviet Union, they would return to the Soviet Union as representatives of the Hungarian people. He denied that this statement was contradictory, since the Soviet and

Hungarian people had the same goals of building socialism and communism: 'while being a Hungarian patriot one can also be a Soviet patriot, a patriot of all socialist countries'.[95] According to this theory, it could no doubt be argued that the Soviet troops which put down the Hungarian uprising had assumed the role of 'Hungarian patriots' and their adversaries the role of Hungarian 'traitors'. The idea that it is the patriotic duty of all socialists to defend socialism in every socialist country has provided the Soviets with a doctrinal justification for overriding the principle of sovereignty within the bloc.

'Socialist patriotism' was said by Soviet commentators in this period to derive from the more general principle of proletarian internationalism and therefore no conflict was admitted between the national and international loyalties of socialists, since the two combined in an 'organic unity'. The internationalism of the working class meant that 'all workers belong to the same "nation" – the world army of working people oppressed and exploited in all bourgeois countries by the self-same force, capital. This does not in any way mean, however, that . . . the worker ceases to be a Frenchman, Englishman, Italian etc. Quite the contrary. True and not sham patriotism springs naturally from proletarian internationalism.'[96] Socialist patriotism was manifested in the fact that the people of the Soviet Union rejoiced in the 'labour accomplishments of . . . other socialist countries' and was the 'direct antithesis of nationalism and chauvinism'.[97] The doctrine of 'socialist patriotism', enunciated in the CPSU programme in 1962, served dual functions for Soviet policy in Eastern Europe. Firstly, it sharpened the distinction between 'genuine patriotism' within the bloc and reactionary 'national patriotism' (with the prerogative of distinguishing between the two left to the Soviets); secondly, it entailed the subordination of patriotism to the higher Marxist-Leninist category of proletarian internationalism. Another essential element in the post-1956 Soviet ideological offensive was emphasis upon the need for vigilance against Western subversion: Koretskiĭ identified two trends in relation to fundamental rights: 'a reactionary trend, characterised by intensified attacks upon the principle of sovereignty' and a 'democratic trend characterised by the struggle to affirm the principles of sovereignty . . . and to defend gains won in revolutions and in national liberation struggles'.[98]

'SOCIALIST INTEGRATION' AND SOVEREIGNTY

The Soviet 'normalisation' process following a challenge to Soviet hegemony within Eastern Europe is likely to include a drive for further 'socialist integration' (embracing both ideological and institutional dimensions): this strategy has been pursued after each major crisis within the bloc. It would, therefore, be misleading to dismiss the barrage of hortatory articles in Soviet journals after the traumatic events of 1956 as mere verbiage, since in several respects they did herald a significant shift in Soviet strategy (although not in objectives) toward Eastern Europe. A major by-product of the upheavals of 1956 was that Soviet policy-makers were forced to reassess the efficacy of existing control techniques within the bloc and, in particular, Stalin's essentially bilateral framework of relationships. The Kremlin's response to the emerging crisis of authority within the bloc was to supplement, and in some cases replace, the cruder Stalinist instruments of control with a more elaborate system of functionalist carrots. These new instruments would not only give East Europeans a genuine stake in the survival of the 'socialist commonwealth', but would also serve to distract their attention away from the 'lure of the West'.

The 'inverse image' comparison of socialist and capitalist international relations was applied fully in Soviet conceptualisations of integration processes within the two systems. The principal differences between the two types of integration were identified as:

1. in socialist integration, socialist states were drawn together by an 'objective process of development'. The 'organic analogy' was frequently employed in order to emphasise that such cooperation was not a temporary coincidence of self-interest;[99]
2. integration within the socialist camp constituted no threat to the sovereignty of the participating states and was based on 'full voluntariness' and full social, economic and political cooperation of free sovereign peoples;[100]
3. the CMEA, was not a 'supra-national' organisation: the Soviets had sought to add a supranational planning arm to Comecon in 1962, but this proposal was strongly opposed, in particular by the Romanians. Notwithstanding the formal constitutional position of the CMEA, however, the Soviets have been forced to reassure East Europeans that participation in Comecon poses no threat to the sovereignty of the member states. The failure of the Kremlin

to assuage doubts about the motives behind the Soviet enthusiasm for economic integration has been a major factor in the slow development of Comecon;

4. socialist economic relations had a positive character, based on fraternal collaboration and mutual aid: socialist states assisted each other disinterestedly;[101]

5. unlike capitalist relations, socialist economic cooperation was devoid of 'antagonistic contradictions'. In the West, smaller states were 'appendages of economically more developed states';[102]

6. in socialist international cooperation, national and international interests were harmoniously combined in an organic unity;

7. it was based on the principle of socialist internationalism and the subordinate principle of 'socialist division of labour', which could not be explained solely in terms of the cash nexus: stripped of the verbiage about fraternal mutual aid, this meant that policy-makers in socialist states were expected to take account of the general economic development of the socialist commonwealth, in addition to their own national interests;

8. the Soviet Union's aid played 'a tremendous role in the acceleration of objective processes of development of the world socialist system';[103]

9. integration in the socialist community was beneficial to world peace: integration in Western Europe was part of a new 'cold war strategy' of western imperialism with the objective of financing rearmament;[104]

10. the capitalist camp was declining, whereas the socialist camp was growing in strength (and according to Khrushchev was already outstripping the capitalist model);[105]

11. integration in the West had a 'profoundly anti-popular character', both domestically and internationally.[106]

Khrushchev's enthusiasm for these new departures might, at first sight, be viewed as a bold leap in the dark, attributable to his idiosyncratic temperament. However, the old control techniques had clearly failed and the Kremlin had little choice but to experiment with more sophisticated deviation controls in order to arrest the process of fission. A fundamental drawback of these instruments of 'fusion', however, has been that, although overtly less obtrusive than the old Stalinist methods, they give rise to dangerous ambiguities. Thus the voluntarist and participatory phraseology in which the 'conciliar' approach adopted by the Soviets was expressed was not to be taken at its full face value: the exuberantly fanciful analyses of socialist cooperation which appeared after 1956 were aimed at camouflaging the Soviet Union's underlying objectives in pursuing the new course. One effect of the new approach was that the 'limits of the tolerable' within the Soviet bloc (the extent to which the Peoples Democracies were free to pursue policies which deviated from the Soviet line) became blurred and open to conflicting interpretations. The Soviet mailed fist was not only hidden behind conciliatory slogans: the circumstances in which it would be wielded became less clear.

Soviet theoreticians have been forced to acknowledge that the harmonious pattern of development postulated in orthodox Soviet conceptualisations of socialist integration have not always been confirmed by events. A major source of difficulty, as with integration in Western Europe, has been that functionalism involves a trade-off between the welfare benefits to be derived from 'going it with others' and the limitations placed upon each country's independence by such participation. The political instrumentality of Comecon for the Soviets was evident from its inception, since although the CMEA was said to be an open organisation which could be joined by any state subscribing to its principles, Yugoslavia was neither informed of, nor invited to attend, its inaugural conference. Yugoslavia's expulsion from the Cominform had demonstrated the Soviet Union's willingness to use socialist multilateral organisations as auxiliary weapons in its disputes with other socialist states. The Soviet Union's continuing enthusiasm for socialist economic integration in Eastern Europe, even after Comecon had become an economic liability to the Soviets, is further evidence of the political advantages which the USSR seeks to gain from functional collaboration.

RELATIONS WITH THE WEST

In the early 1960s, the Zhdanovite doctrine of 'struggle between two systems' was replaced by a Soviet peace offensive and renewed emphasis upon the doctrine of peaceful coexistence (reflecting revised Soviet assessments of the balance of forces between socialism and capitalism). Shortly after Stalin's death, the Soviets also reconsidered their view concerning the inevitability of war. This first period of postwar detente led to the Geneva arms talks in 1955. From the late 1950s, Soviet assessments of the balance of forces between the capitalist and socialist systems were infused with optimism. The 'coexistence' doctrine did not literally mean that the two systems merely coexisted as closed systems: indeed, the notion of competition between the capitalist and socialist systems in the fields of economic and social development and struggle in the ideological sphere pervaded Soviet commentaries. The Soviets insisted that peaceful coexistence was a specific form of class struggle between the two systems and excluded only one type of struggle – war as a means of resolving international problems. From around 1958, Soviet commentaries stressed that the socialist system was forging ahead of the West in economic and social development: in the economic sphere, the superiority of socialist development was said to derive from two factors: firstly, the rapid advance of the world socialist community. Kuzminov predicted that the socialist countries would soon outstrip the capitalist states in gross industrial output; secondly, the postwar capitalist cycle, which had led to new economic crises (even though Kuzminov in 1960 could describe it as a local – USA – crisis and not a world crisis)[107] and sharpening of economic contradictions in Western Europe. Korovin in the same year wrote of 'the general crisis of capitalism', leading to a 'stubborn offensive against the principle of sovereignty' by the United States;[108] the capitalist system was riven by contradictions and would collapse of itself. Varga attributed it to a new overproduction crisis;[109] technologically, Soviet superiority was being demonstrated in the space race. The 'overtake' theory served three principal purposes in relation to the Soviet Union's external relations: firstly, it reinforced confidence in Soviet leadership within the movement; secondly, to draw 'dissident' ruling and non-ruling parties back into the fold; thirdly, to increase the appeal of communism in Africa and Asia. The Soviets also expanded their connections with revolutionary movements, through the 'disinterested' provision of economic and technical help.

According to Starushenko, relations between the two systems should be based on the formula of 'no export of revolution, no export of counterrevolution'.[110] These developments constituted a new stage in the competition between the two systems, in which communism was advancing and capitalism retreating all over the world.[111]. In 1958 the distribution of power was said to be increasingly favourable to the socialist camp. From 1959, following Soviet successes, in military technology and in improving relations within the camp, the Soviets began to speak of Soviet preponderance of power over the West.[112] The images developed in Soviet writings in this 'epoch of the rise and consolidation of socialism' were of the 'senile decay of bourgeois ideology', and of a 'Soviet world outlook in its prime'.[113] In relation to the development of the world socialist system, the CPSU continued to be the 'vanguard force for socialism and communism'.[114] It is possible that these ideas principally served 'masking' functions (to disguise a Soviet position of weakness): but it seems more likely that this 'upswing' mood derived from genuine belief that the West could be overtaken in socioeconomic development. Therefore, they may have constituted a serious underestimation of the difficulties of resolving problems within the international communist movement and overestimation of the Soviet Union's short-term potential relative to the West. This mood lasted until 1962–3, when, following various Soviet setbacks, Soviet commentators qualified their earlier optimistic assessments.

The shocks of 1956 precipitated revisions of Soviet doctrines of 'socialist international relations': these reformulations were part of a concerted drive by the Kremlin to reunite the socialist camp under Soviet leadership (although the fact that, by 1961, Khrushchev openly acknowledged that the communist movement no longer had a 'leading centre'[115] was an implicit admission of the increasingly pluralist nature of the communist movement). The doctrinal formulae which were an integral part of this new strategy derived from the 'verticalist' postulates of socialist internationalism: although the Soviets continued to stress the importance of the sovereignty principle in socialist international relations, the higher principle of socialist internationalism nullified its value. Socialist internationalism not only provided an ideological rationale for the strategies of 'duplication' and 'tight coupling', but also for future Soviet interventions within Eastern Europe.

8 'Socialist Internationalism' and the Warsaw Pact Intervention in Czechoslovakia

The 1960s were to provide many examples of the 'masking' function of Soviet ideology: in this decade, the rift between Soviet doctrinal pronouncements and political realities widened considerably, making nonsense of the optimistic forecasts concerning the inexorable advance of the socialist camp trumpeted by Khrushchev at the close of the 1950s. Khrushchev's revision of the doctrine of 'peaceful coexistence' hinged on the notion of 'peaceful competition' between socialism and capitalism and was predicated upon the assumption of the rapid development of a united and expanding socialist camp under Soviet leadership. The Cuban missile crisis led to a serious loss of face for the Kremlin: but Soviet problems in the 1960s were more comprehensive than a single policy failure. By the mid-1960s, it was evident that the Soviet Union's aspiration to overtake the United States in economic development had failed miserably; in space technology the sputnik era had been superseded by the age of Apollo; the Soviet Union's loss of control within the international communist movement continued apace:[1] the CPSU had been forced to deny that it claimed a 'leading role' within the movement; Romania had asserted its rejection of 'unequal' relationships within the socialist camp. By the 1960s, it was also becoming clear that the demise of formal European Imperialism would not decisively tip the balance of world power in favour of the Soviet Union, since the vast majority of newly emancipated countries (included within the 'zone of peace' in Soviet conceptualisations of the international structure) found nonalignment more attractive than entry into the socialist camp. Moreover, in its drive to win the allegiance of newly independent states, the Soviet Union was now forced to engage in ideological competition with China. The worsening Sino-Soviet schism not only constituted a formidable obstacle to the Soviet Union's desire to reassert its ideological hegemony within the movement, but also compounded Soviet security problems and therefore adversely affected the Soviet power balance with the West.

From around 1963–4, Soviet theoreticians enunciated less optimistic assessments of the balance of forces between capitalism and socialism.[2] Although the Soviets made great strides from the mid-1960s in achieving rough strategic parity with the United States in missile development, this meant diverting scarce resources from other fields. Kosygin's economic reforms introduced in 1965 showed no signs of working. In Eastern Europe, the Soviet integration drive had faltered, due to East European suspicions concerning its motives, regional economic slowdown and the 'domesticist' concerns of the local parties. In the 1960s the bloc became increasingly diversified, as the bloc states responded in various ways to the necessity of reform. Nevertheless, Soviet doctrinal pronouncements in this period continued to assiduously foster the 'harmonic' conception of socialist international relations, stressing the growing unity and strength of the socialist camp under Soviet leadership.[3]

The intervention in Czechoslovakia in 1968 settled uncertainties in Eastern Europe about the practical implications of the Soviet definition of 'socialist internationalism'. It constituted a jolting reminder of how the Kremlin proposed to order its priorities in the event of a clash between respect for sovereignty and its policy of maintaining its hegemony in Eastern Europe. Many of the adverse environmental circumstances besetting the Soviet Union in this period were outside the Kremlin's control: however, it still possessed the ability to enforce its conception of 'socialist international relations' within the bloc. According to Soviet commentaries, the entry of Warsaw Pact forces into Czechoslovakia demonstrated the Soviet Union's fealty to the principle of socialist internationalism, and therefore the invasion served to inject empirical substance into the previously somewhat nebulous concepts of 'comradely mutual assistance' and 'international duty'. The invasion threw the Soviet Union's acutely ambivalent attitude towards the sovereignty principle into sharp relief, since Soviet apologists for the intervention placed greater reliance upon the 'verticalist' arguments deriving from 'proletarian internationalism' than had been the case in 1956. In 1968 the Soviets utilised these doctrinal arguments not merely as an *ex post facto* rationalisation, but also as a pressure language, serving to remind the Czechs of the limits of Soviet tolerance. In order to comprehend why the Soviets assigned a central role to the doctrine of 'limited sovereignty' in 1968 – so that outside the bloc it was widely regarded as a bespoke rationale for the

Warsaw Pact invasion – it is first necessary to examine the nature of the Czechoslovakian heresy.

Background. It is not the purpose of this chapter to trace the events which culminated in the invasion, since these have been thoroughly examined elsewhere.[4] Rather, it seeks to examine the significance of doctrine for Soviet control strategies within the bloc. Nevertheless, some contextual analysis is essential in order to comprehend the interrelationships between doctrine and policy in Soviet crisis management. The emerging crisis has to be viewed in the context of the climate of tension within the international communist movement: no less than four ruling parties (Yugoslavia, China, Albania and Romania) were openly challenging the Soviet model of socialist international relations. In February 1968, Romania walked out of the Budapest consultative meeting (called to set the agenda for an international communist conference) following the meeting's decisions on China and the Middle East.

In relation to the crisis in Czechoslovakia, the following causal factors were of special significance: firstly, the comprehensive policy failures of the Novotný regime – the failure of the 1965 economic reform programme to alleviate economic stagnation helped to create a 'last straw' mood in the country; secondly, the 'coiled spring' effect – the delay in 'destalinisation' in Czechoslovakia, followed by the sudden relaxation of Stalinist repression led to the release of powerful pressures from below which the party could not control; thirdly, divisions within the Czech leadership: as elsewhere in the bloc, the communist party leadership was divided, into 'reformers' and 'conservatives' (Dubček, a 'reform communist', had replaced Novotný in January 1968); fourthly, an increasingly restive intelligentsia: as Golan has shown, in the 1960s leading Czechoslovak intellectuals were developing a 'humanistic' interpretation of Marxism at variance with Soviet Marxism-Leninism;[5] fifthly, 'spillover' effects, which were of two types – spillover from intra-party factional struggles to the intelligentsia (and vice-versa) and political spillover from economic reform: it was virtually inevitable that the decentralisation necessary for successful economic reform would spill into the political sphere. It seems likely that Dubček was buoyed by the tide of events (although, Canute-like, he thought that he could control them). Kusin argues that the 1968 changes sought to reform socialism rather than replace it, although the reform movement developed its own momentum, undermining the regime's basic values.[6] Skilling sees the developments as 'revolutionary', involving a gradual, but accelerating, loss of power by the rulers.[7]

UNCERTAINTY CONCERNING SOVIET TOLERANCE THRESHOLDS

The intervention resulted ultimately from misinterpretation of the 'ground rules' for the maintenance of bloc hegemony, i.e. from a failure of the 'signpost' function of rules. Partly this resulted from an inherent defect in the conciliar strategy pursued after the shocks of 1956 – this strategy widened, but also blurred, the margins of Soviet tolerance; secondly, the 'distraction effect' – the Kremlin's preoccupation with domestic problems took its eye off the East European 'ball';[8] thirdly, twists and turns in Soviet policy in the months leading up to the intervention may have been due more to vacillation stemming from disagreements within the Soviet elite rather than from a sure-footed crisis management strategy; fourthly, the incremental, non-violent, nature of the challenge – unlike the Hungarian revolution, it was not a sudden, frontal assault upon Soviet hegemony; fifthly, the leadership sought to avoid the mistakes of the Hungarian government in the crisis (for example by reaffirming Czechoslovakia's alliance commitments – this was a necessary, but insufficient, condition for compliance with the Kremlin's 'ground rules').

Soviet attacks upon the reform movement were buttressed by reminders of Czechoslovakia's sensitive strategic location and of the danger of a West German *drang nach osten*.[9] However, after the invasion, the Soviets did not station a defensive force on Czechoslovakia's Western borders, which suggests that 'Western aggression' anxiety served mainly propagandistic functions: emphasis upon the West German threat may have been aimed at fomenting latent anti-German feeling within the country and at establishing 'guilt by association', by linking the reformers with the West German *bête noire*. Nevertheless, the shrill polemics on this theme reflected a genuine Soviet anxiety that developments in Czechoslovakia, if left unchecked, would imperil Soviet security. Fears that Prague would seek closer relations with the West and that the 'creeping counterrevolution' would lead to a renewal of bourgeois democracy figured prominently in Soviet demonologies of the 'Prague Spring'.

Communist leaders in Eastern Europe are acutely aware of the 'porosity' of intra-bloc state frontiers: the 'spillover' or 'contagion' effect had been a significant factor in the explosions of 1956. The jittery and aggressive response of Gomulka and Ulbricht to events in Prague showed the low resistance of East Europeans to political infection from their socialist neighbours. In analysing Soviet motives, it is Soviet perceptions of events which are significant. In particular, the Soviets came to the view that the Czechoslovak party had lost its grip on the situation and that the reform movement constituted a grave challenge to communist rule in Czechoslovakia – although Dubček had no intention of allowing other parties to reappear. An inflexible ground rule of Soviet control was that democratic centralist principles must be maintained, to avoid a reversion to bourgeois liberalism.[10]

THE SOVEREIGNTY ISSUE IN THE 1968 CRISIS

Whatever the reason for the growing mood of alarm within the bloc, the crisis immediately brought the issue of sovereignty out into the open. Both implicitly and explicitly, sovereignty was at the core of the crisis: with regard to the 'internal' aspect of sovereignty, the fact that there were several formal, and many informal, discussions between the Czech leaders and the heads of other communist parties concerning internal developments within Czechoslovakia was proof that 'socialist sovereignty' was of a special kind. With regard to the 'external' aspect (independence in the international arena), the ultimate purpose of Soviet expositions of the 'solidarist' conception of socialist international relations was to remind the Czechs that deviation from the Moscow line on foreign policy would not be tolerated. The Czechoslovaks also sought to utilise the sovereignty principle as a defensive shield against interference by its allies. Explicit attempts by some Czechoslovak radicals to re-define the sovereignty of Czechoslovakia fuelled the Kremlin's anxiety. Clear breaches of Czechoslovak sovereignty took place throughout the crisis, in both the form and content of Soviet messages to Prague.

a. The forms of message transmission

The Soviets were to employ a full battery of interventionary techniques in order to arrest this 'creeping counterrevolution'. Little[11] has constructed an 'intervention ladder', ranging from verbal to military responses: in this model, the intervening state seeks to influence developments in the target state by means of calibrated increases in pressure. However, the 'ladder' metaphor implies a neat set of sequential rungs: in the case of Czechoslovakia in 1968, many of these techniques were applied simultaneously and the pattern of events was far more complex and fluid than is suggested by the 'ladder' metaphor. The Soviet instruments of deviation control included: statements by high-ranking officials; press comments carrying authoritative messages; commentaries by lower-ranking officials; the 'citing ploy'; fact-finding visits; face-to-face bilateral meetings; multilateral meetings; and military exercise pressure. In the early period, Soviet 'pressure language' tended to be oblique: later, it became much more explicit, as Moscow's patience ran out.

b. The content of the message

The manner in which the Soviets sought to reconcile 'respect for sovereignty' with 'socialist internationalism' exemplified the use of coded messages and signals: statements applauding the sovereignty principle and references to socialist internationalist imperatives were frequently juxtaposed, although a key role was also played by the use of loaded phrases and the omission of significant words: it was the failure of the Czechs to interpret these signals correctly which eventually led to the invasion.[12] The following themes recurred in Soviet commentaries, in both the pre- and post-invasion phases:

1. developments in Czechoslovakia were the concern of the entire socialist community – an argument clearly at odds with the principle of non-interference, since it blurred the distinction between individual and collective interests and legitimised interference by foreign powers in Czechoslovakia's internal affairs;
2. each socialist country had obligations to the socialist community – meaning that there were limits to Czechoslovakia's capacity to act independently of other socialist states and that Czechoslovakia's independence was subordinate to internationalist values: therefore, the 'supremacy' aspect of Czechoslovak sovereignty was less than absolute;
3. 'peculiarities' in each socialist country did not invalidate the general laws of socialist construction: meaning that the range of policy options available to socialist states was limited. Within the

bloc, the exemplar of these laws was the Soviet Union (which also had special responsibilities for their definition and enforcement);

4. the leading role of the communist party in Czechoslovakia was under threat (in Soviet Marxist doctrine, the 'supremacy' aspect of sovereignty is manifested in the supremacy of the party);
5. the danger of capitalist restoration: counter-revolutionary forces were at work within and without Czechoslovakia: the assumption that capitalist restoration was inadmissible again constituted a limitation on Czechoslovakia's sovereignty, since it denied the country the right to change its form of government;
6. the need for revolutionary vigilance against imperialist attempts to exploit 'weak links' in the socialist community;
7. the Soviet Union's readiness to fulfil its international duty to defend the socialist gains of Czechoslovakia;
8. the Soviet Union's scrupulous respect for Czechoslovakia's sovereignty. At no point did the Soviets unequivocally repudiate the principle: the 'logic of images' dictated that they would maintain their formal stance of scrupulous respect for sovereignty.

Relaxation of censorship opened up a Pandora's box of discontent on the subject of Czechoslovakia's sovereignty (perhaps most comprehensively expressed in an article in *Práce* in June by Václav Kotyk entitled 'Sovereignty from Theory into Practice').[13] Explicit challenges to Soviet ideological orthodoxies also appeared in *Literární listy*, *Rudé právo*, *Predvoj*, *Mladá fronta*, *Reporter*, *Smena*, *Student* and other papers. Taken together, these writings challenged Soviet conceptions of the universal validity of the Soviet model; of the harmony of national and international interests; of the direction of Czechoslovak foreign policy and of the Soviet Union's 'leading role'. The Czech leadership explicitly dissociated itself from some of the more radical articles:[14] nevertheless, the fact they had appeared at all was bound to alarm the Kremlin. In relation to Czechoslovakia's foreign policy, an article by Synek in *Rudé právo* in April argued that the political position of a communist state should not be a 'colourless imitation' of Soviet foreign policy.[15] Synek argued that it was the inalienable right of each socialist country to determine its own road, since 'no one has the right to tell any party or country where their international duty lies'.[16] Kotyk complained that socialist parties could pursue their own domestic and foreign policies only in theory.[17]

A second challenge concerned the Soviet concept of monolithic unity. Pavlov cited Polakovíc's article in *Smena* on 14 May which rejected monolithic unity of the socialist camp.[18] In July Kotyk argued that 'the concept of monolithic unity and of a uniform model of socialism' had not been overcome regardless of frequent criticism and new historical circumstances;[19] the third challenge was to the Soviet model of socialism. In June, in *Izvestiia*, Platkovskiĭ attacked Jan Svoboda for advocating the creation of opposition parties.[20] The publication of Vaculík's *Two Thousand Words*, which questioned the automatic right of the communist party to rule the country, inflamed Soviet fears.[21] In *Mladá fronta*, Horéč called for a 'dialogue of reason', urged the CPSU to remember the 'October Declaration' and rejected the idea that there was a 'single type of socialism'.[22] The fourth challenge was to the Soviet Union's 'leading role': Kotyk questioned the Soviet Union's exclusive right to define socialism,[23] criticised the notion of leading parties with special experience and called for open discussion on international and national affairs.[24] An article by Pavlov typified the Soviet response to these heresies; it asked: 'in what context and within what limits can a socialist country have a foreign policy of its own?' In attacking attempts to 'separate foreign policy from the social system', Pavlov castigated an article by Šedivý which had suggested that peaceful coexistence should extend to relations between all states.[25]

The pre-invasion period
At a meeting of Warsaw Pact leaders in Dresden on 23 March (probably called at the instigation of the worried East Germans and Poles), Dubček sought to reassure his allies that socialism was safe in his hands. The Dresden communiqué did not indicate disagreement. The Soviets must have hoped that the Dresden meeting would force Dubček to check the reform process, but the adoption of an 'Action Programme' of reform by the Czechoslovak communist party at its April plenum reawakened their fears. Although the programme affirmed the country's existing alliance relationships, it also recommended electoral and constitutional changes (including relaxation of censorship). In April, the Moscow party boss, V. V. Grishin, affirmed that socialist construction was a collective endeavour and that socialist states were free to pursue independent domestic and foreign policies, providing these were compatible with their wider obligations.[26] He also warned that imperialism's attempts to exploit 'weak links' necessitated constant revolutionary vigilance.[27]

Other developments in Czechoslovakia in April, such as the inclusion of reformers in a new government and the appearance of press articles agitating for radical change, also alarmed Moscow. Dawisha argues that it was in late April that the Soviets first indicated that they were considering the use of force.[28] A new plenum of the Czechoslovak communist central committee affirmed the party's commitment to the Action Programme. Although the plenum went some way to reassure the programme's East European critics (e.g. by rejecting toleration of opposition parties), other developments fuelled Soviet alarm: Novotný and some other hardliners were replaced and there was a purge of 'Muscovites' within the Czechoslovak Ministry of Defence. Dubček's visit to Moscow on 4–5 May failed to reassure Soviet leaders. At a Warsaw Pact meeting on 8 May (to which the Czechs were not invited), the East Germans and Poles pressed for stern measures against Czechoslovakia.[29] The campaign in the Soviet media continued unabated. Nevertheless, at the end of May, a CPCS plenum endorsed the Action Programme and announced that a special party congress would be held in September. In *Pravda* on 14 June, Konstantinov attacked Císař, the Secretary of the Czech party central committee, for suggesting that Marxism-Leninism was not the only possible form of Marxism.[30] On 4–5 July, the Czechs were invited by the Warsaw Pact members (excluding Romania) to discuss developments in Czechoslovakia: the Czechs refused. On 11 July, Aleksandrov in *Pravda* likened Vaculík's *Two Thousand Words* to counterrevolutionary statements which had appeared in Hungary in 1956 and asserted that threats to the socialist foundations of another socialist country could not be ignored.[31] On 22 July, *Pravda* asked whether it was necessary to wait until the counterrevolutionary forces in Czechoslovakia started winning before responding.[32] *Pravda* also published hostile reports from the Bulgarian and Polish press on developments in Czechoslovakia.

Reactions within the bloc

Alone amongst Czechoslovakia's Warsaw Pact allies, the Romanians attacked interference in Czechoslovakia's internal affairs. However, Romania's insistence that 'that each party had the right to determine its policy'[33] did not halt the ominous tone of comments by other bloc states. These comments reiterated Soviet assertions that 'the defence of socialism in Czechoslovakia is a common, sacred and internationalist task'[34] and that anti-socialist forces were engaged in counter-revolutionary activities.[35] On 25 July, the Hungarian 'Homeland radio' compared events in Czechoslovakia to the Hungarian events of 1956 and warned of the danger of 'counterrevolutionary restoration'.[36] The Bulgarian army paper *Narodna armiia* also reaffirmed the 'touchstone doctrine '.[37] At the outset of the crisis, East German and Polish commentaries were more virulent than those emanating from Moscow. The Hungarians and Bulgarians were initially restrained, but then joined the chorus of execration with gusto.

In early July the Soviet, Polish, East German, Hungarian and Bulgarian party leaders met in Warsaw and issued an open letter to their Czech counterparts.[38] The text of the letter asserted that anti-socialist forces had gained control of the media; that, in league with imperialism, these forces were attempting to undermine Czechoslovakia's socialist foundations; and that the Czech leadership appeared to have lost control. The nub of the letter was the ominous distinction between domestic matters and matters concerning the whole socialist movement. One issue falling within the former category would be a rectification of violations of socialist legality (a euphemism for the activities of 'little Stalins'): perhaps another would be a controlled and moderate liberalisation of Czechoslovakia's economic structure. On the basis of this narrow definition of 'domestic' matters, the letter added that Czechoslovakia's allies had no intention of violating the principles of independence in socialist international relations. But the limits of such independence were reached when socialism was in jeopardy. The letter was a forceful restatement that members must pursue the basic aim of socialist construction in accordance with prevailing Soviet orthodoxies. The Czech leadership refused, however, to accept this self-serving distinction between domestic and commonwealth matters. The Czech reply to the Warsaw letter reminded the five allies of statements contained in the October Declaration, which vaunted the principles of equality, independence, territorial integrity and non-interference.[39]

Polemics in the Soviet and East European press reached new heights in late July, orchestrated by Warsaw Pact manoeuvres. The Czech leadership refused to accept an invitation from the Soviet Politbureau to attend a meeting in Moscow, but agreed to talks at Čierná on the Czech-Soviet border. At Čierná, Brezhnev demanded changes, as outlined in the Warsaw letter. The meeting was abrasive and no written agreement was made, although the Czechs agreed to heed Soviet concerns about the reform process. A further meeting at Bratislava on 3 August resulted in a statement which vaunted both proletarian internationalism and sovereignty without attempting to reconcile these principles. At the meeting, Mlynář (a member of the

Czech delegation) requested that the phrase 'it is the common international duty of all socialist countries to support, defend and consolidate these (socialist) achievements' be conjoined to a clause 'while respecting the sovereignty and national independence of each country'.[40] Brezhnev refused, on the grounds that sovereignty was mentioned elsewhere in the draft. Mlynář disclosed that the Soviet leaders talked in the language of power and *realpolitik* and not the language of proletarian internationalism.[41] As the Czechs were soon to discover, references to sovereignty served a cosmetic function: of far greater significance was the declaration that the parties would never permit the socialist states to be divided.[42] But again, the Czechs and the Soviets were talking about different things: the Czech interpretation was that the Czech party had a duty to defend socialism in Czechoslovakia, and maintain close links with other socialist parties, which they would willingly do. For the latter, it was an expression of a determination to halt the liberalisation programme.

Following the Bratislava meeting, the Soviet press echoed the Declaration's reminders of the need for solidarity. On 6 August, *Krasnaia zvezda* noted that the unity of the socialist countries harmonised with the vital interests of each member and that the Warsaw Pact resolutely defended the gains of socialism and the sovereignty of the member states.[43] On the 14th, Pomelov, a chief architect of the doctrinal justification of the Hungarian intervention, wrote in *Pravda* that socialist countries were 'organically connected' by their common aims and economic and class bases.[44] The ulterior purpose of Soviet expositions of the solidarist conception of socialist international relations was to remind the Czechs that deviation from the official line would not be tolerated: *Kommunist* in August affirmed the Soviet people's determination to perform their 'international duty'.[45]

The military intervention

The invasion of Czechoslovakia ended speculation about the Soviet interpretation of the Bratislava concord. Henceforth there could be no doubt about the practical implications of the 'solidarist' conception of socialist international relations espoused in Soviet commentaries. Nevertheless, the invasion prompted Soviet commentators to explain how the protection of Czechoslovakia's socialist gains by military force could be squared with Soviet statements on sovereignty: none of the arguments advanced in answer to this question were new, since they were culled from orthodox Soviet terminology and had been reiterated in the months preceding the invasion.

The 'invitation' argument

Firstly, Soviet commentators sought to side-step the problem altogether, by stating implausibly that the allies had been invited into Czechoslovakia by beleaguered Czech socialists. Tass announced that the people and government leaders of the CSR had asked the Soviet Union and other allied states to render 'urgent assistance, including assistance with armed forces' and declared that 'nobody will ever be allowed to wrest a single link from the community of socialist states'.[46] Iuri Zhukov in *Pravda* on 21 August said that they had responded to a request from party and state leaders of Czechoslovakia and referred to the sacred international duty to assist other socialist countries.[47] An appeal by unnamed members of the Czech central committee, government and national assembly was read by Soviet permanent representative Malik in the Security Council and published in *Pravda* on the 22nd,[48] although a number of conservatives denied that they had issued the invitation. The membership of the National Assembly also denied knowledge of it.[49] However, even if the 'invitation' had been genuine, it did not reflect the views of the Central Committee. Czechoslovakia's acting permanent representative to the UN read out condemnations from the government of the invasion. To further weaken the 'invitation' argument, the Soviets were not immediately able to instal a Czechoslovak 'Kádár': out of prudence, those willing to assume this role were lying low; thirdly, the nature of resistance also gave the lie: massive demonstrations made nonsense of the assertion that the invaders had been invited into Czechoslovakia in accordance with the people's wishes.

'Collective self-defence against aggression'

The action was said to be in accordance with the Warsaw Treaty and with article 51 of the UN Charter. The Soviet self-defence argument had two strands, both hinging on the notion of a legitimate pre-emptive strike against indirect aggression (the Soviets did not allege armed aggression against Czechoslovakia had taken place): firstly, that revanchists in West Germany – a 'hotbed of revanchism and neo-nazism'[50] – constituted a grave danger to Czechoslovakia: secondly, that imperialists were inciting counterrevolution – Gromyko at the UN spoke of self-defence against imperialist intrigues.[51] Both article 51 of the Charter and article 4 of the Warsaw Treaty refer to an armed attack: neither makes reference to threats or incitement as constituting legitimate grounds for military action (article 51 would have entitled the Czechs to resist the invasion on grounds of self defence). Articles 1 and 4 of the Warsaw Treaty state that the parties will act in accordance with the UN Charter. Article 1 of the Treaty states that the parties agree to refrain from the threat or use of force in their mutual relations. Nor could it be justified by reference to the provisions of Czechoslovakia's mutual assistance treaties. The 'foreign aggression' argument was repudiated by the Czech foreign minister at the UN.[52]

Foreign reactions
In August 1968, there was no Suez affair or other major international crisis to divert world attention from the intervention. Foreign reaction to the invasion was generally hostile.

Reactions of ruling and non-ruling parties

At a mass rally in Bucharest on 21 August, Ceauşescu attacked the 'flagrant transgression' of Czechoslovakia's sovereignty[53] and announced the immediate formation of worker and peasant guards as a precautionary measure. Romania was then attacked in the Soviet Press.[54] The Chinese News Agency denounced the invasion as a 'monstrous crime' and claimed that it had 'torn the veil of Brezhnev, Kosygin and their ilk about internationalism, friendship and cooperation and exposed the hideous features of the Soviet revisionists'.[55] On 23 August, Tito commented that the official Soviet explanation was 'absurd'.[56] A resolution adopted at the 10th plenum of the Central Committee of the LCY on the same date declared that the 'intervention against the CSR can in no way be described as protection of socialism . . . (or) justified by ideological reasons drawn from Marxism-Leninism, because it is flagrantly at odds with the ideas of Marx, Engels and Lenin'.[57] Albania demonstrated its opposition by formally withdrawing from the Warsaw Pact. Even Castro, who supported the invasion, admitted that Czechoslovakia's sovereignty had been flagrantly violated.[58] Although the invasion was also supported by North Vietnam, North Korea and Mongolia, this could not disguise the fact that it had divided the socialist camp. A majority of non-ruling communist parties supported the invasion, but a significant number, including most Western parties, opposed it: in Western Europe only four parties, the West German KPD, the SED in West Berlin and the Luxembourg and Cypriot parties, supported it.[59]

Western reactions

The reaction of the West followed the pattern of Western responses to the Hungarian intervention, in that it was largely limited to verbal condemnation, although it led to a temporary postponement of the SALT talks. Johnson sought progress on SALT and the invasion proved to be only a temporary setback to detente. Mlynář suggests that the Soviets sought and received reassurances from Washington that the US response to an invasion would be mild: however, this was denied by Rusk.[60] What is certain is that the US did not robustly oppose Soviet pressure on Czechoslovakia. The Soviets also sought to reassure Washington about the implications of the intervention. In his comments on the invasion, Rusk denied that it confirmed that the superpowers had agreed to the division of Europe into 'spheres of interest'.[61] The mildness of the US response in 1968 served to create a 'never again' syndrome in subsequent US policy: Washington's responses to the Afghanistan and 1980–1 Polish crises were more vigorous.

THE DOCTRINE OF 'LIMITED SOVEREIGNTY': SOVIET THEORETICAL EXPOSITIONS AND FOREIGN REACTIONS

The inability of Soviet apologists to erect a credible defence against these charges of aggression forced them to fall back upon an argument which, in the context of socialist international relations, supposedly transcends bourgeois legal concepts or accusations of international illegality – the theory of 'limited sovereignty'. The best known re-exposition of the doctrine was the article by Kovalev in *Pravda* on 26 September.[62] Although viewed by many Western commentators as a striking and original contribution to Soviet justifications of the invasion, it was really a rehash of the ideas of Korovin, Pomelov, Pavlov, Aleksandrov and other Soviet polemicists. Neither in substance nor in terminology did it differ from statements which had appeared in Soviet journals during the Hungarian crisis. Moreover, between March and August 1968 each of the component elements of the doctrine had been espoused in Soviet statements, including the Warsaw letter and the Bratislava statement. Why, then did it have such a startling impact? Firstly, Kovalev's exposition was not hidden in a maze of circumlocutory jargon but was expressed boldly, and with unusual clarity, in *Pravda*. Moreover, Kovalev went a little further than had previous writers in drawing out the logical implications of the paramountcy of proletarian internationalism over sovereignty, even though the ostensible purpose of the article was to refute international criticism. Kovalev's article was given wide publicity in Soviet foreign language broadcasts. Before the invasion, proletarian internationalism rhetoric could have been viewed as serving primarily a 'masking function', of little relevance to reality. Kovalev's article vividly demonstrated that a weapon never looks so terrifying as when it is covered in blood. The invasion infused concrete meaning into some previously rather vacuous phraseology utilised by Soviet theorists in their post-1956 endeavours to restoring unity to the socialist camp under Soviet leadership. The 'conciliar' strategy adopted by the Kremlin following the traumas of 1956 had, if nothing else, resulted in renewed Soviet emphasis upon the qualitatively superior character of socialist international relations. If ritual incantation of 'solidarist' terminology could not reverse the erosion of Soviet power, at least it might serve to mask it. Moreover, the strategy of unity through collaboration distracted attention from socialist internationalism's 'sting in the tail'. Henceforth, the meaning of Soviet conciliar euphemisms would be apparent. Several members of the Soviet leadership also publicly espoused the doctrine, including Gromyko at the UN, Mazurov, First Deputy of the Council of Ministers,[63] and Brezhnev at the 5th congress of the Polish communist party in Warsaw in November.[64] The doctrine was also expounded in Soviet theoretical journals and in the Soviet press. The Soviets placed a much greater emphasis upon the theory in 1968 than in 1956, which indicates the threadbare nature of other Soviet justifications.

Secondly, the re-emergence of the doctrine helped to destroy the comforting illusion that 'tank and handcuff' diplomacy had been removed from the armoury of Soviet foreign policy. The doctrine not only provided chapter and verse for the military action against Czechoslovakia: lurking behind the doctrine's grandiose phraseology was the ugly prospect of as many August 20ths as were necessary to reassert Soviet authority over socialist states within reach of Soviet tanks. No wonder, therefore, that the enunciation of the doctrine at a time when Soviet tanks were patrolling the streets of Prague was greeted with alarm in Bucharest, Belgrade, Peking and Tirana.

Kovalev's remarks were predicated upon the orthodox assumption that socialism is an international creed and, therefore, that developments within each socialist country concern the whole socialist commonwealth. Implicit in this assumption is the notion that sovereignty is a secondary principle, subordinate to the general aims of socialism. However, Kovalev does not explicitly admit it had been necessary to violate the sovereignty of Czechoslovakia in order to protect the country's socialist achievements. To have done so would have meant violating a cardinal assumption of Soviet international relations theory – that the USSR is inherently incapable of aggressive acts. Therefore, Kovalev drew an implausible distinction between 'defence of Czechoslovakia's socialist gains' and 'interference in Czechoslovakia's internal affairs'. Thus the five allies had scrupulously respected Czechoslovakia's sovereignty and were in favour of the Czechoslovak people's 'right to determine their own future . . . without counterrevolutionary threats and revisionist and nationalist demagogy'.[65] For Kovalev, sovereignty was a delicate flower indeed, which could only flourish in a special (socialist) environment, otherwise it would develop into a nationalist mutation, which was not genuine sovereignty at all. The 'popular sovereignty' of Czechoslovakia (the only type permissible in Soviet theory) was clearly not a robust organism and was highly susceptible to counterrevolutionary infections. Kovalev's article exposes (unintentionally but nonetheless starkly) the fundamental contradiction in Soviet attitudes towards the sovereignty principle: on the one hand it is regarded as the keystone of international law, and on the other, it is secondary to the aims of Soviet policy. Therefore, at various points in Soviet history it has been necessary for Soviet commentators to downgrade the principle by disparaging its bourgeois genealogy. This dualism in Soviet thinking was clearly evident in Kovalev's article, which counterpointed laudatory references to sovereignty with reminders that relations between socialist states were founded on higher values.

Kovalev attempted to solve this fundamental contradiction by arguing that the allied action had been a struggle for the sovereignty of Czechoslovakia against those who had sought to destroy it.[66] To the uninitiated, Kovalev may sound at this point like a rapist attempting to justify himself by arguing that his motive for the crime was to protect his victim's virginity: because different standards apply in relations between socialist states, the five allies were the chaperons, rather than the rapists, of Czech sovereignty. The distinction between 'abstract' (i.e. formal) and 'genuine' (i.e. 'popular') socialist sovereignty had also been advanced in the aftermath of the Hungarian crisis: Kovalev's article did not even have the distinction of adding new terminological clothing to old ideas, since even the nomenclature he used was culled from the common stock of approved Soviet slogans. Contained within Kovalev's article was a form of 'domino theory', in which 'weak links', endangered by internal and external subversion, jeopardised the whole socialist camp. At one point, he drops all attempts at sophistry and states bluntly that fraternal countries could not be guided by 'abstract sovereignty', when socialism in Czechoslovakia was imperilled.[67]

The central tenets of his article were to be reiterated obsessively in Soviet commentaries on the invasion. On 29 September in *Izvestiia*, Farberov (one of the main architects of the Soviet theory of 'People's Democracy') reaffirmed the validity of 'general laws' governing the building of socialism.[68] *Kommunist* in September asserted that national sovereignty could not be opposed to the class solidarity of workers.[69] Colonel Cherniak in *Krasnaia zvezda* argued that for Marxist-Leninists, the sovereignty concept had a 'class content' and that, for a socialist state, 'independence and sovereignty' meant independence from capitalism. He saw no 'contradictions' between proletarian internationalism and national interests, since they existed in deep organic union.[70] In November, 'Sovetov' contended that accusations that the sovereignty of Czechoslovakia had been violated were based on an 'abstract interpretation of the content of sovereignty, which stems solely from formal logic'.[71]

The theoretical ground had already been laid for Brezhnev's Warsaw speech on 12 November. Brezhnev's remarks were reiterative: nevertheless, his enunciation gave the doctrine the stamp of authority. He spoke of the 'class basis' of sovereignty; of attempts by imperialist powers to exploit socialism's weakest links in order to restore capitalism; of objective and subjective 'difficulties' within the socialist camp and of the validity of the common laws of socialist construction. Enemies of socialism both within and without were engaging in actions which threatened the entire socialist commonwealth. Of greater significance were Brezhnev's prescriptions for dealing with these threats: a renewed ideological offensive, involving a reassertion of the role of the communist parties; the need for integration of the socialist community; and vigilance against the forces of imperialism.[72]

Reactions in Yugoslavia and China

The re-emergence of the doctrine in the wake of the invasion provoked a voluble reaction from socialist states which had reason to fear its implications. There was nothing in the theory which limited its relevance to the borders of the Soviet bloc. The Yugoslavs rejected the Soviet notion of 'socialist internationalism', and maintained that relations between socialist states should be based on the generally accepted principles of international law, including sovereignty. Kovalev's references to the special responsibilities of the Soviet Union were anathema to the Yugoslavs. Sanduc, Belgrade's former correspondent to Moscow, said on Belgrade Radio on 3 October that the doctrine was a 'pseudo-Marxist theory', incompatible with international law and the UN Charter: Kovalev's reasoning suggested that the Soviet Union appeared to regard the socialist system as an extension of its own borders. Furthermore, in order to avoid the danger of a Soviet military intervention, a country must virtually abandon socialism.[73] Tito condemned the doctrine as contrary to international law and the interests of socialism. He concluded that the theory was far more likely to be invoked against smaller nations.[74] Perović asserted that the theory 'could not conceal the naked fact . . . that a socialist country had been militarily overrun and occupied by a group of countries which are also socialist, against the will of its people'.[75] The doctrine was a 'strange Marxism indeed, and even stranger dialectics', since it constituted an attempt to 'squeeze socialism into a procrustian bed of petrified dogmas' and involved a 'colossal mystification of concepts': its purpose was to intimidate other states into submission.[76] Misko Kranjeć in *Komunist* (Belgrade) had already warned that if proletarian internationalism became 'the monopoly of a sole state, sufficiently strong to rush arbitrarily with its bayonets to help the suppressed proletariat, then . . . harmful . . . consequences must appear'.[77]

In an article in *Peking Review* entitled 'Theories of Limited Sovereignty and International Dictatorship are Social-imperialist Gangster Theories', the doctrine was described as a 'fascist theory', a rationale for Soviet colonialism in Europe. According to the

gangster logic of the Soviet revisionist renegade clique other countries can only exercise 'limited sovereignty' while Soviet revisionism itself exercises unlimited sovereignty . . . these theories of the Soviet revisionist renegade clique are . . . merely the shop-worn junk picked up from the ideological arsenal of the Russian Tsars, Fascists and imperialists . . . the only difference is that the Soviet revisionist renegade clique have given this junk a 'socialist internationalist fig leaf'.[78]

At the 9th party congress, Lin Piaó said: 'what does all this stuff (about limited sovereignty) mean? It means that your sovereignty is limited, while his is unlimited.' He likened the doctrine to the Nazi 'New Order in Europe' and the Japanese 'Greater East Asia Co-Prosperity Sphere'.[79]

Reactions within the bloc

Within the Soviet bloc, reaction to the doctrine assumed a predictable pattern: it could hardly have found favour in Bucharest, since the Romanians had even more reason to fear the dubious gift of Soviet fraternal aid than the Yugoslavs or the Chinese. In *Scînteia* on 30 November, Ceauşescu insisted that Marxist doctrine could not be used to negate the principle of sovereignty, nor twisted to suit the aims of Soviet foreign policy;[80] the doctrine was also rejected by deputy foreign minister Sandru in December.[81] At the 10th party conference in August 1969, Ceauşescu denied that the notion of a socialist world system implied a renunciation of sovereignty.[82] Romania's differences with the Soviet Union on sovereignty embraced a wide range of issues, viz.:

a. 'limited sovereignty': specific works on sovereignty by Romanian theoreticians (e.g. Duculescu, Florea, Voicu, Radulescu, Nastasescu[83]) have reiterated that the sovereignty of socialist states is not 'limited' in any way and that it is not subordinate to 'socialist internationalism'. Rather, the Romanians strongly endorse the conception of sovereignty enshrined in general international law;

b. the role of small and medium powers in the international system. The Romanian attitude that a basic conflict in contemporary international relations is between large and small states and also that the participation of smaller and medium-sized powers is one of the main features of the contemporary era[84] was bound to constitute a thorn in the side of Soviet-Romanian relations, since it challenged orthodox Soviet conceptions of how small and medium-sized powers within the Soviet orbit should behave.

Romania's pursuit of an independent line on foreign policy questions (particularly with regard to relations with the West and China) since the 1960s is at odds with the Soviet 'synchronisation' model of bloc foreign policies;

c. the special status of the CPSU: the Romanians have rejected the Soviet Union's claims to a special status within the camp of socialism and the notion that there can be a 'guiding centre' for socialist states, responsible for laying down 'general laws';[85]

d. 'fraternal aid': during the Czechoslovakian crisis, the Romanians explicitly rejected the notion that Czechoslovakia's internal problems could be solved by outside interference;

e. functional collaboration: the Romanian position has been that 'the steady strengthening of economic interdependence has a necessary and normal character, as long as these are taking place *between* national economies and not *beyond* or over them'.[86]

There are many reasons why the Soviet Union has not heeded the call of proletarian duty and rendered 'military assistance' to Romania. Firstly, Romania has pursued a neo-Stalinist domestic policy and therefore the Soviets could not plausibly argue that communist rule in Romania was in jeopardy. Soviet official statements, and perhaps more significantly Soviet behaviour, since 1956, strongly suggest that the prospect of Soviet military intervention in Eastern Europe is greatest whenever the Kremlin believes that a local communist party is in danger of losing control. De-satellitisation and de-stalinisation, however, are not necessarily parallel phenomena: indeed, Romanian 'de-satellitisation', although incomplete, has depended in large measure upon the maintenance of Stalinist political and social structures. Unlike Dubček's Czechoslovakia, Ceauşescu's Romania is hardly likely to serve as a potential model for other bloc members. Romania is a 'southern tier' country and therefore fulfils a less important role in the Soviet Union's overall European strategy than 'Northern tier' states. The Romanian military elite, unlike its counterparts elsewhere in the bloc, is not enmeshed into the Soviet control system: the integration of other bloc armies into the Warsaw Pact effectively neutralises their capacity to act as autonomous defence forces: conversely, the Romanians have developed their own military doctrines of self-defence. Since the Romanians could be expected to resist a Soviet or Warsaw Pact invasion, the possibility of a relatively bloodless 'surgical intervention' against Romania seem remote.

The Romanians have developed a sophisticated diplomatic 'sign language' in order to express their differences with the Soviet Union: the oblique verbal strategies adopted by the Romanians in order to express dissent from the Soviet line are exemplified by the tendency to avoid direct criticisms of the USSR and to temper the pursuit of independence with a judicious measure of caution and restraint. The Romanians have displayed sensitivity towards the Soviet Union's perceptions of its vital security interests and have been prepared to make conciliatory overtures to the Kremlin so that the strains in Soviet-Romanian relations have never degenerated into a total breach. As Kirk Laux notes, a 'militant nationalist' phase (1966–9) was replaced by a phase of 'selective cooperation' after 1970–1.[87]

Poland, the GDR and Bulgaria were the most enthusiastic advocates of the theory (the response from the Hungarians was more guarded). On 8 September 1968, Gomulka said that 'if the enemy tries to lay dynamite under our house, under the community of the socialist countries, it is our duty, patriotic, national and internationalist, to prevent this'.[88] In October *Novoe vremia* reported that Gomulka had said that 'socialist ethics and the principle of internationalism cannot be reduced to sitting back when the socialist system is being abolished in a fraternal country'.[89] Waclawek in the *World Marxist Review* wrote that 'the sovereignty of each socialist country is conditioned by the international interests of socialism, with which the sovereignty of each must combine'.[90]

The zeal with which theoreticians in the GDR espoused the theory reflected the regime's insecurity. On 10 September, the *Berliner Zeitung* called for a campaign of 'ideological purification' and on the 13th *Neues Deutschland* reiterated the 'touchstone' doctrine of internationalism.[91] In *Neues Deutschland* on 13 October, Herman Axen lauded the principles of proletarian internationalism over sovereignty and rejected polycentrism.[92] In *Einheit*, Axen attacked the PCI for condemning the invasion and reaffirmed that the highest principle between communist parties and socialist states was not sovereignty, but proletarian internationalism.[93] In *Deutsche Aussenpolitik*, Kroger affirmed that every socialist country is answerable not only to its own working class but to the socialist community.[94] Kroger's article was hardly an imaginative exposition of the doctrine: he emphasised the need for a class approach to the question of sovereignty, which far from being restricted, was enhanced and safeguarded within the socialist community. Kroger referred to the limited sovereignty doctrine as 'an instrument of imperialist psychological warfare'.[95] Kroger's article was attacked by Obren Milićević in *Borba*, who in turn was criticised in *Deutsche Aussenpolitik*.[96] The Czech journal *Svobodné slovo* scornfully asserted that 'the sovereignty of states cannot be handled like chewing gum. It cannot be chewed as it suits one'.[97] 'Normalisation' in Czechoslovakia naturally involved a return to ideological orthodoxy: the doctrine was soon to be endorsed in *Rudé právo*, and in the June *World Marxist Review*, by Štrougal, in which he affirmed that 'the sovereignty of our socialist state and its international contacts represent an organic entity. Socialist countries must be prepared jointly to defend their socialist gains against imperialist attacks'.[98] It was given legal force in the Soviet-Czech mutual assistance treaty of 1970.[99] The 1975 treaty with the GDR included a similar provision, although the Soviet treaty with Romania signed two months after the Czech treaty contained no such references to 'international duty': this suggested that the doctrine would be applied selectively, in accordance with Soviet priorities and the structure of Soviet power within the bloc.

The lessons of the 'Prague Spring' no doubt influenced the Hungarian reform programme introduced in the late 1960s. The Hungarian reforms were introduced without the provocative fanfare that heralded Czechoslovakia's experiments. Moreover, the party remained in firm control of the programme and did not proclaim their programme to be a 'new model' – i.e. an alternative to the Soviet model. Nor did the Hungarians explain the need for reform by reference to 'crises of socialism'. The Hungarian leadership also sought to reassure the Soviets concerning the nature of the reform programme.[100]

Western analyses

Analyses of the doctrine in the West concentrated on the following aspects:

1. Origins and parallels in Soviet Marxist thought

Although the theory was to become known in the West as the 'Brezhnev Doctrine', Western Sovietologists soon demonstrated that Brezhnev was not its 'father', nor was it 'born' in 1968. Nor indeed was Brezhnev the first Soviet leader to give it official approval, since Khrushchev had rationalised the intervention in Hungary in similar terms. Western scholars discerned three parallels with Bolshevik thought: firstly, there were the Bolshevik justifications for Moscow's assumption of ideological hegemony over the Comintern. As noted in Chapter 2, Lenin had insisted that the Comintern, like the Bolshevik party, be highly centralised: the 'democratic centralist' imperatives governing the operation of the Comintern could be viewed as having been transmuted into a rationale for Soviet hegemony over other socialist states; secondly, there were the hortatory references to revolutionary intervention made by Bolshevik leaders and theoreticians in the first years of the regime.[101] This was not to say that Bolshevik ideas had been borrowed intact, since the 'verticalist' doctrine of the Bolsheviks was designed to hasten the demise of the state system. The Brezhnev Doctrine on the other hand is state-centric and status-quo-oriented. Nor is it founded on an explicit repudiation of the concept of sovereignty: indeed, its exponents are at pains to emphasise the Soviet Union's unblemished record with regard to support for sovereignty. Thirdly, the doctrine probably has most in common with Bolshevik justifications for the suppression of 'counterrevolutionary' separatist movements in the independent Soviet Republics prior to the formation of the USSR.[102] These justifications were formulated before sovereignty was elevated to an exalted place in Soviet international relations doctrine. Nevertheless, the ambivalent attitude of the Bolsheviks towards self-determination meant that their justifications for 'fraternal aid' were (like those of Kovalev and Brezhnev) hedged with qualifying riders.

2. Comparisons with non-Marxist interventionary doctrines

Western scholars also sought to compare it with other justifications for 'hegemonial intervention':

a. The Monroe Doctrine. The similarities with the Monroe Doctrine were noted by Glazer,[103] Franck and Weisband[104] and many others. Romaniecki pointed to the Larreta Doctrine, propounded by the Uruguayan foreign minister in 1945, which asserted that the American states had a right to intervene against 'un-American' (undemocratic and illiberal) regimes.[105] These comparisons can be categorised on the basis of their central assumption concerning the relationship between the two doctrines

1) superpower 'verbal and behavioural symmetry'
2) superpower verbal symmetry, but behavioural 'asymmetry'
3) superpower verbal and behavioural 'asymmetry'.

The first category is based on the assumption that the two superpowers behave and explain themselves in virtually identical ways in their respective spheres – i.e. that the US and the Soviet Union use the same techniques of hegemonial control and justify their interventions in very similar terms. This line of argument has been popular with 'New Left' writers and with analysts of the 'rules of the superpower game'. Secondly, Franck and Weisband note the similarity with the Johnson Doctrine (justifying intervention in the Dominican Republic in 1965). They argue that this similarity is no coincidence: rather, the superpowers 'echo' each other's explanations.[106] However, they point out that, unlike the invasion of Czechoslovakia, the intervention in the Dominican Republic was followed by free elections. Thirdly, the similarity between the doctrines is denied by Glazer[107] and Moore:[108] for Glazer, the difference is one of legality: US intervention in the Dominican Republic was in accordance with international law, in that it followed a genuine request for assistance and conformed to article 19 of the OAS Charter and article 8 of the Inter-American treaty of Reciprocal Assistance.[109] Moore rejects the comparison between Soviet policy in Eastern Europe and US policy in Central America and repudiates the conventional wisdom that the Monroe Doctrine continues to form part of US foreign policy.[110]

b. Pre-war European doctrines. Zorgbibe drew parallels with the doctrine of counterrevolutionary intervention formulated by the 'Holy Alliance' in the early nineteenth century: the protocol of Troppau in 1820 provided for a revolutionary state to be forcibly re-incorporated into the Great Alliance.[111] Romaniecki compared the doctrine to other theories of collective regional intervention: e.g. to the Greater East Asian Congress of the States of East Asia, held in Tokyo in 1943, which resolved to engage in collective defence against Western imperialist powers on the basis of mutual aid and defence of sovereignty of the member states; and to the Nazi Karl Schmitt's theory of *Grausraum*, based on the idea that a powerful state had the right to intervene against any state within its sphere of interest.[112] Thus the Brezhnev Doctrine, stripped of its ideological fancy dress, began to reveal its age.

3. *The geographical and systemic scope of the doctrine*

a. Socialist states outside the bloc. The difference between prewar non-Marxist interventionary doctrines and the Brezhnev Doctrine, according to Romaniecki, was that the perimeters in which the former were operative were defined by geography, whereas the Brezhnev Doctrine had no territorial limits.[113] Davletshin[114] argued that the doctrine was capable of being extended outside the bloc. The senior Soviet commentator Pavlov argued that, in rendering support to the Vietnamese people, the socialist countries 'are carrying out their international duty, which is not limited by any geographical boundaries. The events in Vietnam and Czechoslovakia are essentially of the same order, though expressed in different ways'.[115] Nevertheless, it seems plausible to assume that considerations of power and geography will determine the doctrine's scope. For example, the Kremlin has never given the Castro regime a firm guarantee that the doctrine would be invoked in the event of an American attack upon Cuba – even though Castro endorsed the doctrine at the 1969 World Communist Conference (nor did the Soviets invoke it in support of the Allende regime in Chile in 1973).

b. Pro-Soviet progressive regimes. In the wake of the invasion of Afghanistan, it was suggested that the doctrine had again been extended to embrace states of a 'socialist orientation' – i.e. to developing countries with leftist governments.[116] The caution with which the Soviet Union bestows the term 'socialist' on progressive regimes may stem in part from the complications it would add to its burden of 'international obligations'.

c. Western states. Kovalev had stated that Franco's Spain, Salazar's Portugal or the Greek colonels did not have the right to shelter behind the sovereignty principle. This argument recalled Litvinov's and Korovin's justifications for overriding the sovereignty of fascist regimes. It should be noted that the invasion of Czechoslovakia was, according to Soviet explanations, a pre-emptive strike. Therefore, it provided a rationale for pre-emptive strikes across system boundaries against perceived threats to socialism located in the capitalist world (Kovalev had argued that progressive regimes had a right to protest against neo-Nazism in West Germany[117]).

4. Motives

The doctrine was widely interpreted as an attempt to bestow legitimacy on Soviet actions, compensating for the implausibility of other Soviet justifications.[118] Mitchell saw in the theory a revision of the 'two camps' doctrine, towards a more pessimistic interpretation of socialism's current prospects. Vigilance against counterrevolutionary forces was viewed as necessary in order to prevent capitalist restoration, a far cry from Khrushchev's optimistic forecasts of inexorable revolutionary advance. The core of the doctrine, according to Mitchell, was the need to protect the socialist commonwealth from imperialist subversion by preventing 'weakening of links'[119] and was thus status-quo-oriented (although Mitchell later argued that the doctrine was revised in the mid-1970s and harnessed to expansionary objectives).[120] Romaniecki saw it as the beginning of an expansionary phase in Soviet foreign policy.[121] The two approaches are not necessarily incompatible, since 'pessimism' concerning boundary security has led to aggressive actions throughout history.

The Brezhnev Doctrine and relations with the West

For Keal[122] and Mathieson,[123] the doctrine confirmed the 'tacit understandings' and informal agreements concerning spheres of interest between the superpowers. In his reference to the doctrine in the UN General Assembly, Rusk hinted that it could jeopardise detente, denying that the Soviet Union had the right to make decisions for other socialist states.[124] Rusk had denied shortly after the invasion that the United States had ever entered into spheres of influence agreements or understandings: rather, Johnson, like Eisenhower, recognised the 'reality of Soviet control' in Eastern Europe, so that there was little which could have been done without risking war.[125] The Khrushchev doctrine of 'peaceful coexistence' (based on the notion of peaceful competition, and ideological struggle) was revised in 1969, by two senior theoreticians and members of the CPSU Central Committee. Suslov in *Kommunist* in October gave an optimistic assessment of the prospects for revolutionary progressive forces.[126] Ponomarev in *Kommunist* in December wrote of peaceful coexistence as a form of class warfare, embracing revolutionary warfare against imperialists.[127]

Tongue-in-cheek speculation in the West that the Helsinki accords had 'outlawed' the Brezhnev Doctrine were based on literal interpretations of the provisions of the agreements.[128] In practice, the vocabulary of detente (like the vocabulary of Yalta) was interpreted very differently by the contracting parties: the Soviets continue to insist that Helsinki reaffirmed the principle of sovereignty. As Von Geusau has observed, the common aim of the signatories to promote detente masked widely differing interpretations of its nature and implications.[129] According to Lebedev, the Final Act is based on acceptance by the signatory states that 'no nation has the right to dictate to any other nation how to live and what its political and economic system must be'.[130] The Final Act made no mention of peaceful coexistence, despite Lebedev's assumption that the purpose of 'detente' was 'to make the principle of peaceful coexistence of states with different social systems a law of international life'.[131] That Helsinki was primarily about peaceful coexistence between the two camps is taken as self-evident in Soviet theoretical writings: thus in his examples of the Soviet Union's fidelity to the Helsinki agreements, Lebedev referred only to agreements reached between the USSR and capitalist regimes.[132] At Helsinki, Yugoslavia and Romania dissented from the Soviet assumption that the purpose of the CSCE was primarily about the reduction of tension between blocs and therefore had no relevance for socialist international relations. The Soviet record of 'strict observance' of the Helsinki accords is in the eye of the beholder: the Soviet Union's formal commitment to the Helsinki principles did not prevent the Brezhnev Doctrine from being affirmed in the GDR-Soviet treaty of October 1975. Nor did it result in a modification of the Soviet theory of socialist international relations as expounded in subsequent Soviet academic works.

Helmut Sonnenfeldt, Kissinger's counsellor for European affairs, raised some eyebrows in the West in December 1975 when he advocated Western recognition of the 'organic' relationship between the Soviet Union and the other bloc states – meaning that the West should accept elementary geopolitical realities in Eastern Europe, as a means of developing a more relaxed and productive relationship with the region.[133] The Sonnenfeldt Doctrine, although officially denied, accorded far more closely with the reality of Western policy towards Eastern Europe than did legalistic interpretations of a 'new dawn' for Eastern Europe stemming from the Helsinki accords. In fact, although both Presidential candidates in the elections the following year disavowed the Sonnenfeldt view, it was based on an acknowledgement of *de facto* Western policy towards Eastern Europe since the Second World War – i.e. that Eastern Europe lay firmly within the Soviet sphere of influence.

The Brezhnev Doctrine and international law

Western scholars had no difficulty in identifying incongruities between the doctrine and the UN Charter – with article 2(4) which requires members to refrain from use of force and article 51 on the right to self-defence against armed attack. It contravenes the principle of sovereign equality and respect for the principle of self-determination and equal rights (article 1.2). The doctrine also contravenes articles 1 and 4 of the Warsaw Pact. In the 1970s there was renewed Soviet emphasis on socialist international law and upon the salutary influence of the Soviet state upon general international law, deriving from the development of international relations of 'a new, historically superior type'.[134] 'Socialist internationalism' was elevated into a principle of international law in the Soviet-Czech mutual assistance treaty in 1970. Kozhevnikov and Blishchenko emphasised the need for a class approach to sovereignty and affirmed that the democratic principles of international law were injected with a socialist character.[135] The Yugoslavs and Romanians continued to insist that there was one international law for all states, regardless of their socioeconomic systems. In the words of a leading Romanian scholar, 'a plurality of international peremptory laws would amount to nihilism in international law'.[136]

Soviet rejoinders to foreign criticism of the doctrine

Adverse foreign reaction prompted the Soviets to dismiss the doctrine as nothing more than a malicious invention of the Western propaganda machine. In the aloof denials of Soviet theorists and statesmen, it existed only in the fevered imaginations of anti-Soviet fanatics and was one of the latest weapons in imperialism's ideological campaign against socialism.[137] Soviet commentators normally prefix their references to the doctrine with nullifying adjectives, such as 'notorious', and castigate it as a 'gross slander against the principle of socialist internationalism'.[138] At a meeting of the Helsinki review conference in Vienna in November 1986, Soviet delegate Shikolov said the doctrine was a fabrication and that Kovalev's views were simply his own, not those of the Soviet government.[139]

THE SOVIET IDEOLOGICAL COUNTER-OFFENSIVE: 'SOCIALIST INTERNATIONALISM' REAFFIRMED

The Soviet post-invasion reflex followed the pattern established by

Khrushchev after 1956, i.e. an attempt to restore Soviet ideological hegemony within the international communist movement. The *deus ex machina* underlying this drive for ideological cohesion was the doctrine of socialist internationalism: however, by the late 1960s the obstacles to the restoration of unity had become virtually insurmountable. In the following decade, the Soviets were to face challenges on several fronts: the Eurocommunist alternative to the Soviet model, spearheaded by the Italian and Spanish parties; further assertions of independence by Romania; the aggressive hostility of Peking; and the possibility that the Chinese would form an axis of discontent with the Yugoslavs and Romanians. The Soviet ideological counter-offensive had four inter-related dimensions.

1 Reaffirmation of the universal validity of the Soviet model

The Soviet attempt to re-impose its version of 'orthodoxy' upon the movement was manifested in a campaign against 'revisionism', 'left and right opportunism' and national communism.[140] The Soviets emphasised that 'real socialism' was Soviet socialism, not the Chinese 'deformation' or the alternative model advocated by the Italian party.[141] In the late 1950s, Khrushchev had proclaimed that the Soviet Union was a 'state of all the people': since no other state had yet entered this exalted plane of development, a doctrinal justification was provided for the Soviet Union's assumption of pre-eminence within the movement. At the 24th congress of the party in 1971, Brezhnev advanced the theory of 'developed socialism': this theory, which was expounded at length in Soviet academic works from late 1971, centres on the notion of stages of socialist development. The Soviet Union was said to be a developed socialist society from the early 1960s – the highest level prior to the attainment of communism: no other socialist state was assumed to have reached this level. Therefore, by placing the USSR on a higher plane of development, the theory reinforced the Soviet Union's claim to a unique status.[142] In the early 1970s several bloc leaders proclaimed their aim of building a 'developed socialist' society.[143]

At a round table conference of academics from within the bloc in 1971, Zarodov, the editor of the *World Marxist Review*, sought to reaffirm the existence of general laws and regularities of socialist development: knowledge of these 'objective laws' was distilled from the experience of 'building socialism in the USSR and other socialist countries'.[144] According to Shvetsov in a monograph which sought to justify the CPSU's special role in the communist movement, solidarity with the USSR and the CPSU was and remained the highest principle of internationalism.[145] Attacks upon Maoism and Yugoslav revisionism were key features of this counter-offensive: after some hesitation and ambivalence in Soviet commentaries, from 1971 China was no longer categorised as a member of the socialist camp and was accused of pursuing a 'great-power chauvinistic policy . . . concealed behind pseudo-revolutionary catchwords'.[146] Underlying this offensive was the assumption that 'the ideological struggle was intensifying, not fading away'.[147]

2 The need for unity

The paramount importance of unity was an insistent theme of Soviet commentaries on socialist international relations and was manifested in attacks upon 'splitters' and in expositions of the proper relationship between national and international interests. In relation to the quest for unity, two approaches are discernible: at international party conferences (1969 and 1976) the Soviets were prepared to forgo references to socialist internationalism, 'universal laws of socialism' and 'limited sovereignty' in the interests of unity: however, statements by senior party figures underlined the Soviet commitment to these concepts.[148] The International Conference of Communist and Workers Parties held in Moscow in 1969 (planned prior to the invasion) revealed the extent of disunity within the movement. There was disagreement over the extent to which parties were free to choose their own road to socialism. Criticism of the invasion was made by Berlinguer and by Ceauşescu, although in a muted form. The conference declaration repeated Brezhnev's references to the internal and external enemies of socialism and to the international duty of communists to resist such aggression. Although the conference failed to restore unity, it could be judged as a partial success for the CPSU in that it went further than some had expected in dampening down the potentially corrosive effects of the Intervention, even though the Italians and Romanians signed the main document with reservations.

3 Ideological collaboration

Far from limiting themselves to hortatory calls for unity, the Soviets sought ideological consensus through a network of inter-party contacts throughout the 1970s. Brezhnev also instituted annual meetings in the Crimea with the leaderships of the bloc states from 1973. An insight into the profusion of academic congresses, conferences and symposia held in this period can be gained by perusing the announcements of these meetings in *Social Sciences* (a journal of the Soviet Academy of Sciences, started in 1972). For example, several 'round table' conferences were sponsored by the *World Marxist Review* in the early 1970s: on 'Leninism and the Present Day' organised by the Soviet Academy of Sciences in November 1969; on 'Socialism's place in history'; on 'anticommunism' held in Moscow in January 1970; and on 'Laws Governing the Development of the Socialist World System' in 1971, providing a vehicle for the Soviets to push their 'solidarist' line. Cultural links were expanded through academic exchanges and conferences in many disciplinary fields.

These conferences did not always result in unqualified support for Soviet positions. In the 'round table' on the laws of the socialist world system in 1971, two Romanian scholars dissented from the views of Zarodov on the 'laws' and 'common regularities' of socialist development. Zarodov named these regularities as a 'convergence of socialist nations and states on the basis of proletarian socialist internationalism; socialist economic integration; planned proportional economic development; gradual levelling out of the degree of development of countries; continuous exchange of the experience of socialist and communist construction . . . ; close cooperation in foreign affairs and military cooperation in combatting imperialism'.[149] He emphasised that building the world socialist system was not a spontaneous process and that it required the parties and states to perform 'their international duty and defend socialism's gains'.[150] For Zarodov, 'the sovereignty of socialist nations is tied in organically with proletarian socialist internationalism and is in fact inconceivable without it'.[151] Bogomolov, director of the Soviet Institute of the Economics of the Socialist World System, argued that the most important regularities operating in the national context were 'identical with those operating internationally'.[152]

The Romanian scholar Hutira rejected the notion of common economic laws advanced by Zarodov and Bogomolov on the grounds that 'objective laws manifested themselves in different forms'.[153] In support of the Soviet position, Král, of the Czechoslovak Academy of Sciences, contended that 'to deny common laws in building socialism . . . is to fertilise the soil for a counter-revolutionary assault on the socialist system'.[154] Hutira defined the world socialist system as consisting 'of the separate independent national economies of fourteen sovereign independent states'.[155] On the subject of economic integration, Hutira would agree to the term 'integration' only if it implied voluntary, mutually advantageous, cooperation between states. Zaharescu of Romania also rejected the idea of integration conceived as a single economic plan for all socialist countries.[156]

4 A Renewed Integration Drive

The intervention in Czechoslovakia was an impetus for a Soviet attempt to enhance functional links with the bloc states, through the strengthening of Comecon and the Warsaw Pact. In December 1968, Sorokin wrote of the need for an integrated world socialist economy guided by a single plan.[157] The Soviets pushed for further integration at the 23rd session of the Comecon in April 1969. This drive did not meet with universal acceptance within the bloc. Romania, Hungary and Czechoslovakia expressed opposition to the centralisation plans.[158] At the 24th session in May 1970, Romania refused to agree to the establishment of an Investment Bank.[159] The 1969 Warsaw Pact Political Consultative Council meeting in Budapest established a committee of defence ministers, military and technical councils and a permanent joint staff.

Rakowska-Harmstone has shown that from around 1972–3, Soviet theoretical formulations appeared which sought to apply to the socialist commonwealth a solidarist conception of socialist international relations derived from the salutary example of nationality relations within the USSR.[160] Hodnett's study of the Soviet debate on federalism in the 1960s showed that there was no 'firm party line' on the future of Soviet federalism or on the pace at which the Soviet nationalities would merge ('pro-federalist' theorists advocated the retention of the Union Republics whereas 'liquidationists' favoured the creation of a unitary state).[161] Nevertheless, a dominant premise of the Soviet theory of federalism has been that the 'national sovereignty' of the Union Republics and the state sovereignty of the Union are not only compatible but mutually reinforcing: these sovereignties exist in an 'organic unity' and are 'integral concepts'.[162]

Chkhikvadze asserted that only in socialist federation were the principles of sovereignty and federation compatible and that the principle features of sovereignty of a socialist state could only be understood by applying Marxist-Leninist methodology and a party class approach.[163] The merger formula which was used to explain integration within the USSR (e.g. in 1970 Korkmasova wrote of the convergence and eventual merger of nations and peoples in the USSR through the fading of national boundaries)[164] was also used to explain the processes by which merger would take place amongst socialist states. Paletskis asserted that the experience of the Soviet national commonwealth was a firm basis for socialist construction within the socialist commonwealth.[165]

Rakowska-Harmstone argued that three assumptions underpinned this theory: firstly, that the character of socialist international relations and of intra-state nationality relations within the USSR were identical; secondly, that socialist states were moving inexorably towards unity, which would lead eventually to their merger (*sliianie*); thirdly, that this process had already started within the socialist commonwealth. Also central to the theory was acceptance of the leading position of the CPSU which, because of its experience and strength, had special responsibilities within the movement.[166] This process of convergence was said to require greater cooperation between socialist states: it was not considered to be a 'natural' process, but depended to some degree upon 'subjective' factors.[167] In 1973, Katushev, Secretary of the CPSU Central Committee, wrote of the 'material foundation for the further flourishing of socialist nations and their increasing convergence'.[168] Although Katushev wrote of the 'organic harmony' of socialist states, and denied that there was an 'objective basis for antagonistic contradictions', he also acknowledged the role of subjective factors in the process of comprehensive convergence of socialist nations, such as the necessity for joint efforts and a united foreign policy.[169]

The central assumptions of the doctrine can be summarised as :

1. the vulnerability of the international socialist system to insidious internal decay and imperialist penetration;
2. the need for revolutionary vigilance against class enemies and a counter-offensive against left and right deviations;
3. the paramount role of the communist parties in socialist societies;
4. recognition of the universal validity of the Soviet model of socialism;

5. consolidation and integration of the socialist system;
6. acknowledgement of the role of 'subjective factors' in these processes.

Both the process and the content of Soviet doctrinal revision following intervention in Czechoslovakia bear close resemblances to the shifts in doctrine which took place after the Hungarian revolution: both were precipitated by the shock of an intra-bloc crisis; both resulted in an affirmation of solidarist concepts and a multifaceted attempt to restore unity to the movement under Soviet leadership: in both cases, 'socialist internationalism' was regarded as the lodestar of socialist international relations: most of these concepts were culled from the post-1958 integration drive in Eastern Europe, suggesting that little premium was set upon theoretical innovation. However, there were some differences between these ideological campaigns: for example, in the recognition of 'difficulties' or 'contradictions' impeding cooperation between socialist states and in the importance given to the subjective factor in post-1968 conceptualisations of the future course of socialist international relations: but the main difference between the post-1956 and post-1968 ideological offensives was that the latter encountered far more resistance within the movement. The alternative models of socialism being advanced in Peking and Western Europe represented a defeat for the claims to universal validity of the Soviet system.

The enunciation of the Brezhnev Doctrine worsened the Soviet Union's relations with states outside the bloc: it was a major stimulus to the trend towards 'Eurocommunism' in Western Europe (generating the counter-doctrines of 'socialist pluralism' and of the 'new internationalism'); it exacerbated the Sino-Soviet conflict and the ideological competition between Soviet Marxism-Leninism and Maoism. The rapid improvement of relations between the US and China in the early 1970s was also cause for alarm in the Kremlin. However, the enunciation of the doctrine served to clarify the 'ground rules' of Soviet hegemony within the bloc: when the next potential explosions occurred (in Poland, in 1970, 1976 and 1980–1) the doctrine may well have served to establish the psychological parameters which constrained these challenges to the status quo. Nor did the doctrine seriously impede the process of detente with the West: indeed, as a means of maintaining Soviet hegemony, it may have served to create the short-term stability within the region necessary for the progress of detente.

9 Soviet 'Correlation of Forces' Analysis and Afghanistan

Soviet responses to the crises in Afghanistan and Poland provide object lessons in the scope and nature of the Brezhnev Doctrine. Despite the vagueness of the terminology in which the doctrine was couched, its scope was, until 1979, widely assumed to be limited to the Soviet bloc (an assumption reinforced by the relatively mild Soviet response to the downfall of Allende in Chile in 1973). The invasion of Afghanistan led to speculation in the West that the Doctrine had been extended in two principal ways: firstly, in a geostrategic sense, to embrace 'extra-bloc' interventions in geographical zones outside Europe, where the 'rules of the game' had not been settled between the superpowers. Speculation in the West that Soviet foreign policy had entered an expansionist phase – and that 'limited sovereignty' had become an offensive, global, rather than a defensive, regional, doctrine – had distinct plausibility in the light of the Soviet Union's rise to the status of a global power in the 1970s: the invasion was said to provide insights into the implications of optimistic Soviet assessments of the 'correlation of global forces' in the 1970s;[1] and secondly, to embrace regimes which, in current Soviet theory, are not members of the socialist community of states. At the time of the invasion, Afghanistan was still a 'non-aligned' country, despite its increasing dependence on the Soviet Union. In May 1978, Taraki, then head of the Khalq government, had declared that Afghanistan would not become a satellite of any country and would remain fully independent and non-aligned.[2] Nor did Afghanistan have a mutual assistance treaty with the Soviet Union: the treaty signed between the two countries in December 1978 was a friendship treaty, not a military alliance.[3] Moreover, Afghanistan had never been part of the Tsarist Empire.

Afghanistan was classified by the Soviets as a country of 'socialist orientation' – i.e. a less developed country pursuing a non-capitalist and progressive path of development in close cooperation with the socialist world. These states exhibited characteristics which placed them firmly on the road leading to eventual entry into the socialist community[4] through progression to the status of Soviet Marxist-Leninist regimes.[5] Although these countries were directed by 'revolutionary democratic', rather than Marxist-Leninist, parties they proclaimed socialism as their goal and sought to eliminate imperialist monopoly, the big bourgeoisie and feudal elements.[6] They also pursued an anti-imperialist foreign policy: Brutents noted that revolutionary democratic governments took an anti-imperialist position with regard to the 1968 Czech crisis.[7] They were not, however, regarded as fully-fledged socialist states: they had not yet left the world capitalist economy since 'the international division of labour links countries of socialist orientation with capitalist countries';[8] in the socialist oriented countries, the state structure was undoubtedly the dominant one,[9] but 'a lengthy coexistence of state and private sectors' was envisaged;[10] communist power in Afghanistan still had to be consolidated and therefore the Soviets could not plausibly claim to be defending a stable and well-entrenched socialist government against subversion by an unrepresentative bourgeois minority.

Soviet intervention in Poland in 1980–1 did not take a direct military form: however, unless we define the term 'intervention' narrowly, to mean a direct and convention-breaking military attack, there is no doubt that Soviet policy towards Poland amounted to 'intervention'. The doctrine was invoked at an early stage of the Polish crisis and constituted an important component of the 'psychological environment' of decision-makers on all sides. The fact that Poland was spared the full implications of Soviet 'fraternal assistance' does not mean that the doctrine was not invoked: indeed, the doctrine works best when developments unacceptable to the Soviet Union can be arrested without resort to actual (as distinct from threatened) use of Soviet force: thus the lessons of 1968 had been well learned. The Polish crisis provided insights into the 'prophylactic' function of the Brezhnev Doctrine and into the range of interventionary responses available to the Kremlin.

The issue of sovereignty was central to both crises, viz.:

a. Soviet use of the vocabulary of 'socialist internationalism' as a pressure language during the Polish crisis and as an *ex post facto* rationale for intervention in Afghanistan;
b. direct and indirect Soviet pressure on Poland – by reaffirming the real rules of the system, the Kremlin sought to redefine the 'limits of the tolerable' within the bloc;
c. in both cases, Soviet fraternal aid was justified as a response to

imperialist penetration and breaches of sovereignty of the target state by Western powers (and, in the case of Afghanistan, by China and Pakistan also);

d. in both cases, the Soviets responded to a challenge to its perceived interests by effecting a leadership change in the target state;

e. in both cases, there were pro- and anti-Soviet factions within the target state's governing elite;

f. the Soviets had penetrated the military elites in both countries;

g. in both cases, Soviets rebutted Western arguments that the sovereignties of the target state had been violated by the USSR;

h. the response of the United States as a factor shaping Soviet behaviour during the two crises: the US pressure on the Soviets was particularly strong during the Polish crisis and may well have influenced the mode of intervention;

i. in both cases, Soviet actions exacerbated the Kremlin's disputes with several major ruling and non-ruling communist parties.

The purpose of Chapters 9 and 10 is not to retrace the histories of the Afghanistan and Polish crises, but rather to gauge the extent to which the Brezhnev Doctrine was applied and adapted to these specific situations. Neither the intervention in Afghanistan nor the proxy intervention in Poland, however, can be understood unless they are placed in the broader context of the Soviet Union's external relations and, in particular, of changing Soviet assessments of the 'correlation of forces' between the capitalist and socialist camps: these assessments may well have influenced Soviet behaviour during the crises: in turn, the crises impacted upon Soviet perceptions of the correlation – suggesting reciprocity between doctrinal formulations and events.

THE SOVIET ASSESSMENT OF THE 'CORRELATION OF FORCES' IN THE 1970S

Soviet correlation of forces analysis has a long genealogy in Soviet thought, although its main strands derive from Stalin's 'ebb and flow' doctrine of the dynamics of power between the capitalist and socialist camps. In its modern form it also includes some (unacknowledged) ideas derived from Western systems theory.[11] By seeking to analyse the current global power ratio between socialism and capitalism, it provides the Soviets with a view of the world and a guide to action.

Soviet evaluations of the correlation of forces are, therefore, no mere academic exercises, since they are designed to inform policy: in Zagladin's words, the Marxist-Leninist science of international relations provides a 'reliable compass' that enables socialist society to 'steer to the right road amid the stormy sea of world events and confidently avoid reefs and shoals'.[12] It is not to be equated with Western 'balance of power' concepts, which Soviet scholars explicitly reject: the focus of analysis in both classical and contemporary Western balance of power theories is upon military balances achieved through alliances between states. By contrast, correlation of forces analysis embraces many dimensions of power and is not solely concerned with the military capabilities of states: the international system is recognised as being complex and multi-layered, with overarching and interacting socioeconomic, political and military dimensions (for example, the class and anti-imperialist struggle in the capitalist camp and national liberation struggles in the Third World are regarded by the Soviets as positive factors in the correlation).[13] However, the Soviets have laid greatest stress upon the military power of states in their assessments and therefore correlation of forces analysis is not far removed from Western balance of power theory: rather, it might be regarded as another Soviet example of an unhappy compromise between Marxist-Leninist postulates and the realities of power in the international system.

The value of correlation of forces analysis

As a means of comprehending the dynamics of power and the forces of change in the world, Soviet correlation of forces analysis has a number of defects. Firstly, it seems biased towards an assumption of the growing power and strength of the socialist camp: if acted upon, these assessments might embolden the Kremlin to overextend itself in the international arena: the reason for these tendentious presentations is that correlation of forces analysis serves hortatory, as well as analytical, functions – i.e. it is meant to serve as a kind of morale booster for the rest of the socialist camp. Secondly, its crudity: despite its recognition of the multilayered nature of the categories, it is ultimately rooted in a dualistic ('two camps') approach. As an analytical framework, therefore, it is ill-suited to cope with the heterogeneity and complexity of the contemporary international system (a problem recognised by some contemporary Soviet international relations specialists); thirdly, vagueness: both the conceptual categories and the power relationships between systems defy precise measurement and rest on subjective evaluations and broad generalisations (the specific roles of states and classes are left undefined); fourthly, the danger of 'number magic': since it is possible to obtain at least a crude measure of the military balance, less tangible factors may be undervalued or ignored; fifthly, the reaction of the opposing system: statements of favourable correlations could be perceived by the leadership of the imperialist camp as the prelude to expansion and therefore may provoke a counterreaction – what Lider refers to as a 'boomerang effect'.[14]

From around 1972, Soviet assessments of the correlation of forces and the 'restructuring' of international relations reflected an optimistic Soviet mood. Western analysts, for example Deane,[15] Mitchell,[16] Aspaturian[17] and Meissner,[18] noted that, in Soviet analyses of the world situation, the Soviet Union was deemed to be growing in strength relative to the United States, and close to becoming the world's most influential state. The perceived shift in power relationships in favour of the Soviet Union was articulated by Brezhnev, Suslov and many other Soviet commentators from the mid-1970s.[19] Brezhnev had stated at the 24th party congress in February 1976 that there was probably no place on earth where the USSR could be excluded from consideration.[20] This change in the correlation of forces in favour of the socialist world system was, according to Lebedev, 'an objective natural law of world development'.[21] Butenko has dated the shift to the beginning of the 1970s: he argues that this change resulted partly from 'changes in objective conditions' and partly from 'subjective factors', the most important being the 'foreign policy activity vigorously pursued by the CPSU and the fraternal Marxist-Leninist parties'.[22] Ponomarev noted the shift in the balance of world forces 'in favour of the international working class, in favour of socialism'.[23] The 'correlation' doctrine which emerged in this period comprised the following elements:

1. Global dualism

The Soviets advanced the notion of polarisation between two antagonistic and irreconcileable systems (capitalism and socialism), engaged in unceasing struggle in the world arena. Soviet commentators rejected analyses based on the assumption of 'North-South' cleavages, which placed the Soviet Union in the same category as the United States; Chinese 'three worlds' typologies of the international system were also strongly condemned.[24] The Soviets took a dim view of 'middle way' or 'third force' concepts of development. As Korolev argued, for developing countries 'equidistance' between the USA and the USSR was 'a direct threat to their . . . national interests, since in practice it means drawing away from the socialist countries, thus bolstering . . . neocolonialism'.[25]

2. A struggle of opposites

The two systems were said to differ fundamentally in their socioeconomic bases and characteristics: each system was comprised of a socioeconomic formation made up of a substructure (an economic base or system of production relations) and a superstructure (the state, political relations and culture, legal relations, ideology); Soviet scholars now acknowledge that substructure and superstructure exert influence upon each other.[26]

3. Multidimensional struggle

The 'struggle of opposites' had political, economic, ideological and military dimensions: the modern Soviet peaceful coexistence doctrine, unlike Stalin's 'two camps' theory, does not assume the inevitability of war between the principal protagonists: the socialist camp must nevertheless be prepared to defend itself against imperialist aggression. Moreover, the anti-imperialist struggle permitted the use of revolutionary violence. Armed struggle by national liberation movements was both inevitable and legitimate: at the 25th congress of the CPSU in 1976, Brezhnev said that the CPSU would continue to support peoples fighting for freedom.[27] However, between the centres of the two systems, a rule of the game was 'no export of revolution or counterrevolution'.[28] In non-military spheres, the struggle was ceaseless: between the two systems, there could be no ideological 'ceasefire'.[29] In the Soviet interpretation, detente allowed for struggle with the West in non-military forms and support for national liberation struggles. In this sense it might be argued that the Bolshevik policy of global revolution was being pursued by other means – not in Western Europe, but in the Third World, the soft underbelly of world imperialism.

4. Global class cleavage

The paramount importance of the 'class factor' in foreign policy was repeatedly stressed (although states as organisational forms expressing class interests are assigned a prominent role in contemporary analyses).[30] Both intra- and inter-state class alignments were taken into consideration – e.g. alignments of states, movements, classes, parties, etc.

5.   The interconnectedness of subsystems
Weakness in one part could jeopardise the whole system: therefore, the members could not remain indifferent to events in other parts of the system. Systemic interdependency meant that the national and international were intertwined. Although each socialist country acted as an independent entity in international relations, it was very important 'both theoretically and practically to ascertain the general international essence of its vital interests';[31] in other words, there could be no such thing as purely domestic interests.

6.   The permeability of camp boundaries
The boundaries of both systems were deemed to be porous: e.g. the socialist camp had to be on its guard against penetration aimed at the erosion of socialism[32] through strategies of quiet infiltration by imperialist forces (necessitating revolutionary vigilance and a special role of boundary maintenance for the Kremlin); the ideological struggle waged by the Soviets against the capitalist camp also hinged on the assumption that capitalism's boundaries are permeable.[33]

7.   Systemic disequilibrium
The struggle between two systems was essentially dynamic: the international system would remain in a state of disequilibrium until the triumph of the socialist camp. Soviet assessments of the correlation of forces at any given moment embrace the notion of 'upswings and downswings' in the fortunes of the socialist camp (even though these Stalinist terms were not used). The 1970s version of the theory embraced the possibility of serious setbacks for the socialist camp – e.g. the danger of bourgeois restoration within 'weak link' states – and therefore accorded with Stalin's 'zig zag' theory of revolutionary progress. Socialist advance would not occur as a smooth linear progression: in the short run, the correlation could favour either system, although there were tendencies towards growth and consolidation within socialism and towards internal decay within capitalism, which would eventually assure victory for socialism.[34]

8.   'Objective' and 'subjective' factors in the correlation
The power ratio between the two systems was determined by their

shifting relative strengths and weaknesses, which were products of both objective and subjective factors in the world revolutionary process. 'Objective factors' are elements of the substructure and 'subjective factors' are part of the superstructure. For example, 'objective' aspects of the socialist countries' unity (unlike subjective aspects) did not depend upon 'the will and consciousness of people, parties and governments'[35] (in contemporary theory greater emphasis is placed upon subjective factors in the correlation[36]). Therefore, outcomes were strongly influenced by foreign policy decisions.

9. 'Contradictions' exist within both systems

The capitalist camp was riven with antagonistic contradictions (e.g. the presence of antagonistic classes; uneven levels of development, leading to rivalry and conflict between capitalist powers). 'Contradictions', euphemistically described as 'difficulties', were acknowledged within the socialist camp: however, these difficulties were 'non-antagonistic' and could be overcome through cooperation.[37]

10. Internal opposition

Forces inimical to the system existed within both camps – there were anti-imperialist forces in capitalist states: e.g. the proletariats of the developed states, the emerging proletariats in Third World states of capitalist orientation, sections of the intelligentsia, anti-fascist movements, the peace movement, national minorities, etc. 'Counterrevolutionary' or 'unhealthy' forces linked to world imperialism also existed within socialist states; it was thus necessary for Marxist-Leninist parties to struggle against 'bourgeois, revisionist and Maoist ideologies'.[38]

11. The moral legitimacy of socialism's struggle

Both systems engaged in struggle, but only the struggle of the socialist camp was regarded as legitimate: not only was history on the side of socialism, but there were also fundamental moral differences between the bases of the two systems and in the means used to gain relative advantage – for example, the socialist states engaged in ideological struggle, capitalist states pursued 'psychological warfare'.[39] 'Psychological warfare' 'whips up war hysteria . . . and contributes to material war preparations, rationalises the arms race and spreads gross lies about the socialist countries';[40] the socialist camp's military might was defensive and a force for peace whereas the military power of imperialist states was a danger to peace.

12.   Systemic growth and decay

The size of the two systems was not fixed: rather, the socialist camp would continue to expand and the capitalist camp contract due to the inherent strengths of the former and the inherent weaknesses of the latter. Developing countries were regarded as natural allies of socialist states: even though they were not considered part of the socialist camp, they were 'turning against the power of capital'.[41] According to Inozemtsev, both the capitalist and socialist systems were subject to the 'scientific, technological revolution' ('STR') but in the capitalist world STR intensified the general crisis of capitalism by aggravating its economic and socio-political contradictions.[42] Fragmentation was manifested in intensified struggle between the three main capitalist centres (the USA, Western Europe and Japan). The influence of the workers' movement in the capitalist world was said to be greater than ever.[43]

13.   The role of the CPSU and the Soviet Union in 'restructuring' international relations

'Restructuring' would not happen by itself (it was not simply determined by objective conditions), but depended for its realisation upon the progressive forces, in particular the actions and initiatives of the CPSU and the Soviet state in relations between capitalism and socialism.[44] Thus the USA had been forced to abandon its 'cold war' strategy in favour of an acceptance of peaceful coexistence and detente because of the might and peace policy of the USSR.[45] The role of the CPSU in enhancing the unity of the world socialist system was assumed to be a key factor in supplementing and consolidating the favourable changes in objective conditions.[46]

By the late 1970s, the Soviet Union was a global power, with a global reach: the Soviet shift from a 'continental' to a 'global' policy had begun under Khrushchev – encouraged by Soviet successes in space technology – and was continued by Brezhnev.[47] The shift was reflected in both deeds and words – in the Soviet Union's widening network of relationships with Third World countries; in growing Soviet military power (particularly the rapid build-up of Soviet naval forces); in Soviet actions outside its geographical sphere; and in Soviet support for revolutionary movements (in Angola, Ethiopia, Somalia and South Yemen via its Cuban proxy). There had also been victories for socialism in Vietnam, Laos and Cambodia. By 1980 the Soviet Union was the largest arms exporter. The United States was perceived as weak, possibly handicapped by a 'Vietnam syndrome'.

The weak US response to Soviet challenges in Angola and the horn of Africa bolstered this perception. Valenta has suggested that incoherence in American policy could have emboldened the Soviets in the late 1970s.[48] Therefore, by the late 1970s, it might have been predicted that the Soviet Union would seek to extend its power, mindful of possible American responses, but confident of future success.

THE INVASION OF AFGHANISTAN: SOVIET MOTIVES AND JUSTIFICATIONS

Although a Soviet-Afghan friendship treaty had been signed in 1921, the Soviets appear to have assigned a low priority to Afghanistan until after the Second World War.[49] The Soviet-Afghan relationship after the war was crucially affected by the modernisation goals pursued first by the Afghan royal family and later by the Daoud regime prior to the 1979 coup.[50] The modernisation drive stimulated an 'aid' competition between the superpowers in the 1950s and 1960s, which was won by the Soviets, largely due to American half-heartedness. Soviet advisers reorganised, and thereby gained considerable influence within, the Afghan military. Nevertheless, even after the overthrow of the King in 1973, Afghanistan under the leadership of Daoud remained non-aligned. In return for extensive Soviet military aid, Daoud supported Soviet foreign policy, although he also sought to diversify the country's foreign relations. Daoud's 'Peoples Democratic Party of Afghanistan' was riven by factionalism and was unable to control dissent within the country, even through harsh repression: Daoud was neither willing nor able to subject the country to total Soviet control: to complicate matters further, there were two pro-Soviet factions, the Parcham (Flag) wing (headed by Karmal) and the somewhat more independent Khalq (Mass), headed by Hafizullah Amin. Moscow pursued a policy of duplicity, keeping on good terms with both Daoud and the pro-Soviet factions. In April, Daoud and his family were killed in a bloody coup by Taraki (who had united the two pro-Soviet factions in 1977). Taraki became President, Prime Minister and head of the armed forces, with Amin as foreign minister. The Soviets immediately recognised the new regime and increased the number of Soviet advisers in the country. However, Taraki was not subservient to Moscow and in July 1978 purged the Parcham faction.

The Taraki regime's modernisation drive exacerbated popular unrest and increased the regime's dependency upon Soviet aid. Widespread guerrilla warfare and a major uprising in Herat compounded the government's problems. In March 1979, Amin became Prime Minister and launched a bloody campaign of repression, forcing the regime into even greater dependency upon the Soviet Union. There was an uprising in Kabul in August and in September Taraki was assassinated by Amin. Both Amin and the Soviets blamed the unrest upon interference from outside powers: *Pravda* specifically mentioned the US, China and several other states as providers of aid to the counterrevolutionaries.[51] By the winter of 1979, the Khalq was heavily dependent upon Soviet support and there was serious doubt about Amin's future. Following his fact-finding mission to Kabul in late 1979, the Commander-in-Chief of the Soviet ground forces, General Pavlovskiĭ (who had commanded the Soviet invasion force into Czechoslovakia in 1968), advocated military intervention in order to avert the regime's downfall.[52] However, Amin refused to agree to Soviet intervention, despite Soviet pressure. The Kremlin suspected that Amin was seeking to heal the rift with the West. In December, the Soviets increased their troop presence on their border with Afghanistan from three to five divisions. The Soviets also sent a military mission headed by General Paputin (Soviet Internal Security Forces) to gain Amin's permission for Soviet military aid (Amin rejected this suggestion) or to prepare the ground for his overthrow.[53] The Soviet invasion on 27 December took the form of a massive surprise attack. Amin was killed and a new regime installed, under Karmal (who had been serving in Czechoslovakia as Ambassador since July and who probably did not arrive in the country until a week after the invasion).

The intervention decision appears to have been made by a small group within the Soviet Politburo (Brezhnev, defence minister Ustinov, Andropov and Gromyko). There was little sign of the extended debate within the Soviet leadership (or within the bloc states) which had taken place before the invasion of Czechoslovakia: nor was there the extended campaign of verbal pressure of the kind employed against the Czechs. Indeed, in the month preceding the invasion, Soviet media coverage of developments in Afghanistan was distinctly thin. A complex web of factors may have precipitated the invasion. Firstly security considerations: the downfall of the pro-Soviet regime in Kabul would have altered the strategic balance in favour of the Kremlin's principal adversaries, the US and China. The danger to the Soviet state was mentioned by most Soviet commentators, including Brezhnev, Andropov and by Gromyko at the UN. Brezhnev spoke of the danger of a military bridgehead, expressing the fear of anti-socialist encirclement (with perhaps the US, China and Pakistan forming an anti-Soviet alliance[54]). By 1979, Sino-American relations had improved significantly, whereas Soviet relations with these adversaries had deteriorated as a result of the Sino-Vietnamese war, and the Vietnamese invasion of Cambodia.

Soviet correlation of forces analysis provided the Soviet Union with a rationale for defending this key strategic zone. A self-confident tone was discernible in statements of top Soviet officials in the wake of the invasion.[55] Ustinov said on 14 February in *Pravda* that there had been fundamental changes in the global correlation in favour of socialism (in fact, it was military strength which was the most obvious factor). Some Western analysts linked such assessments to Soviet 'probing' strategies outside Europe in Angola, Ethiopia and South Yemen.[56] The ascendancy of hard liners in the Kremlin gave to Soviet policy a decisiveness it had frequently lacked. Rees has suggested that the invasion was part of a 'strategy of denial' in relation to the rimlands of the Middle East oil-producing states, which would jeopardise the West's oil supplies.[57] Petrov wrote in *Pravda* of the 'strategic arc' of the Soviet Union being imperilled.[58] The Soviets may well have been concerned about the danger of a stronger American presence in Iran. The 'loss of prestige' factor is also worthy of consideration: the fall of a socialist-oriented country on the borders of the Soviet Union would have been a blow to the main support of progressive forces struggling against imperialism; it would have weakened the credibility of the Soviet doctrine of the irreversibility of socialist revolution (even though Afghanistan was not fully 'socialist') and would have been a corrective to the Soviet theory of the inexorable expansion of the world socialist system: it would have been more serious than the fall of Allende, since in the latter case the country was clearly in the American sphere of interest. The Soviets were far more committed in Afghanistan (e.g. advisers and heavy investment) than they had been in Chile. Although developments in Afghanistan were unlikely to have a spillover effect in Eastern Europe, the success of Muslim fundamentalism in Afghanistan could have unsettled the Soviet Union's own Muslim population. If Afghanistan had detached itself from Soviet control, the Soviets would have confronted four hostile Muslim states in the area.

The Soviets must have braced themselves for a fierce reaction from the West – but there was also to be hostile response in the Third World, resulting in a UN General Assembly resolution (passed by 104 to 18, with 18 abstentions) condemning the intervention as inconsistent with the principle of sovereignty. There were to be boycotts of the Moscow Olympic games and of a Soviet-hosted International Islamic Conference in September 1980. Compared to the US response to the invasion of Czechoslovakia, Washington's reaction was robust: the 'rules of the game' did not apply to an 'extra-bloc' country like Afghanistan. The Americans had warned the Soviets several times against military intervention, most forcefully after the assassination of the US Ambassador to Kabul in March.[59] The US saw the invasion as a threat to its vital interests in a key strategic area accounting for the bulk of the West's oil supplies. It imposed a wide range of economic sanctions, boycotted the Moscow Olympics and postponed the ratification of SALT 2. The invasion also resulted in the formulation of the 'Carter Doctrine': in his state of the Union address on 23 January 1980, Carter said: 'any attempt by any outside force to gain control of the Persian Gulf region will be regarded as an assault on the vital interests of the USA and . . . will be repelled by any means necessary including military force'.[60] Britain followed the Americans in applying harsh measures, although the reaction of other Western powers was somewhat less robust.[61]

The intervention was also condemned by several communist states: Romania, China, Yugoslavia and Albania. Others, such as Cuba and North Korea (which has a common border with the Soviet Union), equivocated, whereas Mongolia, Vietnam, Laos and Cambodia supported it.[62] The Yugoslav Ambassador to the UN, Miljan Komatina, attacked the intervention as unjustifiable and accused the Soviets of violating the UN Charter.[63] The three bloc states which had enthusiastically embraced the Soviet concept of 'socialist internationalism' – East Germany, Czechoslovakia and Bulgaria – gave the Soviets full support: Poland and Hungary were more lukewarm, no doubt fearing that the invasion might adversely affect their valued contacts with the West.[64] Unlike other bloc states, Romania did not forward a congratulatory telegram to Karmal.[65] Many non-ruling parties, including (the British, Italian and Spanish) opposed the invasion, although it was supported by the French and Portuguese parties.

There was considerable speculation in the West about the significance of the invasion: did it portend further Soviet expansion or was it motivated by more limited security objectives? The Soviets emphasised the defensive nature of the 'assistance' and sought to reassure the West concerning continuation of oil supplies:[66] the 'traditional expansion' theory of Soviet foreign policy – that the Soviet Union, like the Tsarist regime, has an inexorable desire to expand and does so whenever a 'power vacuum' appears on its borders – supported the former view. However, the 'expansion or defence' debate hinges on a false dichotomy, since an intervention can be defensive in its aims, but offensive in its effects. In addition to the motives outlined above, we should not overlook the possibility that the Soviets were 'pulled' into the Afghan quagmire – i.e. once they had become embroiled in Afghan politics, they could not disengage. The Soviet explanations of its actions in Afghanistan embraced several arguments: these can be summarised as follows:

1. The request for help

The Soviets claimed that military intervention had been undertaken in response to an official request for help by the Afghanistan government: however, their explanations were often vague and contradictory. On 29 December, *Pravda* announced that the government of Afghanistan has appealed to the USSR to provide urgent political, moral and economic assistance, including military assistance.[67] On 31 December Petrov wrote that, guided by international duty, the Soviet Union had acceded to Afghanistan's request for military aid, which would be used for 'repulsing armed intervention from without': he also argued that the Afghan government had made repeated requests in 1978–9.[68] Brezhnev, in a *Pravda* interview of 13 January denied that there was a Soviet intervention: 'we are helping the new Afghanistan at the request of the government to defend the country's national independence . . . against armed aggressive actions from outside.' He said that the Afghan leadership, both during Taraki's rule and afterwards, had made the request.[69] A Tass statement on 6 March 1980 said more specifically that 'the leadership of Afghanistan has asked for military assistance on fourteen occasions, four times in December of last year alone'.[70] On his visit to France, Gromyko asserted that the Soviet Union had responded to a request for military assistance from the Afghan leaders as a result of 'armed encroachments'.[71]

This raised the immediate problem of authorship: Amin was killed in a gun battle on 28 December, but it is highly unlikely that he was responsible, as he had said in September that he was proud that he had not requested military assistance. Moreover, the Soviets were soon to declare Amin a CIA agent.[72] Karmal had been out of the country at the time. In January, Karmal admitted that Amin had not made the request, which had been made by the 'revolutionary council': however, he later argued that Amin did make it.[73] In the Security Council debate on 6 January, Dost, Afghanistan's representative at the UN, said that requests had been made by both Taraki and Amin.[74] The 'invitation' rationale advanced in December and January, which was the lynchpin of the Soviet case, received a resoundingly bad international press, perhaps worse than the Soviets anticipated.[75]

2.   Fulfilment of treaty obligations

A second explanation advanced by the Soviets (including by Brezhnev in *Pravda* on 13 January) was that the Soviet Union was fulfilling its treaty obligations under the terms of the Soviet-Afghan friendship treaty of December 1978. On 28 December, it was reported that Karmal had invoked the Treaty on seizing power.[76] In *Novoe vremia* in early January, Anatol'ev wrote that Soviet assistance in repelling the armed imperialist intervention accorded with article 4 of the Treaty and article 51 of the UN Charter relating to self-defence.[77] However, the Treaty was a friendship treaty, not a military alliance and did not contain a mutual assistance clause of the type the Soviet Union had concluded with the bloc states. Nor did it refer to 'socialist internationalism': indeed, the Treaty affirmed the independence of the two states and did not detract from Afghanistan's non-aligned status.

THE BREZHNEV DOCTRINE AND AFGHANISTAN: THE 'REVERSIBILITY OF SOCIALISM'?

An additional Soviet justification for military intervention – the imperative of international duty – transcended arguments about formal requests for help. In his 31 December article, Petrov wrote that, in agreeing to the Afghan government's request, the Soviet Union was guided by its international duty.[78] In his interview for *Pravda* on 13 January, Brezhnev had said that to act otherwise would 'have meant abandoning Afghanistan to imperialism, enabling aggressive forces to repeat their success in Chile'.[79] The 'Chile analogy' was also to be used by Chervonenko, Soviet Ambassador to France, on 22 April, when he said that the USSR 'would not permit another Chile' and would repel, if necessary, the threat of counterrevolution and foreign intervention.[80] Chervonenko had been Ambassador to Czechoslovakia during the 1968 crisis. On 6 February, Grishin, the Moscow party boss who had enunciated the 'limited sovereignty' doctrine at an early stage of the Czech crisis, wrote in the Moscow *Pravda* that the Soviet Union's obligations to 'socialist internationalism' required it to defend 'revolutionary gains'.[81]

An unsigned article in *Novoe vremia* in January asserted that the intrigues of imperialism necessitated effective international revolutionary solidarity: by coming to Afghanistan's aid, the Soviet Union had fulfilled its international duty.[82] In an obvious reference to 'Eurocommunist' criticisms of the Soviet action, it noted that a 'lively discussion' was taking place, including amongst the left, concerning the nature and forms of international solidarity and whether these were compatible with the principles of sovereignty and noninterference. It asked the rhetorical question: 'does the international solidarity of revolutionaries consist only of moral and diplomatic and verbal support, or also of material, including military, assistance, rendered in . . . a situation of flagrant, massive outside interference?' The history of revolutionary movements – of China in the 1920s and 1930s and Spain in the 1930s – legitimated military assistance of this kind. Otherwise, imperialism would be free to stifle revolutionary movements.[83] The defence minister Ustinov said on 13 February that 'faithful to its international duty, the Soviet Union has always rendered aid to peoples struggling for their sovereignty and revolutionary achievements'.[84]

The similarity between Soviet explanations of the interventions in Czechoslovakia and Afghanistan was unmistakable: the Soviet use of the Brezhnev Doctrine to buttress its explanations of the 'military assistance' rendered to Afghanistan was greeted with alarm in the West and, indeed, within the international communist movement. Meissner suggested that Soviet intervention into a 'grey zone' raised questions about interventions in 'grey zones', in Europe such as Yugoslavia, Albania or Finland.[85] The line of argument used in 1956 and 1968 – i.e. that a successful socialist revolution had been endangered by external forces – did not transfer well onto the Afghan case. The Yugoslavs attacked the Soviet application of the doctrine to Afghanistan: Radio Belgrade criticised an article by Suslov which had stated that no 'genuine national interest' has ever been at odds with proletarian internationalism.[86] However, an article in *Novoe vremia* by Golovin implicitly denied that the Brezhnev Doctrine had been extended to Afghanistan, when he attacked the theoretical journal of the Spanish Communist party for alleging that 'Soviet forces were sent to Afghanistan to save its socialist or near-socialist system',[87] since 'nobody in the USSR could have used such terms'. Rather, Afghanistan's independence was being defended against external aggression.[88] Instead he emphasised the 'assistance and treaty obligations' arguments. However, he went on to say that 'only those who struggle against imperialist aggression in deeds are true internationalists',[89] which could be regarded as a restatement of the Brezhnev Doctrine in different words.

This denial and down-playing of the Brezhnev Doctrine argument may have been designed to reassure the West that the intervention was not part of a new offensive strategy. However, in the light of Brezhnev's and Chervonenko's statements, it seemed less than convincing. Nevertheless, in the early 1980s the Soviets adopted a less assertive international posture, no doubt influenced by the Afghanistan embroglio, the Polish crisis, setbacks in Africa and tougher American policy. Although, in February 1981, Brezhnev gave Castro assurances of 'full support',[90] this fell short of a cast-iron pledge of 'fraternal aid': moreover, this vague commitment was of long standing and therefore did not represent a new departure in policy. The invasion demonstrated that the doctrine could be applied outside Europe and outside the accepted Soviet sphere of interest; it could be applied against regimes which were outside the category of socialist states as defined by the Soviet Union. Did the doctrine extend to other states of socialist orientation? The precarious stability of many of these regimes meant that the possibility of other Soviet extra-bloc interventions in the future could not be ruled out.

In the 1980s, as Valkenier has shown, there was greater emphasis in Soviet theory upon the extent to which revolutionary democratic parties fell short of being Marxist-Leninist parties.[91] From around 1980, the Soviets began a reassessment of Third World radical movements, which led to a revision of the optimistic forecasts of the 1970s concerning the revolutionary potential of the 'newly freed' countries.[92] In addition to 'scientific socialism' some revolutionary democratic parties were said to pursue 'petty bourgeois and even utopian ideas'.[93] It was admitted that they were not necessarily mass organisations and that 'sometimes, the revolution "from above" is not matched by the movement "from below"'.[94] They were viewed as being in an embryonic, preparatory phase of development. A more cautious line on links with Third World movements was advocated by Brutents, a leading expert on 'newly freed' states.[95]

A literal interpretation of the implications of the doctrine's application to Afghanistan can be summarised as:

1. Once a regime had been categorised by the Soviets as 'socialist' or 'socialist-oriented', it would be entitled to Soviet military assistance: 'capitalist restoration' would be prevented by Soviet armed force;
2. Any state threatened by imperialist aggression (defined by the Soviet Union) could be subject to the Soviet Union's call to proletarian duty;
3. The dubious circumstances in which the Kabul regime had been installed meant that, on the pretext of a request from the target state's government, the Soviet Union had the right to intervene in any country in the world, to thwart the plans of 'aggressive imperialist forces'.

In practice, Soviet assessments of costs and benefits – including the risk of confrontation with the United States – would determine the extent of Soviet assistance: the extra-bloc 'probe' into Granada in 1983 was easily repulsed by the United States, the Soviet Union declining to render fraternal assistance in order to prevent 'capitalist restoration'. Far from being a neat 'surgical intervention', the Kremlin's fraternal military assistance to Afghanistan caused the Soviet 'surgeon' to suffer a debilitating bleeding wound. Gorbachev's decision to pull out of Afghanistan (an agreement was signed in April 1988 for withdrawal of all Soviet troops by February 1989) was prompted not only by the dismal prospects for victory over the Mujahedeen, but also by the war's unacceptably high economic and political costs to the Soviet Union: the war was a serious impediment to Gorbachev's reform objectives, both domestically and internationally. Withdrawal would remove a thorn in the side of Soviet relations with China and the Muslim world and would undermine Western 'Soviet aggression' propaganda. Two articles in *Literaturnaia gazeta* in February and March 1988 contained admissions that the invasion decision was a serious miscalculation. In February, the journalist Prokhanov questioned the purpose of the Soviet troop presence in Afghanistan: not only did socialism not exist in the country (he noted that the Afghanistan government had even discarded the socialist symbols of red flag and star), it was doubtful if it could exist there in present conditions. However, in his view, Soviet withdrawal from this seething cauldron would not lead to the creation of either an Iranian or an American type system either: rather, it would result in a system peculiar to Afghanistan.[96]

Soviet statements in April 1988, announcing Soviet withdrawal from Afghanistan, made no reference to 'defending socialism': rather, they emphasised 'traditional friendships' between the two countries.[97] The 'pull out' decision, which was said to be an application of the 'new thinking' in Soviet foreign policy, raises interesting questions concerning the Soviet commitment to the doctrine of the irreversibility of socialism: it was the first example of a Soviet withdrawal following a full blooded attempt to render 'fraternal military aid' to another socialist state. Did it mean that the Kremlin would no longer seek to secure the survival of socialism within the Soviet bloc by military means? Four points are worth noting: firstly, the pull out decision was a rational Soviet response to the problem of imperial overextension: by reducing its burdens in Afghanistan, the Soviet regime placed itself in better shape to respond to centrifugal forces within its critical defence zone in Europe; secondly, the pull out agreement did not concede capitalist victory, since it allows for 'positive symmetry' between Moscow and Washington in the supply of arms to the government and rebels: even in the event of a total victory by the Mujahedeen, Afghanistan would be likely to become a non-aligned, faction-ridden Muslim state rather than a pliable invasion platform for the West (the possibility that the Soviets and Afghan communists will seek to establish a buffer communist enclave on Afghanistan's northern borders cannot be ruled out[98]). Thirdly, Afghanistan is not Eastern Europe: the spillover effect between Afghanistan and Eastern Europe is weaker than between the East European states themselves. Fourthly, before the intervention, Afghanistan was a non-aligned, economically backward socialist-oriented country rather than a fully fledged socialist state. In 1988, a leading Soviet specialist on 'countries of socialist orientation', Kiva, admitted that Soviet theorising on this subject in the 1970s and early 1980s had been distorted by wishful thinking and subjectivism, since many countries included in this category were in no sense socialist:[99] by splitting doctrinal hairs, we might argue that the pull out created no precedent for Eastern Europe. However, no amount of rationalisation could disguise the fact that a Soviet application of the Brezhnev Doctrine had failed.

10 The Soviet Proxy Intervention in Poland

THE CHALLENGE OF SOLIDARITY

The Brezhnev Doctrine performs two principal functions in Soviet foreign policy: firstly, it used as an *ex post facto* rationalisation for military intervention; secondly, it is a prophylactic signalling device, serving to remind East Europeans that the 'ground rules' necessary for the maintenance of Soviet bloc hegemony are still in force (the intimidatory or 'damocletian sword' function of the doctrine). In 1968, the signals concerning the 'ground rules' emanating from Moscow, East Berlin, Warsaw, Sofia and Budapest were misinterpreted by Dubček, who overestimated his ability to persuade his anxious neighbours that socialism in Czechoslovakia was in good hands. In the case of Poland between 1980 and 1982, the 'damocletian' function was successfully deployed, in that the possibility of Soviet military intervention loomed large during the crisis and constituted an important component of the 'psychological environment' of both opponents and proponents of radical change in the country (it was also the dominant factor in Western responses). The Brezhnev Doctrine was the principal reason why the Polish revolution was 'self-limiting' (if we regard the Polish military elite as exclusively part of the Polish 'self')[1] and therefore its deployment demonstrated that the lessons of 1968 had not been forgotten.

In modern usage, the term 'intervention' has become virtually synonymous with military intervention by an external power. This definition is too restrictive. The challenge of Solidarity to the rule of the Polish United Workers Party was, in large measure, brought to an end by an extensive Soviet counterrevolutionary intervention, which took two principal forms: firstly, the Kremlin employed a familiar battery of deviation control techniques (all of which had been applied against Czechoslovakia in 1968) in order to arrest and reverse internal developments with Poland; secondly, the imposition of martial law constituted a 'sharp break'[2] with previous events and received its impetus from Moscow (even though the Kremlin may not have been in full control of the imposition of martial law). This 'proxy intervention' was implemented by the Polish armed forces, headed by personnel well attuned to Soviet thinking and well integrated into the Soviet system of control. In the Polish case, a 'proxy intervention' was probably the best option available for the Kremlin: it carried fewer risks and may have been more effective in thwarting Solidarity's challenge than a fully fledged 1968-style of intervention.

The underlying cause of the upheavals was the regime's profound 'legitimacy crisis', which derived from four principal factors: firstly, the regime was still regarded by many Poles as an alien implant and therefore an obstacle to national self-realisation and an affront to Polish national dignity. In 1978 a discussion group of over 100 prominent Poles (both party and non-party) was established under official auspices (the 'DiP' or 'Experience and the Future' group), with the task of investigating Poland's domestic and international problems. The report was denied official publication, but was published unofficially in Poland and the West. A contributor to the report had stated that Poles did not consider the nation to be 'synonymous with the state';[3] secondly, there existed an alternative focus of popular loyalty in the Catholic church, which symbolised Poland's historical links with the West and which was inextricably bound up with the Polish sense of national identity. The PUWP was never able to uproot this tenacious alternative to its own self-appointed role as the 'leading force' in Polish society. Moreover, as Kolakowski noted, the official ideology deteriorated into lifelessness, so that PUWP leaders sought to justify their policies to the Polish people by appeals to the national interest and *raison d'État* rather than to Marxist-Leninist values (even within the party, the ideology had lost its motivating force[4]). The existence of a lively and truculent intelligentsia also served to undermine the party's authority: 'elite delegitimation' emboldened the opposition and weakened the PUWP's response to challenges to its authority;[5] thirdly, the weakness and incompetence of the governing elite: not only was the party debilitated by endemic factionalism: its failure to develop successful economic programmes widened the regime's 'legitimacy deficit', causing it to lurch from one crisis to another. Poland's postwar history, therefore was a dismal cycle of economic crisis, popular disturbances and lavish, but unfulfilled, promises of reform.

The announcement of food price rises in December 1970 detonated strikes and riots in Gdansk, Gdynia and elsewhere which led to the shooting of workers on Gomulka's orders. Gomulka resigned and was replaced by Gierek in January 1971. The workers were still in a rebellious mood, however, and Gierek was forced to placate them with promises of reform and appeals to patriotism. Remington has observed that the Brezhnev Doctrine was tested in relation to Poland during the crisis: of three possible Soviet responses to the crisis – 'hands off'; buying time by granting economic aid during the period when Gierek was strengthening his position; or military intervention – the 'buying time' alternative enabled the Soviets to avoid (at least temporarily) the horrendous consequences of military intervention.[6] Gierek launched on an ambitious programme of development (fuelled by Western and Soviet credits) which was initially successful.

The Doctrine of 'Developed Socialism'

The ideological packaging around Gierek's reform programme was the Soviet doctrine of 'developed socialism': at the 1971 party congress, Gierek proclaimed that Poland was moving towards becoming a developed socialist society,[7] meaning that Polish socialism was entering a mature phase and therefore that a high level of socialist development had already been attained in all aspects of Polish life: orthodox party ideologists pointed to the existence of high degrees of social consensus, social equality and economic and technological development, stimulated by the 'scientific technological revolution' and directed by the PUWP.[8] However, there seemed to be no relationship between official doctrine and actual policy. Rather, the doctrine was used to justify the status quo and therefore served 'masking' functions. However, some reform-oriented intellectuals, such as Wiatr, Zawadski and Szczepanski, sought to employ the concept of developed socialism in order to address Poland's fundamental problems – these writers focused upon political rather than technical reform issues and advocated greater involvement of citizens in decision-making.[9]

By the mid-1970s, the Polish economy was in dire straits due to the superficial nature of Gierek's reforms. In 1976, labour unrest centred in Radom and Ursus (detonated by announcements of food price increases) was brutally suppressed by the police: the government backed down and postponed the increases. After the 1976 crisis, cooperation between workers and dissident intellectuals led to the formation of new opposition groups. In September 1976, the Committee for the Defence of the Workers (KOR) was formed, which not only challenged the party's leading role, but was also dismissive of the system's capacity for genuine reform. Gierek's solution to the 1976 crisis had been the familiar package of borrowing and promises, but the workers had seen it all before. Moreover, a major factional struggle was raging within the PUWP. Although Gierek secured economic assistance from the Soviets in November 1976, Poland's economic problems were too serious to be solved by a modest infusion of Soviet aid. The crisis in the summer of 1980 was precipitated by an announcement of a rise in meat prices at the beginning of July. The refusal of the government to rescind these increases in response to workers' protests led to a wave of strikes in July and August. Up to this point, the crisis may have seemed like a re-run of 1976. A number of contributory factors however, ensured that the crisis could not be easily contained:

a. the 'last straw' factor: a serious crisis of regime credibility manifested in widespread disillusionment – indeed, exasperation – with the party's rule. This had spread to all levels and led to cooperation between workers and intellectuals (unlike the situations in 1968 and 1970, when students and workers had not acted in unison). As Gerner has argued, a 'revolutionary situation' had developed, in which the rulers were losing their ruling ability and the people were losing patience with the rulers.[10] The DiP report had exposed the extent of corruption and mismanagement within the country:[11] all that was needed was a trigger to detonate a further explosion. Living standards were lower than in 1978 and were expected to drop even further. There was no more room for manoeuvre: the government was too deeply in debt, and too lacking in prestige, to be able to fob the workers off. Most Poles regarded it as axiomatic that, far from being due to specific and rectifiable policy mistakes (as the party claimed), Poland's plight was caused by the system's inherent defects;

b. conflict and demoralisation within the party (a factor common to the crises in Hungary and Czechoslovakia in 1956 and 1968). Party membership declined by one third between 1980 and 1983 and many party members joined Solidarity. In Czechoslovakia in 1968, it had been the party which regarded itself as being in the vanguard of the reform process. In Poland the party was disintegrating, partly from internal processes of 'elite delegitimation' and partly under the onslaught of a 'revolution from below' – a powerful popular movement for change which had developed outside party structures;

c. the existence of credible alternative foci of loyalty (the Church and later the independent trade union movement): the first free trade union had been formed in Silesia in 1978 and on May Day 1978 the Founding Committee of the Independent Trade Unions on the Coast was established in Gdansk. Whereas the party was weakened by factional struggle, the opposition was stronger, more united and better coordinated than ever. Moreover, the opposition was disciplined enough to avoid the outbursts of violence which had played into the government's hands in previous crises;

d. dissatisfaction with the country's relationship with the Soviet Union. This was, of course, a perennial source of discontent: a section on 'sovereignty and national identity' in the DiP report had said that 'the awareness of limited national sovereignty . . . weighs painfully on the Poles and imposed a ceiling on their national aspirations': a respondent argued that 'power in our country should reside in Warsaw and nowhere else'.[12] The decline of the German threat in the 1970s undermined the principal justification for Poland's alliance with the Soviet Union. Nevertheless, the 'unofficial opposition' in its public pronouncements showed an awareness of Poland's 'geo-political situation' and avoided provocative statements on international affairs, to avoid antagonising the Soviets.

The strikers were both determined and well-organised. The government resorted to divide and rule tactics, by insisting on separate negotiations with each plant: however, the strikers refused and therefore the government had to deal with an inter-factory strike committee, which advanced several fundamental demands, including the right to form independent unions and the right to strike. A 'social contract' was signed on August 31, between Walesa and Deputy Prime Minister Jagielski, in which most of the workers' demands were met. In return, the Committee agreed to respect the Constitution, to refrain from intrusion into the political sphere, and to respect Poland's alliance system. The government entered into over 600 similar agreements with strike committees elsewhere. However, in doing so the government was buying itself time: it was a tactical manoeuvre, an admission of temporary weakness, a truce, rather than a peace. No doubt the leadership felt that it could renege on these concessions when circumstances were more propitious. A week after the Gdansk agreements, Gierek was replaced by Kania. There were to be many personnel changes within the government in this period. On 18 September, following a meeting of free union delegates in Gdansk, the National Confederation of Independent Trade Unions came into being under the name Solidarity. On 23 September, Solidarity sought to register as a trade union. The authorities insisted that the union accept the party's leading role, Poland's existing alliance obligations and restrictions on the right to strike as the price of registration. Solidarity refused to pay this price and threatened strike action. However, on 10 November, the Polish supreme court upheld Solidarity's application for registration. By August 1981, Solidarity had about 10 million members. Conversely, communist party membership declined by about one third in the same period.

International responses

Strategic imperatives fuelled Soviet anxieties concerning developments in Poland: the geographical location of Poland – the heart of the main Soviet security zone in the region and the main military communications channel between the Soviet Union and East Germany – secures its pivotal role in Soviet strategy. Poland had been a staunch defender of Soviet positions: it had played its full part in the extirpation of the Prague Spring and had supported Soviet policies on Eurocommunism and detente. The danger of spillover – the possibility that Poland's industrial unrest might infect other parts of the bloc – was well recognised by Poland's conservative neighbours. The 'Polish August' could not be localised effectively: within a hegemonic system, there is no such thing as a purely 'domestic' crisis, since threats to any part of the structure have reverberative effects and inevitably involve those responsible for its design and maintenance.

The fact that strikes had occurred at all was bound to cause alarm in Moscow, since they represented a blatant manifestation of organised opposition to a communist government within the bloc – a direct challenge to a Soviet article of faith concerning the inviolability of communist party rule and of the 'transmission belt' function of trade unions. However, the failure of the government to crush the workers' movement gave additional cause for alarm. In particular, the fact that the government had been forced to grant the workers' committee the crucial concession of the right to organise their own union inevitably meant that the Kremlin would be drawn into Poland's developing crisis. Walesa's distinction between 'political' and 'industrial' issues was hardly a conceptual categorisation which would soothe Soviet fears.

The overall objective of the Kremlin from the emergence of Solidarity to the imposition of martial law – to maintain Poland within the Soviet security system – remained unaltered. However, the specific circumstances of the Polish crisis of 1980–1 required the Kremlin to display some degree of flexibility and tactical finesse. It is possible to make a case for the argument that the Kremlin's response to the crisis showed evidence of 'fancy footwork' in the art of deviation control (overt Soviet concern about developments in Poland tended to fluctuate, from phases of quiescence to bouts of hostility). There may be some truth in this, although the relatively low-key Soviet attitude in the early part of the crisis is likely to have had at least as much to do with indecision as with rational calculation.

The Soviets were to employ a battery of tried and tested techniques in order to force the PUWP to arrest the process of decline. Initially it pursued a dual strategy of support for the PUWP and attacks upon 'antisocialist elements'.[13] Later it attacked revisionists and capitulationists within the PUWP. The content of Soviet messages to the Poles in this period included references to: 1) the danger of 'bourgeois restoration' emanating from counterrevolutionary forces operating within and outside the country. Both the leading role of the Polish party, and the position of 'healthy' (pro-Soviet) forces within it, were in jeopardy; 2) Western penetration and aggression: from West German revanchists, American imperialists and a Catholic 'fifth column' directed from the Vatican; 3) attacks on the concept of 'independent' trade unions; 4) assurances of Soviet support in the protection of Poland's 'socialist gains'; 5) assurances of the inviolability of Poland's existing alliance obligations; 6) emphasis upon the international implications of the unrest in Poland; 7) references to the 'indissoluble' nature of the socialist community and the duty of all member states to defend common interests; 8) rejection of 'alternative models of socialism' and attacks upon 'revisionism'; and 9) accusations of 'anti-Sovietism'.

In addition to vitriolic press campaigns, the Soviets also used the following methods of deviation control: 1) military exercise pressure; 2) meetings between the Soviet and Polish leaderships; 3) Warsaw Pact meetings, at which the situation in Poland was discussed; 4) the 'citing ploy': the use of favourable references to hostile comments on developments in the country; 5) letters from Soviet leaders to their Polish counterparts; 6) 'fact finding' tours by Soviet delegations to

Poland; 7) direct contacts between the Soviet and Polish military elites.

The utilisation of these techniques strongly pointed to the possibility of military intervention, which was widely predicted in the West (even though Soviet writers scorned such speculation).[14] It is highly likely that the Soviets had well advanced contingency plans to intervene in order to arrest Solidarity's challenge. However, it is probable that the Kremlin was divided on the question of the precise circumstances in which to use force. The possibility of Soviet military intervention was a major theme of the crisis, although, as de Weydenthal notes, it did not act as a constraining factor in the early phases, possibly because the initial Soviet response was muted and wary.[15] However, this was replaced by increasing diplomatic and military activity of the kind that had preceded the intervention in Czechoslovakia: the precise effect of these threats is hard to judge. The sheer determination for change amongst the Polish people may have caused them to brush aside the danger of intervention. Leading dissident Jacek Kuron openly discussed this danger in the underground paper *Robotnik*.[16] Klasa, the head of the PUWP's department for the media, conceded the possibility of Soviet intervention on 4 December 1980, but also stated that this would be unnecessary if the people united behind the party.[17]

The Soviets were probably initially constrained in their response to the emerging crisis by a host of situational factors: firstly, the crisis erupted suddenly and probably took the Soviets unawares; secondly, the Kremlin may still have had some faith in the ability of the Polish party to reassert its dominance (as it had done in earlier crises); thirdly, they may well have assumed that the prospect of a relatively bloodless surgical intervention in Poland was remote: they had baulked at military intervention in 1956, 1970–1 and 1976, no doubt seeking to avoid a bloody calamity: this restraint took the form of toleration – within limits – of Polish peculiarities: on balance, this had proved to be a successful strategy; fourthly, the nature of Solidarity's challenge – in the form of a mass movement of up to ten million Poles drawn from all spheres of national life – may have appeared less amenable to a swift military solution than either the Hungarian Revolution or the Prague Spring; fifthly, the likely effect of a heavy handed Soviet response upon relations with the West: at the time of the Polish crisis, the Soviets were engaged in nuclear arms limitation talks with the US in Geneva, and were attending the Helsinki Review Conference. Furthermore, following the invasion of Afghanistan and the Iran crisis, the Americans would be likely to take a tough (albeit non-military) stance in the event of a Soviet intervention in Poland. Carter made it abundantly clear that it would have strained Soviet-American relations to breaking point.[18] It would have added weight to fears prevalent in the West (and Peking), that Soviet foreign policy had entered an aggressive phase.

The Soviets had no intention of allowing the Polish party to share power with 'independent' forces within Poland. It was not, as Dubček had discovered, sufficient for the party leadership to express fealty to the Warsaw Pact, or for Solidarity to deny that it had any political ambitions. The seepage of communist party members into Solidarity was a dangerous threat to the principle of democratic centralism. Moreover, the party had its own 'reform movement' to contend with. The conservative wing's grip on key party posts was increasingly attacked. The state of the party was probably a more worrying factor than Solidarity, since if the party had remained united and resolute, it is likely that it would have won back its concessions from Solidarity incrementally.

In July and August 1980, the Soviet response to the Gdansk crisis was muted. It was not until the 19 August that the Soviet media mentioned industrial unrest (referring to 'stoppages' rather than 'strikes') in Poland.[19] The spectre of counterrevolution in Poland was raised by Petrov in *Pravda* on 1 September who asserted that 'anti-socialist' elements in Baltic Coast factories were using economic problems as a pretext for counterrevolutionary activity.[20] The Soviet media did not report the Gdansk agreements for a day but then responded with a vigorous attack upon the strike leadership.[21] On 2 September, *Izvestiia* accused KOR of wishing to change Poland's political system.[22] On 10–11 September, Jagielski had meetings with Brezhnev, Suslov and Rakhmanin in Moscow. On 20 September in *Pravda*, Petrov warned of anti-socialist subversion in Poland and discerned efforts by German revanchists to revise Poland's Western borders.[23] On the 25th in *Pravda*, Alekseev affirmed that in a socialist society, the links between trade unions and the communist party were inextricable.[24] Initially, it was elements of Solidarity and KOR that were specifically condemned: later, it was the movement itself. Solidarity was not mentioned by name in a Soviet newspaper until 29 October.[25] At a meeting between the Soviet party and government leaders and their Polish counterparts on 30 October, Brezhnev assured Kania of continuing support, expressing confidence in Poland's ability to solve its problems.

The hostile tone of *Pravda* again increased in November 1980, in response to the Polish Supreme Court's decision to uphold Solidarity's appeal to register as an independent union.[26] On 8 November, Polish-Soviet military manoeuvres were shown on Polish television at the time when the Court's decision on Solidarity's registration was imminent. In November and December 1980, and in the spring of 1981, the Soviets engaged in military build-ups on the Polish border. The Soviets extensively cited conservative criticisms of Solidarity in the Polish press. For example, on 17 November 1980, *Pravda* published excerpts from *Trybuna Ludu* attacking the concept of independent trade unions.[27] The events in Poland were also subject to fierce criticism in the media of other bloc states (with the harshest diatribes emanating from the GDR and Czechoslovakia).[28] Solidarity's challenge was viewed not as a domestic, industrial struggle, but as a threat to international peace: General Oliwa and several other Polish military leaders expressed concern about the security implications of the strikes.[29]

In December 1980, the prospects of an imminent Soviet invasion seemed high: there were Western reports that the Soviets were finalising their invasion preparations. On 5 December, Kania headed a Polish delegation to a Warsaw Pact meeting in Moscow. The meeting affirmed Poland's status within the WTO and stated that 'Poland was, is and will remain a socialist state, a firm link in the family of socialist countries'.[30] On 25–6 December, the Polish foreign minister, Czyrek, held talks with Gromyko in Moscow. The communiqué issued at the end of the talks reiterated the 'was, is, and will remain a socialist state' formula and stated that relations between the two countries were based 'on the principles of Marxism–Leninism and proletarian internationalism'.[31] During Czyrek's visit, *Pravda* launched an attack upon the notion of independent trade unions and affirmed the principle of democratic centralism.[32] On 28 December *Krasnaia zvezda* affirmed that Poland was a full member of the WTO and could count upon the fraternal support of other members.[33]

Following an upsurge of industrial unrest in January 1981, the Soviet media published other fierce attacks upon events in Poland. This pattern of lull and frenzy continued right up to the imposition of martial law. The Soviets became more hostile with each concession that Solidarity wrung out of the leadership: they also directed fire against the internal threat within the PUWP.[34] *Pravda* on 3 February said that the 'working class expected that the counterrevolution would be resisted'.[35] At the CPSU Congress on 23 February,

Brezhnev assured his audience that socialist gains would be defended.[36]

A summit meeting took place between Brezhnev and Kania on 4 March, which was followed by extensive Soviet media coverage of Polish events.[37] In the communiqué issued after the talks, and on Radio Moscow on 8 March, the 'was, is and will be' formula was replaced by the phrase 'was and will be', which implied that the Soviets would not tolerate Poland's present situation.[38] On 7 March Tass accused the Confederation for an Independent Poland of seeking to destroy the Polish Constitution by force.[39] Joint military exercises, codenamed 'Soiuz 81' were announced for March 1981: although the exercises straddled several Warsaw Pact countries, the Soviet media concentrated on those in Poland.[40] after the 9th plenum of the PUWP in March 1981, the party was explicitly criticised by the Soviet press for insufficient resolve in dealing with the crisis.[41] At the 16th congress of the Czechoslovak communist party in April, Brezhnev, responding to perceived American threats against Cuba, affirmed that 'Cuba, like Poland, is an inseparable part of the community of socialist states'.[42] Suslov and Rusakov, party secretary for bloc relations, visited Warsaw in April shortly after the Polish party plenum in order to convey the Soviet leadership's concern about the deteriorating situation: in May, a delegation comprised of heads of central committee departments of the CPSU undertook a five-day visit to Poland.

On 5 June the Soviet Central Committee communicated its dismay at the deterioration of the situation in Poland in a letter reminiscent of the 1968 'Warsaw letter': it accused Kania and Jaruzelski of failing to deal with the causes of the crisis and condemned Solidarity as 'counterrevolutionary'.[43] Tass on 11 June 1981 declared that a Marxist–Leninist party had no moral and political right to reduce its role 'only to serving the working class. It . . . is duty bound . . . to direct it'.[44] There were also thinly-veiled criticisms and snubs directed at Kania in the Soviet media. Gromyko visited Warsaw on 3 July, a week before the PUWP plenum. On 31 July, in *Pravda*, Kosolapov, editor of *Kommunist*, attacked Western infiltration strategies in Poland.[45] Naval manoeuvres in the Baltic close to Northern Poland took place in August, followed by troop manoeuvres in Belorussia and the Baltic in September. Averchenko in *Pravda* assured Polish workers that they could count on the support of friends and allies.[46] The contents of a second Soviet letter to the Polish leadership sent on 10 September were made public on 19

September 1981: the letter criticised the Polish party and government for defeatism and complained that 'anti-Sovietism' was widespread in Poland.[47]

'Creeping militarisation' of the Polish government had been under-way since February (despite Soviet disdain of 'Bonapartism').[48] Throughout the crisis, the Soviets had sought to prevent the party from making concessions to Solidarity and were also concerned to ensure that 'democratisation' of the party did not go too far. However, they had more faith in the Polish military than the party. The imposition of martial law derived directly from the extent to which the higher echelons of the Polish armed forces were integrated into the Soviet system (and also demonstrated the efficacy of the Soviet investment in the cultivation of military and other key elites within the bloc, so that, as Rupnik notes, 'when a party is torn apart, the security apparatus remains'[49]). After Jaruzelski's appointment to the post of first secretary to the PUWP, Soviet attacks on events in Poland declined markedly, possibly to minimise the extent of overt pressure.[50]

A wave of industrial unrest in the autumn of 1981 prompted a storm of Soviet media criticism: two Solidarity congresses held in September and October had provided a focal point for Soviet anger. As Ploss's study has shown, there were more 'high crisis' headings on the Polish situation in *Pravda* in September and October 1981 than any other time.[51] Petrov in *Pravda* on 13 October called for decisive measures against counterrevolution.[52] Jaruselski refused to counte-nance the demands of Solidarity. A meeting of central committee secretaries of the ruling parties (attended by representatives of the USSR, Bulgaria, Hungary, the GDR, Poland, Romania, Czechoslo-vakia, Vietnam, Laos, Mongolia and Cuba) issued a statement affirming their solidarity with the 'communists and all the patriots of socialist Poland in their struggle against counterrevolution and anarchy'.[53] On 1 December, three conferences of Warsaw Pact states opened: a defence ministers' conference in Moscow, a news agency chiefs' conference in Prague; and a foreign ministers' conference in Bucharest. *Le Monde* said that the conferences were informed of the decision to impose martial law.[54] In the week before the declaration of martial law on 13 December, Kulikov was again in Warsaw (he had made many visits to Poland in the preceding months). The Polish government admitted on 13 December that the Soviets had been informed that martial law was to be imposed.[55] As Porter has argued, although the consultation which preceded martial law could have been informative, cooperative, and coercive, there was a strong bias towards the coercive.[56]

Reactions of ruling and non-ruling parties

The East Germans and Czechs were more forthright in their criticisms and took practical measures to insulate their own countries from the spillover effects of the Polish crisis. In the autumn of 1980, travel and currency exchange restrictions were imposed by the East Germans and Czechoslovaks respectively in an effort to place Poland in quarantine.[57] The principal themes of East German and Czech commentaries were that counterrevolutionary forces were at work in Poland and that the principle of communist rule was under attack: 'healthy' political forces were being driven from office by counterrevolutionaries.[58] In October, Honecker assured his party that Poland would remain a socialist state.[59] Husák drew parallels between the Polish events and the events in Czechoslovakia in 1968, and indicated that the remedy for this problem was the same.[60] The Prague Spring analogy was a common theme in Czech commentaries on events in Poland.[61] Radio Prague claimed that there was Vatican support for 'anti-socialist counterrevolution', in the form of a Catholic fifth column.[62]

The Bulgarians and Hungarians were initially more restrained, but later joined in this litany of execration, especially after the letter sent by the Soviet party leaders to their Polish counterparts in July 1981.[63] Ceauşescu's attitude to the Polish crisis was ambivalent: on the one hand, the notion of independent trade unions was anathema; on the other hand, to sanction interference in Poland's internal affairs would have been glaringly inconsistent with his position on sovereignty. He therefore pursued a dual course, criticising the Polish party for its errors and attacking the independent union concept, but opposing intervention.[64] The Yugoslavs supported the reform process and opposed intervention. Yugoslav press comment was distinguished by its reflective, analytical quality: the grievances of Poles were acknowledged as legitimate and the full text of the Gdansk agreement was published in *Vjesnik* on 6 September.[65] The Chinese were somewhat ambivalent, welcoming developments which weakened the Soviet Union's hegemony in Eastern Europe, but critical of the concept of independent unions.[66]

The non-ruling parties in Europe took a keen interest in developments in Poland. The Italian party was particularly strident in its support of the reform process and voiced strong opposition to intervention. This led to an open quarrel between the PCI and the Soviets, centring on the relevance of the Soviet model for other countries. In other words, it intensified the debate about the relative merits of 'Eurocommunism' and 'real socialism', which had been simmering since the mid-1970s.[67] Ponomarev launched a fierce attack upon the concept of the 'new internationalism' (the Eurocommunist alternative to 'proletarian internationalism') in *Kommunist* in May 1981.[68] Several other Western parties supported the reform movement.[69]

Western responses

Strongly influenced by National Security Advisor Brzezinski, the Carter administration pursued a policy of 'differentiation' in Eastern Europe, favouring regimes which were more independent of Moscow and more 'liberal' and criticising those with poor human rights records, with the aim of advancing 'the larger goal of gradually transforming the Soviet bloc into a more pluralistic and diversified entity'.[70] Brzezinski argued that 'the consolidation of a freer system in Poland would significantly affect the East-West balance and some felt that it might create preconditions for the fading of the post WW2 division of Europe'.[71] Carter saw Poland as the most important East European country: he increased commodity credits and loans to Poland and established contacts with both governmental and non-governmental groups.[72]

Brzezinski and Carter were determined to avoid the 'mistakes' of the Johnson administration in 1968.[73] On 25 August 1980, Carter sent letters to Thatcher, Giscard, Schmidt and the Pope concerning retaliatory action in the event of Soviet intervention. In November, the Chairman of the US Senate's Foreign Relations Committee, Senator Percy, had warned the Soviets against intervention.[74] In December, there were many Western press reports about Soviet troop movements on Poland's borders with the Soviet Union and East Germany. On 2 December, East Germany closed its borders with Poland for foreign military attachés. Carter sent a message to Brezhnev on 3 December, outlining the consequences of an invasion on relations between East and West.[75] On 5 December information reached Brzezinski that Soviet troops were poised to attack.[76] Carter issued a public statement on Poland on 6 December and also contacted other governments. The aim according to Brzezinski was to deprive the Soviets of surprise, to encourage Polish resistance, to calm the situation by making it clear that an intervention was imminent and to deter the Soviets through an intensification of international pressure.[77] On 12 December, the NATO council also warned the Soviets against intervention, provoking a stern rebuke from Petrov in *Pravda* on 18 December.

The imposition of martial law

The Soviets expressed their approval of the clampdown, but also sought to give the impression that they had no hand in it. A statement on Moscow Radio on 14 December stated that, in advancing an anti-socialist counterrevolutionary programme, Solidarity created a direct threat to Poland's fulfilment of its alliance commitments under the Warsaw Treaty that affected the security of all signatories.[78] Although the means of removing a dire threat to communist rule had been different, this statement would not have been out of place as a justification of the invasion of Czechoslovakia. However, the strategy of intervention by proxy nevertheless had costs for the Soviet Union: it provoked a fierce reaction from the West and led to US sanctions. Gromyko informed the American Ambassador that the US should stop interfering in the internal affairs of the sovereign state of Poland.[79]

The Polish case indicates the 'situational' character of the doctrine, in that the language in which its central tenets are couched is sufficiently vague for it to be applied flexibly, and to be adapted to suit the requirements of new situations. The outcome of the Polish crisis also demonstrated the efficacy of flexible Soviet control strategies: the threat from Solidarity, which loomed so large during the crisis, was effectively removed and Poland remained an integral – albeit an unstable – part of the Soviet system. The intimidatory function of the Brezhnev Doctrine had kept the issue of Poland's sovereignty and its relationship with the Soviet Union off the political agenda during the crisis. Nevertheless, the Polish challenge constituted a grave threat to the Soviet Union's international aspirations: a main plank of the optimistic Soviet assessments of the correlation of forces in the late 1970s was the supposed contrast between the incohesion and decay of the capitalist camp and the growing unity and strength of the socialist camp. Solidarity's challenge demonstrated that there were 'weak links' at the core of the socialist community. Moreover, although the Soviets repeatedly emphasised that peaceful coexistence meant an intensification of the ideological struggle, the Polish crisis exposed the bankruptcy of Marxist–Leninist ideology in a key socialist state. It also constituted a major failure for the Soviet duplicative policy, in that a party (the principal pillar of Soviet bloc hegemony) had virtually collapsed. Soviet setbacks in Afghanistan, the Polish challenge, a more resolute US approach to perceived Soviet expansionism and the Soviet desire for detente, caused the assertive, 'upswing' phase of Soviet foreign policy to peak in the early 1980s.

SOVIET ANALYSES OF THE CAUSES OF THE POLISH CRISIS: 'DEFORMATIONS OF SOCIALISM'?

The Soviets could not admit that the Polish crisis had been caused by systemic failures, and therefore their official explanations centred on 'subjective' factors – in particular, upon the errors and mistakes of the PUWP leadership and the activities of the internal and external enemies of Polish socialism.[80] In December 1983, Kuznetsov in *Voprosy filosofii* attacked the Director of the Polish party's Marxism-Leninism Institute, Jerzy Wiatr, for attributing Poland's recurring crises to fundamental systemic weaknesses, and in particular to the Soviet model on which Polish socialism was based.[81] According to Kuznetsov, Wiatr's alternative Polish model was derived from the experience of Poland's prewar capitalist past: he accused him of denying the leading role of the Polish communist party.[82] In his view, the crisis had been caused by situational factors deriving from Poland's lower phase of development. At a conference in Prague in 1982, Kosolapov also blamed the crisis upon situational factors (the large private agricultural sector, consumerism and economic links with the West) and called for an intensification of class struggle in Poland.[83]

However, the Polish crisis stimulated a lively debate between reformist and conservative Soviet commentators:[84] Butenko, of the Institute of Economics of the World Socialist System, acknowledged that events in Poland held lessons for other socialist countries – it was an example of 'a deformation of socialism' (along with the crises in Hungary and Czechoslovakia in 1956 and 1968, and Maoism), in that the party had become separated from the masses and a rift had developed between the managers and the managed.[85] 'Deformations' could be attributed to either excessive centralisation ('bureaucratism') or excessive decentralisation. He drew the analogy with the Kronstadt revolt in Russia in 1921, which in his view had resulted from errors of the party in failing to take sufficient account of the interests of the masses: fortunately, however, Lenin adopted the correct remedial measures by introducing the new economic policy.[86] Butenko's Kronstadt analogy is another example of the Soviet assumption that other socialist states are at a lower stage of development than the USSR and that crises are caused by failure to heed Soviet lessons. Butenko's Kronstadt analogy was developed by Ambartsumov (also of the IEWSS institute and an advocate of economic reform) in *Voprosy istorii* two years later.[87] In an analysis of the major crises within socialist states, he concentrated on internal causes – incorrect policies and bureaucratic dysfunctions – rather than the official rationale of external subversion. Like Butenko, he advocated a relaxation of bureaucracy and decentralisation.[88] Ambartsumov's article drew fire from orthodox theorists who argued that Poland was at a much lower stage of development than the USSR (i.e. was still in the phase of transition from capitalism to socialism) and had been susceptible to imperialist penetration: this was another way of saying that the Polish débâcle could not happen in the Soviet Union. The editorial board of *Voprosy istorii* repudiated the 'Kronstadt analogy' in December 1984.[89]

A related controversy stimulated by the Polish crisis was the issue of 'contradictions within socialism'. According to Soviet Marxist-Leninist orthodoxy, 'antagonistic contradictions' exist only between classes with different interests: analyses of 'capitalist contradictions' have constituted the core of Soviet theories of capitalist crisis in various periods. In socialist societies, contradictions are 'nonantagonistic' and can be solved through cooperation. However, in this period, the philosopher Fedoseev, Butenko and Semenov (editor of *Voprosi filosofii*) acknowledged the possibility of antagonistic contradictions within socialist societies. Butenko argued that the essential contradiction of socialism was between the growing productive forces and the real system of socialist production. He pointed to the Polish crisis as an example of the serious consequences of ignoring contradictions.[90] Semenov argued that the basic contradictions were between productive forces and production relations, between industry and agriculture and between production and management.[91] He also conceded that under certain circumstances, non-antagonistic contradictions could be transmuted into antagonistic contradictions, where the situation was exploited by counterrevolutionary forces. A decisive role, in his view, was played by subjective factors, in particular by the leading role of the communist party. He denied that this situation could arise in conditions of developed socialism (i.e. in the Soviet Union).[92] The orthodoxy that there could be no antagonistic contradictions under socialism was reiterated by Kosolapov in *Pravda* in 1983.[93] In 1984, Butenko questioned the assumption that contradictions could be attributed solely to 'residual' antagonisms or 'vestiges of capitalism'. In his view, 'objective' causes also exist: thus references to 'residual social antagonisms should not be used to hide problems which needed to be addressed': if rulers lost links with the ruled, there was a possibility of a 'backward evolution'.[94] Semenov acknowledged the possibility of certain antagonistic contradictions developing as a result of internal and external counterrevolutionary forces (even strata within the working class could be antisocialist).[95]

These debates were significant for several reasons: they were manifestations of an acknowledgement by some senior Soviet theoreticians of serious weaknesses within the socialist world system: the triumphalist rhetoric of the mid-1970s was being replaced by sober, and in some cases, more realistic and sophisticated, assessments of the causes of economic stagnation and recurring crises within socialist societies; they also showed that, to some scholars at least, the orthodox tenets of Marxism–Leninism were inadequate to explain the causes of these weaknesses. The fact that there was a debate at all on an article of faith such as 'contradictions within socialism' constituted a retreat from ideology (although not its abandonment, since they agreed, for example, that socialist contradictions differed from contradictions within the capitalist world). The Polish crisis demonstrated the dangers of the policy of 'tight coupling': despite the official assumption that the Soviet Union, as a developed socialist society, was more advanced than other socialist states, the Polish crisis was a stimulus to the processes of self-examination and ideological revision within the Soviet system itself.[96]

11 Superpower Doctrines of Intervention: Comparisons and Contrasts

THE MONROE AND BREZHNEV DOCTRINES COMPARED

We have noted that the emergence of the Brezhnev Doctrine in 1968 stimulated a search by Western scholars for parallels and historical comparisons. Comparisons with the Monroe Doctrine (or rather its modern variants) positively invited themselves, for a multitude of reasons:[1] firstly, both the Monroe and Brezhnev Doctrines are explained in terms of ideological motivations and seek to exclude alien systems from protected zones (European monarchism and colonialism in the original version, and Marxism–Leninism in contemporary variants, of the Monroe Doctrine; capitalism and imperialism in the case of the Brezhnev Doctrine); secondly, both are, purportedly, defensive, anti-interventionist doctrines, formulated to prevent other powers from interfering in the internal affairs of weaker states; thirdly, they both derive from the geopolitics of regions (even though the Brezhnev Doctrine is unlimited in scope, it was widely thought until December 1979 to apply in practice exclusively to the Soviet bloc); fourthly, although both the United States and the Soviet Union formally repudiate 'spheres of interest', they have nevertheless claimed special roles within the regions of Latin America and Eastern Europe respectively; fifthly, both the Monroe and Brezhnev Doctrines are couched not in terms of self-interest, but rather in the altruistic vocabulary of duty and responsibility. As Connell-Smith has argued, the exclusion of extra-continental powers has been justified by the US in terms of its self-image as a 'benevolent paramount power in the Americas';[2] sixthly, both hinge upon the assumption that the protector power is a special type of state, endowed with a 'manifest destiny' or a special role in the 'world revolutionary process' (Duroselle refers to 'American moralism' as 'the essence of American tradition in foreign policy'[3]); seventhly, they both assume an essential harmony of interests between protector and ward (reflected in solidarist doctrines of 'pan-americanism' and 'socialist internationalism' respectively): in both cases, relations between the protector power and the other states in the region have been presented as a new, superior, type of relations; eighthly, in neither case has the hegemonial power's assumption of regional guardianship, or its doctrine of harmony of interests, been universally accepted by the 'protected' states.

Ninth, the doctrines have both been used to justify interventions by the hegemonial power within the protected zone: both powers have engaged in counterrevolutionary interventions, aimed at removing unacceptable governments; tenth, in both cases, conspiracy theories (hinging on the assumption of communist or imperialist subversion) have been employed to justify preemptive actions within the protected zone; eleventh, both the Monroe and Brezhnev Doctrines have played an important role in the propaganda war between the two superpowers: the US and the USSR have held up each other's doctrine to the world as proof of their rival's contempt for the sovereignties of smaller states (both superpowers proclaim respect for sovereignty as a cardinal principle of their foreign policy); twelfth, neither doctrine has been incorporated into international law – indeed, both are widely regarded as being incompatible with international legal principles.

The US has used a wide range of overt and covert interventionary techniques in Central America and the Caribbean in the postwar era: economic pressure: e.g. Cuba, Chile, Nicaragua and Panama; proxy interventions: Cuba (1962) and Nicaragua from 1983; CIA involvement in a coup: Chile (1973); and direct intervention: Guatemala (1954), Dominican Republic (1965) and Grenada (1983); Washington has sought both to change governments (Cuba, Grenada, Nicaragua, Panama) and to prevent their fall (El Salvador). Similarly, it has advanced several justifications for its actions, including invitations from the government of the 'target' state; protection of US nationals; self-defence; and refusal to tolerate the establishment or continuation of a communist regime. Although the United States has a long history of interventions in the region, since its rise to superpower status it has been concerned to prove that its interventions are fully compatible with international law (in keeping with its superpower self-image as a champion of sovereignty, its 'moral competition' with the USSR and its recognition of Third World sensitivities).

Striking parallels have been observed between US interventions in

Central America and the Caribbean basin and Soviet interventions in Eastern Europe. Franck and Weisband, for example, have argued that American interventions in Guatemala, Cuba and the Dominican Republic and the Soviet intervention in Czechoslovakia are evidence of a 'reciprocal two-ghetto system' for Central America and Eastern Europe, in which the superpowers accept each other's right to intervene within their respective spheres, and in which they justify their interventions (and condemn the interventions of the other) in very similar terms.[4] Kaufman refers to this as a form of 'bipolar legitimation'.[5] Parallels between the verbal behaviour of the Soviet Union and the US in the Dominican and Czechoslovak crises were, according to Franck and Weisband, 'as symmetrical as a classical ballet, with the two powers in the second movement neatly changing roles'. They have characterised this reversal of roles as an 'echo phenomenon' in which American justifications are countered by Soviet criticism of violations of international law and of the UN Charter.[6] In both regions, the action of the other superpower has been largely limited to verbal condemnation and both have shown a willingness to observe the 'rules of the game' and engage in 'tacit understandings'.[7] Franck and Weisband argue that the verbal strategies of the superpowers in the Dominican and Czechoslovakian episodes have 'transformational impacts' on the international system,[8] in that the superpowers mimic each other's rhetoric: put bluntly, their argument is that the American rationale for its intervention in the Dominican Republic set a bad example which the Soviets followed in 1968 (this argument ignores the fact that the Brezhnev Doctrine had already been developed in relation to Hungary). Following their interventions, both superpowers have sought to limit the role of the United Nations and 'hide' behind regional organisations in which they play a dominant role. Connell-Smith sees similarities between US relations with Latin America (especially the Caribbean) and the Soviet system in Eastern Europe in that both hegemons seek to prevent the breakaway of a *second* satellite (Yugoslavia and Cuba being the original defectors[9]).

The comparison between the Monroe and Brezhnev Doctrines has been rejected by several American scholars. Moore sees the two doctrines as being 'poles apart'[10] and elsewhere has dismissed these comparisons as having the logic of the 'upside down world of the mad hatter'.[11] Moore argues that no American statesman has invoked the Monroe Doctrine as a legal justification for contemporary US policy in Central America. Indeed, he argues, it has been defunct as a legal or political doctrine since Franklin Roosevelt proclaimed the 'good neighbour' policy in the 1930s.[12] In addition, he argues that the original Monroe Doctrine sought to affirm the principles of sovereignty and self-determination and therefore is fully compatible with the UN Charter.[13] Glazer sees fundamental differences between the two doctrines, in that the Monroe Doctrine was concerned with self defence against aggression by European powers and said nothing about self defence against perceived threats emanating from the internal structures or policies of the Latin American states.[14] This is of course true of the original doctrine, but not of some of its modern variants. Central to these comparisons is the perceived incongruity between stated policy and actual behaviour: between superpower commitment to the norms of non-intervention and the record of superpower disregard for the sovereignties of smaller states. The 'self images' of the superpowers require the Kremlin and Washington to insist that there are qualitative differences between, say, Soviet actions in Czechoslovakia and US actions in Grenada. However, the similarities between the behaviour of the superpowers in their respective spheres deserve further investigation.

Spheres of interest

We have noted that the term embraces a wide spectrum of meanings, ranging from influence to annexation. It normally refers to geographical regions, although Romanian scholars in the 1970s extended the concept to embrace global 'spheres of interest' by states seeking world hegemony.[15] In order to get to grips with these putative symmetries in superpower behaviour, it seems necessary to explore the following issues:

1. the nature and form of the mutual acceptance of spheres of interest by the superpowers: for example, the extent to which the 'rules of the game' are tacit or explicit;
2. the types of asymmetric relationship which exist within each sphere and the instruments used by the regional hegemon to enforce its dominance;
3. the extent to which the 'ground rules' governing state behaviour within the sphere are understood and accepted by the subordinate states;
4. the verbal strategies of superpowers in relation to their respective spheres;

5. boundary maintenance: reactions to perceived probes and intrusions by one power into its rival's sphere of interest.

The Monroe, Johnson and Reagan Doctrines

The Monroe Doctrine dates from a presidential address to Congress in 1823, in which Monroe argued that intrusions into any portion of the hemisphere were 'dangerous to our peace and safety'.[16] The specific threat lay in the aim of the European powers to reconquer the Spanish colonies in Latin America. It had, therefore, in part an ideological motivation (to prevent the intrusion of alien powers and doctrines). It also rested on the assumption that the US had a responsibility to keep out imperialistic European powers because of its superior strength (even though at the time the US lacked the power to perform its protector role and Britain and France continued to intervene). The doctrine was accepted by Britain and later received recognition in the League of Nations Covenant.

Although extra-continental intervention was viewed as a threat to US interests, the doctrine was also based on the explicit assumption of hemispheric solidarity. The doctrine was at first welcomed in Latin America, because it was viewed as beneficial to the interests of smaller powers, protecting them from encroachments by European imperialism. As a doctrine of non-intervention it was widely supported and even the Soviets have regarded the early doctrine as progressive.[17] However, a modern Western critic has argued that 'the Monroe Doctrine of 1823 was no less one-sided and self-interested than its outgrowth, the modern Monroe Doctrine, with the qualification that the latter is in conflict with the sovereignty and self-respect of the Latin Americas'.[18] Therefore, the doctrine could not be justified on the grounds of an inherent and perpetual harmony of interests, but only on the basis of temporary coincidences of national interest, deriving from perception of a common external threat.

It is the manner in which the doctrine has been interpreted and applied by Monroe's successors which has made it unpopular in Latin America, where it has been widely viewed as a doctrine justifying US intervention in the region in the interests of US security. According to Quantanilla, 'instead of meaning America is not for Europe, it (now) means America is for the US'.[19] Thus it has frequently been argued that there are two Monroe Doctrines, the one formulated by Monroe, and the distorted doctrine of the 'corollaries'. The corollaries added by Roosevelt, Grant, Olney[20] and others transmuted the Monroe formula into an offensive doctrine, capable of justifying American intervention in the hemisphere, even when no direct or tangible 'foreign threat' was present. The 'corollaries' altered the original doctrine in two ways: firstly, they introduced the notion of pre-emptive action, taken in order to forestall foreign intervention (it is probable that all foreign interventions could be justified in some sense, by reference to the need for a pre-emptive strike); secondly, they broadened the doctrine to embrace intra-hemispherical threats – dangers to American security emanating from within the 'protected' states.[21]

From the enunciation of the doctrine to the Spanish-American war, US interventions tended to derive from 'on the spot' decisions by naval commanders rather than from coherent government policy. However, between 1900 and 1914, US policy became less idiosyncratic, leading to interventions and the establishment of protectorates in several Latin American states between 1895 and 1915. There were US interventions in Cuba in 1906–9 and 1917; Nicaragua was occupied in 1909 and 1912; Haiti and the Dominican republic were subject to American military rule in 1915 and 1916. US intervention took the form of economic 'dollar' diplomacy as well as military action.[22] The most well known of the amendments to the Monroe Doctrine was the Theodore Roosevelt corollary, which justified intervention on the grounds of protection of US interests or when 'chronic wrong doing or . . . a general loosening of the ties of civilised society may in America as elsewhere, ultimately require intervention by some civilised nation'.[23] Not only did the corollary imply an inherent moral and ideological superiority over 'extra continental' powers; it also asssumed a racial and cultural superiority over the protected states. The Roosevelt corollary transformed a doctrine of non-intervention into one of intervention, by giving to the US a regional policing role. The Roosevelt corollary required the Latin American countries to develop political systems acceptable to the United States and therefore bears resemblance to the Brezhnev Doctrine, which also assumes the right of the hegemonial power to regulate the internal affairs of 'protected' states. It has been argued that the Roosevelt corollary has been an anachronism since the 'Good Neighbour' policy of the mid-1930s: the Roosevelt corollary was officially renounced in the Clark memorandum of 1928. US ratifications of the UN and OAS Charters also constituted implicit refutations of the corollary[24] (although, by the same token, the

USSR is also a signatory to the UN Charter and to many treaties which proclaim respect for sovereignty).

Since the formulation of the Monroe Doctrine, the US has risen to superpower status, Latin America has suffered chronic regime instability and the region has become heavily dependent upon the US. In addition, the global conflict between the superpowers has meant that a stronger ideological dimension had been injected into Washington's protector role, so that it is now justified in terms of keeping the region free of communism.[25] The term 'Monroe Doctrine' is not officially used by contemporary American governments. However, the American policy analyst Ronfeldt has recently proposed that the doctrine be 'modernised', by involving other interested powers in the Caribbean basin (a form of 'collective hegemony') and by invoking it not against all 'revolutionary' regimes, but only those involved in 'extra-hemispheric entanglements' – i.e. those which present tangible and direct threats to the security of neighbouring states.[26]

Soviet Views of the Monroe Doctrine

References to the Monroe Doctrine have figured prominently in postwar Soviet expositions of American imperialism. In the interwar era, the Soviets showed little interest in the doctrine, (or indeed in Latin America).[27] However, in the post-Stalin period, the Soviets have shown greater attention to the region. The modern Soviet view of the Monroe Doctrine is that it now serves the interests of the American monopolies and underpins the American drive for world hegemony.[28] The doctrine is said by Soviet analyses to have undergone a transformation, from being a 'progressive' doctrine of non-intervention to its present role as a rationale for US global aggression: as Korovin argued in 1960 'the original motto of the doctrine – America for the Americans' has been turned into 'America (and the whole world!) for the USA'.[29] Korovin saw in American policy 'a systematic disregard for sovereignty bordering on international brigandage'. He noted that the doctrine was mentioned in the League Covenant but not in the UN Charter, or the OAS Charter. However, the 'mildewed Monroe Doctrine' was now a favourite screen for modern US interventionist doctrines, such as the Dulles-Eisenhower Doctrine, which justified US intervention in the Middle East. He included financial, diplomatic and military interference in this category.[30] Gonionsky argues that even in its early days, it was only 'superficially defensive' because European intrusion was scarcely feasible. It was an 'unburied corpse', an instrument of oppression, plunder and enslavement of Latin Americans, through military interventions, coups d'état and other means.[31] For Modzhorian, it is an example of American expansion and hegemony, of 'plunder and brigandage' deriving from the predatory nature of capitalism and the struggle for markets between capitalist states for spheres of interest and domination.[32] Thus it is now a theoretical substantiation of the USA's expansionist policy in Latin America.[33] For Khachaturov, 'pan-American solidarity is solidarity between the oppressor and the oppressed'.[34] The Monroe Doctrine has served three principal aims in Soviet propaganda: firstly, to exacerbate anti-American sentiments in a zone crucial to US security; secondly, to underscore Soviet theories concerning the aggressive nature of American foreign policy; thirdly, to expose American hypocrisy concerning respect for sovereignty and human rights.

POSTWAR US INTERVENTIONS IN LATIN AMERICA AND THE CARIBBEAN

The aim of this section is to identify the pattern of US intervention in the postwar period, in order to provide a basis for comparison between Soviet and US interventionary doctrines in their respective spheres. Scott has described the main features of the US 'style' of intervention as a tendency to associate leftist movements with communist threats; frequent resort to covert operations; and use of the 'invitation' rationale.[35]

Guatemala (1954)
The intervention in Guatamala derived from the motive to remove an unacceptable regime, the 'proto-communist' system of Jacobo Arbenz Guzman. The Arbenz government had expropriated unused lands belonging to the United Fruit company of Boston. Although the regime denied American claims that it was an 'outpost of Soviet Communism', it had communist support and had developed links with the Soviets (an arms shipment had arrived from Czechoslovakia in May). The US found support for intervention from some other OAS states, who regarded Guatemala's land expropriation measures and external policies as evidence that the regime was spearheading a communist drive in the region. The 9th Conference of the OAS in

Caracas in March 1954, denounced the 'interventionist tendency' of international communism, which was said to be incompatible with American freedom, and resolved to protect themselves against this threat. US intervention took the form of bombing raids and the use of ground forces (comprised of US Marines and Guatemalans opposed to the regime). The intervention was explained as a counter-intervention against a communist threat to the peace of the region. The Soviets sought to refer the matter to the UN Security Council, but the US rejected this request, preferring to confine it to the OAS.

The Cuban revolution

The uprising which brought Castro to power was not a socialist revolution in the Soviet Marxist sense. Nevertheless, the fact that the regime was anti-American and had developed close relations with the Soviet Union raised the possibility of American intervention. Although Kennedy had pledged during his election campaign not to use US forces to overthrow Castro, he nevertheless resolved to remove him by other means. This took the form of an abortive 'proxy intervention' undertaken by anti-Castro exiles. The attempt failed badly, and Castro, no doubt seeking to gain protection from the Soviets, declared himself a 'Marxist-Leninist'. At a meeting of the consultative organ of the OAS at Punta de la Este in January 1962, it was agreed that 'the adherence of any member of the OAS to Marxism-Leninism is incompatible with the inter-American system and the alignment of such a government with the communist bloc breaches the security and solidarity of the Hemisphere'.[36] The Cuban blockade of 1962 was justified on grounds of self-defence against an aggressive power, supported by external powers (principally the Soviet Union), which constituted a threat to US security interests. The US also argued that Cuba belonged to the American bloc of states and therefore was subject to its jurisdiction.

The Dominican Republic

In 1963, there was a successful military coup against the leftist Bosch government elected the previous year. Two years later, a civil war broke out between pro- and anti-Bosch factions. The intervention was undertaken by an 'Inter-American Force' (comprised largely of

US Marines). It was at first justified by President Johnson and by the American Ambassador on humanitarian grounds – i.e. that US citizens had to be rescued and that it was in compliance with a request of the Dominican Republic to help restore law and order.[37] Johnson said it was law enforcement and military officials who made the request, although this is disputed. Shortly afterwards, the US administration developed an ideological justification, in terms of a responsibility to preserve democracy against the threat of tyranny.[38] The Johnson doctrine may have emerged as a result of the disclosure that the 'invitation' was made not by the Dominican government *per se* but by a faction within it, after this faction had failed to restore order. Johnson declared: 'the American nations cannot, should not and will not permit the establishment of another communist government in the Western hemisphere'.[39] This doctrine received Congressional ratification in the Selden Resolution, which affirmed the right of the US to prevent the establishment of communist regimes in the region: the leaders of the Dominican revolution denied that they were communist, even though a small communist faction was active in the revolution.

The US government sought to minimise the international repercussions of the intervention by justifying its actions on several grounds: that it derived from an invitation from the government; that it was undertaken to protect US nationals; that the threat to order emanating from the Republic was recognised by other states, which contributed to the 'Inter-American Force'; and that any attempt to establish a government deemed incompatible with the principle of the American system could be brought down. The 'protection of US nationals' argument was subjected to critical scrutiny in the American press. The OAS supported the intervention on humanitarian grounds, but refused to endorse the 'Johnson Doctrine': several Latin American states condemned the intervention as a contravention of the OAS Charter. The Soviets branded it as a blatant violation of the UN Charter. However, they observed the 'rules of the game' and limited their response to verbal condemnations. Nevertheless, the Dominican intervention has figured prominently in Soviet demonologies of US aggression.[40]

Chile

Allende was elected to president of Chile in 1970, as head of a popular front government. Although Allende described himself as a socialist, Kissinger viewed the Allende regime as proto-communist, anti-American and a danger to neighbouring states.[41] Nixon also regarded Allende as a crypto-communist and applied various forms of economic pressure against Chile.[42] Allende's ambitious nationalisation programme, his revolutionary rhetoric and contacts with Cuba and the Soviet Union exacerbated US fears. By 1973, the country was racked by industrial unrest and rampant inflation and appeared on the verge of civil war. Allende declared a state of emergency in May, but was overthrown by Pinochet in September. Kissinger refers to the widespread assumption of US involvement in the coup as a 'testament to the power of political mythology'.[43] Kissinger has argued that Chile was given low priority by the US administration and that Allende was toppled by internal forces. However, he saw him as a 'geo-political challenge' and admits that the Nixon administration explored the possibility of a military coup in order to prevent Allende's accession to the presidency.[44] Although the Soviet response to the coup was mild, the Chile episode provided a 'never again' rationale for Soviet intervention in Afghanistan. The Soviets blame the Allende government for failing to heed the 'general laws' of revolution: far from coming to Allende's aid, at the 25th congress of the CPSU it was argued that the 'Chilean tragedy [was] a forceful reminder that a revolution must know how to defend itself'.[45]

The intervention in Grenada

The US invasion of Grenada in October 1983 followed an internal struggle within the communist government of the country (the 'New Jewel Movement' which had seized power in 1979). Prime Minister Bishop was murdered by the more extreme communist faction led by Coard.[46] Grenada was a 'socialist-oriented' country rather than a fully-fledged socialist state in Soviet terminology.[47] At the time of the invasion, Grenada was near to becoming part of the world socialist system. There were Cuban advisers in all government departments in 1983 and Coard was committed to a policy of 'communist restructuring'. The Soviet Union has been wary of entering into formalised commitments with states in the region. Even pro-Soviet communist regimes outside the Warsaw Pact (Cuba, Vietnam, Laos and North Korea) are not linked to the USSR by military treaty. However, it should be remembered that a country of socialist orientation had been invaded by the Soviet Union in 1979, in order to protect its 'socialist gains' (Grenada supported the Soviet invasion of Afghanistan). There had also been a military build-up within the country: in March 1983 Reagan declared Grenada to be a threat to US security.[48]

The turmoil within the communist ranks in Grenada provided the opportunity for action. On 21 October 1983, a meeting of the Organisation of East Caribbean states requested the UK, the US, Trinidad, Jamaica and Barbados to participate in an invasion (the UK declined). A US force and token contingents from several Caribbean states invaded Grenada and gained control against stiff opposition from mainly Cuban troops. The intervention was justified by the US on several grounds: humanitarian (to protect the lives of US nationals); restoration of order (where authority had broken down); and legitimate self defence against a threat to US security interests posed by the communist Grenadian regime. The Johnson Doctrine argument appeared to take second place behind the others, although Washington argued that Bishop and his colleagues sought to use the country as a launching pad for Soviet expansion in the region.[49] Little use was made by the US of a request from the Grenadian Governor-General.

It has been argued by Moore that the Grenada intervention was a lawful regional peacekeeping action undertaken in accordance with the UN Charter and under the aegis of the OECS treaty.[50] He denies that it was analogous to the Brezhnev Doctrine, because it followed a request from the Governor-General (a claim doubted by Doswald-Beck in her study of justifications for intervention[51]) and was undertaken at the behest of several states. In any case, he argues, the US government had tolerated a Marxist regime in Grenada for some time. He discerns several differences between the Brezhnev Doctrine and US actions in Grenada, viz.:[52]

a. the Brezhnev Doctrine is not based on a request from constitutional authorities (following a breakdown in authority);
b. or on the protection of nationals;
c. the Brezhnev Doctrine is antithetical to genuine self-determination;
d. the Soviet doctrine seeks to suppress human rights and is contrary to the UN Charter;
e. it has never been welcomed anywhere it has been applied (the Soviet invasion of Afghanistan was opposed by the majority of the population).

This positive view of the Grenadian intervention was not shared by all American jurists. In the same journal, nine professors of law referred to the Grenadian episode as 'international lawlessness'[53] and questioned whether chronic disorder in a neighbouring state permitted unilateral intervention. Article 8 of the OECS charter states that external aggression is the *casus foederis*. Article 18 of the OAS charter prohibits interference in the internal affairs of other signatory states. They likened the intervention to Roosevelt's 'big stick' policy of the early twentieth century.[54] Joyner has argued that 'it appears to have been a case of unilateral intervention by the US, expressly approved in advance by neighbouring island states and undertaken without due regard for the territorial sovereignty or political independence of Grenada'.[55] Similar discussions about the legality of Soviet 'fraternal aid' have yet to take place in Soviet academic journals.

The Soviets responded with a battery of condemnatory rhetoric, but made no attempt to come to Grenada's aid. The 'irreversibility of socialism' notion which is the cornerstone of the Brezhnev Doctrine is armatured to power considerations and estimates of risk. The support given to Grenada prior to the intervention was an example of a Soviet 'probe' into an American sphere and has been interpreted as a sign of boldness on the part of the Soviets. However despite increasing Soviet confidence and global military strength, the Grenada episode demonstrated that the Kremlin accepted the 'rules of the game' with regard to the US sphere of interest.

El Salvador and Nicaragua

Both the Carter and Reagan administrations supplied arms to governments in El Salvador, to aid the struggle against a leftist guerrilla movement. Carter suspended military aid to the government on the grounds that it had violated human rights. Reagan resumed this aid: the democratic elections of 1982 have provided Washington with a rejoinder to the Soviet charge that it is propping up an unpopular right-wing 'puppet' regime. Reagan's support for the 'contra' guerrillas in Nicaragua has also been categorised as a modern application of the Monroe Doctrine, in that it has been viewed as an attempt by the US to remove an unacceptable government by armed force. Although some non-communists were included in the first Sandinista government, the commandantes who led the revolution against Somoza have a strong leftist orientation. The Sandinista government has been viewed by the US as a thorn in its side since it came to power in 1979. US support for the 'contras' has been justified on several grounds: self-defence against Sandinista aggression (against El Salvador and other neighbouring states); humanitarian; and the Johnson doctrine.[56] However, the refusal of Congress to allow direct or indirect military aid to the contra rebels imposed severe limitations upon Reagan's ability to provide effective support to the opponents of the regime. The description of Reagan's policy towards Nicaragua as a kind of reverse 'Brezhnev Doctrine' is strongly criticised by Moore, who has argued that American (and 'contra') policy has been geared to changing the domestic and foreign policies of the Sandinistas rather than bringing the government down.[57] Reagan has spoken publicly in these terms. But the 'Irangate' scandal showed that at least part of the US administration was seeking the overthrow of the Sandinistas in breach of congressional decisions. Moore also argues that legal restraints govern US policy in Central America (the Boland amendment prohibits use of funds to aid attempts to overthrow the Nicaraguan government).[58] However, this argument requires qualification in the light of the 'Irangate' disclosures.

SUPERPOWER INTERVENTIONS: THE 'RULES OF THE GAME'

In relation to intervention by the superpowers, we can distinguish between:

I. intra-bloc interventions – i.e. interventions within the superpowers' spheres of interest;

II. interventions outside recognised spheres of interest – e.g. the US in the Middle East, the Soviet Union and Cuba in Angola or the horn of Africa;

III. intrusions into the opposing superpower's sphere.

I. Intra-bloc interventions

The similarities and differences between the interventionary behaviour of superpowers within their regional subsystems can be summarised as follows:

Ia. Similarities

1. The intervening power will stress the legality of its actions: in particular, the intervention will be initially justified in terms of an invitation from the government of the target state. Other arguments (e.g. treaty obligations, self-defence, humanitarian) which justify the intervention in terms which accord with international law are also likely to be employed;
2. both superpowers assume special duties and roles to protect smaller states within their zone from falling under the sway of the other;
3. these duties are justified on the grounds of the superpowers' might and special responsibilities and are couched in terms of altruism rather than of self-interest;
4. the intervention will also be explained in ideological terms. The opposing ideology is presented as inherently aggressive and expansionist (evidence will be produced to prove internal and external subversion);
5. it will be presented as a defensive measure and therefore the intervening power will describe the action as aimed at restoring or preserving the status quo (the latter by means of a pre-emptive strike);
6. the intervening power will base its action on an assumption that the other superpower will not respond militarily;
7. the superpower will seek to present the action as a collective endeavour, pursued jointly with neighbouring states; it will utilise where possible a regional organisation in which it plays a dominant role;
8. the intervening power will seek to limit UN involvement;
9. 'intervention' may take the form of direct military involvement, but may also involve economic pressures, threats or internal subversion;
10. the intervening power will be willing to endure a tarnished international image in order to protect its perceived 'core interests';
11. the other power will point to the intervention as a blatant example of the 'hegemonism' of its rival

Ib. Differences

1. Domestic opposition in the US may be a powerful constraint on

foreign policy (Nicaragua). As Kaufman has argued, forms of control derive from differences in the internal systems of the hegemonial powers (an 'open' system in the US and a 'closed' system in the USSR[59]). However, the domestic unpopularity of the Afghanistan War may have been a factor in the Soviet 'pull out' decision. The Gorbachev era has ushered in a freer climate of debate on foreign affairs (within the framework of party control);

2. toleration of regime diversity: the US has been prepared to tolerate a variety of regime types within its sphere (excluding communist regimes). It should, however, be remembered that there are now significant differences between the regimes within the bloc and that the USSR has a higher tolerance threshold than hitherto;

3. the extent of control: the USSR has enmeshed the regimes of Eastern Europe into the Soviet system through a complex network of ideological, institutional and economic linkages, whereas the US has not sought such a high degree of integration – although US multinational corporations are said by the Soviets and by Western 'dependency' theorists to be inextricably bound up with the ends and means of American policy in the region;

4. many states within the American sphere refer to themselves as non-aligned. This is not acceptable within the Soviet bloc (even though Romania has moved to a position of 'partial alignment');

5. there is a greater degree of geographical contiguity between the Soviet Union and its 'wards' in Eastern Europe than is the case between the US and the Latin American states (military exercise pressure has been an important instrument of Soviet intervention);

6. Within the Soviet bloc, several states are wealthier than, and regard themselves as culturally superior to, the hegemonial power. Not only is the United States richer by far than any Latin American state, it does not suffer from feelings of cultural inferiority *vis à vis* its 'wards'.

In general, US responses to Soviet interventions in Eastern Europe and Soviet responses to US interventions in Central America and the Caribbean have been muted, taking the form of verbal condemnations and (in the case of Poland after the imposition of martial law) limited sanctions. The rules of the game will not be explicitly stated, but can be observed from conduct and statements by the parties during crisis periods. On the intervening power's side:

1. the superpower will seek to deny or minimise its involvement, partly in order to maintain its world image, but also to avoid antagonising the other power;
2. there may be signals to the other power, indicating that the intervention has limited objectives;
3. the intervening power will indicate that the action involves no change in policy and is defensive in character;
4. the intervening power will seek to realise its objectives quickly, in order to create a *fait accompli* and forestall the possibility of any effective action by the other power.

Similarly, the response of the other power is also likely to follow well-established rules of the game. These include:

1. verbal condemnations: references to gross violations of sovereignty and of international law;
2. attempts to turn the other power into a pariah amongst nations; to elicit international condemnation of the intervention; and to apply international sanctions;
3. the opposing power will avoid actions which might lead to war;
4. the response will be limited in duration and will not fundamentally disrupt the relationship between the superpowers (for example, in relation to arms control negotiations);
5. the tacit acceptance of 'rules of the game' and the limited response of the opposing power will serve to clarify the 'ground rules' of superpower interaction, thereby redefining sphere boundaries. However, neither power will admit that they have agreed to a partial division of the world on the basis of spheres of interest.

II. Interventions outside 'spheres of interest' ('extra-bloc interventions')

These are characterised by the absence of agreed rules, and the high risk of 'showdowns' between the superpowers. The nature and forms of extra-bloc intervention will be conditioned by superpower perception of the prevailing balance of power – in particular any developments within the sphere of interest likely to upset the superpower balance will call forth a response. Superpower explanations of their interventions within their spheres normally contain some reference to the opposing powers' efforts to destabilise the region and upset the prevailing balance of power. It might also be argued that superpower assessment of the overall balance of power may also result in interventions. We have noted that Western commentators have frequently accused the Soviets of seeking to 'globalise' the Brezhnev Doctrine. Similarly the Soviets have accused the US of pursuing a 'neo-globalist' drive for world hegemony.[60]

The Monroe Doctrine has also been linked to extra-hemispherical American doctrines in the postwar era, notably to the 'Eisenhower Doctrine',[61] the 'Carter Doctrine' and the Reagan Codicil to the Carter Doctrine. The Eisenhower Doctrine was formulated in 1957 as a means of preventing the establishment of communist governments in the Middle East: in January Eisenhower had requested Congress to allow him to use armed force to protect any state in the Middle East that requested aid against international communist aggression. According to Eisenhower, US forces were sent to Lebanon to protect American lives and to help the Lebanese government defend its sovereignty from the communist threat.[62] The Carter Doctrine was formulated in response to the Soviet invasion of Afghanistan and is based on Carter's statement that any attempt by an outside power to gain control of the Persian Gulf would be regarded as an assault upon vital US interests and would be resisted by armed forces.[63] In 1981, Reagan said that Saudi Arabia would not become another Iran. This has been interpreted as meaning that the US would intervene to prevent a change of regime in Saudi Arabia, even if pressures for change emanated from within the country.[64] These 'doctrines' are characterised by the Soviets as blatant examples of attempts to justify American expansion and aggression.

Favourable assessments of the correlation of forces by the Soviets from the mid-1970s may have resulted in attempts to extend its sphere of influence to other zones. Such actions have been described by Fawcett as taking place along the power frontiers of the world, which he defines as 'an area of inward and outward pressure between two power systems'.[65] Power frontiers, according to Fawcett, are dynamic: interventions along them 'will appear as defensive or aggressive according to the direction in which it is conceived as moving'.[66] Afghanistan might be considered as one example of a 'power frontier': given its geographical contiguity to the USSR, it was more likely that the Soviets would intervene than the US. Soviet policy has been far bolder in Africa than in Central America or the Caribbean in three ways: firstly, through the use of Cuban proxies: secondly, through a major increase in diplomatic contacts from the 1960s; and thirdly, through arms sales.[67]

III. Intrusions (or probes) into the sphere of interest of the other superpower

These are the most dangerous to world stability, in that they are likely to provoke a robust response from the regional hegemon: for example, Soviet involvement in Cuba and Grenada might be described as probes into the US sphere. It has been suggested by Aspaturian that Soviet support for the Bishop regime in Grenada may have derived in some measure from Soviet assumptions that the US response to Soviet incursions was likely to be less than robust.[68] The response to these challenges by the US would be indications of US determination to resist an extension of Soviet power elsewhere. Despite these examples, determined efforts to penetrate the opposing superpower's sphere of interest have been rare: rules of the game and tacit understandings have been accepted by both sides.[69]

In comparing the two doctrines, it is not always clear whether or not commentators are implying that there exists a behavioural (and moral) symmetry between the two superpowers, or whether the similarity refers to the official explanations of US and Soviet interventions. It is undeniable that there are similarities between the two doctrines. However, the US has not sought to impose a 'duplicative' policy on Latin America, by forcibly transforming Latin American regimes into democracies on the US model. But Washington is now less tolerant of right-wing dictatorships. In the Gorbachev era the Soviet Union's 'tolerance threshold' has widened further and therefore there could be a 'partial convergence' of US and Soviet policies in their respective spheres.

12 Challenges to Soviet Doctrines of Sovereignty in the 1980s

Contemporary challenges to the Soviet doctrine of sovereignty stem from three broad environmental pressures: firstly, changes in the 'texture' of the international system, deriving from what the Romanian scholar Brucan has termed 'technological interdependence pressure'[1] – i.e. increased global interdependence and internationalisation; secondly, the threat to the survival of all states from the danger of nuclear annihilation; thirdly, explicit criticisms of Soviet conceptions of 'socialist' sovereignty, emanating from within the international communist movement. This chapter examines Soviet doctrinal responses to these challenges in the light of the Gorbachev 'revolution' and Soviet 'new thinking' on international relations. The first two sets of influences impinge in some measure on all states, regardless of their social system: we noted in Chapter 1 that, in the early postwar years, the Soviet response to Western 'mondialism' (prescriptions for 'world government') was a vigorous reassertion of the paramountcy of the sovereignty principle in international relations. It will be useful to briefly compare more recent Western and Soviet perspectives on the prospects for sovereignty in an increasingly interdependent world:

CONTEMPORARY WESTERN AND SOVIET PERSPECTIVES ON 'CHALLENGES TO SOVEREIGNTY'

Western perspectives

The theme of the 'vanishing substance' of sovereignty[2] has constituted a central theme of Western 'functionalist' and 'neofunctionalist' analyses in the postwar period. This concern is not a new phenomenon: in 1925, Politis wrote that sovereignty had been virtually abolished.[3] The trend in Western thought has been towards an acknowledgement that these forces have led to some *de facto* diminution of sovereignty. Some writers have gone further: in 1954,

Loewenstein asserted that 'in reality, the notion of sovereignty and its corollaries are largely semantic and escapist formulae'.[4] Although he later modified his views, in 1959 Herz argued that the 'permeability' of nation-states to nuclear attack had undermined the logic of the state system.[5] Vernon, in his influential work *Sovereignty at Bay* outlined the threat to sovereignty from multinational companies;[6] Western 'neofunctionalists' (for example, Haas, Schmitter and Nye) have sought to identify the conditions and processes which are conducive to the development of 'supranationalist' regional political communities: the main focus of this work has been upon the dynamics of integration in Western Europe.[7]

Schwarzenberger has noted that international society contains both centripetal and centrifugal forces and therefore the trend is not solely towards the lessening of sovereignty: in his words, it is neither 'evanescent' nor 'triumphant':[8] nevertheless, it is also widely accepted in the West that interdependency is altering the 'texture' of the international system, so that, according to Burton, 'cobweb' models – based on the assumption of multiple interdependency – afford a better insight into the nature of the international system than 'billiard ball' (states as sole actors) conceptions.[9] Western thought on the subject embraces a diverse range of opinion concerning the value of sovereignty – thus it is regarded by some as a laudatory principle, embodying the notions of independence, non-interference and self-determination; others have emphasised the role of the sovereign state as a factor inhibiting, or threatening, human progress, viewing it as an obstacle to cooperation between peoples; a barrier preventing a fairer distribution of global wealth; a source of antagonism and international lawlessness; and a drain on scarce resources through expenditure on defence.[10]

Soviet perspectives

In 1970, the subject area of 'internationalisation, integration and the problem of sovereignty' was identified by Shakhnazarov and Burlatskiĭ – two of the most innovative Soviet political theorists – as a topic requiring greater research.[11] The significance of the growing trend towards interdependence, and of 'global problems which pass beyond national boundaries and permeate the fabric of world events'[12] is acknowledged in contemporary Soviet theory: Lukin recognises that 'the present system of international relations is characterised by the expansion and multiplication of functional, all-embracing ties and interdependence between its elements'.[13] His reference to 'reciprocal dependence' could easily have been written by a Western functionalist (even though he attributes his understanding of the internationalisation of social life to Marx and Lenin).[14] The driving force of this process is the 'scientific technological revolution' (STR), which, according to Inozemtsev (writing before the emergence of the 'new thinking') aggravated the contradictions within capitalism, but enhanced the development of the world socialist system.[15] However, Soviet theorists do not explicitly concede that interdependence pressures have led to a 'modified'[16] or 'relativised'[17] sovereignty. In Soviet international relations thought, interdependence perspectives have been counterbalanced by a shift in emphasis from transnational, class-based analyses toward state-centric conceptions of global relations. Although Soviet international relations theorists display familiarity with contemporary Western ideas, and incorporate Western concepts into their analyses, they do not accept Western premises concerning the processes by which state sovereignty will be eroded.[18] Soviet commentators have continued to insist that international cooperation must impose no limitation of sovereignty.[19] Korovin's statement that, without recognition of the sovereignty principle, 'there would be no voluntary cooperation between states and no international law'[20] still has a contemporary ring.

In the postwar era, a large Soviet literature has also emerged on the threat to the sovereignty of states from the activities of transnational companies (TNCs). Soviet writers display a familiarity with Western literature on the subject, but attribute the seminal work on the internationalisation of monopoly capitalism and 'supermonopolies' to Lenin. The focus of Soviet writing on this theme has broadened since the early postwar years (when it concentrated on American economic penetration of Western Europe) to embrace the threat of monopoly capitalism to the sovereignty of Third World countries. Until the Gorbachev era, the Soviet attitude to TNCs was unremittingly hostile. As the 'shock force of neo-colonialism'[21] these carriers of the internationalisation of capital[22] were said to constitute a menace to the sovereignties of states subject to capitalist penetration[23] – i.e. to states outside the world socialist system.[24] In Soviet conceptions, TNCs are linked organically to bourgeois state power: thus US multinationals have been anathematised as an outward extension of the US military-industrial complex and as the principal organisational vehicles for the US 'neo-globalist' drive for world hegemony.[25] Soviet attitudes towards international economic organisations (other than those established within the world socialist system) have also been hostile: thus Volkov in 1986 described the IMF and the World Bank as vehicles for 'interfering in the internal affairs of developing countries, undermining their sovereignty'.[26]

A conventional wisdom of Soviet writing on regional integration has been that, whereas economic integration in the West constitutes a dire threat to the sovereignty of the participating states, within the socialist community sovereignty is enhanced by interstate cooperation. The Soviets have insisted that 'under socialist integration no country suffers any infringement of its sovereignty'[27] and that the CMEA is not a supranational body. Faithful to Marxist–Leninist doctrine, modern Soviet writers have predicted that all states will eventually merge into one international community with a single economy: but this not expected to occur for a long time.[28] In 1973, Gubin argued that the simultaneous entry into communism formula was not relevant to the monopoly phase of capitalism, since uneven development prevented simultaneous world-wide revolution.[29]

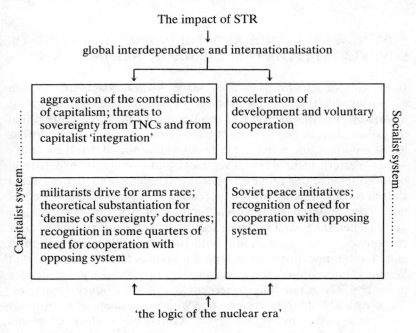

Figure 12.1   Pressures from the global environment

According to Shakhnazarov the logic of the nuclear era demands 'the renunciation of national self-interest and, unreserved preference of the international interest to the national'.[30] However, he refuses to concede that the danger of nuclear 'midnight' challenges the logic of the state system itself. Shakhnazarov took a Western writer to task for accusing 'advocates of the very idea of sovereignty of the seven deadly sins':[31] rather, he pointed to the progressive role of sovereignty in the modern world. A cardinal assumption of contemporary Soviet thinking is that the nuclear danger is forcing states with different social systems to cooperate in the interests of human survival. However, the Soviet Union is said to play a major role in peace initiatives, whereas in bourgeois states some elements are using nuclear technology as a rationale for accelerating the arms race or for undermining the logic of state sovereignty.[32] These challenges emanating from the global environment (as perceived by Soviet international relations specialists in the early 1980s) are depicted in Figure 12.1.

THE 'NEW THINKING' AND THE SOVIET DOCTRINE OF SOVEREIGNTY: THE EMERGENCE OF A 'THIRD AXIS'?

In the Gorbachev era, there is evidence that a fundamental revision of Soviet doctrine on the subject of global interdependence is underway. The driving force of this doctrinal shift is recognition that the policy of insulating the Soviet Union from the global economy has led to economic and technological backwardness and that the country needs Western technology, investment and managerial expertise in order to reverse this process of decline. Therefore, there has been a shift in Soviet thinking towards recognition of the positive aspects of interaction between states with different socioeconomic systems. In a period when the Soviet Union is seeking joint ventures with capitalist enterprises, closer cooperation with the EEC, and participation in global economic institutions, the traditional Soviet doctrine that Western transnational and international organisations are a menace to sovereignty is not fully congruent with Soviet policy objectives. The possibility of Soviet cooperation with world financial institutions has been raised by Aganbegyan, Gorbachev's chief economic adviser:[33] the Soviet Union has also sought to join the GATT, as a means of boosting its foreign trade (China has already been admitted). There are signs that the Soviets may be adopting a less dismissive attitude towards the EEC: in 1988, Borko acknowledged that, in some measure, the EEC serves the national interests of the member states and raised the possibility of cooperation between the two European systems in the economic field.[34] In marked contrast to its aggressively hostile posture towards global institutions in the early post-war years, the Soviet Union has showed increasing enthusiasm for participation in UN agencies (particularly the economic commissions[35]).

But the most striking modification of Soviet doctrine has been advanced by Shakhnazarov, who has argued that the rapid pace of change in the world requires the 'ruthless scuttling' of dogmas.[36] In his view, there is a need to enhance the 'governability' of an increasingly interdependent and integral world. He therefore favours the creation of a 'world government' comprised of states with different socioeconomic systems in order to address common global problems. He acknowledges that the traditional Soviet attitude towards Western 'mondialism' (e.g. early postwar Western proposals for 'world government') were strongly hostile. He still considers these proposals to have been reactionary, because they were based on a denial of sovereignty and were designed to foster global imperialism. There were two specific reasons why these proposals were unacceptable: firstly, the predominance of US economic power in this period meant that a world government would have resulted in 'legalisation of the world supremacy of US capital';[37] secondly, the colonial territories were not yet free and therefore 'mondialism' provided a rationale for denying colonial peoples their right to independence.

However, he argues that these objections to 'world government' no longer apply: thus political and economic power in the world is now more diffused than in the early postwar period (e.g. Japanese economic power and the rise of the Soviet Union to superpower status). Therefore, there is now a possibility of a 'world government' based on a 'balance of interests' between states with different socioeconomic systems. Shakhnazarov's 'world government' would not, however, mean the demise of sovereignty (an idea he still considers reactionary). Rather, it would be an international body (not a world state) based on the voluntary agreement between states, since 'sovereignty is not infringed in any way by the voluntary delegation of part of one's powers to an international or supranational agency'.[38] Like other Soviet 'interdependence' theorists, Shakhnazarov seeks to give his ideas proper Marxist credentials by referring to Marx's references to 'internationalisation'. He also quotes a 1923 Soviet work on the state by Adoratskiĭ, which recognised the significance of 'global interdependency'.[39] The striking feature of Shakhnazarov's theory is the extent to which it is prepared to contemplate cooperation between states with different socioeconomic systems. Shakhnazarov recognises that the struggle between systems is not the only Soviet concept of world development.[40]

The 'interdependence' perspective might be viewed as constituting a 'third axis' in Soviet orientations towards sovereignty: this does not mean that the 'legal-positivist' and 'class' orientations have been abandoned. Rather, the 'interdependence' axis is reflective of a current Soviet strain of thought or 'mood'. Nor is the interdependence orientation likely to give TNCs a clear bill of moral health. Nevertheless, this shift in orientation justifies a modification of the 'biaxial' model of sovereignty. Figure 12.2 depicts these three axes: the Soviet orientation towards sovereignty in specific contexts is viewed as influenced by a situational 'force field' – e.g. fear of Western interference in the 'positivist' orientation; and of the break-up of the socialist camp in the 'class' orientation; the fear of economic decline and backwardness in the 'interdependence' orientation.

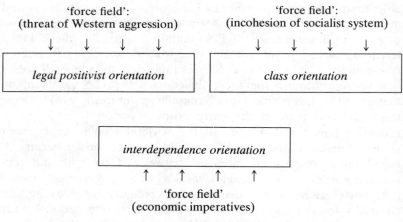

Figure 12.2   The emergence of a 'third axis'

Challenges from within the international communist movement

In this section, we concentrate upon the challenges to the Soviet conception of sovereignty emanating from within the international communist movement. A preliminary distinction is necessary between challenges from outside and from within the Soviet power zone in Eastern Europe: in practice, however, 'intra-bloc' and 'extra-bloc' challenges cannot be considered in isolation, since they tend to feed upon each other. Taken together, the substance of the challenges have involved rejection of: 1) Soviet conceptions of the relationship between national and international interests; 2) Soviet ideological hegemony within the movement; 3) the 'general laws of socialism' and of the universal applicability of the Soviet model; 4) superpower blocs and spheres of interest; 5) the 'Brezhnev Doctrine'; 6) Soviet theories of socialist integration.

The two decades following the Prague Spring have demonstrated that, in responding to challenges to bloc cohesion, the Kremlin has been vainly struggling against a hydra-headed monster. No sooner had one 'head' – the Prague Spring – been lopped off, than others were to appear to threaten the structure of power and influence upon which the Soviet hegemonial system had been built. Despite Soviet ideological offensives designed to restore unity, each of the bloc states, in different ways, presented challenges to Soviet interests in the 1970s and 1980s. Underlying these challenges were a number of inter-related environmental factors to which the Soviets could not effectively respond. These factors can be summarised as follows:

1. Detente and the 'lure of the West'
Improvement of relations with the West has an unsettling effect upon the region, since it tends to expose and exacerbate divergences of interest between the Soviet Union and the bloc states: the Soviets have found it increasingly difficult to synchronise the policies of the bloc states towards the West: Soviet efforts to make East Europe march in step with each shift in its policy towards the West has been a continuing source of friction within the bloc.

2. The challenge of Eurocommunism
The Eurocommunist alternative to Soviet socialism, which was most forcefully expressed by the Italian and Spanish parties, involved acceptance of pluralism, multiparty systems, press freedom and national roads of socialist construction. The rejection by these parties of one-party rule and of the 'general laws of socialist construction' was bound to draw fire from the Soviets. At the East Berlin conference of European and Western parties in 1976, the Soviets

were forced to compromise with the Eurocommunists since, as Triska
has argued, they still needed the ideological endorsement of the West
European parties.[41] Conversely, the West European parties needed
to distance themselves from the Moscow line for electoral reasons. At
the 1976 conference, Brezhnev denied that the CPSU favoured a
'leading centre' and the final conference document made no reference to socialist internationalism.[42] Nevertheless, from 1976, polemics between the Western parties and the CPSU intensified: Suslov,
Ponomarev, and other hardline ideologues launched fierce attacks
upon the Eurocommunist heresy and reaffirmed the 'general laws of
socialist construction'.[43]

3. Economic ossification
There were inherent and irremediable weaknesses in the economic
systems imposed on Eastern Europe, which no amount of 'reform'
could remedy. These were exemplified by slow growth rates, recur-
rent economic crises and heavy borrowing from the West. 'Buying
time' strategies – Western credits and Soviet loans – merely postponed the agony of future explosions. The failure of the East
European communist parties to meet the economic aspirations of
their populations has been a major contributory factor to bloc
instability. Moreover, although the East German and – for a time –
Hungarian economies performed creditably, their systems implicitly
represented a repudiation of the Soviet economic model. The
increased economic dependency of the East European regimes upon
the Soviet Union (deriving from the poor competitiveness of East
European products on world markets, Soviet economic aid and
Soviet integration drives) served to increase the sense of 'regional
claustrophobia' amongst East Europeans. Moreover, since the Soviet
system itself was in deep economic trouble, the ill-health of the bloc
economies could only worsen. The worsening economic situation
which led to a reduction in real terms of Soviet economic subsidies
(particularly in the energy sphere) also contributed to East German
and Hungarian drives to free themselves from strict conformity to the
Moscow line.

4. Conflicting definitions of 'national' and 'international interests'
The attempts by some of the East European communist leaderships
to narrow regime 'legitimacy deficits' also had implications for Soviet
hegemony, in that greater stress upon national, as distinct from
international, interests raised awkward questions concerning East

European commitment to socialist internationalism as the cardinal principle governing relations within the bloc.[44]

5. *Inertia and division within the Soviet leadership*
Inertia within the Soviet elite during the Brezhnev years contributed to economic and political stagnation within the Soviet bloc. In the interregnum before the accession of Gorbachev Soviet policy towards Eastern Europe was unimaginative and designed to preserve the status quo rather than to develop policies appropriate to rapidly changing conditions. The turnover in Soviet leadership created uncertainty in Eastern Europe, delaying the formulation of solutions to the region's developing crisis.

6. *Soviet policy failures*
The Kremlin's failure to prevent the deployment of Cruise and Pershing missiles also increased the mood of disillusionment with Soviet handling of relations with the West. The Soviet Union's failure to reach a *modus vivendi* with China and its embroilment in Afghanistan further dented the Soviet image as an effective international actor.

The Soviet response to these challenges was to seek to bind the states of Eastern Europe more closely into the Soviet sphere, through a renewed ideological offensive and integration drive. Emphasis was thus placed upon the primacy of the international over the national, the need for revolutionary vigilance and the shortcomings of the West (a form of 'negative legitimation').[45] Institutional integration was pursued through an expanding network of functional contacts between bloc representatives, thereby further enmeshing the East European elites into the Soviet control system. This 'solidarist' strategy was, to some extent, counter-productive and led to open disagreements between the Soviet Union and the bloc states: partly this was manifested in coded polemics and partly in open rejection of Soviet integration plans at Comecon 'summits'.

'NATIONAL AND INTERNATIONAL INTERESTS' WITHIN THE BLOC

In the early 1980s, the dissatisfaction of Eastern Germany and Hungary with a range of Soviet policies led to an insidious, rather than a dramatic, erosion of Soviet authority within the bloc. Moreover, these challenges were made by parties in firm control: it was as if the 'children' had suddenly grown to adulthood and were demanding to be treated on near equal terms with the 'parent'. The limits which Soviet foreign policy placed upon the ability of East Germany and Hungary to develop economic links with the West contributed to the assertion of independence by Honecker and Kádár. But one of the most significant developments was the refusal of the GDR to fully support a renewed campaign of hostility towards NATO in general and West Germany in particular.[46] Honecker's determination to develop relations with West Germany in a 'coalition of reason', would have previously been unthinkable. There had been serious difficulties in Soviet–East German relations before – notably in the latter period of Ulbricht's rule: but the issue then had been Ulbricht's refusal to follow the Soviet lead in opening up links with the West. In 1984, there were open disagreements between the Kremlin and Berlin over INF deployment.[47] It would be an overstatement to refer to a Berlin–Budapest axis of dissension from Moscow: nevertheless, the regimes developed an alliance against the restrictions imposed upon them by the Kremlin. The Hungarians and East Germans (non-Slav peoples), have anti-Russian traditions and are westward-looking. Moreover, due to their respective 'legitimacy crises', the regimes have sought to increase their domestic popularity through appeals to popular sentiments – East Germany through rapprochement with West Germany and Hungary through economic reforms. In 1982, Hungary joined the IMF and the World Bank; in 1983 it sought to improve its ties with China and in 1984, it welcomed Craxi, Kohl and Thatcher. Soviet criticism of 'nationalism' and 'revisionism' in Hungary in 1984 and 1985 showed that the Kremlin would not accept these developments passively.[48]

An article by Mátyás Szürös, the International Affairs Secretary of the Hungarian Communist Party Central Committee, published in a party journal in January 1984, rejected the notion that the interests of each socialist country had to be secondary to interests defined by Moscow[49] – i.e. that the Peoples Democracies had to accept the role of obedient foot soldiers in superpower conflicts. Szürös's arguments were hardly original, since they had been asserted more stridently by China, Yugoslavia, Romania and Albania. What was striking was that these arguments were being advanced by Hungary, a country which had been allowed a wide measure of latitude in internal affairs in return for fealty to Moscow in international affairs. It had participated in the invasion of Czechoslovakia and was not regarded as a 'problem country' by Moscow: indeed, it may have been seen as a kind of future model of relations between the Soviet Union and the other bloc states. Szürös's article had been prompted by the new 'cold war' between the Kremlin and Washington and in particular by the prospect of INF deployment. Szürös gave several examples of the positive effects of the new diplomacy of small- and medium-sized powers (visits of Trudeau and Thatcher to Budapest). He was not saying that national and international interests were incompatible, but rather that the pursuit of national interests could be conducive to the achievement of common objectives.[50]

These assertions provoked a vigorous response from Soviet and Czech commentators, who re-emphasised the primacy of international over national interests.[51] An article in *Rudé právo* in March 1984 stressed the need for bloc unity and criticised the pursuit of independent foreign policies by allies departing from their genuine national interests[52] (the article was published in *Novoe vremia*, which showed that Moscow was not prepared to sit on the sidelines). The Czech response to the Szürös article was predictable: less so was the attitude of East Germany. Almost immediately, *Neues Deutschland* reprinted Hungarian reassertions of the independent line articulated by Szürös.[53] East Germany's incongruous role as a 'bloc dissident' was manifested in independent initiatives in relation to West Germany and in open debates on theoretical issues. These debates were a good example of the 'rules of the game' relating to intra-bloc conflicts in that the actors observed the rule of 'auto-limitation' and restraint: disagreements were articulated not by the leaders, but by second level officials and publicists; secondly, the debate was expressed in the coded language of ideology, which provides a rich store of euphemisms, so that explicit criticism of the other side was avoided. An additional strategy was that of 'echo support' – reprinting favoured articles emanating from other parts of the bloc.[54]

An article by 'Borisov' (believed to be Oleg Rakhmanin, first deputy of the central committee's department for relations with ruling communist parties) in *Voprosy istorii KPSS* in April 1984 attacked certain East European countries for favouring national over international policies. It pointed to the existence of petty bourgeois elements in some socialist countries, which were seeking to subvert the general laws of socialist construction.[55] It also detected signs of political instability in East Germany, manifested in the clergy and the peace movement. The article represented a 'no change' policy on the part of the Chernenko leadership. It was virtually inevitable that

Romanians would join in this debate, since the remarks by Szűrös echoed what they had been saying for years about the proper relationship between national and international interests. *Era Socialista* in September rejected the idea of the assimilation of socialist nations and the notion of unity between national and international interests.[56]

GORBACHEV AND EASTERN EUROPE: THE BREZHNEV DOCTRINE REPEALED?

For virtually the whole of the postwar period, Western analyses of the Soviet hegemonial system in Eastern Europe have been predicated on the assumption that the stimulus for change in the region would emanate primarily from outside the Soviet Union: the Kremlin was like a fixed post against which the East European states had to strain in order to achieve greater latitude in domestic and foreign policy. Although some Western analysts predicted that fundamental changes could soon occur within the Soviet Union,[57] most assumed that a radical reform of the Soviet system was several decades away. Gorbachev's assumption of power in March 1985 raised the possibility that reform pressure might emanate from the centre in several ways: firstly, given the Soviet Union's 'vanguard' role, initiation of radical reform in the Soviet Union could not leave bloc states untouched; secondly, from the outset, Gorbachev indicated that he intended to assign top priority to relations with Eastern Europe (the large number of intra-bloc meetings held in the first two years bore out the seriousness of his intentions[58]). The policies with which Gorbachev has become associated during his rule – radical reform through *uskorenie* (acceleration), *perestroika* (restructuring), *demokratizatsiia* (democratisation), *glasnost'* (publicity, openness); a new detente with the West; and the achievement of European denuclearisation – obviously had implications for the bloc states, regardless of whether or not Gorbachev had a clearly worked out strategy for Eastern Europe; thirdly, given the extent to which the Soviet Union is dependent upon trade with the region, Gorbachev's domestic objectives – rapid economic growth, improvements in organisational efficiency, higher quality goods and technological innovation – would be meaningless without corresponding improvements within the bloc states. According to Gorbachev's chief economics adviser Aganbegyan, '*perestroika* in one area reinforces *perestroika* in another':[59] he was referring to the domestic connections between economic and social reform: however, it could also be applied to linkages between domestic and foreign policy.

Fourthly, the 'new thinking' has, in various ways, served to undermine the principal doctrinal assumptions upon which the Soviet hegemonial system is based. For example, Gorbachev's explicit rejection of 'omniscience' within the international communist movement and his call for greater sophistication in relations between communist parties raises interesting questions concerning the future pattern of international relations within the bloc. The 'new thinking' has also led to ambivalence in Soviet policy postures: in contemporary Soviet foreign policy journals, it is possible to find both reiteration of, and challenges to, Soviet international relations dogmas: according to Kortunov, the imperative of the 'new thinking' necessitates the abandoning of 'old stereotypes'.[60] However, these commentaries tend to be counterpointed by renewed calls for international solidarity and a principled Leninist stand.[61] Although the current trend in Soviet commentaries on international relations is to downplay or ignore the 'dualist' dogma that the world is essentially split into two competing socioeconomic systems (the underlying rationale for bloc solidarity), the traditional assumption that the trend of world development is leading to the 'irreversible replacement of capitalism' by socialism has by no means been abandoned.[62] Gorbachev has contributed to this ambivalent posture: at the CPSU central committee plenary meeting in February 1988, he called for 'fundamentally different international relations' but also said that the 'new thinking rests on the Leninist theory of imperialism' and that he had 'no illusions' about imperialism, 'which will never become good'.[63] Indeed, the current Soviet mood for self-criticism and questioning is counterpointed by renewed emphasis upon the faults of capitalism (another example of 'negative legitimation'): the 'new thinking' is regarded as an adaptation of Marxism–Leninism, not its abandonment.[64]

Economic necessity is the mother of *perestroika*. Shlapentokh has characterised the Gorbachev reforms as an example of a preventative change in ideology, in that they derive from fear of danger (economic and technological backwardness, leading to Soviet weakness relative to the West).[65] An article in *Kommunist* in 1987 suggested that the threat to the Soviet Union from Western economic warfare is now more salient than the threat of military attack from the West.[66] Aganbegyan also admits the danger of economic exhaustion through

Old Thinking	New Thinking
emphasis upon class struggle	emphasis upon inter-state cooperation
necessity of ideological struggle	ideological differences downplayed
emphasis upon 'struggle and competition between two systems'	emphasis upon internationalisation and interdependencies within and across system boundaries
main threat to Soviet Union: military aggression	main threat: economic exhaustion from a new arms race and failure to reform
capitalism decaying rapidly	acknowledgement of the resilience of capitalism
positive changes in international result from Soviet initiatives	international progress results from a 'dialectical' process of dialogue
capitalist integration bad	capitalist integration has some positive features
no cooperation between EEC and Comecon	possibility of mutually beneficial cooperation between European economic systems
global economic institutions tools of capitalism	some global economic institutions mutually beneficial
'world government' impossible as long as capitalism exists	'world government' between states with different socio-economic systems feasible (Shakhnazarov)
support for CPSU, the 'touchstone' of internationalism	no 'omniscient' parties

Figure 12.3   The 'old' and 'new' political thinking

military rivalry.[67] The means sought to respond to this threat have been a renewed efficiency drive, a reduction in the crippling burden of military expenditure, an inflow of Western technology, retrenchment in foreign policy (reduction in aid to third world clients; reduction in subsidies to the bloc states; and suture of the 'bleeding wound' of Afghanistan) and arms agreements which 'liberate resources for peaceful construction' (Aganbegyan).[68] Regardless of its underlying motives, the 'new thinking' on international affairs represents a significant departure from old orthodoxies, as Figure 12.3 shows.

Western scholars are divided on the issue of the nature and

significance of 'Gorbachevisation'. The 'reform pessimism' school comprises several strands of thought: firstly, cynicism concerning the underlying motives of Gorbachev's foreign policy initiatives, which have been attributed to the Soviet need for a temporary respite from the arms race (a policy consistent with previous Soviet behaviour patterns when the correlation of forces is deemed unfavourable to the Kremlin); secondly, perceptions of Gorbachev as a man of limited aims and restricted vision (notwithstanding his dynamism) – i.e. as essentially an *apparatchik* seeking to overhaul, rather than fundamentally transform, the system.[69] For Zhores Medvedev, Gorbachev is 'neither a liberal nor a bold reformer'.[70] Despite Gorbachev's 'revolutionary' pronouncements, his is an ideology oriented towards system maintenance rather than system transformation, *perestroika* being a controlled reform from above rather than a revolution from below: in May 1988, Gorbachev reassured Soviet media chiefs that 'restructuring' would not endanger the party's vanguard role;[71] thirdly, although there may be doubt about Gorbachev's intentions, there can be no doubt about the Soviet system's formidable resistance to change: Soviet history is littered with failed attempts at economic reform (a fact acknowledged by Aganbegyan[72] who has admitted that economic restructuring is proceeding 'with difficulty and pain').[73] Schroeder notes the similarity between *perestroika* and the decentralisation measures of 1965 and the economic planning decree of 1979, neither of which resulted in fundamental changes.[74] Similarly, Hofheinz has noted that Gorbachev's insistence on high growth rates from the outset inhibited the chances of successful reform and discerns parallels with Khrushchev's abortive attempts to improve the Soviet economy.[75] Moreover, Gorbachev (as he himself has acknowledged) faces opposition from vested interests at various levels. Gorbachev has been remarkably successful in forcing through personnel and organisational changes within the Kremlin leadership. For example, in September 1988, he removed his conservative rival Ligachev from the post of party second secretary and retired several other leading members of the party's old guard from key posts. At the same time, he restructured the party's apparatus and promoted his own men to key positions within the central committee secretariat. However, it is far easier to shuffle personnel, or to alter institutional structures, than it is to change systemic values, or to eliminate 'inertia prone' behaviour patterns. Vested interests could ensure that Gorbachev's domestic policy initiatives are washed out at the implementation stage.

Fourthly, the destabilising effects of Gorbachev's modernisation drive (within the Soviet Union and Eastern Europe) may, at some point, force a retreat from reform in the interests of the system maintenance: *glasnost'* has also opened a hornet's nest of powerful nationalist pressures within the Soviet Union, which may distract the Kremlin's attention from other policy areas. Nationalist protests within the Baltic republics and intercommunal violence between Armenians and Azerbaijanis over the status of Nagorno-Karabakh in 1988 are unlikely to be isolated instances of dissatisfaction with the nature and structure of the Soviet multinational state. The dispatch of Soviet troops to the Armenian capital in order to quell nationalist unrest is an example of the use of the Brezhnev Doctrine to maintain the unity and cohesion of the Soviet Federation. Any attempt by a Soviet nationality to transform its fictional 'national sovereignty' into a genuine state sovereignty would receive a resolute rebuff from the Kremlin. In November 1988, the Estonian parliament's decision to grant itself the power to veto laws made in Moscow was annulled by the praesidium of the Supreme Soviet. According to Gorbachev, the Estonian decision had been made under pressure from extremists and demagogues. However, although centralist counter-measures may temporarily contain these nationalist pressures, they are unlikely to eradicate them.

The 'reform optimism' school lays stress upon Gorbachev's personal qualities (his drive, determination and leadership skills) and upon the differences between Gorbachev's initiatives and previous reform programmes: thus Cohen, Schmidt-Hauer and Frankel discern substance and promise in Gorbachev's professed determination for reform.[76] Service argues that Gorbachev uses the reform terminology of Khrushchev, but places more emphasis on democratisation and openness.[77] Similarly, 'reform optimists' stress that the logic of the situation (the Soviet Union's dire economic situation) will provide the driving force of radical change and that, if it is to be successful, modernisation cannot be confined to questions of technical efficiency. Gorbachev's vigorous attacks upon bureaucratic inertia are not empty rhetoric; in his first two years of office, he initiated reform decrees and directives on organisational reform, planning targets, pricing policy, quality control and elections for management and minor party posts.[78] Nevertheless, Gorbachev remains something of a mystery wrapped in an enigma: the vagueness of many of Gorbachev's pronouncements has often been noted.[79] Hofheinz attributes this imprecision to the fact that Gorbachev is a politician appealing to different audiences.[80]

An additional debate has focused upon the implications of 'Gorbachevisation' for the West: Urban has suggested that if Gorbachev is successful, the Soviet Union would become a more powerful adversary (militarily stronger and more attractive to leftist movements); conversely, if the reforms fail badly, the Kremlin would sink back into its old ways: the best scenario, for Urban, is for a middle-range outcome, which bogs the Soviet Union down in a continual struggle for modernisation: he argues that the Soviets ought to pay tangible prices for Western cooperation.[81] Conversely, Hough[82] and Frankel[83] interpret Gorbachevisation as a manifestation of the current ascendancy of 'Westerners' in the struggle between Western-oriented and 'Slavophile' factions which dates back to Tsarist times. In Frankel's view, a stronger, Western reform-oriented Soviet Union is preferable to a weaker 'Slavophile' one.

Gorbachev's objectives towards Eastern Europe appear to be in the direction of greater efficiency, through domestic reform and functional collaboration: they are designed to invigorate, rather than transform or dismantle, the Soviet hegemonial system in the region. Although some Soviet commentators have admitted that the invasion of Afghanistan was a mistake, they have not (openly and explicitly) drawn the same conclusions about the invasion of Czechoslovakia. The Warsaw Pact meeting in Sofia in October 1985 provided Gorbachev with a forum to explain the meaning of his new style of leadership for Eastern Europe. His statements were generally low key and guarded. It is possible that, despite his expressed determination to improve bloc relations, the broad sweep of Gorbachev's vision – global and domestic – left little time to focus on Eastern Europe. Gorbachev seems in favour of greater elbow room for the bloc states, although this by no means extends to abolition of the bloc's basic ground rules: even if Gorbachev himself was in favour of a fundamental revision of these rules, it seems unlikely that he would have the capacity to deliver.

Gorbachev has eschewed the 'solidarist' vocabulary which underpins the Brezhnev Doctrine. Neither during his speech at the 27th congress nor at the June 1986 meeting of the Political Consultative Committee of the Warsaw Pact in Budapest did he mention 'socialist internationalism'. In his book *Perestroika* he affirms that relations between states should be based on the principle of independence.[84] His statements during his visit to Yugoslavia in March 1988 have been interpreted in the West as an 'implicit retreat' from the Brezhnev

Doctrine;[85] the joint communiqué issued at the end of his talks with Yugoslav leaders eschewed reference to 'socialist internationalism' and contained an unqualified repudiation of interference in the affairs of other states. It also affirmed the value of dialogue between the two parties on the issue of socialist construction (socialist parties were considered free to determine their own path of development) and rejected the notion that there was a monopoly of truth. But Yugoslavia is outside the bloc and Khrushchev had made similar statements concerning Soviet-Yugoslav relations. Nevertheless, the 'equity effect' may result in some degree of 'Yugoslavisation' of Soviet-East European relations.[86] Furthermore, after the announcement of the Soviet pull-out of Afghanistan, conditions have never been better for a bloc state to pursue independent policies. Gorbachev's approach to Eastern Europe has so far been conciliatory: he has relied on exhortation and has not attempted to force reform initiatives on the bloc states (in the manner that 'destalinisation' was forced on local parties): nevertheless, reform in Eastern Europe is vital if he is to realise his domestic goals.

East Europeans had good reason to be confused by the contradictory signals emanating from Moscow after Gorbachev's accession: these contradictory messages were a reflection of the divisions within the Kremlin. On the one hand, at the 27th congress of the CPSU, Gorbachev explicitly rejected the idea that relations within the socialist community were based on hierarchy and laid stress on the need for open and candid discussions.[87] On the other hand, the new programme of the CPSU in its somewhat vague references to Eastern Europe had reiterated the conventional 'solidarist' line. A battery of articles in Soviet journals and newspapers in June and July 1985 served to underline Moscow's positions concerning international versus national interests.[88] In June 1985 in *Pravda*, 'Vladimirov' had cautioned against the paramountcy of national over international interests. 'Vladimirov' was believed to be the pseudonym of Oleg Rakhmanin, the deputy head of the Central Committee of the CPSU's department dealing with ruling parties. He explicitly criticised the bridge-building policies of certain unnamed socialist countries and attacked domestic economic policies which deviated from centralised direction.[89] Moscow's new integrationist policy was also laid down at the Warsaw summit meeting of Comecon in June, where the Soviets stressed the need for unity. An article by Biriukov in *Pravda* in December 1985 condemned the Prague Spring and reaffirmed the Brezhnev Doctrine: it also called for greater cohesion between socialist countries.[90]

However, in the first three years of Gorbachev's rule, some prominent Soviet intellectuals have sought to lay the theoretical ground for a new model of socialist international relations and have (implicitly) challenged the central assumptions of the Brezhnev Doctrine. In July 1985, Bogomolov, the head of the Soviet 'Institute of the Economics of the World Socialist System', asserted in *Kommunist* that the differences in the national interests of socialist states had to be acknowledged, in the interests of unity.[91] In September, Iuri Novopashin, a senior official in the same Institute, was more explicit in his repudiation of hierarchical forms of socialist international relations. Writing in the journal *Rabochii klass i sovremennyĭ mir* he rejected the view that relations between socialist states should take 'domineering forms', or be based upon the subordination of one socialist country to another (i.e. upon an international variant of the principle of 'democratic centralism').[92] In statements published in 1987 and 1988, another high-ranking member of the Institute, Leonid Iagodovskiĭ, drew laudatory parallels between some aspects of the 'Prague Spring' and the Gorbachev reforms and also criticised the negative response of the Brezhnev leadership to Dubček's reform programme (without, however, going so far as to say that the invasion itself was a mistake).[93]

New Soviet theories concerning socialist international relations inevitably raise the issue of the role assigned to the principle of 'socialist internationalism' in these formulations. Since the late 1950s, the principle had been used by Soviet commentators to explain the distinctive nature of socialist international relations: it has also provided the ideological rationale for Soviet intervention. In the Gorbachev era, the tendency has been for Soviet reformists to eschew explicit reference to the principle. However, in July 1988, Aleksandr Bovin, (*Izvestiia*'s chief political commentator) sought to reinterpret 'socialist internationalism' by fusing it with the principle of 'peaceful coexistence'. In 1968, the Soviets had accused 'unhealthy forces' in Czechoslovakia of seeking to base Czechoslovakia's relations with other socialist states upon 'peaceful coexistence', a principle said to apply only to relations between states with *different* socialist systems. Twenty years later, Bovin argued that socialist internationalism 'complements and enriches' peaceful coexistence rather than displaces it: in his view, socialist international relations have matured to the point where the potential for genuine fraternal cooperation between socialist countries can be maximised, and the negative consequences of contradictions between them minimised, through enhancement of the 'management mechanism' for regulating socialist international relations.[94]

In the era of 'new thinking', Soviet commentators enjoy greater freedom to develop idiosyncratic theoretical positions. It is therefore now more difficult to assess the degree of 'authoritativeness' of Soviet commentaries. Nevertheless, the ideas of Bogomolov, Novopashin, Iagodovskiĭ and Bovin do not seem out of line with the conciliatory thrust of Gorbachev's own comments on the subject of socialist international relations. We should not, however, leap to the conclusion that the Brezhnev Doctrine has now been permanently displaced by a 'Gorbachev Doctrine' (a term used by Iagodovskiĭ), since current Soviet 'tolerance thresholds' in relation to Eastern Europe have yet to be put to the test.

Gorbachev's foreign policy initiatives also had implications for Eastern European stability. The talks between Reagan and Gorbachev on arms control at Reykjavik took place without prior consultation with the bloc states and exemplified the preference of the superpowers for bilateralism. The end of the 'new cold war' was also likely to give the bloc states a freer hand to develop their own forms of detente with individual Western powers. A fundamental purpose of Gorbachev's reform programme in the economic sphere is to enable the Soviet Union to compete more successfully with the West on every level: in this sense, it represents a shift from the optimistic assessments of the global correlation of forces in the late Brezhnev period, which led to overextension of Soviet power. By contrast, Gorbachev's global strategy seems aimed at preventing a major shift in the correlation in favour of the West.

Given that the East European leaderships had been in power for many years, it was unlikely that they would embark upon radical reform, since this would imply criticism of their records. Moreover, the ageing leaders of the bloc states had seen Soviet reform initiatives (and Soviet leaders) come and go. The potentially destabilising effects of Gorbachev's domestic initiatives upon Eastern Europe derive from several factors: it could lead to a revolution of rising expectations – the events of 1956 had been detonated in part by confusing signals from Moscow concerning revision of the bloc's ground rules, while the crisis in Czechoslovakia had been preceded by Brezhnev's limited experiments in economic reform. It is in periods when the Kremlin is divided and preoccupied with its own internal problems that explosions tend to occur in Eastern Europe. Gorbachev's reform drive could exacerbate intra-party struggles by emboldening the reform factions. Economic liberalisation cannot be divorced from political liberalisation and, given the fragile legitimacy of the bloc regimes, Gorbachev's programme involves a high-risk strategy for the bloc.

The varied response of the East European leaderships to the Gorbachev reform drive was yet another manifestation of the diversity of the bloc. It received a frosty reception in Prague, Bucharest and East Berlin, since the leaderships of these states rightly viewed 'reconstruction' as a threat to their survival.[95] Kádár had neither the energy nor enthusiasm for reform. However, reform pressures soon developed both within and outside party structures: by 1988, Hungary had the biggest hard currency debt in the bloc and there was a growing rift between the intelligentsia and the party: the Hungarian Academy of Science in criticism of party conference draft standpoints said that 'crisis symptoms are multiplying at an accelerating rate'.[96] Some officials were advocating a shift from party monopoly towards a form of pluralism. Szűrös in 1988 championed the concept of 'all-European interests' and argued that the 'new thinking' should lead to the forging of new contacts with the West.[97] In April 1988, a new opposition group (the Network of Free Thinkers) called for multiparty democracy and removal of Soviet troops from Hungary.[98] In May 1988, Kadar was replaced by the pragmatic Karoly Grösz. By the spring of 1989, the party had announced plans for the introduction of a *de facto* multiparty system in the 1990s. However, popular agitation for reform continued apace: in March 1989, demands for genuine democracy and independence were reiterated at a National day rally in Budapest, organised by a coalition of 22 opposition groups and attended by 90 000 people.

Poland is ahead of the Soviet Union in economic decentralisation, but remains in a parlous economic state. The Polish people's rejection of the government's reform plans in the November 1987 referendum, and a new wave of strikes in 1988, were indications of continuing popular dissatisfaction with the regime. Less than a decade after 'crushing' Solidarity, the PUWP was forced to seek a *modus vivendi* with it: in March 1989, an agreement was reached between the government and Solidarity for the introduction of a partial form of democracy based on a two chamber parliament: however, since the agreement guaranteed the PUWP a majority in the most important chamber (the *Sejm*) it seemed like a classic attempt by a threatened ruling elite to coopt, and thereby deradical-ise, a troublesome out-group without relinquishing the levers of power. Nevertheless, for Solidarity it represented a significant step forward. Gorbachev has enjoyed good relations with Jaruzelski (in 1987 they affirmed 'socialist internationalism' as a principle governing Soviet–Polish relations).[99]

The divisions within the Soviet party hierarchy on the desirability of radical reform are paralleled within the Bulgarian party. The dominant element within the Bulgarian leadership favours economic reforms, but has been concerned to ensure that this does not spill over into demands for greater political freedom. Despite Zhivkov's favourable references to the Soviet example, he indicated that he was prepared to take only half the loaf: reconstruction, but not *glasnost'*. In April 1987, after stalling on the reform question, Zhivkov announced measures designed to introduce self management. From the summer of 1987, Bulgarian reform measures proceeded at a rapid pace.[100]

Honecker has reason to fear *glasnost'* and has already introduced some limited economic reforms. Moreover, the relative success of the East German economy gave Honecker a plausible argument for not following the Soviet model in the economic sphere. *Glasnost'* for East Germany could mean the resurgence of the unofficial peace move-ment and demands for greater political freedoms: the chanting of Gorbachev's name by East German youths in the shadow of the Berlin wall in the summer of 1987 was indicative of the potentially destabilising effects of Gorbachev's initiatives. The East Germans were lukewarm about the reform programme passed at the 27th congress and indicated that they could learn little from the Soviets in the economic sphere.[101] In 1988, in an effort to insulate itself from the winds of reform blowing from Moscow, the East German regime began censoring Soviet publications.

The Czechoslovak regime maintains itself in power through Stalin-ist repression and rejection of reform initiatives. Therefore, the parallels between 'Gorbachevisation' and Dubček's Prague Spring are too close for comfort (on 4 January 1988, *Rudé právo* derided the argument that the programme of the 'unprincipled' Dubček had anything in common with 'reconstruction'). The striking parallels between Dubček's reform programme – for example, decentralisa-tion, and self-criticism – were not lost on the Czechs. The initial strategy of the Czech leadership was to respond to Gorbachev's reformist speeches with a deafening silence. At the 17th party congress, Husák acknowledged the need for reforms in the area of economic planning, but did not concede that this was due to fundamental structural weaknesses and made no mention of *glasnost*'. He did, however, promise economic reforms over the next four years. Prior to his visit to Prague in April 1987, Gorbachev had said that he would be glad if Soviet experience could be useful to Czechoslovakia: but he was no doubt aware that a 'big stick' policy could be dangerous and his comments during the visit were low key. Charter 77 wrote to Gorbachev prior to his visit and four members of the Dubček government sent him a congratulatory letter. The fact that he left early in order to prepare for the impending meeting with Schultz on arms control was indicative of the cool relations between Moscow and Prague. The replacement of Husák by the conservative Miloš Jakeš in late 1987 was further evidence of the regime's resistance to genuine reform: in April 1988, Jakeš assured a *Time* correspondent that the regime was capable of dealing with challenges without Soviet military assistance.[102]

Ceauşescu largely ignored Gorbachev's initiatives, pursuing the line that reforms in Romania were unnecessary, as 'restructuring' had taken place many years before.[103] The Romanians continued to reject 'socialist internationalism' as a basis of socialist international relations. Following the visit of the Romanian Prime Minister to Moscow in March 1985, Gorbachev said that cooperation between the two countries must be based upon 'friendship'. He made no mention of 'socialist internationalism' during his visit to Romania in the Spring of 1987: Gorbachev was politely but not enthusiastically received by Ceauşescu, who showed no signs of accepting the Soviet leader as a superior. The Romanians rejected the need for greater coordination as stressed by Gorbachev: they also rejected Gorbachev's plans for joint enterprises, which must have seemed reminiscent of the joint Soviet-Romanian companies (Sov-Roms) of the Stalin years. Prior to the extraordinary session of the CMEA council in December 1985, *Scînteia* published a theoretical rebuttal of the notion that sovereignty had to be renounced in favour of participation in supranational bodies.[104] Ceauşescu made his opposition to the Gorbachev reforms clear in his speech to the 42nd CMEA session in Bucharest in November 1986. Ceauşescu distanced himself from the Soviet position at Reykjavik by arguing that a nuclear arms agreement should not be conditional upon US renunciation of SDI.

The response of the West

Western commentaries on the implications of the Gorbachev reform programme for Eastern Europe have centred on its potentially destabilising effects within the bloc: although the reform programme has been generally welcomed in the West, there has been less discussion of its implications for Western strategy towards the region. Put bluntly, what should the West do? A number of possible options suggest themselves: firstly, to continue the minimalist policy – to sit on the sidelines, in the expectation that the 'decomposition' process within the bloc will continue, regardless of *perestroika* and *glasnost'*: the merit of this policy may be that, to seek to accelerate the process of reform could prove counterproductive, by undermining Gorbachev's position and by strengthening the hand of the conservatives. Moreover, a policy of Western 'engagement' might encourage the peoples of Eastern Europe to overestimate Western intentions and capabilities: although East Europeans are unlikely to repeat the mistake of the Hungarian revolutionaries in 1956, nevertheless a sharp break in Western policy in the direction of engagement could lead to further explosions which ultimately would lead to further repression and a halt to the reform programme.

A second option is that of 'constructive engagement' – a policy of rewards and punishments designed to accelerate the reform process in the region. William Luers, a former American Ambassador to Czechoslovakia, has called for a more 'energetic' policy towards the region, based on a revival of the 'differentiation' or 'selective wooing' policy pursued by Nixon, Kissinger and Ford.[105] This would involve widening of US contacts in the bloc states (not only at the 'official' level but also with opposition elements); selective relaxation of trade restrictions; encouraging the East European regimes to pursue independent policies; and pushing for the implementation of the provisions of the Helsinki Final Act. We should not expect, of course, the Kremlin to meekly accept a Western 'engagement' policy: for over forty years they have blamed every bloc crisis upon Western interferences and are unlikely to respond benignly to an explicit policy of engagement. When, for example, in 1984, Vice President Bush outlined a policy of 'differentiation' towards Eastern Europe, he was vigorously denounced by the Soviets.[106] The 'new thinking' is unlikely to alter the Soviet attitude towards direct Western involvement in the region.

All Western initiatives depend for their success upon Soviet reactions. Ionescu[107] sees the most realistic solution as being a form of 'Finlandisation' – neutrality guaranteed by both sides. The European states would be granted 'internal' sovereignty – i.e. domestic jurisdiction – but, in acknowledgement of Soviet security interests, would have limited independence in the international arena. However, the Soviets have shown no interest in neutralist solutions and it would require a major upheaval for these options to become attractive to the Kremlin. Indeed, a fundamental purpose of Gorbachev's integration drive is to obviate the need to invoke the more brutal means by which the doctrine is enforced. Optimistic assessments of the implications of 'Gorbachevisation' for Eastern Europe need therefore to be tempered by the following riders:

1. Gorbachev's drive for greater economic cooperation within the bloc would, if successful, bind the Peoples Democracies more closely to the Soviet Union;
2. The Brezhnev Doctrine has been consistently upheld within the bloc by successive Soviet leaders. There has been no sign that Gorbachev is willing to renounce the Soviet commitment to communist party rule in Eastern Europe. If there was a real possibility that a bloc state would detach itself from the socialist camp, some form of intervention could not be ruled out (despite Gerasimov's terse reassurance to the contrary in December 1987[108]);
3. We should not underestimate the determination of the East European and Soviet ruling elites to retain power *de facto* (notwithstanding the 1989 Soviet elections, which revealed widespread discontent with the party establishment);
4. The prospects of success of the economic reform programme seem poor and therefore 'Gorbachevisation' is raising hopes which are destined to remain unfulfilled.

Western speculation concerning the continuing validity of the Brezhnev Doctrine now hinges upon the likely response of Gorbachev to a challenge to Soviet hegemony within the bloc. Put bluntly, in the event of a new Hungarian revolt, a Prague Spring or a Polish Summer, would he follow his predecessors and opt for a policy of suppression? The answer to this question depends upon several imponderables: firstly, upon the aims of Gorbachev towards Eastern Europe, and of his perception of how Soviet security interests in the region can be maintained (the 'Northern triangle' states will continue to be the principal zone of Soviet concern). Secondly, upon the capacity of any figure in the Soviet leadership to shape decisions (i.e. the decision would depend upon prevailing power balances within the

Kremlin). Thirdly, upon the Kremlin's assessments of the costs and benefits of Intervention: in the Gorbachev era, the intervention option is especially unattractive, for several reasons: resort to this option would probably kill Gorbachev's reform initiatives stone dead and would strengthen the position of conservative factions throughout the bloc; it would be a devastating blow to the Soviet Union's modernisation drive, by depriving the Soviet Union of necessary Western technology and investment and by provoking another arms race. Moreover, the 'post-Afghanistan' syndrome has sapped the Soviet faith in the efficacy of 'surgical interventions'.

Fourthly, upon Soviet perceptions of the nature of the challenge: in the postwar era, Soviet counterrevolutionary interventions (direct or 'proxy') can be roughly divided into two types, although actual situations are never as clear cut as this dichotomy would suggest: a) 'rescue mission' interventions – to prevent the overthrow of a party by forces opposed to communist rule; b) 'deviation control' interventions – to prevent a reformist party from pursuing a radical alternative to the Soviet model of socialism. In a period when the Soviets themselves are deviating from old orthodoxies, a 'rescue mission' type of intervention would seem more likely – i.e. it would follow a breakdown of order and a request for assistance from a beleaguered party (although the Kremlin no doubt hopes that the local ruling elites would be sufficiently strong to impose a 'Jaruzelski solution' on the population). If the Soviet Union did intervene directly, it would probably justify its decision by emphasising treaty obligations rather than defence of socialist gains.

Fifthly, the likely response of the West: notwithstanding the postwar 'rules of the game' with regard to Eastern Europe as a Soviet sphere of interest, the Western states may nevertheless perform an increasingly important 'balance tipping' role in relation to intra-bloc crises: the vacillations within the Kremlin during the Prague Spring and the 1980/1 Polish crisis were signs that the Soviet leadership were acutely aware of the costs and benefits of military action. A vigorous demonstration by the West of its dissatisfaction with the Soviet response to the crisis could serve to strengthen the hand of the opponents of intervention in the Kremlin. The West is not therefore helpless in relation to the changes which are taking place in Eastern Europe: its response should be to offer rewards for behaviour which widens the margins of freedom for the East European peoples and to 'punish' policies which seek to freeze Eastern Europe in the mould created by Stalin over four decades ago.

Conclusion

The emergence of the 'Brezhnev Doctrine' following the invasion of Czechoslovakia in 1968 in no sense represented a qualitative shift in Soviet attitudes towards the concept of sovereignty: rather, it constituted a continuation of the Soviet Union's traditional use of the concept as a weapon in the armoury of Soviet foreign policy, a weapon employed for both offensive and defensive purposes. In Eastern Europe after the Second World War, this 'weapon' was used (albeit ineffectively) by the Kremlin to cover the ugly fact of Soviet domination. However, as the postwar history of Soviet-Yugoslav relations, and the history of international relations within the Soviet bloc of states has shown, this weapon has put itself at the service of more than one East European master. From the first years of 'socialist international relations', Yugoslavia insisted upon its right to genuine, as distinct from purely formal, sovereignty. Within the Soviet bloc, the gap between the idea of sovereignty and (for the Soviet Union) its disagreeable reality has narrowed since the Stalin era – unless we regard sovereignty as an all-or-nothing condition, it seems reasonable to argue that the Peoples Democracies contained within the Soviet bloc are more 'sovereign' now than in the late 1940s. However, if three eventful decades have loosened the Soviet grip on Eastern Europe, they have not weakened the Soviet grasp of elementary logic: thus the phrase 'independent sovereign state', if taken literally, necessarily implies 'independent of the Soviet Union'.

The response of Soviet theorists and statesmen to these challenges to Soviet regional hegemony has been to subordinate the sovereignty principle to 'higher' Marxist–Leninist values, to resurrect the concept of an 'international relations of a new type' and to remind those who adhere to a literal interpretation of the sovereignty principle that sovereignty within the socialist community must be viewed from a transnational class perspective. Despite Gorbachev's conciliatory overtures to Eastern Europe, Western speculation concerning the imminent or actual demise of the doctrine must be treated with caution: Soviet statements vaunting the principles of sovereignty and independence in socialist international relations were made long before the emergence of Gorbachev. Even though conditions within the region have undoubtedly changed in the last three decades, history has repeatedly demonstrated that Soviet references to the sovereignty of the bloc states should not be taken too literally.

The theoretical foundations of the Brezhnev Doctrine are firmly rooted in Soviet Marxist thought and therefore cannot be dismissed as a novel by-product of the five allied powers' invasion of Czechoslovakia. Each of the component elements of the doctrine can be traced back to earlier periods in Soviet history and had been employed by the Kremlin as part of its overall strategy of control in Eastern Europe prior to the emergence of the Prague Spring. Indeed, it can be argued that the most novel aspect of the doctrine as it emerged in 1968 was the extent of its impact in the West and within the international communist movement, an impact attributable to the fact that the Warsaw Pact tanks patrolling the streets of Prague constituted a graphic illustration of its implications for Eastern Europe. As had been the case with regard to the Soviet invasion of Hungary in 1956, military intervention in Czechoslovakia removed the Soviet doctrine from the sphere of abstract theorising onto the plane of *realpolitik*: the invasion constituted a more eloquent exposition of the doctrine's implications than the dialectical casuistry of Soviet Marxist theoreticians: in this sense, the invasion of Czechoslovakia served to breathe life and meaning into concepts which could previously have been dismissed as little more than vacuous slogans.

The unsullied Marxist pedigree which Soviet theoreticians have bestowed upon the Soviet conceptualisation of 'socialist sovereignty' should not, of course, be taken at its face value: rather, it must be viewed as the product of a marriage between political expediency and Soviet state-centric interpretations of Marxist–Leninist doctrine. The ostensible purpose of the doctrine is to preserve the unity and cohesion of the socialist commonwealth by safeguarding the 'socialist gains' of each socialist state: it is therefore couched not in the language of 'national interest' but rather in the solidarist terminology of proletarian internationalism. In this sense the doctrine rests upon the assumed paramountcy of 'vertical' cleavages within the international system (manifested in the struggle between capitalism and socialism) over the horizontal division of mankind into separate states. However, between the idea and the reality of the Soviet approach to sovereignty falls the shadow of the Kremlin's fixation with national security. The Soviet conception of 'socialist sovereignty' as espoused by Soviet theoreticians in relation to the interventions in Hungary, Czechoslovakia and Afghanistan has its roots in the Soviet assumption that the national security of the USSR is dependent upon the continuing existence of a *cordon sanitaire* of Sovietised regions on the USSR's borders. Hence the survival of 'socialism' (in its Soviet Marxist–Leninist brand) within the bloc is perceived as inextricably linked to the survival of the Soviet Union itself. In practice, the Soviet Union's interpretation of its 'international duty' to defend socialism abroad has been a dependent variable of the Kremlin's current evaluation of the costs and benefits of rendering 'fraternal military aid'.

As a means of legitimising Soviet military intervention, the theory has hardly proved effective. However, the prominence it has assumed in the Soviet theory of international relations (and in international perceptions of the Kremlin's foreign policy preoccupations in Eastern Europe) has provided short term benefits to the Soviet Union in a number of respects. Firstly, the Brezhnev Doctrine represents a clarification of the hegemon's 'ground rules' – the extent to which the bloc states are free to stray from the path of orthodoxy defined by the Soviet Union. In particular, the enunciation of the doctrine in relation to the invasion of Czechoslovakia in 1968 and of Afghanistan in 1979, and during the Polish crisis of 1980–1 served to demonstrate that the Soviet Union would not tolerate 'anti-socialist degeneration' (perceived threats to communist rule) beyond a certain point. Secondly, it is an indication of the Soviet Union's continuing determination to utilise its 'power of last resort' in order to maintain its control within the bloc. Thirdly, the doctrine, as enunciated in Soviet statements during periods of crisis within the bloc, serves as an instrument of Soviet pressure whenever a bloc state seems in danger of loosening its ties with the Soviet Union. Therefore, in addition to providing a theoretical justification for military intervention *ex post facto*, the theory of limited sovereignty serves as a prophylactic signalling device, which, by sending a clear warning to East Europeans may prove sufficient to redirect an East European communist state along a path of development acceptable to Moscow.

Neither the 'conflict prophylaxis' nor the 'intervention-legitimation' functions of the doctrine are without their drawbacks for the Soviet Union. Not only is the doctrine repudiated by the major non-ruling parties, it has constituted an added thorn in the side of the Soviet Union's relations with China, Yugoslavia, Romania and Albania. Moreover, critics of the limited sovereignty doctrine have explicitly rejected the Soviet Union's claim that the theory has an authentic Marxist–Leninist pedigree. Nor does the theory have any basis in international law: rather, it is at odds with generally recognised legal principles. It has been argued by Soviet commentators that the Warsaw Pact provided the legal justification for the invasions of Hungary and Czechoslovakia: therefore, the Pact might be regarded as an institutional expression of the Brezhnev Doctrine. However, a literal reading of the text of the Treaty provides no justification of this view, except if one's definition of 'aggression' was to be stretched so wide as to encompass any threat to Soviet control within Eastern Europe.

The doctrine has proved to be an adaptable instrument of Soviet policy. Indeed, in a classic example of historical irony, one of the first tangible results of *glasnost'* could be that the doctrine will be employed for one of its original purposes. As this book has shown, the notion of 'limited sovereignty' partly derives from Bolshevik attempts to bestow an ideological rationale upon the enforced integration of non-Russian nationalities into the Soviet multinational state (by emphasising the primacy of proletarian internationalist imperatives over the principle of national self-determination). In the Gorbachev era, centrifugal pressures within the Soviet multinational empire (the emergence of powerful nationalist currents in the Baltic republics and in the Caucasus) may result in history repeating itself, not as farce but as further tragedy.

Moreover, by further destabilising Eastern Europe, the 'Gorbachev revolution' could indirectly give the Brezhnev Doctrine a renewed prominence: Gorbachev's controlled 'revolution from above' within the Soviet Union could indirectly detonate uncontrollable 'revolutions from below' within the Peoples Democracies. The ruling elites of these states know that Moscow remains the ultimate guarantor of their power: history never repeats itself in exactly the same way. However, the possibilities of an explosion in some part of the Soviet bloc seem high: the great economic slowdown of the 1980s has created a crisis psychology within the region. Efforts by the communist party leaderships to arrest this process of decline are likely to go the same dismal way as previous reformist programmes, since there are limits to the extent to which economic decentralisation can be introduced without impinging upon core political structures. Ruling elite strategies of 'out-group cooptation' (through the introduction of limited forms of political pluralism, as in Poland), seem more likely to fuel, rather than satisfy, urgent popular demands for fundamental change.

The 'new thinking' and the 'post-Afghanistan syndrome' have created dangerous ambiguities concerning Soviet toleration thresholds in Eastern Europe. The encouragement of reform in the region is a high-risk strategy which has proven costly to the Soviet Union in the past. The Soviets are likely to be sucked, albeit unwillingly, into Eastern Europe's developing crisis. The principal factors which could mitigate these dangers are that, after forty years, lessons have been learned on both sides. The Soviet Union is undoubtedly more tolerant of East European aspirations, and East Europeans have learned a certain finesse in dealing with Moscow. The defusion of East–West tension and the seemingly genuine commitment of Gorbachev to reform have further widened the margins of independence enjoyed by the bloc states. However, it would be unwise to assume that these margins have been abolished altogether: the terms and conditions of the 'Gorbachev Doctrine' for Eastern Europe have by no means been clearly enunciated. The real test of current Soviet tolerance thresholds will come when a ruling party seems on the verge of losing power *de facto*, or when a state seeks withdrawal from the Warsaw Pact (which could yet undermine Gorbachev's position, or force him to bare his 'iron teeth').

But even in these circumstances Soviet responses would be difficult to predict. There seems little possibility, in the near future, that the Soviet Union will accept the wholesale 'Finlandisation' of Eastern Europe: however, if constitutional reforms in Hungary do lead to the end of the communist party's rule, it may well be that the Soviets will accede to the country's aspirations for neutral status (underpinned by guarantees from the West). Although the Soviets would be unlikely to extend the same status to the strategically more important 'Northern Triangle' states, a neutralised Hungary could in time serve as a prototype for other countries within the bloc. However, this line of development is by no means inevitable: for example, a violent upheaval within the bloc could yet lead to a 'counter-reformation' in which a revivified Brezhnev Doctrine (possibly dressed in a new terminological livery) would be assigned a prominent role – even though, given the current fluid situation in Eastern Europe, the specific forms and scope of this new role cannot be confidently presaged. Although the doctrine has already been pronounced 'dead' by some Western commentators (and, also, though more obliquely, by some Soviet spokesmen), it may yet emerge from the graveyard of history to which it has been prematurely consigned in these assessments. It is still too early to write the obituary of the Brezhnev Doctrine.

Notes and References

1 Introduction

1. E. A. Korovin, *Sovremennoe mezhdunarodnoe publichnoe pravo*, Gosudarstvennoe izdatel'stvo, Moscow, 1926, p. 42.
2. L. Ratner, 'Mezhdunarodnoe pravo v marksistkom osvshchenin', *Sovetskoe gosudarstvo i pravo (SGP)*, no. 6, 1935, pp. 128–37, at p. 132.
3. Ibid.
4. E. A. Korovin, *Mezhdunarodnoe pravo perekhodnogo vremeni*, Gosudarstvennoe izdatel'stvo, Moscow, 1924, p. 60.
5. See Mark Vishniak, 'Sovereignty in Soviet Law', *Russian Review*, Jan. 1949, pp. 34–45.
6. A. Ia. Vyshinskiĭ, 'Mezhdunarodnoe pravo i mezhdunarodnaia organizatsiia', *SGP*, no. 1, 1948, pp. 1–23, at p. 21.
7. A. Zhdanov, 'The International Situation', *For A Lasting Peace, For A People's Democracy, (FALP)*, no. 1, 1947, pp. 2–4, at p. 3.
8. V. M. Koretskiĭ, 'General Debate on the Draft Declaration on the Rights and Duties of States', 9th Meeting, 25 April 1949, *Yearbook of the International Law Commission*, 1949, New York, 1956, pp. 70–3.
9. Comprising the USSR, Poland, Czechoslovakia, East Germany, Hungary, Romania and Bulgaria.
10. See Paul Keal, *Unspoken Rules and Superpower Dominance*, St Martin's Press, New York, 1983, ch. 3.
11. E. Korovin, 'The Second World War and International Law', *American Journal of International Law (AJIL)*, vol. 40, 1946, pp. 742–55, at p. 743.
12. K. A. Baginian, *Narushenie imperialisticheskimi gosudarstvami printsipa nevmeshatel'stva*, Izdatel'stvo akademii nauk SSSR, Moscow, 1954, p. 3. Soviet international relations literature is studded with references to the Soviet Union's unblemished record with regard to respect for sovereignty.
13. See W. Seton-Watson, *The Pattern of Communist Revolution*, Methuen, London, 1960, ch. 13.
14. Paul Shoup, 'Communism, Nationalism and the Growth of the Communist Community of Nations after World War II', *American Political Science Review (APSR)*, vol 56, 1962, pp. 886–98, at p. 890.
15. See Richard Pipes, *The Formation of the Soviet Union: Communism and Nationalism 1917–1923*, Atheneum, New York, 1980, ch. 6.
16. W. B. Ballis, 'The Political Evolution of a Soviet Satellite: the Mongolian People's Republic', *Western Political Quarterly*, vol. ix, June 1956, pp. 293–328.
17. See ch. 2.
18. N. Farberov, 'Obshchestvennoe i gosudarstvennoe ustroĭstvo stran narodnoĭ demokratii', *Bol'shevik*, no. 24, 1948, pp. 30–43, at p. 42.

262

19. See Ruth Amende Rosa, 'The Soviet Theory of "Peoples Democracy"', *World Politics*, vol 1, 1948, pp. 489–510; H. G. Skilling, '"People's Democracy" in Soviet Theory', *Soviet Studies*, vol 3, 1951–2, pp. 16–31, 131–49.

20. A. Orlov, 'Ideĭnoe i organizatsionnoe ukreplenie kommunisticheskikh i rabochikh partii stran narodnoĭ demokratii', *Bol'shevik*, no. 2, 1950, pp. 39–52, at p. 52.

21. Farberov, 'Obshchestvennoe i gosudarstvennoe . . .'

22. O. Kuusinen, 'Vy za ili protiv sovetskogo soiuza?', *Novoe vremia (NV)*, no. 39, 1948, pp. 3–12, at p. 5.

23. V. Tikhomirov, 'Ukreplenie soiuza rabochikh i trudiashchikhsia krest'ian v stranakh narodnoĭ demokratii', *Bol'shevik*, no. 7, 1950, pp. 41–8, at p. 41; N. P. Farberov, 'O klassakh i partiiakh v stranakh narodnoĭ demokratii tsentral'noĭ i iugo-vostochnoĭ evropy', *SGP*, no. 9, 1949, pp. 8–22, at p. 12.

24. B. S. Mankovskiĭ, 'Novyĭ etap v razvitii narodno-demokraticheskikh gosudarstv kak gosudarstv sotsialisticheskogo tipa', *SGP*, no. 7, 1950, pp. 1–13, at p. 2.

25. A. Ia. Vyshinskiĭ, 'Razoblachit' klevetnikov do kontsa', *Pravda*, 24 Oct. 1949, p. 3.

26. See M. Paromov, 'Formy i metody ekonomicheskogo sotrudnichestva SSSR i stran narodnoĭ demokratii', *Voprosy ekonomiki (VE)*, no. 12, 1950, pp. 34–50, at p. 34.

27. See I. Volges, 'The Hungarian Dictatorship of 1919: Russian Example versus Hungarian Reality', *East European Quarterly*, 1970, vol. 4, no. 1, 1970, pp. 58–71.

28. Pipes, *The Formation of the Soviet Union* . . . , pp. 254–5.

29. F. Konstantinov, *Socialist Internationalism*, Progress Publishers, Moscow, 1978, p. 97.

30. Ibid. See also I. D. Ostoia-Ovsianyĭ, A. I. Stepanov, V. D. Shchetinin (eds), *Diplomatiia sotsializma*, IMO, Moscow, 1973, p. 23.

31. T. T. Hammond, 'The Communist Takeover of Outer Mongolia: Model for Eastern Europe?', *Studies on the Soviet Union* (Munich), vol. xi, no. 4, 1971, pp. 107–44, at p. 108.

32. Sh. Sanakoyev, 'Formation and Development of Socialist International Relations', *International Affairs*, (Moscow) *(IA(M))*, no. 10, 1967, pp. 3–11, at p. 7.

33. See V. V. Aspaturian, 'The Union Republics and Soviet Nationalities as Instruments of Soviet Territorial Expansion', in V. V. Aspaturian, *Process and Power in Soviet Foreign Policy*, Little Brown, Boston, 1971, p. 473.

34. See for example, E. V. Tadevosian, 'Internatsionalizm sovetskogo mnogonatsional'nogo gosudarstva', *Voprosy filosofii*, *(VF)*, no. 11, 1982, pp. 16–29, at p. 21.

35. A. A. Gromyko and B. N. Ponomarev, *Istoriia vneshneĭ politiki SSSR (1945–80)*, tom 2, Izdatel'stvo nauka, Moscow, 1981, p. 48.

36. Konstantinov, *Socialist Internationalism*; Sanakoyev, 'Formation and Development of Socialist International Relations', p. 7.

37. See K. Marx and F. Engels, 'The Communist Manifesto', *Collected*

Works, (*CW*), vol. 6, Lawrence and Wishart, London, 1976, pp. 476–519, at p. 503.

38. Ibid., p. 488; Engels, 'Principles of Communism', *CW*, vol. 6, pp. 341–57, at p. 345; Engels, 'The Origin of the Family, Private Property and the State', in K. Marx and F. Engels, *Selected Works vol. II*, Lawrence and Wishart, London, 1962, pp. 170–307, at p. 302.

39. See 'Manifesto', p. 487.

40. Ibid., p. 503.

41. K. Marx, 'The Future Results of British Rule in India', in N. J. Smelser (ed.), *Karl Marx on Society and Social Change*, University of Chicago Press, 1973, p. 139.

42. 'Manifesto', *passim*. See also S. Avineri (ed.), *Karl Marx on Colonialism and Modernisation*, Doubleday Anchor, New York, 1969, pp. 133–7.

43. 'Manifesto', p. 486.

44. Ibid., p. 497.

45. K. Marx, 'Critique of the Gotha Programme', in K. Marx and F. Engels, *Selected Works In One Volume*, Lawrence and Wishart, London, 1968, pp. 311–31, at p. 327.

46. R. N. Berki, 'On Marxian Thought and the Problem of International Relations', *World Politics*, vol. 24, 1971–2, pp. 85–105.

47. V. Kubálková and A. Cruickshank, *Marxism-Leninism and Theory of International Relations*, Routledge and Kegan Paul, London, 1980, esp. ch. 2.

48. Berki, 'On Marxian Thought . . .', p. 85.

49. Kubálková and Cruickshank, *Marxism-Leninism and Theory of International Relations*, p. 62. They nevertheless argue that the predominant attitude of Marx and Engels towards international relations was a negative one (p. 241).

50. 'Manifesto', p. 503.

51. K. Marx, 'Letter to P. V. Annenkov, 28 Dec. 1846', *CW*, vol. 38, 1982, pp. 95–106, at p. 98.

52. F. Engels, *Anti-Dühring*, Lawrence and Wishart, London, 1954, p. 315. As S. Avineri has noted, it was Engels, in *Anti-Dühring*, who used the biological term 'withering away', whereas Marx always referred to the 'abolition and transcendence (aufhebung)' of the state, a philosophical description: *The Social and Political Thought of Karl Marx*, Cambridge University Press, 1968, p. 203.

53. F. Engels, 'Introduction To Karl Marx, "Civil War in France" ', in *Marx and Engels on the Paris Commune*, Progress Publishers, Moscow, 1971, p. 27.

54. For an examination of these issues, see Eliot Goodman, *The Soviet Design For a World State*, Columbia University Press, New York, 1960, esp. ch. 1; P. Mayer, *Cohesion and Conflict in International Communism*, Martinus Nijhoff, The Hague, 1968, ch. II.

55. V. I. Lenin, *Sochineniia*, tom 31, p. 209; see also his speech at a stone-laying ceremony for a monument to Marx: *Soch.*, tom 42, p. 150. All references to Lenin's works refer to the 4th edition (*Sochineniia*, Gosudarstvennoe izdatel'stvo politicheskoĭ literatury, Moscow, in 45

volumes published between 1941–67) unless otherwise stated.
56. See his speech on the founding of the Communist International in 1919: *Soch.*, tom 28, p. 461.
57. G. Zinoviev, *Kommunisticheskiĭ internatsional: doklad na vos'mom s''ezde RKP(B)*, Izdatel'stvo kommunisticheskogo internatsionala, Petrograd, 1919, p. 38.
58. I. V. Stalin, *Marksizm i natsional'no-kolonial'nyĭ vopros*, Gosudarstvennoe izdatel'stvo politicheskoĭ literatury, Moscow, 1939, p. 125.
59. Iu. L. Piatakov, in *Vosmoĭ s''ezd RKP(B) Stenograficheskiĭ otchet*, Izdatel'stvo gubern RSFSR, Saratov, 1919, p. 49.
60. L. Trotsky, *My Life*, Peter Smith, Gloucester, Mass., 1970, p. 341.
61. Ibid.
62. Engels, 'Principles of Communism', p. 352.
63. Lenin, 'Doklad o taktike RKP(B)', 5 July 1922, *Soch.*, tom 32, pp. 454–72, at p. 456.
64. Lenin, at 8th party congress, March 1919, *Soch.*, tom 29, pp. 126–43, at p. 133.
65. Lenin, *Soch.*, tom 22, pp. 132–45, at p. 135.
66. Lenin, 'O lozunge soedinennykh shtatov evropy', *Soch.*, tom 21, pp. 308–11, at p. 311.
67. Lenin, *Soch.*, tom 28, p. 309.
68. Lenin, 'Pervonachal'nyĭ nabrosok tezisov po natsional'nomu i kolonial'nomu voprosam', *Soch.*, tom 31, pp. 122–8, at p. 124.
69. G. Gurvich (ed.), *Konstitutsii SSSR i soiuznykh respublik*, Izdatel'stvo "vlast' sovetov", Moscow, 1933, pp. 5–19, at p. 7.
70. 'Statutes of the Communist International', adopted at the Second Comintern congress, 4 August 1920, in Jane Degras (ed.), *The Communist International 1919–43*, Oxford University Press, 1956, vol. 1, pp. 161–6, at p. 163.
71. I. V. Stalin, *Voprosy Leninizma*, 11th ed., Gospolitizdat, Moscow, 1947, p. 606.
72. N. S. Khrushchev, speech in Leipzig, 7 March 1959, reported in *Pravda*, 27 March 1959, p. 1. See also G. A. Brinkley, 'The "Withering" of the State under Khrushchev', *Review of Politics*, vol. 23, no. 1, 1961, pp. 37–51.
73. Ratner, 'Mezhdunarodnoe pravo v marksistskom ovshchenin', p. 132.
74. Korovin, 'The Second World War and International Law', p. 740.
75. E. Korovin, 'Absoliutnyĭ suverenitet ili absoliutnaia nepravda?', *NV*, no. 41, 1947, pp. 14–15, at p. 15.
76. See I. D. Levin, *Printsip suvereniteta v sovetskom i mezhdunarodnom prave*, Izdatel'stvo 'pravda', Moscow, 1947, p. 6.
77. V. N. Durdenevskiĭ and S. B. Krylov (eds), *Mezhdunarodnoe pravo*, Iuridicheskoe izdatel'stvo ministerstva iustitsii SSSR, Moscow, 1947, pp. 122–3.
78. E. B. Pashukanis, *Ocherki po mezhdunarodnomu pravu*, Gosudarstvennoe izdatel'stvo sovestskoe zakonodatel'stvo, Moscow, 1935, p. 91.
79. Editorial, 'Sovetskiĭ Soiuz-oplot mira i nezavisimosti narodov' *Bol'shevik*, no. 19, 1947, pp. 1–8, at p. 3.

80. Levin, *Printsip suvereniteta* . . . See also his *Suverenitet*, Iuridicheskoe izdatel'stvo ministerstva iustitsii SSSR, Moscow, 1948, and Korovin, 'Absoliutnyĭ . . .', pp. 14–15.
81. G. F. Aleksandrov, 'Kosmopolitizm-ideologiia imperialisticheskoĭ burzhuazii', *VF*, no. 3, 1948, pp. 174–92, at p. 177.
82. Editorial, 'Vospitanie sovetskogo patriotizma-vazhneĭshaia zadacha ideologicheskoĭ raboty', *Bol'shevik*, no. 14, 1947, pp. 1–7, at p. 1.
83. E. A. Korovin, 'Za sovetskuiu patrioticheskuiu nauku prava', *SGP*, no. 7, 1949, pp. 6–12, at p. 10. Levin had already recanted his 'mistakes' (see Levin, 'K voprosu o sushchnosti i znachenii printsipa suvereniteta', *SGP*, no. 6, 1949, pp. 33–46, at p. 33).
84. A. Ia. Vyshinskiĭ, 'O nekotorykh voprosakh teorii gosudarstva i prava', *SGP*, no. 6, 1948, pp. 1–17, at p. 7.
85. V. F. Gubin, 'Karl Marks i mezhdunarodnoe pravo', *Sovetskiĭ ezhegodnik mezhdunarodnogo prava (SEMP) 1968*, Izdatel'stvo nauka, Moscow, 1969, pp. 16–34.
86. Zhdanov, 'The International Situation', p. 3.
87. See Levin, 'K voprosu o sushchnosti i znachenii printsipa suvereniteta', p. 38.
88. Iu. Frantsev, 'Ideologiia burzhuaznogo natsionalizma na sluzhbe imperialisticheskoĭ reaktsii', *Bol'shevik*, no. 8, 1947, pp. 39–47, at p. 42.
89. Ibid.
90. K. Ia. Chizhov, 'Amerikanskiĭ imperializm-razrushitel' mezhdunarodnogo prava', *SGP*, no. 2, 1952, pp. 52–9, at p. 53.
91. Aleksandrov, 'Kosmopolitizm-ideologiia imperialisticheskoĭ burzhuazii', p. 182.
92. O. V. Bogdanov, 'Amerikanskaia mezhdunarodno-pravovaia doktrina na sluzhbe imperialisticheskoĭ expansii', *SGP*, no. 5, 1952, pp. 70–5, at p. 73.
93. Korovin, 'Mezhdunarodnoe pravo na sovremennom etape', *Bol'shevik*, no. 19, 1946, pp. 24–39, at p. 27.
94. Korovin, 'The Second World War . . .', p. 747.
95. Ibid.
96. A. Ia. Vyshinskiĭ speech to the UN on 10 Dec. 1948, in *Vneshniaia politika Sovetskogo Soiuza: dokumenty i materialy 1948*, Gosudarstvennoe izdatel'stvo politicheskoĭ literatury, Moscow, 1951, pp. 503–12, at pp. 505–6.
97. V. M. Koretskiĭ, 'General Debate on the Draft Declaration on the Rights and Duties of States', pp. 71–2.
98. Ibid., p. 71.
99. Ibid., p. 72.
100. Levin, 'K voprosu o sushchnosti i znachenii printsipa suverenita', p. 33. See also O. Kuusinen, *O pretendentakh na opeku nad narodami evropy*, Ogiz gospolitizdat, Moscow, 1947.
101. Levin, 'K voprosu o sushchnosti i znachenii printsipa suverenita'. See also, V. I. Lisovskiĭ, 'Evropeĭskiĭ sovet-orudie anglo-amerikanskikh imperialistov', *SGP*, no. 1, 1952, pp. 74–8.
102. A. A. Anisimov, 'Mezhdunarodnaia protivopravnost' atlanticheskogo

pakta', *SGP*, no. 1, 1952, pp. 62–8, at p. 63.
103. M. Marinin, 'Strategiia, politika i ekonomika v "plan Marshalla"', *Bol'shevik*, no. 14, 1948, pp. 48–62, at p. 62.
104. Durdenevskiĭ and Krylov (eds), *Mezhdunarodnoe pravo*, pp. 140–3.
105. Editorial, 'Sovetsko-bolgarskiĭ dogovor', *NV*, no. 13, 1948, pp. 1–2, at p. 1.
106. See V. F. Generalov, 'Ob osnovnykh chertakh mezhdunarodno-pravovogo sotrudnichestva Sovetskogo Soiuza i stran narodnoĭ demokratii', *SGP*, no. 7, 1950, pp. 14–26.
107. Zhdanov, 'The International Situation', p. 3.
108. Ts. Dragoĭcheva, 'Druzhba slavianskikh narodov', *NV*, no. 46, 1947, pp. 3–5.
109. Gheorghui-Dej, 'The Communist Party of Romania in the Struggle for the Democratisation of the Country', *FALP*, no. 3, 1947, p. 5.
110. See ch. 3.
111. N. Rubinsteĭn, 'Vneshniaia politika sovetskogo gosudarstva', *NV*, no. 12, 1948, pp. 4–7, at p. 6.
112. N. Leonidov, 'Sovetskiĭ Soiuz i strany narodnoĭ demokratii', *NV*, no. 45, 1948, pp. 2–5, at p. 3.
113. Lenin, 'Tretiĭ international i ego mesto v istorii', *Soch.*, tom 29, pp. 279–87, at p. 279.
114. Kuusinen, 'Vy za ili protiv sovetskogo soiuza?', p. 5.
115. Ibid., p. 12.
116. O. Eran, *The Mezhdunarodniki: An Assessment of Professional Expertise in the Making of Soviet Foreign Policy*, Turtledove, Ramat Gan, Israel, 1979.
117. S. Anghelov (ed.), *Socialist Internationalism: Theory and Practice of International Relations of a New Type*, Progress Publishers, Moscow, 1979, pp. 223–4.
118. Thomas M. Franck and Edward Weisband, *Word Politics: Verbal Strategy Among the Superpowers*, Oxford University Press, New York, 1971, ch. 8.
119. Zdeněk Mlynář, *Nightfrost in Prague*, Karz Publishers, New York, 1980, pp. 239–41.

2 The Genealogy of the Soviet Conception of Sovereignty

1. See for example, Alan James, *Sovereign Statehood*, Allen and Unwin, London, 1986, ch. 1.
2. Ibid., p. 1.
3. *Iuridicheskiĭ slovar'*, tom 2, Gosudarstvennoe izdatel'stvo iuridicheskoĭ literatury, Moscow, 1956, p. 460.
4. In Marek Stanislaw Korowicz, 'Some Present Aspects of Sovereignty in International Law', *Recueil Des Cours, Académie De Droit International De La Haye*, no. 1, 1961, pp. 5–118, at p. 8.
5. See F. H. Hinsley, 'The Concept of Sovereignty and the Relations Between States', in John C. Farrell and Asa P. Smith (eds), *Theory and Reality in International Relations*, Columbia University Press, New York, 1967, pp. 58–63, at p. 63.

6. Korowicz, 'Some Present Aspects of Sovereignty in International Law', pp. 35–67, V. Shevtsov, *The State and Nations in the USSR*, Progress Publishers, Moscow, 1982, p. 25.
7. V. A. Vasilenko, 'Gosudarstvennyĭ suverenitet i mezhdunarodnyĭ dogovor', *SEMP*, 1971, pp. 60–79, at p. 65.
8. Korovin, 'Absoliutnyi suverenitet ili absoliutnaia nepravda?'
9. S. V. Chernichenko, 'Sub"ektivnye granitsy mezhdunarodnogo prava i vnutrenniaia kompetentsiaia gosudarstv', *SEMP*, 1985, pp. 101–24, at p. 103.
10. Ia. Vyshinskiĭ, 'O nekotorykh voprosakh teorii gosudarstva i prava'.
11. *Iuridicheskiĭ slovar'*, p. 460.
12. F. Konstantinov, *Socialist Internationalism*, Progress Publishers, Moscow, 1978, p. 183.
13. B. M. Klimenko (ed.), *Slovar' mezhdunarodnogo prava*, Mezhdunarodnye otnosheniia, Moscow, 1982, p. 214; also *Iuridicheskiĭ entsiklopedicheskiĭ slovar'*, Sovetskaia entsiklopediia, Moscow, 1984, p. 359.
14. N. A. Ushakov, *Suverenitet v sovremennom mezhdunarodnom prave*, IMO, Moscow, 1963, pp. 6–8.
15. Shevtsov, *The State and Nations in the USSR*, p. 25.
16. Ushakov, *Suverenitet v sovremennom mezhdunarodnom prave*, p. 8.
17. V. V. Aspaturian, *Union Republics in Soviet Diplomacy*, Librairie E. Droz, Geneva, 1960, pp. 24–7.
18. G. Schwarzenberger, 'The Forms of Sovereignty', *Current Legal Problems*, vol. 10, Stevens, London, 1957, p. 276.
19. F. I. Kozhevnikov (ed.), *Mezhdunarodnoe pravo*, Gosudarstvennoe izdatel'stvo iuridicheskoĭ literatury, Moscow, 1957, p. 97.
20. Durdenevskiĭ and Krylov (eds), *Mezhdunarodnoe pravo*, p. 122.
21. I. Traĭnin, 'Voprosy suvereniteta v sovetskom soiuznom gosudarstve', *Bol'shevik*, no. 15, 1945, pp. 12–23, at p. 13.
22. Konstantinov, *Socialist Internationalism*.
23. F. I. Kozhevnikov and I. P. Blishchenko, 'Sotsializm i sovremennoe mezhdunarodnoe pravo', *SGP*, no. 4, 1970, pp. 88–95, at pp. 94–5.
24. V. Chkhikvadze, 'Historic Significance of the Formation of the Soviet Federal State', *Social Sciences* (Moscow), no. 4, 1972, pp. 33–46, at p. 37.
25. Durdenevskiĭ and Krylov (eds), *Mezhdunarodnoe pravo*, p. 114.
26. See ch. 12 for an analysis of current Soviet thinking on sovereignty.
27. See Franklyn Griffiths, 'Origins of Peaceful Coexistence', *Survey*, no. 50, Jan. 1964, pp. 195–201, at p. 195.
28. See Anthony Adamovich, 'Towards a Single Socialist Nation', *Studies on the Soviet Union* (Munich), no. 3, vol. 1, 1962, pp, 33–40; and I. A. Kurganov, 'The Nationality Policy of Communism', *Bulletin of the Institute for the Study of the USSR* (Munich), vol. viii, no. 1, 1961, pp. 12–17.
29. Pashukanis, *Ocherki po mezhdunarodnomu pravu*, pp. 16–18.
30. See W. Korey, 'The Comintern and the Genealogy of the "Brezhnev Doctrine" ', *Problems of Communism* vol. 18, 1969, pp. 52–9.
31. Hans Kelsen, *The Communist Theory of Law*, Stevens, London, 1955, p. 193.

32. P. Stuchka, *Uchenie o gosudarstve i konstitutsii RSFSR*, Izdatel'stvo 'krasnaia nov"', Moscow, 1923, p. 30; Korovin *Sovremennoe Mezhdunarodnoe publichnoe pravo*, pp. 42–3. In *Ocherki* . . . , Pashukanis defines 'sovereignty' as: independent authority (*vlast'*), not deriving from a higher power; and meaning 'complete self-determination' (p. 88).

33. See V. L. Verger, *Pravo i gosudarstvo perekhnogo vremeni*, Moscow, 1924, p. 200, quoted in Kubálková and Cruickshank, *Marxism-Leninism* . . . , pp. 129–30.

34. See Korovin, *Sovremennoe mezhdunarodnoe publichnoe pravo*, pp. 42–6. On the development of the Soviet theory of international law in the interwar period, see T. Taracouzio, *The Soviet Union and International Law*, Macmillan, London, 1935.

35. Vishniak, 'Sovereignty in Soviet Law', p. 38; he associates the rise of the 'positivist' doctrine of sovereignty in the late 1930s to Vyshinskiĭ.

36. F. Kozhevnikov, in *Sovetskoe gosudarstvo i revoliutsiia prava*, no. 3, 1930, pp. 147–8, in Ivo Lapenna, 'The Soviet Concept of "Socialist" International Law', *Year Book of World Affairs (YBWA)*, 1975, pp. 242–64, at p. 252.

37. Korovin, *Sovremennoe mezhdunarodnoe publichnoe pravo*, p. 42; Ratner, 'Mezhdunarodnoe pravo v marksistkom osvshchenin', p. 132.

38. E. A. Korovin, review of Taracouzio, *The Soviet Union and International Law, Harvard Law Review*, vol. 49, 1936, pp. 1392–5, at p. 1393.

39. K. Radek, 'The Bases of Soviet Foreign Policy', *Foreign Affairs*, Jan. 1934, pp. 193–206.

40. Korovin, review of *The Soviet Union and International Law*, p. 1394.

41. See G. Ginsburgs, 'A Case Study in the Soviet Use of International Law: Eastern Poland in 1939', *AJIL*, vol. 52, 1958, pp. 69–84; A. Shtromas, 'Soviet Occupation of the Baltic States and their Incorporation into the USSR, pt. 2, *East European Quarterly*, vol. xix, no. 4, 1986, pp. 459–67.

42. M. Jakobson, *The Diplomacy of the Winter War*, Harvard University Press, Cambridge, Mass., 1961, p. 166. In an article entitled 'The Creative Contribution of the USSR to the Equitable Solution of Territorial Problems', published in a Polish legal journal in 1950, the Soviet lawyer F. I. Kozhevnikov reaffirmed the notion of a just war by asserting that the USSR had the right to 'defend itself' by 'adjusting' the boundaries of another state if that state constituted a threat to Soviet security (F. I. Kozhevnikov, 'Twórcza rola ZSRR slusznym rozwialzywaniu zagadnień terytorialnych', *Państwo i Prawo*, vol. 5, no. 12, 1950, pp. 3–36, at p. 3 (contains English summary).

43. G. Aleksandrov (ed.), *Politicheskiĭ slovar'*, Gosudarstvennoe izdatel'stvo politicheskoĭ literatury, Moscow, 1940, p. 553.

44. Pipes, *The Formation of the Soviet Union*, p. 296.

45. Litvinov, speech delivered at the League of Nations, 1 July 1936, text in M. Litvinov, *Protiv aggressii*, Ogiz gosudarstvennoe izdatel'stvo politicheskoĭ literatury, Moscow, 1938, p. 22.

46. D. B. Levin, 'K voprosu o poniatii diplomatii', *SGP*, no. 9, 1948, pp. 14–28, at p. 27.

47. Pipes, *The Formation of the Soviet Union*, p. 296.

48. G. Zinoviev, 'Die Russische Revolution und das Internationale Proletariat', *Die Kommunistische Internationale, (KI)*, Feltrinelli reprint, Milan, 1967, no. 6, 1919, pp. 12–24, at p. 24.
49. G. Zinoviev, 'Die Perspectiven der Proletarischen Revolution', *KI*, no. 1, 1919, pp. 9–14, at p. 9.
50. G. Zinoviev, 'O kominterne', in *Desiatyi s"ezd RKP(B)*. *Stenograficheskoi otchet*, Gosudarstvennoe izdatel'stvo, Moscow, 1921, pp. 270–80, at p. 271.
51. Marx to Engels, 13 Feb. 1863, in Karl Marx and Friedrich Engels, *Correspondence 1846–1895*, Martin Lawrence, London, 1934, p. 144.
52. Korey, 'The Comintern and the Genealogy of the "Brezhnev Doctrine"'.
53. 'Appeal of the Second World Congress of the Communist International', in Alan Adler (ed.), *Theses, Resolutions and Manifestos of the First Four Congresses of the Third International*, Ink Links, London, 1980, pp. 61–3, at p. 62.
54. Council of Peoples Commissars Declaration, 28 Jan. 1920: text in Iu. V. Kliuchnikov and A. V. Sabanin (eds), *Mezhdunarodnaia politika: noveishego vremeni v dogovorakh notakh i deklaratsiiakh*, Izdanie litizdata NKID, Moscow, 1928, pp. 4–5.
55. N. Bukharin and E. Preobrazhenskiĭ, *Azbuka kommunizma*, Gosudarstvennoe izdatel'stvo, Moscow, 1920, p. 109.
56. *KPSS v rezoliutsiiakh i resheniiakh*, Izdatel'stvo politicheskoĭ literatury, Moscow, 1970, p. 69.
57. G. Tunkin, *Teoriia mezhdunarodnogo prava*, IMO, Moscow 1970, argues that Lenin opposed 'pushing revolutions' in a *Pravda* article on 28 Feb. 1918, p. 17. However, as the Yugoslav commentator Milos Prelević has noted, Lenin did favour the 'export of revolution', or 'socialist bonapartism' in 1920: 'Armed Conflicts Between Socialist Countries', *Survey* (Sarayevo), nos. 1–2, 1980, pp. 61–80, at p. 68.
58. Lenin, *Soch.*, tom 33, pp. 106–12, at p. 107.
59. Lenin, 'K istorii voprosa o neschastnom mire', *Soch.*, tom 26, pp. 401–8, at p. 408.
60. N. Bukharin, 'Speech on the Draft Programme at the Fourth Comintern Congress', in J. Degras (ed.), *Soviet Documents on Foreign Policy 1917–24*, vol. 1, RIIA, Oxford University Press, 1951, p. 322.
61. Ibid.
62. L. Trotsky, *Lenin*, Harrap, London, 1925, p. 220.
63. Trotsky, 'O voennom polozhenii i voennoĭ politike' in *Vosmoi s"ezd RKP(B)*, pp. 91–8, at p. 92.
64. See T. Davletshin, 'The Soviet Claim to Intervene in the Defence of Socialism', *Bulletin of the Institute for the Study of the USSR*, vol. XVI, August 1969, pp. 3–9.
65. M. N. Tukhachevskiĭ, 'K voprosu o sovremennoĭ strategii', in D. B. Riazanov *et al.*, *Voina i voennoe iskusstvo v svete istoricheskogo materializma*, Gosudarstvennoe izdatel'stvo, Moscow, 1927, pp. 103–35.
66. See Katriel Ben Arie, 'M. N. Tukhachevskiĭ and the Theory of Civil War', *East European Quarterly*, vol. XV, no. 4, 1982, pp. 441–521.

67. Warren Lerner, 'Attempting a Revolution from Without', *Studies on the Soviet Union*, vol. XI, no. 4, 1971, pp. 94–106, at p. 101.
68. Stalin, 'K itogam rabot XIV konferentsii RKP(B)', *Sochineniia* (Gosudarstvennoe izdatel'stvo politicheskoĭ literatury, Moscow, 1947–51, in 13 volumes), tom 7, pp. 90–132, at p. 101.
69. D. A. Gaĭdukov, V. M. Kotok, S. L. Ronin (eds), *Istoriia sovetskoĭ konstitutsii-sbornik dokumentov 1917–57*, Izdatel'stvo akademii nauk SSSR, Moscow, 1957, Doc. 124, pp. 226–37, at p. 226.
70. Korovin, *Mezhdunarodnoe pravo perekhodnogo vremeni*, p. 60.
71. Ibid.
72. Korovin, *Sovremennoe mezhdunarodnoe publichnoe pravo*, p. 42.
73. Ibid.
74. Korovin, *Mezhdunarodnoe pravo perekhodnogo vremeni*, p. 61.
75. Ibid.
76. Ibid.
77. E. Pashukanis, 'Mezhdunarodnoe pravo', in P. Stuchka (ed.), *Entsiklopediia gosudarstva i prava*, Kommunisticheskoĭ akademii, tom 2, Moscow, 1930, pp. 622–6, at p. 626.
78. E. Pashukanis, *Ocherki . . .* , ch. 1.
79. See Kelsen, *The Communist Theory of Law*, pp. 89–112.
80. Pashukanis, 'Interventsiia', in Stuchka (ed.), *Entsiklopediia . . .* , pp. 162–7.
81. Pashukanis, 'Interventsiia', p. 166.
82. Ibid., pp. 166–7.
83. Korovin, review of Taracouzio, p. 1393.
84. John N. Hazard, 'Cleansing Soviet International Law of Anti-Marxist Theories', *AJIL*, vol. 32, no. 2, 1938, pp. 244–52.
85. See Arie, 'M. N. Tukhachevskiĭ . . .'
86. M. Iroshnikov, D. Kovalenko, V. Shiskin, *Genesis of the Soviet Federative State (1917–25)*, Progress Publishers, Moscow, 1982, p. 18.
87. 'Sotsialisticheskaia revoliutsiia i pravo natsii na samoopredelenie', *Soch.*, tom 22, pp. 132–45, at pp. 135–6.
88. L. Kamenev, quoted in Jurij Borys, *The Russian Communist Party and the Sovietisation of the Ukraine*, Norstedt, Stockholm, 1960, p. 337.
89. V. V. Aspaturian, 'The Theory and Practice of Soviet Federalism', *Jl. of Politics*, vol. 12, no. 1, 1950, pp. 20–51, at p. 22.
90. See Lenin, 'Natsional'nyĭ vopros v nasheĭ programme', *Iskra*, 19 July 1903, in *Soch.*, tom 6, pp. 412–20, at p. 412.
91. Pavel Urban, 'The Nationality Question', *Studies on the Soviet Union*, vol. IX, no. 1, 1969, pp. 56–72, at p. 58.
92. Iroshnikov *et al.*, *Genesis of the Soviet Federative State*, p. 18.
93. Ibid.
94. Lenin, 'Doklad o partiĭnoĭ programme', 19 March 1919, *Soch.*, tom 29, pp. 144–73, at p. 171.
95. See Iroshnikov *et al.*, *Genesis of the Soviet Federative State*, pp. 18–19.
96. Lenin, 'Sotsialisticheskaia revoliutsiia . . .', pp. 135–6.
97. Urban, 'The Nationality Question', p. 59.
98. Lenin, 'K istorii voprosa o neschastnom mire', p. 408.
99. Lenin, 'Sotsialisticheskaia revoliutsiia . . .', p. 138.

100. 'Deklaratsiia prav narodov Rossii', in Gaĭdukov *et al.*, *Istoriia sovetskoĭ konstitutsii*, pp. 19–20.
101. Text in Gaĭdukov *et al.*, *Istoriia sovetskoĭ konstitutsii*, pp. 76–87, at p. 76.
102. See Pipes, *The Formation of the Soviet Union*, pp. 250–55.
103. See Taracouzio, *The Soviet Union and International Law*, pp. 30–31.
104. Text in Gaĭdukov *et al.*, *Istoriia sovetskoĭ konstitutsii*, pp. 44–46.
105. 'Ob obrazovanii SSSR', *Soch.*, tom 5, pp. 156–9, at p. 158.
106. 'Ob ob"edinenii sovetskikh respublik', *Soch.*, tom 5, pp. 145–55, at p. 150.
107. Borys, *The Russian Communist Party and the Sovietisation of the Ukraine*, pp. 131–53.
108. Ibid., pp. 32–5.
109. Pipes, *The Formation of the Soviet Union*, pp. 253–4.
110. Stalin, 'Ob ob"edinenii sovetskikh respublik', p. 150.
111. Stalin, 'Zakliuchitel'noe slovo po dokladu o natsional'nykh momentakh v partiĭnom i gosudarstvennom stroitel'stve', 12 s"ezd RKP(B), 25 April 1923, *Soch.*, tom 5, pp. 264–75, at p. 265.
112. Stalin, 'K itogam rabot XIV konferentsii RKP(B)', p. 101.
113. Stalin, 'O proekte konstitutsii Soiuza SSR', 25 Nov. 1936, *Voprosy Leninizma*, Gospolitizdat, Moscow, 1952, p. 551.
114. A. Alymov and S. Studenikin, 'Sovetskiĭ federalizm i demokraticheskiĭ tsentralizm', *Sovetskoe gosudarstvo*, 1933, nos. 1–2, pp. 13–20, at p. 19.
115. See Shvetsov, *The State and Nations in the USSR*, p. 6.

3 Sovereignty and Stalin's Policy towards Eastern Europe

1. Raymond L. Garthoff, 'The Concept of the Balance of Power in Soviet Policy Making', *World Politics*, vol. 4, 1951–2, pp. 85–111.
2. See M. Rubinsteĭn, 'Bor'ba imperialisticheskogo i antiimperialisticheskogo lagereĭ', *Mirovoe khoziaĭstvo i morovaia politika', ('MKhMP')*, no. 11, 1947, pp. 78–94.
3. Declaration of the first Cominform conference, *FALP*, no. 1, 10 Nov. 1947, p. 1.
4. Frederick C. Barghoorn, 'The Varga Discussion and its Significance', *American Slavic and East European Review*, vol. 7, no. 3, 1948, pp. 214–36.
5. L. Mendel'son, 'Krizisy i tsikly epokhi obshchego krizisa kapitalizma', *MKhMP*, no. 11, 1947, pp. 42–77.
6. I. Lemin, 'Ekonomicheskie protivorechiia i bor'ba mezhdu amerikanskimi i angliĭskimi imperialistami', *VE*, no. 7, 1949, pp. 61–82.
7. Stalin, 'K itogam rabot XIV konferentsii RKP(B); also 'Politicheskiĭ otchet tsentral'nogo komiteta (XIV s'ezd VKP(B))', *Soch.*, tom 7, pp. 261–391, at p. 265.
8. Ibid., pp. 92–3.
9. Stalin, at the 15th Congress, Dec. 1927, *Soch.*, tom 10, pp. 271–371, at pp. 282–9.
10. Stalin, 'Politicheskiĭ otchet tsentral'nogo komiteta XVI s"ezdu

VKP(B), June 1930, *Soch.*, tom 12, pp. 235–373, at p. 235. For an analysis of Stalin's theory of revolutionary 'ebbs and flows', see 'Historicus', 'Stalin on Revolution', *Foreign Affairs*, vol. 27, no. 2, 1949, pp. 174–214, at pp. 192–3.

11. This assumption has been questioned by Gati: see Charles Gati, 'The Stalinist Legacy in Soviet Foreign Policy', in E. P. Hoffman (ed.), 'The Soviet Union in the 1980s', *Proceedings of the Academy of Political Science*, New York, vol. 35, no. 3, 1984, pp. 214–26, at p. 218.

12. In *Desiatyi s"ezd RKP(B)* . . . , p. 20.

13. Letter to Lenin 1 Jan. 1920, in Lenin, *Soch.*, (3rd edition), Partizdat tsk VKP(B), Moscow, 1936, tom 5, p. 624.

14. See Urban, 'The Nationality Question', pp. 56–7.

15. See Pipes, *The Formation of the Soviet Union*, p. 272.

16. Stalin, 'Ob ob"edinenii sovetskikh respublik', *Soch.*, tom 5, pp. 145–55, at pp. 149–50.

17. See V. V. Aspaturian, 'The Union Republics and Soviet Nationalities as Instruments of Soviet Territorial Expansion', in V. V. Aspaturian (ed.), *Power and Process in Soviet Foreign Policy*, Little Brown, Boston, 1971, pp. 473–4.

18. Ivan Bernier, *International Legal Aspects of Federalism*, Longman, London, 1973, pp. 106–7.

19. Traĭnin, 'Voprosy suvereniteta . . .', p. 21.

20. On Soviet federalism in this period see V. V. Aspaturian, 'The Theory and Practice of Soviet Federalism', *Jl. of Politics*, vol. xii, 1950, pp. 20–51.

21. See I. Dzyuba, *Internationalism or Russification? A Study of the Soviet Nationalities Problem*, Weidenfeld and Nicolson, London, 1968, p. x.

22. E. Korovin, 'Mezhdunarodnoe pravo na sovremennom etape', *Bol'shevik*, no. 19, 1946, pp. 24–39, at p. 27.

23. Ibid.; Traĭnin argued that the Soviet multinational state marked a higher stage in the solution of the national question: 'Voprosy suvereniteta . . .', p. 22.

24. Stalin, 'Politika sovetskoĭ vlasti po natsional'nomu voprosu v Rossii', *Soch.*, tom 4, pp. 351–363; 'counter-revolutionary' at P. 354; 'bondage' at p. 352.

25. Ibid., pp. 352–3.

26. See Traĭnin, 'Voprosy suvereniteta'.

27. *Pravda*, 7 Feb. 1946, p. 1.

28. Milovan Djilas, *Conversations With Stalin*, Rupert Hart-Davis, London, 1962, p. 160.

29. Ibid.

30. Ibid.

31. See Aurel Brown, *Romanian Foreign Policy since 1965*, Praeger, New York, 1978, p. 59.

32. See Stephen Clissold (ed.), *The Soviet-Yugoslav Dispute*, RIIA, London, 1948, Doc. 120, pp. 183–197, at p. 187; P. Auty *Tito*, Longmans, London, 1970, p. 250.

33. See Charles S. Maier (ed.), *The Origins of the Cold War in Contemporary Europe*, New Viewpoints, New York, 1978.

34. See Seton-Watson, *The Pattern of Communist Revolution*, p. 256.
35. I. Deutscher, *Stalin*, Penguin, Harmondsworth, 1966, p. 549. See also F. Claudin, *The Communist Movement*, Penguin, Harmondsworth, 1975, p. 452.
36. On the Cominform see Adam B. Ulam, 'The Cominform and the Peoples Democracies', *World Politics*, vol. 3, no. 2, 1951, pp. 200–17.
37. For the text of the Blad proposals, see *Jl. of Central European Affairs*, vol. VII, 1947, pp. 416–17. These plans were denounced as 'counterrevolutionary': see Piotr S. Wandycz, 'Recent Traditions of the Quest for Unity: Attempted Polish-Czechoslovak and Yugoslav-Bulgarian Confederations 1940–48', in Jerzy Lukaszewski, *The Peoples Democracies After Prague*, (College of Europe), De Tempelhof, Bruges, 1970, pp. 85–93, at p. 91.
38. Z. Brzezinski, *The Soviet Bloc: Unity and Conflict*, Harvard University Press, Cambridge, Mass., 1960, pp. 81–2.
39. See Sh. Sanakoyev, 'The 21st. Congress on the Socialist Countries' Transition to Socialism', *IA(M)*, no. 5, 1959, pp. 32–8, at pp. 35–7. On convergence and levelling up, see: M. Z. Aïrapetian and V. V. Suzhodeev, *Novyĭ tip mezhdunarodnykh otnosheniĭ*, Mysl, Moscow, 1964, p. 181; K. Katushev, 'Ukreplenie edinstva sotsialisticheskikh stran-zakonomernost' razvitiia mirovogo sotsializma', *Kommunist*, no. 16, 1973, pp. 17–54, at p. 18.
40. Soviet integration theory lays stress on the voluntariness of integration processes: see E. T. Usenko, 'Mezhdunarodno-pravovye problemy rashirenia i uglubleniia sotrudnichestva sotsialisticheskikh gosudarstv', *SEMP*, 1983, pp. 28–40, at p. 37.
41. Z. Brzezinski, *The Soviet Bloc.* . . .
42. A. B. Ulam, *Expansion and Coexistence*, Secker and Warburg, London, 1968, p. 109.
43. N. Jamgotch Jr, *Soviet–East European Dialogue: International Relations of a New Type?*, Stanford University Press, 1968, p. 25.
44. S. Kovalev, 'Suverenitet i internatsional'nye obiazannosti sotsialisticheskikh stran', *Pravda*, 26 Sept. 1968, p. 4.
45. Konstantinov, *Socialist Internationalism*, p. 192.
46. Ibid.
47. Lynn Etheridge Davis, *The Cold War Begins: Soviet-American Conflict Over Eastern Europe*, Princeton University Press, 1974, 282–4.
48. See F. A. Vali, 'Soviet Satellite Status and International Law', *JAG Journal*, Oct.–Nov. 1961, pp. 169–72.
49. James Rosenau, 'Pre-theories and Theories of Foreign Policy', in R. Barry Farrell (ed.), *Approaches to Comparative and International Politics*, Northwestern University Press, Evanston, Ill., 1966.
50. V. V. Aspaturian, *Union Republics in Soviet Diplomacy: a Study of Soviet Federalism in the Service of Soviet Foreign Policy*, Librairie E. Droz, Geneva, 1960.
51. See William Zimmerman, 'Dependency Theory and the Soviet-East-European Hierarchical Regional System: Initial Tests', *Slavic Review*, vol. 37, no. 4, 1978, pp. 604–21.
52. Valerie Bunce, 'The Empire Strikes Back: The Evolution of the

Eastern Bloc from a Soviet Asset to a Soviet Liability', *International Organisation*, vol. 39, no. 1, 1985, pp. 1–46.

53. Vali, 'Soviet Satellite Status and International Law', p. 172.
54. Korowicz, 'Some Present Aspects of Sovereignty . . .', p. 95.
55. Ibid.
56. Aspaturian, *Union Republics in Soviet Diplomacy* . . . , pp. 25–9.
57. Ibid.
58. Ibid.
59. See Henry Bernstein (ed.), *Underdevelopment and Development: the Third World Today*, Penguin, Harmondsworth, 1978.
60. Paul Marer, 'Has Eastern Europe become a Liability to the Soviet Union?', in Charles Gati (ed.), *The International Politics of Eastern Europe*, Praeger, New York, 1976, pp. 59–81.
61. Bunce, 'The Empire Strikes Back . . .'.
62. M. S. Vazquez, 'Zones of Influence', *YBWA*, 1973, pp. 301–15, at pp. 301–2.
63. Edy Kaufman, *The Superpowers and their Spheres of Influence*, Croom Helm, London, 1976, p. 10.
64. G. N. Curzon, 'Frontiers', *The Romanes Lecture 1907*, Clarendon Press, London 1907, p. 42. See also G. W. Rutherford, 'Spheres of Influence: An Aspect of Semi-Suzerainty', *AJIL*, vol 20, no. 2, 1926, pp. 300–25.
65. See Lynn Etheridge Davis, *The Cold War Begins* . . . , p. 141.
66. W. S. Churchill, *The Second World War, Triumph and the Tragedy*, Houghton Mifflin, Boston, 1951, pp. 227–8.
67. Dean Rusk, in a speech at New Haven on 12 Sept. 1968, *Keesings Contemporary Archives*, 26 Oct.–2 Nov. 1968, p. 22994.
68. See B. Rychlowskii, 'The Yalta Conference and the Present Day', *IA(M)*, no. 7, 1984, pp. 89–97; Vera Tolz, 'The Soviet Press Marks the Anniversary of the Yalta Conference' *Radio Free Europe-Radio Liberty, Radio Liberty Research (RLR)*, RL54/85, 19 Feb. 1985, pp. 1–6.
69. R. Lowenthal, 'The Logic of One Party Rule', in Alexander Dallin (ed.), *Soviet Conduct in World Affairs*, Greenwood Press, Westport, Conn., 1961, pp. 58–74, at p. 66.

4 Early Postwar Soviet Theories of Socialist International Relations

1. E. Varga, 'Demokratiia novogo tipa', *MKhMP*, no. 3, 1947, pp. 3–14.
2. See Ivo Lapenna, 'The Soviet Concept of Socialist International Law', *YBWA*, 1975, pp. 242–64, at p. 255.
3. See W. Zimmerman, *Soviet Perspectives on International Relations 1956–67*, Princeton University Press, 1969, ch. 2.
4. See Samson Soloveitchik, 'International Law as "Instrument of Politics"', *University of Kansas City Law Review*, vol 21, 1953, pp. 169–83.
5. Richard T. de George, *Patterns of Soviet Thought*, University of Michigan Press, 1968, p. 238.
6. See F. I. Kozhevnikov, 'Nekotorie voprosy mezhdunarodnogo prava v

svete truda I. V. Stalin "Marksizm i voprosy iazikozneniia"', *SGP*, no. 6, 1951, pp. 25–36.

7. N. Leonidov, 'Novaia polosa v istorii slavianskikh narodov', *NV*, no. 9, 1946, pp. 3–6, at p. 6.
8. W. Gomulka, in *FALP*, no. 1, 1947, p. 8.
9. Iu. Frantsev, 'Natsionalizm-oruzhie imperialisticheskoĭ reaktsii', *Bol'shevik*, no. 15, 1948, pp. 45–55, at p. 55.
10. Zhdanov, 'The International Situation . . .', *FALP*, p. 4.
11. See ch. 5.
12. N. Farberov, 'Obshchestvennoe i gosudarstvennoe ustroĭstvo stran narod'noĭ demokratii', *Bol'shevik*, no. 24, 1948, pp. 30–43, at p. 42.
13. Iu. Frantsev, 'Ideologiia burzhuaznogo natsionalizma na sluzhbe imperialisticheskoĭ reaktsii', *Bol'shevik*, no. 8, 1947, pp. 39–47, at p. 47.
14. 'Bratskiĭ privet vsem narodam boriushchimsia za pobedu demokratii i sotsializma', *Pravda*, 4 Nov. 1949, p. 1.
15. Gheorghiu-Dej, 'The Soviet Union, Leading Force in Camp of Democracy and Socialism', *FALP*, no. 21, 1948, p. 3.
16. K. Gottwald, 'Fraternal Alliance with USSR – Basic Principle of People's Democratic Policy', *FALP*, no. 21, 1948, p. 3.
17. See, for example, Stanislaw Ehrlich 'Demokracja Ludowa', *Państwo i Prawo*, vol. 4, no. 3, 1949, pp. 3–11.
18. N. Leonidov, 'Velikaia sokrovishchnitsa', *NV*, no. 46, 1949, pp. 4–9, at p. 8.
19. See I. Dudinskiĭ, 'Ekonomicheskoe sotrudnichestvo SSSR i stran narodnoĭ demokratii', *Bol'shevik*, no. 6, 1950, pp. 9–19; N. D. Kazantsev, 'Zemel'nye reformy v stranakh narodnoĭ demokratii', *SGP*, no. 6, 1949, pp. 18–32, at p. 18.
20. Leonidov, 'Velikaia sokrovishchnitsa'.
21. A. Orlov, 'Ideĭnoe i organizatsionnoe ukreplenie kommunisticheskikh i rabochikh partii stran narodnoĭ demokratii', *Bol'shevik*, no. 2, 1950, pp. 39–52, at p. 52.
22. Frantsev, 'Natsionalizm-oruzhie imperialisticheskoĭ reaktsii'.
23. N. Leonidov, 'Sovetskiĭ Soiuz i strany narodnoĭ demokratii', *NV*, no. 45, 1948, pp. 3–7, at p. 7.
24. Ibid., p. 5.
25. G. Dimitrov, in *FALP*, no. 21, 1948, p. 2.
26. F. Chernov, 'Burzhuaznyĭ kosmopolitizm i ego reaktsionnaia rol'', *Bol'shevik*, no. 5, 1949, pp. 30–41, at p. 31.
27. Editorial, 'Against Nationalism, For Proletarian Internationalism', *FALP*, no. 10, 1949, p. 1.
28. Ibid.
29. See Dudinskiĭ, 'Ekonomicheskoe sotrudnichestvo . . .'; P. Figurnov, 'Stroitel'stvo sotsialisticheskoĭ ekonomiki v evropeĭskikh stranakh narodnoĭ demokratii', *Bol'shevik*, no. 20, 1949, pp. 49–61.
30. A. Leont'ev, 'Ekonomicheskie osnovy novoĭ demokratii', *Planovoe khoziaĭstvo (PKh)*, no. 4, 1947, pp. 63–79; V. Karra, 'Ob ekonomicheskom razvitii Rumynskoi narodnoĭ respubliki', *VE*, no. 4, 1948, pp. 74–81, at p. 77.
31. N. Leonidov, 'Sovetskiĭ Soiuz . . .', p. 6; V. F. Kirichenko, 'Bor'ba s

prestupnymi posiagatel'stvami na ekonomicheskiĭ stroĭ evropeĭskikh gosudarstv narodnoĭ demokratii', *SGP*, no. 6, 1951, pp. 37–46.

32. Speech at the 6th Congress of the Yugoslav Communist Party in November 1952, in Clissold (ed.), *Yugoslavia and the Soviet Union* ..., Doc. 162, pp. 245–7.
33. See, for example, A. Zauberman, *Economic Imperialism: The Lesson of Eastern Europe*, Bellman Books, London, 1948.
34. Rákosi described 'peoples democracy' as a dictatorship of the proletariat without the Soviet form, *The New York Times*, 23 Jan. 1949.
35. Leonidov, 'Sovetskiĭ Soiuz ...', Leonidov's quotation is taken from a speech by Stalin in August 1927: *Soch.*, tom 10, p. 51.
36. See Gheorghiu-Dej, 'Betrayal of Revolutionary Marxism', *FALP*, no. 13, 1948, p. 3.
37. P. Lendvai, 'How to Combine Détente with Soviet Hegemony?', *Survey*, vol. 77, Autumn 1970, pp. 75–92, at p. 76.
38. See Rosa, 'The Soviet Theory of "Peoples Democracy"'; Skilling, '"People's Democracy" in Soviet Theory'.
39. K. Grzybowski, 'The Commonwealth of Socialist Nations', in A. Larson and C. W. Jenks (eds), *Sovereignty Within the Law*, Dobbs Ferry, New York, 1965, pp. 319–31, at p. 322.
40. S. Yakubson, 'The Soviet Concept of Satellite States', *Review of Politics*, vol. 2, April 1949, pp. 184–95. See also W. B. Ballis, 'Soviet Russia's Asiatic Frontier Technique: Tannu Tuva', *Pacific Affairs*, vol. 14, March 1941, pp. 91–6.
41. Claudin, *The Communist Movement*, p. 182.
42. Editorial, 'Deviatnadsatsaia godovshchina' in *Kommunisticheskiĭ Internatsional*, vol. 16, Oct. 1936, pp. 8–14. See Joan Barth Urban, 'Moscow and the PCI in the 1970s: Kto Kovo?', *Studies in Comparative Communism*, Summer/Autumn 1980, pp. 99–167, at p. 104.
43. B. Schwartz, 'China and the Soviet Theory of People's Democracy', *Problems of Communism*, Sept.–Oct. 1954, pp. 6–15.
44. Rosa, 'The Soviet Theory of People's Democracy', p. 490.
45. A. Ross Johnson, *The Transformation of Communist Ideology: The Yugoslav Case 1945–53*, The MIT Press, 1972, pp. 11–12.
46. Ibid.
47. See G. Skilling, '"People's Democracy" in Soviet Theory'.
48. Varga, 'Demokratiia novogo tipa'.
49. Johnson, *The Transformation of Communist Ideology* ..., pp. 13–19.
50. Ibid.; also Skilling, '"People's Democracy" in Soviet Theory'.
51. For example, in each of the Peoples Democracies 'the leading role belongs to the communist parties': I. Konstantinovskiĭ, 'Strany narodnoĭ demokratii-novaia bresh' v sisteme imperializma', *NV*, no. 49, 1947, pp. 3–9, at p. 5. B. S. Mankovskiĭ emphasised the importance of democratic centralism: 'Narodno-demokraticheskaia respublika-politicheskaia forma diktatury rabochego klassa', *SGP*, no. 10, 1949, pp. 12–21, at p. 18.
52. N. P. Farberov 'O klassakh i partiiakh v stranakh narodnoĭ demokratii tsentral'noĭ i iugo-vostochnoĭ evropy', *SGP*, no. 9, 1949, pp. 8–22, at p. 12.
53. Rosa, 'The Soviet Theory of "Peoples Democracy"', p. 490.

54. At the Bulgarian Party Congress in December 1948, in Skilling, '"People's Democracy" in Soviet Theory', p. 25.
55. N. Farberov, 'Novye momenty v razvitii narodnoĭ demokratii', *SGP*, no. 1, 1949, pp. 40–54; V. Karra, 'Druzhba i sotrudnichestvo stran narodnoĭ demokratii', *NV*, no. 5, 1948, pp. 3–6.
56. B. S. Mankovskiĭ, 'Klassovaia sushchnost' narodnodemokraticheskogo gosudarstva', *SGP*, no. 6, 1949, pp. 7–17, at p. 11.
57. N. D. Kazantsev, 'Zemelnie reformy stranakh narodnoĭ demokratii', *SGP*, no. 6, 1949, pp. 18–32, at p. 18.
58. A. Kosmin, 'Demokraticheskii tsentralizm-nezyblemyi zakon partiinoi zhizni', *Bol'shevik*, no. 2, 1950, pp. 53–63.
59. Konstantinovskiĭ, 'Strany narodnoĭ demokratii . . .'.
60. Ibid.
61. B. S. Mankovskiĭ, 'Novyĭ etap v razvitii narodno-demokraticheskikh gosudarstv kak gosudarstv sotsialisticheskogo tipa', *SGP*, no. 7, 1950, pp. 1–13, at p. 5.
62. Ehrlich, 'Democracja Ludowa'.
63. H. Draper, 'The Dictatorship of the Proletariat', in M. Curtis, (ed.), *Marxism*, Atherton Press, New York, 1970, pp. 285–96.
64. Ibid.
65. R. Tucker, 'The Proletarian State', in Curtis (ed.), *Marxism*, pp. 297–302, at p. 300.
66. Lenin, 'Proletarskaia revoliutsiia i renegat' Kautskiĭ', *Soch.*, tom 28, pp. 209–309, at p. 217.
67. Ibid., pp. 219–21.
68. Ibid.
69. Ibid., p. 220.
70. Ibid., pp. 226–7.
71. Lenin, 'Doklad o partiinoĭ programme', *Soch.*, tom 29, pp. 144–63, at p. 161.
72. Ibid.
73. Lenin, 'Detskaia bolezn' "levizny" v kommunizme', *Soch.*, tom 31, pp. 5–97, at p. 26.
74. Ibid., p. 26.
75. Ibid., p. 27.
76. M. Paromov, 'Formy i metody ekonomicheskogo sotrudnichestva SSSR i stran narodnoĭ demokratii', p. 34.
77. Editorial: 'Basis of Fraternal Cooperation Between Free Peoples', *FALP*, no. 30, 1951, p. 1.
78. E. Korovin, 'Mezhdunarodnoe pravo na sovremennom etape', at p. 27.
79. Leonidov, 'Sovetskiĭ Soiuz . . .', p. 4.
80. Paromov, 'Formy i metody'.
81. J. Berman, 'Stran narodnoĭ demokratii na poroge novogo goda', *NV*, no. 1, 1951, pp. 7–12, at p. 7.
82. Gheorghiu-Dej, *FALP*, no. 3, 1947, p. 5.
83. See A. Marinin, 'Strategiia, politika i ekonomika v "plan Marshalla"', at p. 62.
84. O. Petrovskiĭ, 'Vneshnetorgovaia politika stran narodnoĭ demokratii',

NV, no. 2, 1948, pp. 3–10, at p. 6.
85. Dudinskiĭ, 'Ekonomicheskoe sotrudnichestvo . . .', p. 9.
86. A. Kashkarov, 'Dve linii ekonomicheskogo razvitiia v evrope', *NV*, no. 50, 1948, pp. 7–12, at p. 10; also M. Rubinshteĭn, 'Kapitalisticheskie monopolii SShA podzhigateli novoĭ voiny', *Pkh*, no. 3, 1949, pp. 66–83.
87. K. Ia. Chizhov, 'Ekonomicheskaia ekspansiia SSha-ugroza suverenitetu gosudarstv', *SGP*, no. 6, 1951, pp. 47–61, at p. 60.
88. A. Leont'ev, 'O kosmopolitizme i internatsionalizme', *NV*, no. 15, 1949, pp. 10–14, at p. 11.
89. A. Leont'ev, 'Plan Marshalla v svete deĭstvitel'nosti', *NV*, no. 26, 1948, pp. 3–9, at p. 5.
90. Conference Declaration, *FALP*, no. 1, 1947, p. 1.
91. M. Marinin, 'Strategiia, politika . . .'.

5 Marxist–Leninist Doctrine and the Soviet Theory of Sovereignty

1. 'Platform of the Communist International', adopted by the first congress (drafted by Bukharin), 4 March 1919, in Degras (ed.), *The Communist International 1919–43*, vol. 1, p. 23.
2. Lenin, *Soch.*, tom 31, p. 148.
3. I. Pomelov, 'Splochenie sil sotsializma i nekotorye voprosy ideologicheskoĭ bor'by i Vengrii', *Kommunist*, no. 10, 1957, pp. 73–90, at p. 82.
4. Sh. Sanakoyev, 'Proletarian Internationalism: Theory and Practice', *IA(M)*, no. 4, 1969, pp. 9–15, at p. 14.
5. Sh. Sanakoyev and N. I. Kapchenko, *Nachinye osnovy vneshneĭ politiki sotsializma*, Izdatel'stvo 'znanie', (Seriia mezhudunarodnaia, no. 11), Moscow, 1971, p. 17; Editorial: 'Pod znamenem proletarskogo internatsionalizma', *Kommunist*, no. 18, 1968, pp. 3–7.
6. G. Shakhnazarov, 'The "Great Power" Approach to International Politics', *WMR*, no. 5, 1972, pp. 34–46, at p. 36.
7. Allen Lynch, *The Soviet Study of International Relations*, Cambridge University Press, 1987, p. 140.
8. L. A. Shvetsov, *Internatsionalnaia rol' KPSS v mirovom revoliutsionnom dvizhennii*, Lenizdat, Moscow, 1972, p. 8.
9. Shakhnazarov, 'The "Great Power" Approach to International Politics'.
10. Iu. Ia. Kirshin, 'Mirovaia politika: sushchnost', osnovnye cherty i tendentsii', *VE*, no. 12, 1982, pp. 67–74, at p. 68.
11. G. Shakhnazarov, 'Governability of the World', *IA(M)*, no. 3, 1988, pp. 16–24, at p. 17. See also I. Gur'ev, 'V avangarde istorii', *MEMO*, no. 11, 1987, pp. 3–14.
12. In 'Perestroika, the 19th Party Conference and Foreign Policy', (Guest Club discussion), *IA(M)*, no. 7, 1988, pp. 1–18, at p. 5.
13. E. G. Plimak, 'Novoe myshlenie i perspektivy sotsial'nogo obnovleniia mira', *VE*, no. 6, 1987, pp. 73–89, at p. 78.

14. V. Zagladin, 'An Arduous But Necessary Path', *IA(M)*, no. 9, 1988, pp. 28–37, at p. 34. See also his 'Partiia-narod-sotsializm', *MEMO*, no. 5, 1987, pp. 3–16, at p. 5.
15. T. T. Hammond, 'Leninist Authoritarianism Before The Revolution', in E. J. Simmons (ed.), *Continuity and Change in Russian and Soviet Thought*, Russel and Russel, New York, 1955, pp. 145–6; also, R. G. Wesson, 'The Soviet State, Ideology and Patterns of Autocracy', *Soviet Studies*, vol xx, no. 2, 1968, pp. 179–86.
16. *Soch.*, tom 28, pp. 435–51, at p. 449.
17. 'Rech' o roli kommunisticheskoĭ partii', *Soch.*, tom 31, pp. 210–14, at p. 212.
18. *Soch.*, tom 33, p. 394.
19. Gunther Nollau, *International Communism and World Revolution*, Greenwood Press, Westport, Conn., 1961, ch. 6.
20. 'Conditions of Admission to the Communist International . . .' Aug. 1920, in Degras (ed.), *The Communist International* . . . , vol. 1, pp. 166–72, at p. 171.
21. Ibid., p. 169.
22. *Soch.*, tom 29, p. 125.
23. 'Theses on the Role of the Communist Party in the Proletarian Revolution', Adopted by the Second Comintern Congress, in Degras (ed.), *The Communist International* . . . , vol. 1, pp. 127–35.
24. S. Avineri, *The Social and Political Thought of Karl Marx*, Cambridge University Press, 1968, pp. 256–7.
25. *Soch.*, tom 27, pp. 340–1.
26. *Soch.*, tom 29, p. 283.
27. G. Zinoviev, 'Die Perspektiven der Proletarischen Revolution, *Die Kommunistische Internationale*, no. 1, May 1919, Moskau-Petrograd, Feltrinelli reprint, Milan 1967, pp. 9–14, at p. 11.
28. See Claudin, *The Communist Movement*, ch. 3.
29. Extracts from the Resolutions of the 4th Congress on 'Five Years of the Russian Revolution', in Degras (ed.), *The Communist International* . . . , vol. 1, p. 444.
30. Ibid.
31. See Claudin, *The Communist Movement*, pp. 71–117.
32. In Degras (ed.), *The Communist International* . . . , vol. 3, pp. 512–13.
33. In Adler (ed.), *Theses, Resolutions and Manifestos of the First Four Congresses of the Third International*, p. 62.
34. In Clissold (ed.), *The Soviet Union and Yugoslavia* . . . , Doc. 180, p. 263.
35. O. Kuusinen *et al.*, *Fundamentals of Marxism-Leninism*, Lawrence and Wishart, London, 1961, pp. 775–6.
36. Ibid.
37. Klaus von Beyme, *The Soviet Union in World Politics*, Gower, Aldershot, Hants, 1987, pp. 156–8.
38. V. V. Zagladin (ed.), *Theory and Tactics of the International Communist Movement*, Progress Publishers, Moscow, 1985, p. 47.
39. Iu. Krasin, *The Contemporary Revolutionary Process*, Progress Publishers, Moscow, 1981, p. 164.

40. Zagladin (ed.), *Theory and Tactics* . . . , p. 82.
41. See Shvetsov, *Internatsionalnaia rol' KPSS* . . . , pp. 32–3.
42. See ch. 12.
43. *Pravda*, 3 Nov. 1987.
44. On 'popular sovereignty', see: G. T. Chernobel, 'Kontseptsiia narodnogo suvereniteta', *SGP*, no. 8, 1970, pp. 30–7; G. S. Gurvich, 'Narod, narodnyĭ suverenitet i narodnoe predstavitel'stvo v sovetskoĭ sistemye', *SGP*, no. 12, 1958, pp. 38–47, at p. 47.
45. Lenin, 'Tretiĭ internatsional i ego mesto v istorii', *Soch.*, tom 29, pp. 272–87, at p. 285.
46. Lenin, 'O gosudarstve', *Soch.*, tom 29, pp. 433–45, at p. 445.
47. Korovin, 'Absoliutnyĭ . . .', pp. 14–15.
48. Levin, 'Printsip suvereniteta . . .', pp. 6–8.
49. N. A. Ushakov, *Suverenitet v sovremennom mezhdunarodnom prave*, p. 68.
50. G. Tunkin, 'Novyĭ tip mezhdunarodnykh otnosheniĭ i mezhdunarodnoe prava', *SGP*, no. 1, 1959, pp. 81–94.
51. *Iuridicheskiĭ spravochnik*, Iuridicheskaia literatura, Moscow, 1973, pp. 432–3; A. Ia. Sukharev (ed.), *Iuridicheskiĭ entsiklopedicheskii slovar'*, 1984, Sovetskaia entsiklopediia, Moscow, p. 359.
52. V. A. Vasilenko, 'Gosudarstvennyĭ suverenitet i mezhdunarodnyĭ dogovor', *SEMP*, 1971, pp. 60–70, at p. 64; also Korovin, 'Proletarskiĭ internatsionalizm i mezhdunarodnoe pravo', *SEMP*, 1958, pp. 50–75, at p. 57.
53. Aryeh L. Unger, *Constitutional Development in the USSR: A guide to the Soviet Constitutions*, Methuen, London, 1981, passim.
54. *FALP*, no. 1, 1947, p. 1.
55. F. Chernov, 'Burzhuaznii kosmopolitizm i ego reaktsionnaia rol'', *Bol'shevik*, no. 5, 1948, pp. 30–47, at p. 38.
56. Iu. Frantsev, 'Natsionalizm-oruzhie imperialisticheskoĭ reaktsii', *Bol'shevik*, no. 15, 1948, pp. 45–55, at p. 45.
57. Korovin, 'Respect for Sovereignty, An Unchanging Principle of Soviet Foreign Policy', *IA(M)*, no. 11, 1956, pp. 31–41, at p. 38.
58. G. Tunkin, *Teoriia mezhdunarodnogo prava*, IMO, Moscow, 1970, pp. 496–9.
59. See J. Larrain, 'Base and Superstructure', in T. Bottomore (ed.), *A Dictionary of Marxist Thought*, Blackwell, Oxford, 1983, pp. 42–5.
60. Marx, 'Letter to P. V. Annenkov'.
61. K. N. Waltz, *Man, The State and War: A Theoretical Analysis*, Columbia University Press, 1969, p. 82.
62. Ibid., p. 126.
63. Lenin, 'Imperializm, kak vysshaia stadiia kapitalizma', *Soch.*, tom 22, pp. 173–290.
64. See Lynch, *The Soviet Study of International Relations*, p. 101.
65. See Waltz, *Man, The State and War* . . . , p. 159.
66. Ibid., p. 228.
67. F. V. Konstantinov *et al.*, *The Fundamentals of Marxist-Leninist Philosophy*, Progress Publishers, Moscow, 1982, p. 292.
68. Shakhnazarov, 'Governability of the World'.

69. Larrain, 'Base and Superstructure'.
70. M. Rader, *Marx's Interpretation of History*, Oxford University Press, 1979, ch. 1.
71. Ibid.
72. See his letter to Bloch (21–2 Sept. 1890), K. Marx and F. Engels, *Selected Correspondence*, FLPH, Moscow, 1968, pp. 498–500.
73. Rader, *Marx's Interpretation of History*.
74. Gubin, 'Karl Marks i mezhdunarodnogo prava'.
75. S. B. Krylov, 'Les Notions Principales du Droit des Gens (La doctrine Sovietique du droit internationale)', *Recueil Des Cours, Académie De Droit International De La Haye*, vol. 1, 1947, pp. 407–76, at p. 441.
76. Ibid.
77. G. Tunkin, 'Sorok let sosushchestvovaniia i mezhdunarodnoe pravo', *SEMP*, 1958, pp. 15–49, at pp. 27 and 45.
78. V. F. Gubin, 'Marksizm-Leninizm o mezhdunarodnykh otnosheniiakh kak osobom vide obshchestvennykh otnoshenii i mezhdunarodnoe pravo', *SEMP*, 1974, pp. 39–56, at pp. 47–8.
79. V. Gantman, 'The Class Nature of Present Day International Relations', *IA(M)*, no. 9, 1969, pp. 55–7, at p. 56.
80. Sh. Sanakoyev, 'Foreign Policy of Socialism', *IA(M)*, no. 5, 1975, pp. 108–18, at p. 109.
81. Ibid.
82. Konstantinov *et al.*, *The Fundamentals of Marxist-Leninist Philosophy*, p. 246.
83. Lynch, *The Soviet Study of International Relations*, pp. 5–6.
84. Iu. Krasin, *The Contemporary Revolutionary Process*, p. 136.
85. V. F. Butenko, 'Protivorechiia razvitiia sotsializma kak obshchestvennogo stroia', *VF*, no. 10, 1982, pp. 16–29, at p. 18.

6 The Ideological Dimension

1. See N. Kapchenko and Sh. Sanakoyev, 'Foreign Policy and Ideology', *IA(M)*, no. 9, 1981, pp. 76–86.
2. T. Timofeev, 'Leninizm i nekotorye voprosy ideologicheskoĭ bor'by', *VF*, no. 4, 1980, pp. 86–99.
3. N. Kapchenko, 'Foreign Policy and Ideological Struggle Today', *IA(M)*, no. 3, 1985, pp. 45–54, at p. 45.
4. V. Zagladin 'World Balance of Forces and the Development of International Relations, *IA(M)*, no. 3, 1985, pp. 65–75, at p. 65; also Iu. A. Krasin, 'Revoliutsionnaia teoriia i revoliutsionnaia politika', *VF*, no. 11, 1978, pp. 73–85, at p. 73.
5. See chs. 10 and 11.
6. See F. Vali, *Rift and Revolt in Hungary*, Harvard University Press, Cambridge, Mass., 1961, ch. 3.
7. Ray Taras, *Ideology in a Socialist State: Poland 1956–1983*, Cambridge University Press, 1984, p. 258.
8. E. Kux, 'Contradictions in Soviet Socialism', *POC*, vol. 33, no. 6, 1984, pp. 1–27, at p. 7.

9. G. Shakhnazarov, 'The "Great Power" Approach to International Politics', *WMR*, no. 5, 1972, pp. 34–6, at p. 35.
10. See for example B. Korolev, 'Ideologicheskaia bor'ba na mirovoĭ arene v sovremennykh usloviiakh', *Politicheskoe samoobrazovanie*, no. 12, 1975, pp. 70–79, at p. 70.
11. Kapchenko and Sanakoyev, 'Foreign Policy and Ideology', p. 76.
12. Ibid., p. 83.
13. A. Gromyko, *Leninskim kursom mira*, Politizdat, Moscow, 1984, p. 568.
14. Iu. A. Krasin, *The Contemporary Revolutionary Process*. The Soviets have also condemned doctrines of 'national interest' as the basis of American foreign policy – V. S. Krivokhizha and V. S. Shein, 'Doktrina "natsional'nykh interesov" SShA: istoki, preemstvennost', evoliutsiia', *VF*, no. 8, 1977, pp. 40–53, at p. 44.
15. V. Zagladin, 'Partiia-narod-sotsializm', *MEMO*, no. 5, 1987, pp. 3–16, at p. 5.
16. M. S. Gorbachev, *Perestroika New Thinking For Our Country and The World*, Collins, London, 1987, p. 221.
17. See S. L. Sharp, 'National Interest: Key to Soviet Politics', in A. Dallin (ed.), *Soviet Conduct in World Affairs*, Greenwood Press, West Point, Conn., 1975, pp. 46–58.
18. H. Adomeit 'Ideology in the Soviet View of International Affairs', in C. Bertram (ed.), *Prospects of Soviet Power in the 1980s*, Macmillan, London, 1980, pp. 103–117, at p. 103.
19. D. D. Comey, 'Marxist-Leninist Ideology and Soviet Policy', *Studies in Soviet Thought*, no. 4, 1962, pp. 301–19, at p. 302.
20. C. Keeble, 'The Implications for Foreign Policy', in C. Keeble (ed.), *The Soviet State. The Domestic Roots of Soviet Foreign Policy*, Gower, London, 1985, p. 220.
21. Sharp, 'National Interest . . .'.
22. Comey, 'Marxist-Leninist Ideology and Soviet Policy', pp. 317–18.
23. R. N. Carew-Hunt, 'The Importance of Doctrine', in Dallin (ed.), *Soviet Conduct in World Affairs*, p. 45.
24. Comey, 'Marxist-Leninist Ideology and Soviet Policy'.
25. See, for example, A. Bromke, 'Ideology and National Interest in Soviet Foreign Policy', *International Journal*, vol. xxii, no. 4, 1967, pp. 547–62; Adomeit, 'Ideology in The Soviet View of International Affairs'.
26. See Bromke, 'Ideology and National Interest . . .', p. 555.
27. Adomeit, 'Ideology in the Soviet View of International Affairs', p. 106.
28. Lowenthal, *World Communism*, p. 5.
29. Bromke, 'Ideology and National Interest', pp. 552–3.
30. Martin Seliger, *The Marxist Conception of Ideology*, Cambridge University Press, 1977, p. 26.
31. Taras, *Ideology In a Socialist State: Poland 1956–1983*, pp. 1–5.
32. See D. Bell, 'Ideology and Soviet Politics', *Slavic Review*, no. 4, 1965, pp. 591–603.
33. Seliger, *The Marxist Conception of Ideology*, p. 4.

34. Iu. Krasin, *The Contemporary Revolutionary Process*, p. 140. See also N. B. Bikkenin, *Socialist Ideology*, Progress Publishers, Moscow, 1978.
35. F. V. Konstantinov, 'Marksistko-Leninskaia filosofiia. Ee mesto i rol' v sovremennom mire', *VF*, no. 7, 1982, pp. 37–45; Krasin, *The Contemporary Revolutionary Process*, p. 147.
36. Seliger, *The Marxist Conception of Ideology*, p. 4.
37. Taras, *Ideology in a Socialist State* . . . , p. 28; Seliger, *The Marxist Conception of Ideology*, p. 4.
38. Z. Brzezinski, *Ideology and Power in Soviet Politics*, Praeger, New York, 1962, ch. 5.
39. Ibid., p. 5.
40. Ibid.
41. Taras, *Ideology in a Socialist State*, p. 27.
42. Ibid., p. 26.
43. Krasin, *The Contemporary Revolutionary Process*, p. 153.
44. J. Frankel, *The National Interest*, Macmillan, London, 1970, pp. 31–41.
45. C. Perrow, 'The Analysis of Goals in Complex Organisations', *American Sociological Review*, vol. 26, 1961, pp. 854–66.
46. Carew-Hunt, 'The Importance of Doctrine', p. 46.
47. Seweryn Bialer, 'The Soviet Union and the West in the 1980s: Detente, Containment, or Confrontation?', *Orbis*, vol. 27, no. 1, 1983, pp. 35–58, at p. 41.
48. De George, *Patterns of Soviet Thought*.
49. Comey, 'Marxist-Leninist Ideology and Soviet Policy', p. 315.
50. A. G. Meyer, 'The Functions of Ideology in the Soviet Political System', *Soviet Studies*, vol. xvii, no. 3, 1966, pp. 273–285, at p. 280.
51. Ibid., p. 279.
52. V. Shlapentokh, *Soviet Public Opinion and Ideology: Mythology and Pragmatism in Interaction*, Praeger, New York, 1986, p. 12.
53. Ibid., p. 11.
54. Eran, *The Mezhdunarodniki* . . . , p. 3.
55. A. L. Unger, 'Politinformator or Agitator: A Decision Blocked', *POC*, vol. 19, 1970, pp. 30–43.
56. Comey, 'Marxist-Leninist Ideology and Soviet Policy', p. 315.
57. Ibid., following Mannheim's definition of ideology as a 'mental fiction'.
58. Brzezinski, *Ideology and Power in Soviet Politics*, p. 136.
59. H. Adomeit, *Soviet Risk-Taking and Crisis Behaviour*, Allen and Unwin, London, 1982, p. 330.
60. V. Kubálková and Cruickshank, *Marxism-Leninism* . . . , p. 65.
61. Krasin, *The Contemporary Revolutionary Process*, p. 144.
62. Lowenthal, *World Communism*, p. 100. See also Carew-Hunt, 'The Importance of Doctrine', p. 45; and Brzezinski, *Ideology and Power in Soviet Politics*, p. 143.
63. Kubálková and Cruickshank, *Marxism-Leninism* . . . .
64. B. S. Ukraintsev, 'Marksistsko-Leninskaia filosofiia i metody obshchestvennykh nauk', *VF*, no. 7, 1977, pp. 83–93, at p. 85.
65. See W. Zimmerman, *Soviet Perspectives on International Relations*

1956–67, Princeton University Press, 1969.

66. Von Beyme, *The Soviet Union in World Politics*, p. 11.
67. See ch. 10.
68. Krasin, *The Contemporary Revolutionary Process*, p. 144.
69. See Adomeit, *Factors in Soviet Risk Taking and Crisis Behaviour*, p. 330.
70. See H. Achminov, 'Khrushchev's "Creative Development" of Marxism-Leninism' *Studies on the Soviet Union*, vol. 1, no. 3, 1962, pp. 5–17, at p. 16.
71. Zimmerman, *Soviet Perspectives on International Relations 1956–67*.
72. R. Judson Mitchell, *Ideology of a Superpower. Contemporary Soviet Doctrine on International Relations*, Hoover Institution Press, Stanford, California, 1982, p. 4.
73. Lynch, *The Soviet Study of International Relations*, p. 7.
74. Shlapentokh, *Soviet Public Opinion and Ideology*, p. 94.
75. See ch. 7.
76. Achminov, 'Khrushchev's "Creative Development" . . .'
77. Ibid.
78. Ibid., p. 12.
79. Comey, 'Marxist-Leninist Ideology and Soviet Policy', although Gati has argued that it is difficult to generalise on this point (C. Gati, 'The Stalinist Legacy in Soviet Foreign Policy', in E. P. Hoffman, *The Soviet Union in the 1980s*, The Academy of Political Science, New York, 1984, pp. 214–26, at p. 222).
80. Barrington Moore Jr, 'The Relations of Ideology and Foreign Policy', in Dallin (ed.), *Soviet Conduct . . .* , pp. 75–92, at p. 76.
81. R. Judson Mitchell, 'The Revised "Two Camps" Doctrine in Soviet Foreign Policy', *Orbis*, vol. xvi, Spring 1972, pp. 21–34, at pp. 32–4.
82. Carew-Hunt, 'The Importance of Doctrine', p. 40.
83. Zvi Gitelman, 'The Diffusion of Political Innovation: From Eastern Europe to the Soviet Union', in R. Szporluk (ed.), *The Influence of Eastern Europe and the Soviet West on the USSR*, Praeger, New York, 1975, pp. 11–67.
84. G. Rozman, *A Mirror For Socialism: Soviet Criticisms of China*, Princeton University Press, 1985.
85. Kux, 'Contradictions in Soviet Socialism'; also Alfred B. Evans Jr, 'The Polish Crisis in the 1980s and Adaptation in Soviet Ideology', *Jl. of Communist Studies*, 1986, vol 2, no. 3, 1986, pp. 263–85.
86. E. K. Valkenier, 'Revolutionary Change in the Third World: Recent Soviet Assessments', *World Politics*, no. 3, 1986, pp. 415–34.
87. V. Kortunov, 'Novoe politicheskoe myshlenie-imperativ sovremennosti', *MEMO*, no. 10, 1986, pp. 16–25.
88. Shlapentokh, *Soviet Public Opinion and Ideology*, p. 94.
89. See C. Glickham, 'New Directions for Soviet Foreign Policy', *Radio Free Europe-Radio Liberty*, RB Supplement no. 2/86, 6 Sept. 1986, p. 1.
90. R. Lowenthal, 'The Logic of One Party Rule', in Dallin (ed.), *Soviet Conduct in World Affairs*, pp. 58–74.
91. Ibid., p. 62.

92. Barrington Moore Jr, 'The Relations of Ideology and Foreign Policy', p. 83.
93. Bell, 'Ideology and Soviet Politics'.
94. Lowenthal, 'The Logic of One Party Rule'.
95. R. G. Wesson, 'Soviet Ideology: the Necessity of Marxism', *Soviet Studies*, vol. 21, no. 1, 1969, pp. 64–70, at p. 69.

7 Challenges to Soviet Regional Hegemony in the 1950s and the Soviet Response

1. F. Stephen Larrabee, *The Challenge to Soviet Interests in Eastern Europe*, Rand R-3190-AF, Santa Monica, Calif., 1984, p. 7.
2. Raymond Cohen, *International Politics: The Rules of the Game*, Longman, London, 1981, ch. 3.
3. Ibid., p. 16.
4. Ibid., p. 17.
5. Ibid., p. 19.
6. See L. A. Fituni, 'Pravovye formy ekonomicheskogo sotrudnichestva SSSR i stran narodnoĭ demokratii', *SGP*, no. 6, 1953, pp. 91–103.
7. Editorial, 'Novye proiski vragov mira', *NV*, no. 27, 1953, pp. 1–2; also *Neues Deutschland*, 18 June 1953.
8. See Arnulf Baring, *Uprising in East Germany*, Cornell University Press, 1972, p. 81.
9. Z. Brzezinski, *The Soviet Bloc*, p. 52.
10. See Paul Zinner (ed.), *National Communism and Popular Revolt in Eastern Europe*, Columbia University Press, 1956.
11. *Pravda*, 31 Oct. 1956, p. 1; in *Documents on International Affairs 1956*, RIIA, Oxford University Press, 1959, pp. 465–8.
12. Veljko Mićunović, *Moscow Diary*, Chatto and Windus, London, 1980, p. 130.
13. In *Documents on International Affairs 1956*, pp. 476–7.
14. Sumner Welles, 'Intervention and Interventions', *Foreign Affairs*, vol 26, no. 1, 1947, pp. 116–33, at p. 116.
15. P. H. Winfield, 'The History of Intervention in International Law', *British Year Book of International Law (BJIL)*, vol 3, 1922–3, pp. 130–49, at p. 130.
16. J. N. Rosenau, 'The Concept of Intervention', *Jl. of International Affairs*, vol xxII, no. 2, 1968, pp. 165–76, at p. 167.
17. A. Piradov, 'The Principle of Non-Interference in the Modern World', *IA(M)*, no. 1, 1966, pp. 53–8, at p. 57.
18. L. A. Modzhorian, 'Bor'ba demokraticheskogo lageria za natsional'nuiu nezavisimost' i natsional'yĭ suverenitet', *SGP*, no. 1, 1953, pp. 52–65, at p. 57.
19. In 1950, 1953, 1954, and 1956 the Soviets made submissions to the UN for the definition of aggression.
20. See A. Evgen'ev, 'Pravosub''ektnost', suverenitet i nevmeshatel'stvo v

mezhdunarodnom prave', *SGP*, no. 2, 1955, pp. 75–84, at pp. 82–4.
21. R. Little, *Intervention: External Involvement in Civil Wars*, Martin Robertson, London, 1975, p. 3.
22. *Documents on International Affairs 1956*, pp. 471–2. See Michael G. Fry and Condeleezza Rice, 'The Hungarian Crisis of 1956: The Soviet Decision', *Studies in Comparative Communism*, no. 1, 1983, pp. 85–98.
23. Mićunović, *Moscow Diary*, p. 127.
24. Text in *Documents on International Affairs 1956*, pp. 523–37, at p. 528.
25. Text in *NV*, no. 21, 1955, p. 16.
26. Text in *Documents on International Affairs 1956*, pp. 471–2.
27. See Korovin, 'Respect for Sovereignty – An Unchanging Principle of Soviet Foreign Policy', pp. 37–8.
28. Ibid., p. 38. See also Korovin's 'Proletarskiĭ internationalizm i mezhdunarodnoe pravo', *SEMP*, 1958, pp. 50–73, at pp. 56–7.
29. I. Pomelov, 'Razvitie sotsializma i proletarskiĭ internatsionalizm' *Kommunist*, no. 1, 1957, pp. 15–30.
30. V. Khvostov, 'The Leninist Principles of Foreign Policy', *IA(M)*, no. 4, 1957, pp. 18–26, at p. 18.
31. Pomelov, 'Razvitie sotsializma . . .'.
32. N. Vasil'ev, 'Protiv izvrashcheniia printsipov proletarskogo internationalizma', *Izvestiia*, 9 March 1957, pp. 3–4, at p. 4.
33. *Pravda*, 13 February 1957, pp. 3–5.
34. Korovin, 'Respect for Sovereignty . . .', pp. 37–8.
35. Ibid.
36. Ibid.
37. Pomelov, 'Razvitie sotsializma . . .'.
38. Ibid., p. 23.
39. Ibid., p. 16.
40. I. Pomelov, Splochenie sil sotsializma i nekotorye voprosy ideologicheskoĭ bor'by v Vengrii', *Kommunist*, no. 10, 1957, pp. 73–90, at p. 73.
41. Editorial, 'The Growing Unity of the Socialist Countries', *IA(M)*, no. 2, 1957, pp. 2–12, at p. 10.
42. Ibid., p. 12.
43. A. Berkov, 'Edinstvo i splochennost'-zalog novykh uspekhov mezhdunarodnogo kommunisticheskogo dvizheniia', *Kommunist*, no. 6, 1957, pp. 114–22, at p. 117.
44. T. Timofeev, 'Certain Aspects of Proletarian Internationalism', *IA(M)*, no. 5, 1957, pp. 42–52, at p. 50.
45. *Documents on International Affairs 1956*, p. 504.
46. 'Za dal'neĭshee splochenie sil sotsializma na osnove Marksistsko-Leninskikh printsipov', *Pravda*, 23 Nov. 1956, pp. 2–4, at p. 4.
47. See Nollau, *International Communism and World Revolution*, pp. 286–7.
48. See Deitrich Andre Loeber, 'The Legal Structure of the Communist Bloc', *Social Research*, vol. 27, no. 2, 1960, pp. 183–202.
49. 'Edinstvo sotsialisticheskogo lageria-uslovie postroeniia sotsializma', *Pravda*, 6 March 1957, pp. 4–5.

50. *Pravda*, 22 Nov. 1957, pp. 1–2.
51. Ibid.
52. Pomelov, 'Razvitie sotsializma . . .', p. 21.
53. Nollau, *International Communism and World Revolution*, p. 320.
54. N. P. Farberov, 'Ob izuchenii novogo opyta gosudarstvennogo stroitel'stva stran narodnoĭ demokratii, *SGP*, no. 8, 1958, pp. 3–13, at p. 3.
55. Editorial, 'The Growing Unity of the Socialist Countries', p. 12.
56. Pomelov, 'Razvitie sotsializma . . .', p. 21.
57. Berkov, 'Edinstvo . . .', p. 117.
58. D. Shevliagin, 'Bor'ba bratskikh kommunisticheskikh partii protiv sovremennogo opportunizma', *Kommunist*, no. 18, 1957, pp. 27–44, at p. 39.
59. William Zimmerman, 'International Relations in the Soviet Union: The Emergence of a Discipline', *Jl. of Politics*, vol. 31, 1969, pp. 52–70, at pp. 52–5.
60. See Eran, *The Mezhdunarodniki* . . . .
61. The term 'socialist internationalism' had already entered the Soviet vocabulary (for example, it was mentioned in a *Pravda* article on the Hungarian events in November 1956 (see note 46)). However, it was not used as a conceptual underpinning for a general theory of 'socialist international relations' until the following year.
62. Tunkin, 'Sorok let sosushchestvovaniia i mezhdunarodnoe pravo', *SEMP*, 1958, pp. 15–49, at p. 47.
63. Korovin, 'Proletarskiĭ internatsionalizm i mezhdunarodnoe pravo', pp. 50–3.
64. K. Seleznev, 'Bor'ba Marksa za utverzhdenie printsipov proletarskogo internatsionalizma v rabochem dvizhenii', *Kommunist*, no. 7, 1958, pp. 41–55, at p. 55.
65. On mutual aid, see for example M. Mitin, 'Nerushimoe edinstvo sotsialisticheskikh stran', *Kommunist*, no. 2, 1961, pp. 11–22, at p. 18.
66. Kuusinen *et al.*, *Fundamentals of Marxism-Leninism*, p. 772.
67. G. I. Tunkin, 'Novyĭ tip mezhdunarodnykh otnosheniĭ i mezhdunarodnoe prava' *SGP*, no. 1, 1959, pp. 81–94, at p. 90.
68. Sh. Sanakoyev, 'The 21st. Congress and the Socialist Countries' Transition to Communism', *IA(M)*, no. 5, 1959, pp. 32–8, referred to 'fraternal mutual support (as) an objective law of the development of the world socialist economic system', p. 37.
69. *Pravda*, 2 Dec. 1960, p. 1.
70. N. Inozemtsev, 'Mezhdunarodnye otnosheniia novogo tipa', *MEMO*, no. 4, 1957, pp. 72–85.
71. G. I. Tunkin, 'Sorok let sosushchestvovaniia i mezhdunarodnoe pravo', p. 36.
72. E. T. Usenko in D. B. Levin (ed.), *Mezhdunarodnoe pravo*, Izdatel'stvo iuridicheskaia literatura, Moscow, 1964, p. 62; G. I. Tunkin, *Voprosy teorii mezhdunarodnogo prava*, Iuridicheskoĭ literatury, Moscow, 1962, pp. 325–6.
73. V. M. Shurshalov (ed.), *Mezhdunarodno-pravovye formy sotrud-*

nichestva sotsialisticheskikh gosudarstv, Izdatel'stvo akademii nauk SSSR, Moscow, 1962.

74. Tunkin, 'Novyĭ tip mezhdunarodnikh otnosheniĭ', p. 88.
75. See Ivo Lapenna, 'The Soviet Concept of "Socialist" International Law', pp. 253–5.
76. E. A. Korovin (ed.), *Mezhdunarodnoe pravo*, Akademiia nauk SSSR institut prava, Moscow, 1951, p. 146.
77. O. V. Bogdanov, 'Amerikanskaiia mezhdunarodno-pravovaia doktrina na sluzhbe imperialisticheskoĭ expansii', *SGP*, no. 5, 1952, pp. 70–5, at p. 74.
78. See W. W. Kulski, 'The Soviet Interpretation of International Law', *AJIL*, vol. 49, 1955, pp. 518–34, at p. 521.
79. G. I. Tunkin, 'Mirnoe sosushchestvovanie i mezhdunarodnoe pravo', *SGP*, no. 7, 1956, pp. 3–13, at p. 10.
80. *Pravda*, 21 April 1957, p. 2.
81. Tunkin, 'Sorok let . . .', p. 47.
82. Tunkin, 'Sorok let . . .', p. 45.
83. Korovin, 'Proletarskiĭ internationalizm i mezhdunarodnoe pravo', p. 70.
84. Ibid., p. 71.
85. Ibid. See also Vasilenko, 'Gosudarstvennyi suverenitet . . .', p. 64.
86. Ibid.
87. E. T. Usenko, 'Osnovnye mezhdunarodno-pravovye printsipy sotrudnichestva sotsialisticheskikh gosudarstv', *SGP*, no. 3, 1961, pp. 16–29, at p. 28.
88. E. T. Usenko, '25 let mezhdunarodnoĭ organizatsii novogo tipa', *SEMP*, 1974, pp. 11–38, at p. 20.
89. See, for example, F. I. Kozhevnikov, 'Velikaia oktiabr'skiia sotsialisticheskaiia revoliutsiia i mezhdunarodno-pravovoe znachenie pervykh vneshepoliticheskikh aktov sovetskogo gosudarstva', *SGP*, no. 11, 1957, pp. 50–60, at p. 59; Tunkin, 'Sorok let . . .', p. 47.
90. But these are filled with a new content: F. I. Kozhevnikov *et al.*, 'Sovetskoe gosudarstvo i mezhdunarodnoe pravo, *IMO*, Moscow, 1967, p. 25.
91. Sh. Sanakoyev, 'The Basis of Relations between Socialist Countries', *IA(M)*, no. 6, 1958, pp. 23–33, at p. 27.
92. See V. Khvostov, 'The Leninist Principles of Foreign Policy', *IA(M)*, no. 4, April 1957, pp. 18–26, at pp. 19–20.
93. See J. P. Nettl, *Rosa Luxemburg*, Oxford University Press, 1966, vol. 2, p. 853.
94. See Khostov, 'The Leninist Principles of Foreign Policy', p. 19; Konstantinov, *Socialist Internationalism*, pp. 116–27.
95. *Izvestiia*, 10 April 1958, p. 2.
96. Kuusinen *et al.*, *Fundamentals of Marxism-Leninism*, p. 546.
97. Sh. Sanakoyev, 'Internationalism and Socialist Patriotism', *IA(M)*, no. 12, 1961, pp. 8–13, at p. 11.
98. V. M. Koretskiĭ, 'Problema 'osnovnykh prav i obiazannosteĭ gosudarstv' i mezhdunarodnom prave', *SEMP*, 1958, pp. 74–92, at p. 85.

99. M. Mitin, 'Nerushimoe edinstvo sotsialisticheskikh stran', *Kommunist*, no. 2, 1961, pp. 11–22, at p. 14; A. Alekseev, 'Ekonomicheskoe sorevnovanie mezhdu sotsializmom i kapitalizmom', *MEMO*, no. 2, 1957, pp. 13–25: they were 'diametrically opposed' types of economic system, pp. 23–4.

100. L. Tolkunov, 'Novyĭ etap v razvitii mirovoĭ systemy sotsializma', *Kommunist*, no. 3, 1961, pp. 14–27, at p. 19.

101. I. Dudinskiĭ, 'Ekonomicheskie osnovy edinstva sotsialisticheskikh stran', *Kommunist*, no. 5, 1961, pp. 103–112, at p. 105.

102. V. M. Shurshalov (ed.), *Mezhdunarodno-pravovye formy* . . . , p. 16; J. Lemin, 'K voprosy o protivorechiiakh mezhdu kapitalistichestimi stranamii na sovremennom etape', *MEMO*, no. 8, 1960, pp. 25–40.

103. Aĭrapetian and Suzhodeev, *Novyĭ tip mezhdunarodnykh otnosheniĭ*, p. 32.

104. V. Gantman, 'Imperialisticheskaia "integratsiia" i mezhdunarodnye otnosheniia', *Kommunist*, no. 16, 1962, pp. 96–107, at p. 107.

105. N. S. Khrushchev, 'Narushchnye voprosy razvitiia mirovoĭ sotsialisticheskoĭ sistemy', *Kommunist*, no. 12, 1962, pp. 3–26, at p. 26.

106. Gantman, 'Imperialisticheskaia "integratsiia" . . .', p. 107.

107. I. Kuzminov, 'The Post-War Capitalist Cycle', *IA(M)*, no. 8, 1961, pp. 61–8, at p. 65.

108. E. Korovin, 'Sovereignty and Peace', *IA(M)*, no. 9, 1960, pp. 7–12, at p. 7. Peaceful coexistence meant 'cooperation and competition' – Korovin, *International Law Today*, no. 7, 1961, pp. 18–22, at p. 19.

109. E. Varga, 'Problemy poslevennogo promyshlennogo tsikla i novyĭ krizis pereproizvodstva', *MEMO*, no. 6, 1958, pp. 18–35.

110. G. Starushenko, 'Mirnoe sosushchestvovanie i revoliutsiia', *Kommunist*, no. 2, 1962, pp. 78–89, at p. 86.

111. Ia. Kotkovskiĭ, 'Tendentsii ekonomicheskogo razvitiia sotsializma i kapitalizma', *MEMO*, no. 3, 1958, pp. 14–28.

112. See I. Lemin, 'Mezhdunarodnye otnosheniia na novom etape obshchego krizisa kapitalizma', *MEMO*, no. 4, 1961, pp. 3–18.

113. A. Notkin, 'Sovremennyĭ etap ekonomicheskogo sorevnovaniia SSSR i glavnykh kapitalisicheskikh stran', *VE*, no. 7, 1961, pp. 7–22; A. Alekseev and V. Kubarin, 'Sotsializm pobedit v mirnom ekonomicheskom sorevnovanii s kapitalizmom', *VE*, no. 11, 1960, pp. 3–12.

114. V. Korionov, 'The Historic Mission of Communism', *IA(M)*, no. 9, 1961, pp. 3–8, at p. 8.

115. N. S. Khrushchev, 'Za novye pobedy mirovogo kommunisticheskogo dvizheniia', *Kommunist*, no. 1, 1961, pp. 3–37, at p. 34.

8 'Socialist Internationalism' and the Warsaw Pact Intervention in Czechoslovakia

1. C. Olgin, 'World Communism: Disintegration or Unity in Diversity?', *Bulletin of the Institute for the Study of the USSR*, vol. xvii, no. 6, 1970, pp. 3–16, at p. 5.

2. See Zimmerman, *Soviet Perspectives* . . . , ch. 5.

3. Aĭrapetian and Suzhodeev, *Novyĭ tip mezhdunarodnykh otnosheniĭ*;

Shurshalov (ed.), *Mezhdunarodno-pravovye formy* . . . , ch. 1.
4. See, for example, V. V. Kusin, *The Intellectual Origins of The Prague Spring*, Cambridge University Press, 1971; Karen Dawisha, *The Kremlin and The Prague Spring*, University of California Press, Berkeley, 1984; W. Gordon Skilling, *Czechoslovakia's Interrupted Revolution*, Princeton University Press, 1976, pp. 751–2.
5. Galia Golan, 'Czechoslovak Marxism in the Reform Period', in S. Avineri (ed.), *Varieties of Marxism*, Martinus Nijhoff, The Hague, 1977, pp. 299–316.
6. Kusin, *The Intellectual Origins of The Prague Spring*, pp. 140–2.
7. Skilling, *Czechoslovakia's Interrupted Revolution*, p. 834.
8. C. Gati, 'Soviet Empire: Alive But Not Well', *POC*, March-April 1985, pp. 73–86, at pp. 82–3; Jiri Valenta, 'The Bureaucratic Politics Paradigm and the Soviet Invasion of Czechoslovakia', *Political Science Quarterly*, no. 94, Spring 1979, pp. 56–76.
9. Moscow Radio domestic service referred to revanchist gatherings of Sudeten Germans, *Foreign Broadcast Information Service (Soviet Union), (FBIS.SU)*, vol. 3, no. 144, 24 July 1968, p. A15.
10. V. Stepanov, 'Vedushchaia sila stroitel'stva kommunizma', *Izvestiia*, 11 May 1968, pp. 4–5, at p. 4.
11. Little, *Intervention* . . . , pp. 9–11.
12. On the reasons for Dubček's misinterpretation of these signals, see Dawisha, *The Kremlin and The Prague Spring*, pp. 364–5.
13. V. Kotyk, 'Sovereignty, from Theory into Practice', *Práce*, 11 July 1968, in *Radio Free Europe Research. Czechoslovak Press Survey (RFER.CPS)*, no. 2102, 17 July 1968, pp. 1–6.
14. Dawisha, *The Kremlin and The Prague Spring*, p. 166.
15. I. Synek, 'The Specific Road To Socialism', *Rudé právo*, 19 April 1968, in *RFER.CPS*, no. 2070, 14 May 1968, p. 6; also his article with A. Mikeštic and A. Muller in *Rudé právo*, 22 March 1968 (attacked by O. Pavlov, 'Proletarian Internationalism and Defence of Socialist Gains', *IA(M)*, no. 10, 1968, pp. 11–15, at p. 15).
16. Synek, 'The Specific Road to Socialism', p. 7.
17. Kotyk, 'Sovereignty, from Theory into Practice', p. 2.
18. Pavlov, 'Proletarian Internationalism and Defence of Socialist Gains', p. 14.
19. V. Kotyk, 'International Responsibility', *Práce*, 20 July 1968, *RFER.CPS*, no. 2105, 29 July 1968, pp. 9–10.
20. V. Platkovskiǐ, 'Glavnaia sila v bor'be za kommunizm', *Izvestiia*, 25 June 1968, pp. 4–5, at p. 5.
21. In *Literární listy*, 27 June 1968.
22. J. Horéč, *Mladá fronta*, 27 July 1968, in *RFER.CPS*, no. 2113, 21 August 1968, pp. 3–6, at p. 4.
23. V. Kotyk, 'The Democratisation Process and Our Foreign Policy', *Predvoj*, no. 19, 9 May 1968, *RFER.CPS*, no. 2082, 4 June 1968, pp. 1–4, at p. 2.
24. Kotyk, 'Sovereignty from Theory into Practice', p. 3.
25. Pavlov, 'Proletarian Internationalism and Defence of Socialist Gains', p. 14.
26. V. V. Grishin, 'Pod rukovodstvom KPSS po Leniniskomu puti-k

kommunizmu', *Izvestiia*, 23 April 1968, pp. 1–2.
27. Ibid.
28. Dawisha, *The Kremlin and The Prague Spring*, p. 69.
29. Jeffrey Simon, *Cohesion and Dissension in Eastern Europe. Six Crises*, Praeger, New York, 1983, p. 44.
30. F. Konstantinov, 'Marksizm-Leninizm-edinoe international'noe uchenie', *Pravda*, 14 June 1968, pp. 3–4.
31. I. Aleksandrov, 'Ataka protiv sotsialisticheskikh ustoev Chekoslovakii', *Pravda*, 11 July 1968, p. 4.
32. 'Po pobedu tochki zreniia prezidiuma tsk kpCh', *Pravda*, 22 July 1968, p. 4.
33. *Scînteia*, 22 July 1968, in *RFER. Eastern Europe (RFER.EE)*, no. 9, 29 July 1968, p. 7.
34. *Narodna armiia*, 23 July 1968, *RFER. East European Press Survey (RFER.EEPS)*, no. 2107, 25 July 1968, p. 3.
35. *Poglod*, 22 July 1968, *RFER.EE*, no. 7, 25 July 1968, p. 3.
36. Homeland Radio, 25 July 1968, *RFER.EE*, no. 10, 30 July 1968, p. 6.
37. *Narodna armiia*, 24 July 1968, *RFER.EE*, no. 8, 26 July 1968, p. 2.
38. Text in *Kommunist*, no. 11, 1968, pp. 4–9.
39. In R. A. Remington (ed.), *Winter in Prague*, MIT Press, 1969, Doc. 36, pp. 234–43.
40. See Mlynář's account in *Nightfrost in Prague*, p. 154.
41. Ibid., p. 155.
42. Text in *Kommunist*, no. 12, 1968, pp. 15–23.
43. Editorial: 'Edinstvo i splochennost', *Krasnaia zvezda*, 6 August 1968, p. 1.
44. I. Pomelov, 'Obshchie printsipy i natsional'nye osobennosti v razvitii sotsializma', *Pravda*, 14 August 1968, pp. 3–4.
45. Editorial, 'Proletarskiĭ internatsionalizm-znamia mezhdunarodnogo kommunisticheskogo dvizheniia', *Kommunist*, no. 12, 1968, pp. 24–30, at p. 30.
46. Tass International Service, *FBIS.SU*, vol. 3, no. 164, 21 August 1968, pp. A1–2.
47. Iu. Zhukov, 'Chego oni dobivalis'', *Pravda*, 21 August 1968, p. 4.
48. *Pravda*, 22 August 1968, p. 1.
49. C. Zorgbibe, 'La doctrine soviétique de la "souveraineté limitée"', *Revue générale de droit international publique*, Pédone, Paris, no. 4, Oct.–Dec. 1970, pp. 872–905, at p. 890.
50. See D. Kraminov, 'NATO-orudie diversiĭ i revanchizma', *Kommunist*, no. 14, 1968, pp. 80–6, at p. 86. References to West German aid to counterrevolutionary forces continued in the East German, Bulgarian, Hungarian and Polish press, *RFER.EE*, no. 32, 31 August 1968, p. 3.
51. A. Gromyko, in *Izvestiia*, 5 Oct. 1968, p. 4.
52. Richard M. Goodman, 'The Invasion of Czechoslovakia: 1968', *International Lawyer*, vol 4, no. 1, 1969–70, pp. 44–79.
53. *RFER. Romania*, no. 12, 6 Sept. 1968, p. 2.
54. V. Kudriavtsev, 'Kontrrevoliutsiia pod maskoĭ "vozrozhdeniia"', *Izvestiia*, 25 August 1968, pp. 3–4.
55. *BBC Monitoring Report (BBCMR)*, Far East, no. 2856, 24 Aug. 1968, p. 3.

56. *BBCMR*, Eastern Europe, no. 2855, 23 Aug. 1968, p. 3.
57. See *Yearbook of International Communist Affairs (YICA)*, 1969, Hoover Institution Press, Stanford, Calif., pp. 1075–9.
58. *Granma*, 25th August 1968, in *YICA*, 1969, p. 1021.
59. See Skilling, *Czechoslovakia's Interrupted Revolution*, pp. 751–2.
60. There may not have been a specific agreement, as Mlynář alleges, but signalling beforehand: see Dawisha, *The Kremlin and The Prague Spring*, pp. 292–3.
61. See ch. 9.
62. S. Kovalev, 'Suverenitet i internatsional'nye obiazannosti sotsialistichekikh stran', *Pravda*, 26 Sept. 1968, p. 4.
63. K. T. Mazurov, *Pravda*, 7 Nov. 1968, pp. 1–3, at p. 2.
64. L. Brezhnev speech at the 5th Congress of the Polish United Workers Party, Warsaw, 12 Nov. 1968, *Pravda*, 13 Nov. 1968, pp. 1–2, at p. 2.
65. Kovalev, 'Suverenitet i internatsional'nye obiazannosti sotsialistichekikh stran'.
66. Ibid.
67. Ibid.
68. N. Farberov, 'Ob obshchikh zakonomernostiakh stroitel'stva sotsializma', *Izvestiia*, 29 Sept. 1968, pp. 4–5.
69. 'Pod znamenem proletarskogo internatsionalizm', *Kommunist*, no. 18, 1968, pp. 3–7.
70. Col. N. Cherniak, 'Nezyblemye printsipy sotsialisticheskogo sodruzhestva', *Krasnaia zvezda*, 1 Dec. 1968, p. 3.
71. A. Sovetov, 'The Present Stage in the Struggle Between Socialism and Imperialism', *IA(M)*, no. 11, 1968, pp. 3–9, at p. 6.
72. *Soviet News*, London, no. 4565, 19 Nov. 1968.
73. *BBCMR.EE*, no. 2889, 3 Oct. 1968, p. 2.
74. In Clissold (ed.), *The Soviet-Yugoslav Dispute*, Doc. 223, p. 229.
75. P. Perović, 'Socialism and National Sovereignty', *Socialist Thought and Practice*, no. 32, Oct.–Dec. 1968, pp. 64–81, at p. 65.
76. Ibid., pp. 67 and 74.
77. M. Kranjeć, in *Komunist*, 12 Sept. 1968, p. 3, *RFER Yugoslavia (RFER.Y)*, no. 31, 16 Sept. 1968, p. 3; A Kresić in *Odjec*, 1 Nov. 1968, called upon the international communist movement to emancipate itself from 'Soviet hegemony', *RFER.Y*, no. 59, 15 Nov. 1968, p. 3; S. Dolenć, 'Internationalism is the Option of the Sovereign', *Socialist Thought and Practice*, no. 44, July–Sept. 1971, pp. 71–8.
78. *Peking Review*, 28 March 1969, pp. 23–4, at p. 24.
79. Ibid., 30 April 1969, p. 32.
80. *RFER Romania (RFER.R)*, no. 21, 30 Dec. 1968, p. 2.
81. Radio Bucharest, 20 Dec., *RFER.R*, no. 20, 24 Dec. 1968, p. 2.
82. Radio Bucharest, 6 Aug. 1969, *RFER.R*, no. 17, 8 Aug. 1969, p. 2.
83. See V. Duculescu, 'Statul suveran in relatiile internationale', *Era Socialista*, no. 13, July 1973, pp. 27–9, at p. 27.
84. See M. Malita, 'The Role of Medium Sized Countries in the Resolution of Inter-State Conflicts', *Revue Roumaine d'Etudes Internationales*, (Bucharest), vol 14, 1980, pp. 35–43, at p. 43.
85. Petru Panzaru in *Era Socialista*, no. 24, 1982, attacked the notion of 'general laws' of socialist development, in Anneli Maier, 'The Roma-

nian–Soviet Ideological Dispute', *RFER Radio Background Report (RFER.RBR)* (Romania), no. 27, 8 Feb. 1983, pp. 1–11, at p. 8.

86. Dr Constantin Moisuc, 'On the Main Features of the New Economic World Order', *Revue Roumaine* . . . , vol. 10, 1976, pp. 403–428, at p. 403.

87. J. Kirk Laux, 'Socialism, nationalism and underdevelopment: research on Romanian foreign policymaking', in H. Adomeit and R. Boardman, *Foreign Policy Making in Communist Countries*, Saxon House, Farnborough, Hants., 1979, pp. 49–78, p. 58.

88. Speech at harvest festival 8 Sept. 1968, *RFER. Poland*, no. 64, 11 Sept. 1968, p. 2.

89. W. Gomulka, 'O sobytiiakh v Chekoslovakii', *NV*, no. 42, 1968, pp. 10–11.

90. J. Waclawek, 'The International and National in Communist Policy', *WMR*, no. 8, 1969, pp. 27–30, at p. 30.

91. *RFER,GDR*, no. 15, 17 Sept. 1968, pp. 2–3.

92. Herman Axen, *ND, 13 Oct. 1968, in RFER.GDR*, no. 17, 25 Oct. 1968, pp. 2–3.

93. Herman Axen, 'Proletarischer Internationalismus in unserer Zeit' *Einheit*, no. 10, 1968, pp. 1203–20, at p. 1212.

94. H. Kroger, 'Die sozialistische soweranitat der DDR und der proletarische internationalismus', *Deutsche Aussenpolitik*, vol. 14, 1969, pp. 1419–28, at p. 1426.

95. Ibid., p. 32.

96. Obren Milićević, 'Suverenitet i sotsjalizam' *Borba*, 19, 20 and 21 November 1969; Johannes Kirsten, 'Zum sozialistischen volkerechtichen Prinzip der staatlichen soweranitat', *Deutsche Aussenpolitik*, vol. 15, no. 1, Jan. 1970, pp. 20–30; Dorothy Miller, An East German Defence of the "Limited Sovereignty" Theory', *RFER.GDR*, no. 0396, 21 Nov. 1969, pp. 12–16.

97. *Svobodné slovo*, 27 Feb. 1969, in Oton Ambroz, 'The Doctrine of Limited Sovereignty: its Impact on East Europe', *East Europe*, no. 5, 1969, pp. 19–24.

98. L. Štrougal, 'On The Relevance of Leninism Today', *WMR*, vol 12, no. 7, 1969, pp. 28–32, at p. 31.

99. Dietrich Frenzke, 'New Czech–Soviet Alliance Treaty', *Aussenpolitik*, vol. 21, no. 3, 1970, pp. 321–30.

100. Zvi Gitelman, 'The Diffusion of Political Innovation: From East Europe to the Soviet Union', in R. Szporluk (ed.), *The Influence of Eastern Europe and the Soviet West on the USSR*, Praeger, New York, 1975, pp. 11–67, at p. 49.

101. See Korey, 'The Comintern and the Genealogy of the "Brezhnev Doctrine" ', pp. 55–6.

102. T. Davletshin, 'Limited Sovereignty: The Soviet Claim to Intervene in Defence of Socialism', *Bulletin of the Institute for the Study of the USSR*, vol. xvi, no. 8, 1969, pp. 3–9, at p. 7.

103. See Stephen G. Glazer, 'The Brezhnev Doctrine', *International Lawyer*, vol. 5, no. 1, 1969–70, pp. 168–79.

104. Franck and Weisband, *Word Politics*, p. 6.

105. Leon Romaniecki, 'Sources of the Brezhnev Doctrine of Limited Sovereignty and Intervention', *Israel Law Review*, no. 5, 1970, pp. 527–41, at p. 537.
106. Franck and Weisband, *Word Politics*.
107. Glazer, 'The Brezhnev Doctrine', p. 177.
108. John Norton Moore, 'Grenada and the International Double Standard', *AJIL*, vol. 78, 1984, pp. 145–68.
109. Glazer, 'The Brezhnev Doctrine', pp. 176–7.
110. Moore, 'Grenada and the International Double Standard'.
111. Charles Zorgbibe, 'La doctrine sovietique de la "souveraineté limitée"', *Revue générale de droit international publique*, no. 4, 1970, pp. 872–905, at p. 873.
112. Romaniecki, 'Sources of the Brezhnev Doctrine . . .'
113. Ibid.
114. Davletshin, 'Limited Sovereignty . . .', p. 9.
115. Pavlov, 'Proletarian Internationalism and Defence of Socialist Gains', p. 15.
116. See ch. 9.
117. Kovalev, 'Suverenitet i internatsional'nye obiazannosti sotsialisticheskikh stran'.
118. See Paul Lendvai 'How to Combine Detente With Soviet Hegemony', pp. 75–6.
119. R. Judson Mitchell, 'The Revised "Two Camps" Doctrine in Soviet Foreign Policy', *Orbis*, Spring 1972, vol. xvi, no. 1, pp. 21–34, at p. 24.
120. Mitchell, *Ideology of a Superpower*.
121. Romaniecki, 'Sources of the Brezhnev Doctrine . . .', p. 528.
122. Keal, *Unspoken Rules and Superpower Dominance*, pp. 131–2.
123. Neil Mathieson, *The "Rules of the Game" of Superpower Military Intervention in the Third World*, University Press of America, Washington, 1980.
124. Rusk, speech at New Haven.
125. Ibid.
126. M. Suslov, 'Leninizm i revoliutsionnoe preobrazovanie mira', *Kommunist*, no. 15, 1969, pp. 13–37, at pp. 34–5.
127. B. Ponomarev, 'V. I. Lenin – velikiĭ vokhd' revoliutsionnoĭ epokhi' *Kommunist*, no. 18, 1969, pp. 13–26.
128. See S. M. Schwebel, 'The Brezhnev Doctrine Repealed and Peaceful Co-existence Enacted', *AJIL*, vol. 66, 1972, pp. 816–19; E. McWhinney, *The International Law of Detente. Arms Control. European Security and East West Cooperation*, Sithoff and Noordhoff, Alphen aan den Rijn, 1978, p. 127.
129. F. A. M. Alting Von Geusau, 'Detente After Helsinki. Attitudes and Perspectives', *YBWA*, 1978, pp. 8–22, at p. 15.
130. N. I. Lebedev, *A New Stage in International Relations*, Pergamon, Oxford, 1977, ch. 3.
131. Ibid., p. 69.
132. Ibid.
133. Sonnenfeldt text in *New York Times*, 6 April 1976, p. 4.
134. Glazer, 'The Brezhnev Doctrine', pp. 173, 176.

135. F. I. Kozhevnikov and I. P. Blishchenko, 'Sotsializm i sovremennoe mezhnunarodnoe pravo', *SGP*, no. 4, 1970, pp. 88–104, at pp. 94–5. See also J. N. Hazard, 'Renewed Emphasis Upon a Socialist International Law', *AJIL*, vol. 65, no. 1, 1971, pp. 142–8.
136. E. Glaser, 'International Peremptory Law (jus cogens gentium)', *Revue Roumaine d'Etudes Internationales* (Bucharest), vol. 7, 1973, pp. 57–95, at p. 69.
137. Sh. Sanakoyev and N. Kapchenko, 'Triumph of the Principles of Proletarian Internationalism', *IA(M)*, no. 8, 1969, pp. 32–9, at p. 35.
138. A. I. Lepeshkin, 'Suverenitet v sovetskom gosudarstve i ego ukreplenie v period razvitogo sotsializma', *SGP*, no. 7, 1976, pp. 26–34, at p. 32.
139. Roland Eggleston, 'US Soviet Clash in Vienna over Brezhnev Doctrine and Afghanistan', *Radio Liberty Research (RLR)*, RL445/86, 25 Nov. 1986, pp. 1–2. See ch. 12.
140. See V. Kortunov, 'Lenin i ideologicheskaia bor'ba nashikh dneĭ', *MEMO*, no. 10, 1969, pp. 3–11, at p. 8.
141. Ibid.
142. See Alfred B. Evans Jr, 'Developed Socialism in Soviet Ideology', *Soviet Studies*, vol. 29, no. 3, 1977, pp. 409–28.
143. See J. Seroka and M. D. Simon (eds), *Developed Socialism in the Soviet Bloc*, Westview Press, Boulder, Colo., 1982.
144. K. Zarodov, 'Laws Governing the Development of the World Socialist System', *WMR*, vol. 14, no. 10, 1971, pp. 1–14, at p. 1.
145. Shvetsov, *Internatsionalnaia rol' KPSS v mirovom revoliutsionnom dvizhenii*, p. 57.
146. Katushev, 'Ukreplenie edinstva sotsialisticheskikh stran-zakonomernost' razvitiia mirovogo sotsializma', p. 52.
147. L. Moskvichev, 'Teoriia "deideologizatsii": stoki i sotsial'naia sushchnost'', *MEMO*, no. 12, 1968, pp. 3–15, at p. 15.
148. Suslov, 'Leninizm . . .' and Ponomarev, 'V. I. Lenin . . .'.
149. Round Table: Laws Governing the Development of the World Socialist System', *WMR*, vol. 14, no. 10, 1971, pp. 1–14, at p. 2.
150. Ibid., pp. 2–3.
151. Ibid., p. 2.
152. Ibid., p. 3.
153. Ibid., p. 4.
154. Ibid., p. 5.
155. Ibid., p. 4.
156. Ibid., p. 11.
157. G. Sorokin, 'Problemy ekonomicheskoĭ integratsii stran sotsializma', *VE*, Dec. 1968, pp. 77–86, at p. 85; E. T. Usenko, 'Sotrudnichestvo stran-chlenov SEV i sotsialisticheskiĭ internatsionalizm', *SGP*, no. 4, 1970, pp. 79–87.
158. B. Kovrig, 'Regionalism and Integration in Eastern Europe', *International Journal*, vol. 30, no. 4, 1975, pp. 689–706, at p. 700.
159. Ibid.
160. Rakowska-Harmstone, 'Socialist Internationalism . . .'.
161. G. Hodnett, 'The Debate over Soviet Federalism', *Soviet Studies*,

vol. 18, no. 4, 1967, pp. 458–81.
162. Shevstov, *The State and Nations in the USSR*, p. 112.
163. V. Chkhikvadze, 'Historic Significance of the Formation of the Soviet Federal State', *Social Sciences*, no. 4, 1972, pp. 33–46, at p. 38.
164. K. D. Korkmasova, 'Kriterii form natsional'noi gosudarstvennosti v SSSR', *SGP*, no. 11, 1970, pp. 45–51, at p. 48.
165. Iu. Paletskis, 'V. I. Lenin i velikoe sotruzhestvo natsii', *SGP*, no. 4, 1970, pp. 11–18, at p. 18.
166. Rakowska-Harmstone, 'Socialist Internationalism . . .'
167. Katushev, 'Ukreplenie edinstva . . .', p. 27.
168. Ibid.
169. Ibid., p. 24. 'The distinguishing feature of socialism is not the total absence of contradictions, but the absence of antagonistic contradictions': M. A. Suslov, *Marxism-Leninism – the International Teaching of the Working Class*, Progress Publishers, Moscow, 1975, p. 97.

9 Soviet 'Correlation of Forces' Analysis and Afghanistan

1. See V. V. Aspaturian, 'Soviet Global Power and the Correlation of Forces', *Problems of Communism*, May–June 1980, pp. 1–18.
2. See R. Rand, 'A Chronology of Soviet–Afghan Relations, April1978–Jan. 1980', *RLR*, RL17/80, 2 Jan. 1980, pp. 1–10.
3. Tass, 5 Dec. 1978, in Rand, 'A Chronology of Soviet–Afghan Relations', p. 4.
4. For examples of Soviet analyses of 'countries of socialist orientation' in this period, see A. Kiva, 'Sotsialisticheskaia orientatsiia: nekotorye problemy teorii i praktiki', *MEMO*, no. 10, 1976, pp. 19–32; V. F. Li, 'Politicheskaia nadstroika v obshchestvakh sotsialisticheskoi orientatsii', *VF*, no. 9, 1981, pp. 3–16.
5. Kiva, 'Sotsialisticheskaia orientatsiia . . .'.
6. V. V. Zagladin (ed.), *Theory and Tactics of the International Communist Movement*, Progress Publishers, Moscow, 1985, p. 446.
7. K. N. Brutents, *National Liberation Revolutions Today*, pt. 2, Progress Publishers, Moscow, 1977, p. 125.
8. Ibid., p. 164.
9. Ibid., p. 20.
10. Ibid., p. 54. See also G. Smirnov, 'State Sector in Countries of Socialist Orientation', *Social Sciences*, no. 2, 1980, pp. 157–66, at p. 164.
11. See V. P. Kuz'min, 'Mesto sistemnogo podkhoda v sovremennom nauchnom poznanii i marksistskom metodologii', *VF*, no. 2, 1980, pp. 45–58.
12. V. Zagladin, 'World Balance of Forces and the Development of International Relations', *IA(M)*, no. 3, 1985, pp. 65–73, at p. 65. See also G. Shakhnazarov, 'K probleme sootnosheniia sil v mire', *Kommunist*, no. 3, 1974, pp. 77–89; Julian Lider, *Correlation of Forces: An Analysis of Marxist-Leninist Concepts*, Gower, Aldershot, 1986, pp. 19–55; Sh. Sanakoyev, 'The World Today: Problem of the Correlation of Forces', *IA(M)*, no. 11, 1974, pp. 40–50; Michael J. Deane, 'The

Soviet Assessment of the "Correlation of World Forces"', *Orbis*, vol. 20, no. 3, 1976, pp. 625–36.

13. Zagladin, 'World Balance of Forces . . .', p. 70.
14. Lider, *Correlation of Forces* . . . , p. 30.
15. Deane, 'The Soviet Assessment of the "Correlation of World Forces"'.
16. R. Judson Mitchell, *Ideology of a Superpower*, ch. 5.
17. Aspaturian, 'Soviet Global Power . . .', p. 17.
18. Boris Meissner, 'Soviet Foreign Policy and Afghanistan', *Aussenpolitik*, vol. 31, no. 3, pp. 260–82, at p. 261.
19. See Mitchell, *Ideology of a Superpower*; Brezhnev's speech of 14 June 1974 (*Pravda*, 15 June, pp. 1–2); M. A. Suslov, 'Za plodotvornyĭ trud na blago naroda', *Pravda*, 21 Feb. 1980, p. 2.
20. *Pravda*, 25 Feb. 1976, pp. 2–9, at p. 4.
21. N. Lebedev, *The USSR in World Politics*, Progress Publishers, Moscow, 1982, p. 141.
22. A. P. Butenko, Iu. S. Novopashin, B. M. Pugachev (eds.), *Consolidation of The Socialist Countries' Unity*, Progress Publishers, Moscow, 1981, p. 9.
23. B. Ponomarov, 'Topical Theoretical Problems of the World Revolutionary Process', *Social Sciences*, no. 2, 1972, pp. 7–43, at p. 34.
24. E. Primakov, 'Newly Free Countries: Common Features', *Social Sciences*, no. 4, 1981, pp. 21–36, at p. 23.
25. B. Korolyov (Korolev), *Real Socialism and Ideological Struggle*, Progress Publishers, Moscow, 1985, p. 115.
26. Lider, *Correlation of Forces*, pp. 21–3; also John Lenczowski, *Soviet Perceptions of U.S. Foreign Policy: A Study of Ideology Power and Consensus*, Cornell University Press, 1982, ch. 1.
27. *Pravda*, 25 Feb. 1976, p. 4.
28. B. Korolev, 'Ideologicheskaia bor'ba na mirovoĭ arene v sovremennykh usloviiakh', *Politicheskoe samoobrazovanie*, no. 12, 1975, pp. 70–9, at p. 75.
29. B. Korolyov (Korolev), *Real Socialism* . . . , p. 85.
30. See Lynch, *The Soviet Study of International Relations*.
31. Butenko *et al.* (eds), *Consolidation* . . . , p. 94.
32. Korolev, 'Ideologicheskaia . . .', p. 72.
33. See N. Inozemtsev, 'O Leninskoĭ metodologii analiza mirovogo obshchestvennogo razvitiia', *Kommunist*, no. 12, 1976, pp. 66–77, at p. 76.
34. Shakhnazarov, 'K probleme sootnosheniia sil ĭ mire', p. 80.
35. Butenko *et al.* (eds), *Consolidation* . . . , p. 34.
36. Lider, *Correlation of Forces*, pp. 65–7.
37. M. A. Suslov, *Marxism–Leninism – the International Teaching of the Working Class*, Progress Publishers, Moscow, 1975, p. 97.
38. Korolev, 'Ideologicheskaia . . .', p. 74.
39. Ibid., p. 72.
40. N. Kapchenko and Sh. Sanakoyev, 'Soviet Foreign Policy and Ideology', *IA(M)*, no. 9, 1981, pp. 76–86, at p. 83.
41. G. Mirskiĭ, 'Razvivaiushchiesia strany i mirovoĭ kapitalizm', *MEMO*, no. 3, 1976, pp. 35–45.

42. See N. Inozemtsev, 'The Scientific and Technical Revolution and the Modern World', *Social Sciences*, no. 3, 1980, pp. 8–17, at p. 12.
43. G. Pirogov, 'Nekotorye tendentsii razvitiia mezhdunarodnogo rabochego dvizheniia', *MEMO*, no. 2, 1977, pp. 14–26.
44. Korolev, 'Ideologicheskaia . . .', p. 74.
45. See *Sistema, struktura i protsess razvitiia sovremennykh mezhdunarodnykh otnosheniĭ*, Izdatel'stvo nauka, Moscow, 1984, pp. 415–20.
46. O. Bykov, 'SSha i real'nosti mezhdunarodnoĭ razriadki', *MEMO*, no. 8, 1976, pp. 28–38; V. V. Zhurkin and E. M. Primakov, *Mezhdunarodnye konflikty*, IMO, Moscow, 1972, pp. 218–26.
47. B. Meissner, 'Soviet Foreign Policy and Afghanistan', *Aussenpolitik*, vol. 31, no. 3, 1980, pp. 260–82.
48. Jiri Valenta, 'From Prague to Kabul: The Soviet Style of Invasion', *International Security*, vol. 5, no. 2, 1980, pp. 114–41, at p. 140.
49. See Edward R. Girardet, *Afghanistan, The Soviet War*, Croom Helm, London, 1985, p. 88.
50. See Henry S. Bradsher, *Afghanistan and the Soviet Union*, Duke University Press, Durham, 1985; Joseph J. Collins, *The Soviet Invasion of Afghanistan: A Study in the Use of Force in Soviet Foreign Policy*, Lexington Books, Lexington, Mass., 1986.
51. A. Petrov, 'K sobytiiam v Afganistane', *Pravda*, 31 Dec. 1979, p. 4.
52. Valenta, 'From Prague to Kabul . . .', p. 125.
53. Lawrence Sherwin, 'Soviet Media Coverage of Events in Afghanistan in the Weeks before the Coup', *RLR*, RL62/80, 11 Feb. 1980, pp. 1–5, at p. 5.
54. See Collins, *The Soviet Invasion of Afghanistan*, p. 130.
55. R. Rand, 'The Brezhnev Doctrine, Afghanistan and the Upcoming Warsaw Pact Summit', *RLR*, RL171/80, 7 May 1980, pp. 1–3, at p. 1.
56. Ibid.; Meissner, 'Soviet Foreign Policy and Afghanistan'.
57. David Rees, 'Afghanistan's Role in Soviet Strategy', *Conflict Studies*, no. 118, May 1980, p. 5.
58. Petrov, 'K sobytiiam v Afganistane'.
59. See Margaret Doxey, 'The Soviet Union and Afghanistan', *YBWA*, 1983, pp. 62–80, at p. 65.
60. Z. Brzezinski, *Power and Principle: Memoirs of the National Security Advisor 1977–81*, Weidenfeld and Nicolson, London, 1983, p. 443.
61. See Doxey, 'The Soviet Union and Afghanistan', pp. 68–79.
62. See Rand, 'The Brezhnev Doctrine . . .'.
63. See S. Stankovic, 'Belgrade's Reaction To Afghanistan: "Stalinist Methods"', *RFER Radio Background Report (RBR)* (Yugoslavia), no. 5, 10 Jan. 1980, pp. 1–4, at p. 4.
64. Rand, 'The Brezhnev Doctrine . . .', p. 3.
65. See *RFE.RL Romania*, no. 1, 29 Jan. 1980, p. 4.
66. Brzezinski, *Power and Principle*.
67. Petrov, 'K sobytiiam v Afganistane'; see, Lawrence Sherwin, 'Soviet Press Treatment of Afghanistan's Request for Military Assistance', *RLR*, RL113/80, 20 March 1980, pp. 1–3, at p. 1.
68. Ibid. Petrov also claimed that it was in accordance with Article 51 of the UN Charter.
69. Brezhnev, *Pravda*, 13 Jan. 1980, p. 1.

70. Tass statement in English, 1820 GMT 6 March 1980, in Sherwin, 'Soviet Press Treatment . . .', p. 3.
71. Gromyko, Communiqué on press conference in Paris, *Pravda*, 26 April 1980, p. 4.
72. In *Sotsialisticheskaia industriia*, 16 Jan. 1980, p. 3, in Sherwin, 'Soviet Press Treatment . . .', p. 2. On Kabul Radio on 10 September, Amin said that he was proud that he had not asked foreign countries to fight in Afghanistan, *FBIS Middle East (ME)*, 12 Sept. 1979, p. 2.
73. Kabul Radio, 11 Jan. 1980, *FBIS.ME*, 14 Jan. 1980, pp. 2–3.
74. Security Council Debate, 6 Jan. 1980, UN Doc. 2187.
75. See R. S. Newell, 'International Responses to the Afghanistan Crisis', *World Today*, May 1981, pp. 172–81.
76. Reuters, 28 Dec. 1979, in Sherwin, 'Soviet Media Coverage . . .', p. 5.
77. Gennadii Anatol'ev, 'Otpor imperialisticheskomu umeshatel'stvu', *NV*, no. 2, Jan. 1980, pp. 8–10, at p. 9.
78. Petrov, 'K sobytiiam v Afganistane'. On protection of Afganistan's 'revolutionary gains', see P. Demchenko, 'Afghanistan: na strazhe zavoevanii naroda', *Kommunist*, no. 5, 1980, pp. 71–8.
79. Brezhnev, *Pravda*, 13 Jan. 1980, p. 1.
80. Chervonenko, reported in *New York Times*, 22 April 1980, p. 3.
81. V. V. Grishin, in *Moskovskaia Pravda*, 6 Feb. 1980, pp. 2–3, *FBIS-.SU*, 14 Feb. 1980, R 22.
82. 'Kommunisty solidarny s Afganskoĭ revoliutsieĭ', *NV*, no. 3, 1980, pp. 8–10, at p. 10.
83. Ibid.; also A. Epishev, 'Partiia Lenina-udokhovitel' i organizator pobedy', *Kommunist*, no. 7, 1980, pp. 60–72, at p. 71.
84. Ustinov, 'Vo imia mogushchestva-ot chizny', *Pravda*, 14 Feb. 1980, p. 2.
85. Meissner, 'Soviet Foreign Policy and Afghanistan', p. 281.
86. Z. Antic, 'New Yugoslav Polemics with Soviet Union and Vietnam', RBR.Y./62, 19 March 1980, pp. 1–3, at p. 2.
87. Oleg Golovin, 'O druz'iakh i protivnikakh nezavisimogo revoliutsionogo Afganistana', *NV*, no. 12, 1980, pp. 7–9.
88. Ibid.
89. Ibid.
90. *Izvestiia*, 24 Feb. 1981, p. 2. See also his statement at the 16th Congress of the Communist Party of Czechoslovakia, *Pravda*, 8 April 1981, p. 1.
91. E. K. Valkenier, 'Revolutionary Change in the Third World: Recent Soviet Assessments', *World Politics*, no. 3, 1986, pp. 415–34.
92. Ibid.
93. Zagladin (ed.), *Theory and Tactics*, p. 448.
94. Ibid., p. 450.
95. Valkenier, 'Revolutionary Change in the Third World'.
96. A. Prokhanov, 'Afganskie voprosy', *Literaturnaia gazeta*, 17 Feb. 1987, pp. 1, 9.
97. See 'Joint-Afghan statement', 7 April 1988, *Soviet News*, 13 April 1988, p. 133.
98. S. Sego, 'Will the Afghan Border be Redrawn?', *RLR*, Rl.156/88, 30 March 1988, pp. 1–3.

99. A. Kiva, 'Socialist Orientation: Reality and Illusions', *IA(M)*, no. 7, 1988, pp. 78–86.

10 The Soviet Proxy Intervention in Poland

1. For example, the principal positions within the Polish armed forces are occupied by graduates of Soviet military academies: see D. A. Mac-Gregor, 'Uncertain Allies? East European Forces in the Warsaw Pact', *Soviet Studies*, no. 2, 1986, pp. 227–47, at p. 238.
2. See Rosenau's definition of 'Intervention' in ch. 7.
3. *Poland: The State of the Republic, Reports by the Experience and Future Discussion Group (DiP) Warsaw*, ed. by Michael Vale, Pluto Press, London, 1981, p. 154.
4. Leszek Kolakowski, *Main Currents of Marxism, Vol. 3: The Breakdown*, Clarendon Press, Oxford, 1978, p. 467.
5. See Paul G. Lewis (ed.), *Eastern Europe: Political Crisis and Legitimation*, Croom Helm, London, 1984, pp. 1–41.
6. R. Remington, 'The Warsaw Pact', *YBWA*, 1973, pp. 153–72, at p. 167.
7. See Maurice D. Simon, 'Developed Socialism and the Polish Crisis', in J. Seroka and M. D. Simon (eds), *Developed Socialism in the Soviet Bloc: Political Theory and Political Reality*, Westview Press, Boulder, Colo., 1982, pp. 99–117, at p. 99.
8. Ibid., p. 100.
9. Ibid.
10. Kristian Gerner, *The Soviet Union and Central Europe in the Postwar Era*, Gower, Aldershot, 1985, p. 136.
11. *Poland: The State of the Republic*, p. 77.
12. Ibid.
13. See Bruce Porter, 'The USSR's Dual Approach Towards Poland', *RLR*, RL1/81, 29 Dec. 1980, pp. 1–4, at p. 3; also Richard D. Anderson, 'Soviet Decision-Making and Poland', *POC*, XXI, no. 2, 1982, pp. 22–36.
14. M. Ponomarev, 'Kholodnye vetry nad evropoĭ', *Krasnaia zvezda*, 28 Dec. 1980, p. 3.
15. See J. B. de Weydenthal, 'Party Attempts to Reassert Itself Amid Threats of Soviet Intervention', *RFER RAD.BR*, no. 303, (Poland), 18 Dec. 1980, pp. 1–8, at p. 3.
16. *Robotnik*, no. 68, 23 Nov. 1980, in Peter Raina, *Poland 1981. Towards Social Renewal*, Allen and Unwin, London, 1985, p. 48.
17. Josef Klasa, head of the party's media department, Reuter, 4 Dec. 1980, in de Weydenthal, 'Party Attempts . . .', p. 4. de Weydenthal notes that the party leaders frequently hinted at this possibility, p. 3.
18. See Brzezinski, *Power and Principle*, pp. 300–1.
19. Porter, 'Phases in the USSR's Response to the Labour Unrest in Poland', *RLR*, RL71/81, 17 Feb. 1981, pp. 1–7, at p. 1.
20. A. Petrov, 'Proiski vragov sotsialisticheskoĭ Pol'shi', *Pravda*, 1 Sept. 1980, p. 5.

21. See Sidney Ploss, *Moscow and the Polish Crisis*, Westview Press, Boulder, Colo., 1986, pp. 16–17.
22. *Izvestiia*, 2 Sept. 1980, p. 2.
23. A. Petrov, 'Vmeshatel'stvo vo vnutrennie dela PNR prodolzhaetsia', *Pravda*, 20 Sept. 1980, p. 5.
24. G. Alekseev, 'V. I. Lenin o profsoiuzakh', *Pravda*, 25 Sept. 1980, p. 2.
25. In *Literaturnaia gazeta*, 29 Oct. 1980. See B. Porter, 'Phases . . .', p. 3.
26. *RFER Situation Report (RFER.SR)*, no. 21 (Poland), 21 Nov. 1980, p. 2.
27. *New York Times*, 14 Dec. 1981, in Bruce Porter, 'The USSR and Poland on the Road to Martial Law', *RLR*, RL4/82, 30 Dec. 1981, pp. 1–10, at p. 2.
28. See L. Sherwin, 'Soviet Media Cite Their Socialist Brethren on Poland', *RLR* RL461/80, 2 Dec. 1980, pp. 1–3.
29. de Weydenthal, 'Party Attempts to Reassert Itself . . .', p. 6.
30. The 'was, is and will be' formula was first mentioned on 5 December in the communiqué of the Warsaw Pact Summit Conference, *Pravda*, 6 December 1980, p. 1: see Bruce Porter, 'The USSR's Dual Approach Towards Poland', p. 1.
31. Tass, Dec. 26 1980, in Porter, 'The USSR's Dual Approach Towards Poland', p. 1.
32. M. Baglai, 'Profsoiuzy v usloviiakh sotsialisticheskogo obshchestva', *Pravda*, 26 Dec. 1980, pp. 2–3, at p. 2.
33. M. Ponomarev, 'Kholodnye vetry nad evropoï'.
34. Iu. Krasin, 'Internatsional'noe i natsional'noe v revoliutsionnom prot-sesse', *NV*, no. 7, 1981, pp. 18–20.
35. 'Polozhenie v Pol'she', *Pravda*, 3 Feb. 1981, p. 4.
36. Radio Moscow, 23 Feb. 1981, in Bruce Porter, 'The 26th Party Congress: Brezhnev on Soviet Foreign Policy', *RLR* RL80/81, 23 Feb. 1981, pp. 1–6, at p. 2.
37. Tass 30 Oct. 1981. See Lawrence Sherwin, 'Soviet Coverage of Poland since the Brezhnev-Kania meeting', *RLR*, RL108/81, 9 March 1981, pp. 1–3, at p. 1.
38. Ibid., pp. 2–3.
39. Ibid., p. 1.
40. Tass, 10 March 1981, Bruce Porter, 'Warsaw Pact Manoeuvres and Poland: The Political Implications', *RLR*, RL118/81, 17 March 1981, pp. 1–3, at p. 2. On 23 January, the day before Solidarity's strike for a five-day week, *Krasnaia zvezda* gave front page news to Soviet-Polish manoeuvres, L. Sherwin, 'The Litany of Criticism Continues', *RLR*, RL44/81, 27 Jan. 1981, pp. 1–3, at p. 2.
41. On Soviet 'signalling' during the Crisis, see Thomas M. Cynkin, *Soviet and American Signalling in the Polish Crisis*, Macmillan, London, 1988.
42. *Pravda*, 8 April 1981, p. 1.
43. *Pravda*, 12 June 1981, p. 1.
44. Tass, 11 June 1981.
45. R. Kosolapov, 'Atakuiushchii klass', *Pravda*, 31 July 1981, p. 2.

46. B. Averchenko, 'Mezhdunarodnoe obozrenie', *Pravda*, 9 August 1981, p. 4.
47. *Pravda*, 19 Sept. 1981, p. 4.
48. Jacques Rupnik, 'The Military and Normalisation in Poland', in Paul G. Lewis (ed.), *Eastern Europe . . .*, pp. 154–75, at p. 162.
49. Ibid., p. 158.
50. Lawrence Sherwin, 'Soviet Media Commentary At the Time of the Appointment of the New Polish Premier', *RLR*, RL72/81, 13 Feb. 1981, pp. 1–3, at p. 1.
51. Ploss, *Moscow and the Polish Crisis*, p. 155.
52. A. Petrov, '"Solidarnost" rvetsia k vlasti', *Pravda*, 13 Oct. 1981, p. 4.
53. Tass, 4 Nov. 1981, in E. Teague, 'Meeting of Central Committee Secretaries of Ruling CPs', *RLR*, RL446/81, 6 Nov. 1981, pp. 1–4, at p. 3.
54. *Le Monde*, 18 Dec. 1981, in Porter, 'The USSR and Poland on the Road to Martial Law', p. 8.
55. *New York Times*, 14 Dec. 1981, in Porter, 'The USSR and Poland . . .', p. 2.
56. See Bruce Porter, 'The USSR and Poland . . .', Kulikov had consultations in Warsaw with Poland's military leaders on 24 and 25 Nov., *Pravda*, 26 Nov. 1981, p. 7.
57. Porter, 'Phases in The USSR's Response To The Labour Unrest in Poland', pp. 2–3.
58. Patrick Moore, 'Poland's Allies Rally Behind the Healthy Forces', *RFER*, *RAD.BR*/198 (Eastern Europe), 13 July 1981, pp. 1–3, at p. 1.
59. See Patrick Moore, 'Tougher Line on Poland in Eastern Media', *RFER*, *RAD.BR*/31 (Eastern Europe), 5 Feb. 1981, pp. 1–4; also his 'Eastern Media Critical of Polish Developments', *RFER.BR*/110 (Eastern Europe), 23 April 1981, pp. 1–4.
60. Husák, reported in *Rudé právo*, 16 Feb. 1981, in *RFER.SR* Czechoslovakia/4, 24 Feb. 1981, pp. 1–15, at p. 2.
61. See Moore, 'Tougher Line on Poland . . .'.
62. Radio Prague, 28 Jan. 1981, in Moore, 'Tougher Line on Poland . . .'.
63. Moore, 'Tougher Line on Poland . . .'.
64. Patrick Moore, 'Sharp Editorial in *Scînteia* on Poland', *RAD.BR*/279 (Romania), 30 Sept. 1981, pp. 1–4.
65. Raina, *Poland 1981: Towards Social Renewal*, p. 8.
66. Michael Yahuda, *China's Foreign Policy After Mao*, Macmillan, London, 1983, pp. 194–5.
67. Kevin Devlin, 'Soviet-PCI Polemics over Poland', *RFER*, *RAD.BR*/185 (World Communist Movement), 30 June 1981, pp. 1–4.
68. B. Ponomarev, 'O mezhdunarodnom znacheni XXV s"ezda KPSS', *Kommunist*, no. 5, 1981, pp. 3–17.
69. See Kevin Devlin, 'Western C.P.s Back Polish Renewal, Warn Against Intervention', *RFER*, *RAD.BR*/178 (World Communist Movement), 24 June 1981, pp. 1–4.
70. Brzezinski, *Power and Principle*, p. 300.
71. Ibid., p. 464.

72. Ibid., p. 463.
73. Ibid., p. 468.
74. L. Korbonski and L. Fajfer, 'The Soviet Union and the Two Crises in Poland', in Jonathan R. Adelman, *The Superpowers and Revolution*, Praeger, New York, 1986, ch. 15, at p. 255.
75. Brzezinski, *Power and Principle*, p. 466.
76. Ibid., p. 466.
77. Ibid., p. 467.
78. Moscow Radio, 14 Dec. 1981.
79. Moscow Radio, 29 Dec. 1981, in L. Sherwin, 'Soviet Media Responds to U.S. Sanctions against Moscow', *RLR*, RL8/82, 4 Jan. 1982, pp. 1–3, at p. 1. On U.S. reactions, see Max Kampelman, 'Soviet Responsibility in Poland', *World Affairs*, no. 144, Spring 1982, pp. 502–5.
80. E.g. Korolev, *Real Socialism and Ideological Struggle*, pp. 107–8.
81. A. V. Kuznetsov, 'O teoreticheskikh kontseptsiiakh odnogo Pol'skogo politologo', *VF*, no. 12, 1983, pp. 26–39.
82. Ibid.
83. R. Kosolapov, 'Vklad XXIV, XXV i XXVI s"ezdov KPSS v razrabotkii teoreticheskikh i politicheskikh problem razvitogo sotsializma i perokhoda k kommunizmu', *Kommunist*, no. 5, 1982, pp. 54–67.
84. See E. Kux, 'Contradictions in Soviet Socialism', *POC*, Nov.–Dec. 1984, pp. 1–27, and Alfred B. Evans Jr, 'The Polish Crisis in the 1980s and Adaptation in Soviet Ideology', *Jl. of Communist Studies*, vol. 2, no. 3, 1986, pp. 263–85, upon which the analysis below is largely based.
85. A. Butenko, 'Sotsializm: formy i deformatsii', *NV*, no. 6, 1982, pp. 5–7.
86. Ibid., p. 6.
87. E. A. Ambartsumov, 'Analiz V. I. Leninym prichin krizisa 1921g i putei vykhoda iz nego', *VI*, no. 4, 1984, pp. 15–29.
88. Ibid.
89. 'Ot redakstsionnoi kollegii', *VI*, no. 12, 1984, pp. 97–102.
90. See A. Butenko, 'Protivorechiia razvitiia sotsializme kak obshchestvennogo stroia', *VF*, no. 10, 1982, pp. 16–19, at p. 17.
91. V. S. Semenov, 'Problema protivorechii v usloviiakh sotsializma', *VF*, no. 7, 1982, pp. 17–32, at p. 32.
92. Ibid., p. 21.
93. R. Kosolapov, 'Sotsializm organicheskaia tselostnost' sotsial'noi sistemy', *Pravda*, 4 March 1983, pp. 2–3.
94. A. P. Butenko, 'Eshche raz o protivorechiiakh sotsializma', *VF*, no. 2, 1984, pp. 124–9.
95. V. S. Semenov, 'K teoreticheskomu uglublenniu i konkretizatsii analiza problemy protivorechii v usloviiakh razvitogo sotsializma', *VF*, no. 2, 1984, pp. 130–40.
96. See Kux, 'Contradictions in Soviet Socialism' and Evans, 'The Polish Crisis . . .'.

11   Superpower Doctrines of Intervention: Comparisons and Contrasts

1. A. Ulam, 'The Destiny of Eastern Europe', *Problems of Communism*,

Feb. 1974, pp. 1–12, at p. 6; N. Chomsky, *Turning the Tide: U.S. Intervention in Central America and the Struggle for Peace*, Pluto Press, London, 1985, p. 59.

2. G. Connell-Smith, *The U.S. and Latin America*, Heinemann, London, 1974, p. 11.
3. J. Duroselle, *From Wilson to Roosevelt*, Chatto and Windus, London, 1964, p. 203; Connell-Smith, *The U.S. and Latin America*, p. xii.
4. Franck and Weisband, *Word Politics . . .* , p. 10.
5. Kaufman, *The Superpowers and their Spheres of Influence*, p. 20.
6. Franck and Weisband, *Word Politics . . .* , p. 97.
7. On 'rules of the game' and tacit understandings see Keal, *Unspoken Rules and Superpower Dominance*; and Mathieson, *The 'Rules of the Game' of Superpower Military Intervention in the Third World*.
8. Franck and Weisband, *World Politics . . .* , p. 108.
9. Connell-Smith, *The U.S. and Latin America*, p. 278.
10. J. N. Moore, 'The Secret War in Central America and The Future of World Order', *AJIL*, vol. 80, 1986, pp. 43–127, at p. 116.
11. J. N. Moore, 'Grenada and the International Double Standard', *AJIL*, vol. 78, 1984, pp. 145–68, at p. 165.
12. Moore, 'Secret War . . .', p. 115.
13. Ibid., pp. 115–16.
14. Glazer, 'The Brezhnev Doctrine', pp. 175–6.
15. V. Duculescu, 'Spheres of Interest in International Relations', *Revue Roumaine D'etudes Internationales (Bucharest)*, vol. 15, 1981, pp. 115–22.
16. See Elihu Root, 'The Real Monroe Doctrine', *AJIL*, vol. 8, no. 3, 1914, pp. 427–42.
17. B. Dymritshin and J. Gilmore, 'The Monroe Doctrine: A Soviet View', *Bulletin of the Institute for the Study of the USSR*, vol. II, May, 1964, pp. 3–14, at p. 8.
18. 'G. Nerval', 'A Latin American View: Egoistic from its Pronouncement' in A. Rappaport (ed.), *The Monroe Doctrine*, Holt, Rinehart and Wiston, New York, 1964, pp. 92–8, at p. 98.
19. L. Quantanilla 'Machiavellian due to Corollaries' in Rappaport (ed.), *The Monroe Doctrine*, pp. 99–106, at p. 100.
20. See Quantanilla, 'Machiavellian due to Corollaries'.
21. D. Perkins, *The Monroe Doctrine 1867–1907*, Johns Hopkins Press, Baltimore, 1937, p. 119.
22. See Connell-Smith, *The U.S. and Latin America*.
23. Text in A. S. Link and W. M. Leary (eds), *The Diplomacy of World Power: The U.S. 1889–1920*, Edward Arnold, London, 1970, pp. 72–7.
24. Perkins, *The Monroe Doctrine 1867–1907*, pp. 342–3; Duroselle, *From Wilson to Roosevelt*, pp. 163–4.
25. See text of the 'Selden Resolution' (20 Sept. 1965), House of Representatives 560, 89th Congress Sess., 111 Cong. Rec. 245347.
26. David Ronfeldt, 'Geopolitics, Security and U.S. Strategy in the Caribbean Basin', Rand R-2997-AF/RC, Santa-Monica, Calif., 1983, p. 52.
27. See Dymritshin and Gilmore, 'The Monroe Doctrine: A Soviet View'.

28. See E. Korovin, 'Sovereignty and Peace', *IA(M)*, no. 9, 1960, pp. 7–12; N. N. Bolkhovitinov, 'Doktrina Monro: legendy i deĭstvitel'nost'', *MEMO*, no. 9, 1960, pp. 14–26; L. Minayev, 'American Hegemonism and InterImperialist Contradictions', *IA(M)*, no. 8, 1983, pp. 49–57.
29. Korovin, 'Sovereignty and Peace', p. 8.
30. Ibid., pp. 8–11.
31. S. Gonionsky, 'The Unburied Corpse of the Monroe Doctrine', *IA(M)*, no. 10, 1960, pp. 60–6, at p. 66.
32. L. A. Modzhorian, 'Amerikanskie doktriny grabezha i razboia: ot Monro do Zhonsona', *SGP*, no. 9, 1965, pp. 57–66.
33. See also Iu. M. Mel'nikov, 'Anakhronizm amerikanskoi doktriny i politiki sily', *Voprosy istorii (VI)*, no. 11, 1986, pp. 3–22, at pp. 8–9.
34. K. Khachaturov, 'U.S. Ideological Aggression in Latin America', *IA(M)*, no. 1, 1986, pp. 64–71, at p. 65. On modern variants, see V. Bolshakov, 'Doctrine of International Brigandage', *IA(M)*, no. 11, 1986, pp. 100–8.
35. Andrew M. Scott, 'Military Intervention by the Great Powers: The Rules of the Game', in I. William Zartman, *Czechoslovakia: Intervention and Impact*, New York University Press, 1970, pp. 85–104, at p. 86.
36. In Franck and Weisband, *Word Politics . . .* , p. 61.
37. US Department of State Bulletin, no. 52, 1965, pp. 744–8.
38. Kaufman, *The Superpowers and their Spheres of Influence*, p. 30.
39. Ibid., p. 82.
40. See for example, F. S. Tarasov, *SShA i latinskaia amerika*, Izdatel'stvo politicheskoĭ literatury, Moscow, 1972, pp. 278–92; I. Strok, 'Central America: Greater Opposition to U.S. Policy', *IA(M)*, no. 12, 1986, pp. 65–71.
41. H. Kissinger, *Years of Upheaval*, Weidenfeld and Nicolson, London, 1982, p. 375.
42. Ibid., p. 378.
43. Ibid., p. 374.
44. Ibid., pp. 376–7.
45. Zagladin (ed.), *Theory and Tactics . . .* , pp. 411–12.
46. P. M. Dunn and B. W. Watson, *American Intervention in Grenada*, Westview Special Studies in Military Affairs, Boulder, Colo., 1985.
47. On the concept of 'socialist orientation', see ch. 9.
48. V. V. Aspaturian, 'The Impact of the Grenada Events on the Soviet Alliance System', in V. V. Aspaturian (ed.), *Grenada and Soviet/Cuban Policy. Internal Crisis and U.C./O.E.C.S. Intervention*, Westview Press, Boulder, Colo., 1986, p. 62.
49. Aspaturian, 'The Impact of the Grenada Events . . .'.
50. Moore, 'The U.S. Action in Grenada', p. 156.
51. L. Doswald-Beck, 'The Legal Validity of Military Intervention by Invitation of the Government', *British Yearbook of International Law*, 1985, pp. 188–252, at p. 236.
52. Moore, 'The U.S. Action in Grenada', p. 165.
53. F. A. Boyle *et al.*, 'International Lawlessness in Grenada', *AJIL*, vol. 78, 1984, pp. 172–5.

54. Ibid., p. 174.
55. C. Joyner, 'Reflections on the Lawfulness of Invasion', *AJIL*, vol. 78, 1984, pp. 131–44, at p. 144.
56. See Moore, 'Secret War . . .', pp. 111–20.
57. Ibid., p. 112.
58. Ibid., pp. 113–14.
59. Kaufman, *The Superpowers and their Spheres of Interest*, p. 35.
60. Z. P. Iakhimovich, 'Marksistskaia kontseptsiia mira: traditsii i sovremennost'', *VI*, no. 6, 1986, pp. 3–21, at p. 21.
61. Robert A. Devine, *Eisenhower and the Cold War*, Oxford University Press, 1981, pp. 91–2.
62. State Department Bulletin, no. 997, July 1958.
63. In Brzezinski, *Power and Principle*, p. 426.
64. W. M. Reisman, 'Critical Defence Zones and International Law: The Reagan Codicil', *AJIL*, vol. 76, 1982, pp. 589–91.
65. J. E. S. Fawcett, 'Intervention in International Law', *Recueil Des Cours, Académie De Droit International De La Haye*, 1961, vol. 2, pp. 347–421, at p. 349.
66. Ibid.
67. Peter Shearman, 'Soviet Foreign Policy in Africa and Latin America', *Journal of International Studies*, vol. 15, no. 3, 1986, pp. 339–66.
68. Aspaturian, 'The Impact of the Grenada Events . . .', p. 49.
69. Scott, 'Military Intervention by the Great Powers'.

12 Challenges to the Soviet Doctrines of Sovereignty in the 1980s

1. Silviu Brucan, *The Dialectic of World Politics*, Free Press, New York, 1978, p. 142.
2. W. Levi, *Contemporary International Law: A Concise Introduction*, Westview Press, Boulder, Colo., 1979, p. 93.
3. N. Politis, 'Le Problème de la limitation de la souveraineté', *Recueil Des Cours, Académie De Droit International De La Haye*, vol. 6, 1925, in 'Korowicz, Sovereignty . . .', p. 5.
4. K. Loewenstein, 'Sovereignty and International Cooperation', *AJIL*, vol. 48, 1954, pp. 222–54, at p. 223.
5. J. Herz, *International Politics in the Atomic Age*, Columbia University Press, New York, 1959.
6. R. Vernon, *Sovereignty At Bay*, Basic Books, New York, 1971.
7. See C. C. Pentland, 'Neofunctionalism', *YBWA*, 1973, pp. 345–71.
8. G. Schwarzenberger, *International Law and Order*, Stephens, London, 1971, p. 58.
9. J. Burton, *World Society*, Cambridge University Press, 1972, pp. 35–45.
10. See James, *Sovereign Statehood*.
11. G. Kh. Shakhnazarov and F. M. Burlatskiĭ, 'O razvitii Marksistsko-Leninskoĭ politicheskoĭ nauki', *VF*, no. 12, 1980, pp. 10–23, at p. 22.
12. V. Lukin, '"Power Centres" and World Politics', *Social Sciences*, no. 2, 1985, pp. 95–106, at p. 101.
13. Ibid.
14. Ibid.

15. N. Inozemtsev, 'The Scientific Technological Revolution and the Modern World', *Social Sciences*, no. 3, 1980, pp. 8–17, at p. 12.
16. Brucan, *The Dialectic of World Politics*, p. 84.
17. Ghita Ionescu, 'A Geopolitical Aspect of an Eminently Geopolitical Crisis', *Government and Opposition*, vol. 22, no. 3, 1987, pp. 259–69, at p. 269.
18. G. Shakhnazarov, 'Governability of the World', *IA(M)*, no. 3, 1988, pp. 17–24, at p. 19.
19. Ibid.
20. E. Korovin, in F. I. Kozhevnikov (ed.), *Mezhdunarodnoe pravo*, Gosudarstvennoe izdatel'stvo iuridicheskoĭ literatury, Moscow, 1957, p. 93.
21. M. Volkov, 'The Imperialist Essence of Collective Neocolonialism', *IA(M)*, no. 4, 1986, pp. 64–71, at p. 64.
22. See I. Ivanov, 'Transnational'nyĭ monopolisticheskiĭ kapital i razvivaiushcheesia obshchestvo', *MEMO*, no. 11, 1986, pp. 31–42.
23. N. Sergeyev, 'Developing Nations and the Transnational Corporations', *Social Sciences*, no. 2, 1979, pp. 171–88, at p. 173.
24. See A. Z. Astapovich, *Strategiia transnational'nykh korporatsii*, Izdatel'stvo nauka, Moscow, 1978.
25. I. Frolov, 'Nauchit'sia myslit' i deĭstvovat' po-novomu', *MEMO*, no. 8, 1986, pp. 3–7.
26. Volkov, 'The Imperialist Essence . . .', p. 67.
27. V. S. Shevtsov, *The State and Nations . . .* , p. 167.
28. Butenko *et al.*, *Consolidation of the Socialist Countries' Unity*, pp. 235–7.
29. V. F. Gubin, 'Kommunisticheskiĭ manifest i mezhdunarodnoe pravo', *SEMP*, 1973, pp. 43–62, at p. 53.
30. G. Shakhnazarov, 'The Logic of the Nuclear Era', *Social Sciences*, no. 2, 1985, pp. 37–58, at p. 43.
31. G. Shakhnazarov, 'May Man Never Know "Nuclear Midnight"', *Social Sciences*, no. 3, 1984, pp. 140–59, at p. 156.
32. Zagladin (ed.), *Theory and Tactics . . .* , ch. 4.
33. A. Aganbegyan, *The Challenge: Economics of Perestroika*, Hutchinson, London, 1988, p. 154.
34. Iu. Borko, 'O nekotorykh aspektakh izucheniia protsessov zapadno evropeĭskoĭ integratsii', *MEMO*, no. 2, 1988, pp. 33–50, at p. 42.
35. A. Aslund, 'The new Soviet policy towards international organisations', *World Today*, vol. 44, no. 2, 1988, pp. 27–30.
36. Shakhnazarov, 'Governability . . .', p. 16.
37. Ibid., p. 19.
38. Ibid., p. 24.
39. V. Adoratskiĭ, *O gosudarstve*, Moscow, 1923 in Shakhnazarov, 'Governability . . .', p. 18.
40. Ibid., p. 17.
41. Jan. F. Triska, 'Eurocommunism and the Decline of Proletarian Internationalism' in V. V. Aspaturian, J. Valenta, D. Burke (eds), *Eurocommunism Between East and West*, Indiana University Press, Bloomington 1980, pp. 72–99; also Jiri Valenta, 'Eurocommunism and Eastern Europe', *POC*, March–April 1978, pp. 41–5.

42. J. B. Urban, 'Moscow and the PCI in the 1970s: Kto Kovo?', *Studies in Comparative Communism*, Summer/Autumn 1980, pp. 99–167.
43. See 'Ponomarev Delivers Sharp Attack on Eurocommunism', *RLR*, RL317/81, 21 Oct. 1979, p. 1.
44. R. D. Asmus, 'The National and the International: Harmony or Discord?', *RFER.RBR*/144, 10 Dec. 1985, pp. 1–10.
45. V. Shlapentokh, *Soviet Public Opinion and Ideology*, Praeger, New York, 1986, p. 16.
46. R. D. Asmus, 'The Soviet-East German Dispute Revisited', *RFER.RBR*/66, 16 July 1985, pp. 1–12.
47. A. J. McAdams, *East Germany and Detente*, Cambridge University Press, 1985, pp. 194–201.
48. S. Wise, 'CPSU Journal Outlines Soviet Stance on Warsaw Pact Foreign Policy Dispute', *RLR*, RL173/84, 30 April 1984, pp. 1–6; and E. Teague, 'Debate Over Eastern Europe's National Interests Continues', *RLR*, RL285/85, 29 Aug. 1985, pp. 1–4.
49. In *Társadalmi Szemle*, no. 1, January 1984, pp. 13–21. See A. Reisch and V. V. Kusin, 'National Versus International Interests', in Vojtech Mastny (ed.), *Soviet/East European Survey 1983–84*, Duke University Press, Durham, 1985, pp. 227–36, at p. 227.
50. R. D. Asmus, 'GDR Supports Hungarian Position on Bloc Relations', *RFER.RBR*/75 (Eastern Europe), May 1984, pp. 1–6.
51. Wise, 'CPSU Journal . . .'; also B. Murphy, 'Moscow Forces Postponement of Honecker Visit', *RLR*, RL332/84, 5 Sept. 1984, pp. 1–7.
52. M. Stefanik and I. Hlivka, 'The National and the International in CPCS Policy', in Reisch and Kusin, 'National Versus International Interests', p. 232.
53. *Neues Deutschland*, 12 April 1984, in Wise, 'CPSU Journal . . .', p. 1.
54. On 30 July, *Neues Deutschland* reprinted an article from the Hungarian paper *Nepszava*, supporting Honecker's foreign policy: see Murphy, 'Moscow Forces Postponement . . .', p. 1.
55. O. V. Borisov, 'Soiuz novogo tipa' *Voprosy istorii KPSS (VIKPSS)*, no. 4, 1984, pp. 34–49.
56. A. Maier, 'Party Journal Rejects East-Bloc Assimilation', *RFER.RBR*, Romanian Special Report/16, 14 Nov. 1985, pp. 3–5.
57. See R. V. Burks, 'The Coming Crisis in the Soviet Union', *East European Quarterly*, vol. XVIII, no. 1, 1984, pp. 61–71.
58. He announced on taking office that developing relations with Eastern Europe would be his first commandment, *Pravda*, 12 March 1985, p. 3.
59. Aganbegyan, *The Challenge* . . . , p. 43.
60. V. Kortunov, 'Novoe politicheskoe myshlenie-imperativ sovremennosti', *MEMO*, no. 10, 1986, pp. 16–25, at p. 16.
61. V. Zagladin, 'Partiia-narod-sotsializm', *MEMO*, no. 5, 1987, pp. 3–16, at p. 5.
62. Editorial, 'Seven Decades – the Judgement of History', *IA(M)*, no. 1, 1988, pp. 3–11, at p. 3.
63. *Soviet News*, 24 Feb. 1988, p. 71.
64. E. Primakov, 'Proryv v Vashingtone', *MEMO*, no. 2, 1988, pp. 3–7, at p. 4.
65. V. Shlapentokh, 'The XXVII Congress: A Case Study of the Shaping

of a New Party Ideology', *Soviet Studies*, vol. XL, no. 1, 1986, pp. 1–20, at p. 4.

66. V. Zhurkin, S. Karaganov, A. Kortunov, 'Vyzavy bezopasnosti-starye i novye', *Kommunist*, no. 1, 1988, pp. 42–50; see J. Checkel, '"New" and "Old" Thinking on Soviet National Security', *RLR*, RL 88/88, 2 March 1988, pp. 1–4.
67. Aganbegyan, *The Challenge* . . .
68. Ibid., p. 203.
69. See P. Hofheinz, 'Piecing Together the Gorbachev Puzzle', *Jl. of Communist Studies*, vol. 3, no. 2, 1987, pp. 160–77, at pp. 163–5.
70. Z. Medvedev, *Gorbachev*, Blackwell, Oxford, 1986, p. 285.
71. Tass, 10 May 1988: *BBC Monitoring Report, Soviet Union*/0149, 12 May 1988, p. 1.
72. Aganbegyan, *The Challenge*, p. 40.
73. Ibid., p. xxxv.
74. See Gertrude E. Schroeder, 'Gorbachev: "Radically" Implementing Brezhnev's Reforms', *Soviet Economy*, no. 2, 1986, pp. 289–301, at pp. 296–300.
75. P. Hofheinz, 'Gorbachev's Double Burden: Economic Reform and Growth Acceleration', *Millennium*, vol. 16, no. 1, 1987, pp. 21–48.
76. C. Schmidt-Hauer, *Gorbachev: The Path To Power*, Pan, London, 1986.
77. R. Service, 'Gorbachev's Political Reforms: Future in the Past', *Jl. of Communist Studies*, vol. 3, no. 2, 1987, pp. 276–85, at p. 281. See Hofheinz, n. 69 above.
78. K. Dawisha and J. Valdez, 'Socialist Internationalism in Eastern Europe', *Problems of Communism*, March–April 1987, pp. 1–14, at p. 14.
79. Service, 'Gorbachev's Political Reforms . . .', p. 279.
80. Hofheinz, 'Piecing Together . . .', p. 285.
81. G. Urban, 'Should we help Gorbachev?', *World Today*, Feb. 1988, pp. 19–20.
82. J. Hough, 'Gorbachev's Strategy', *Foreign Affairs*, vol. 64, no. 1, 1985, pp. 33–55.
83. J. Frankel, 'Should we help Gorbachev? – Another View', *World Today*, May 1988, pp. 77–8.
84. Gorbachev, *Perestroika* . . . ,
85. X. Smiley, *Daily Telegraph*, 19 March 1988, p. 1.
86. V. V. Kusin, 'The "Yugoslavisation" of Soviet-East European Relations?', *RFER.RADBR*/57 (Eastern Europe), 29 March 1988, pp. 1–5.
87. Dawisha and Valdez, 'Socialist Internationalism . . .'.
88. See Asmus, 'The National and the International: Harmony or Discord?'
89. O. Vladimirov, 'Vedushchiĭ faktor mirovogo revoliutsionnogo protsessa', *Pravda*, 21 June 1985, p. 3.
90. I. Biriukov, 'Vazhnyĭ politicheskiĭ zavet', *Pravda*, 14 Dec. 1985, p. 5. See E. Teague, 'Pravda Reaffirms Lessons of Prague Spring', *RLR*, RL1/86, 19 Dec. 1985, pp. 1–5.
91. O. Bogomolov, 'Soglasovanie ekonomicheskikh interesov i politiki pri

sotsializme', *Kommunist*, no. 10, 1986, pp. 82–93.

92. Iu. S. Novopashin, 'Politicheskie otnosheniia stran sotsializma', *Rabochii klass i sovremennyĭ mir*, no. 5, 1985, pp. 55–65, at p. 60.

93. For an excellent exposition of Iagodovskiĭ's views (explained in *Novoe vremia* 'Kriterii effektivnosti', *NV*, no. 37, 1987, pp. 17–9; in *Argumenty i fakty*, no. 33, 1988, and elsewhere), see E. Teague, 'Relevance of "Prague Spring" Discussed', *RLR*, RL368/88, 15 August 1988, pp. 1–5.

94. A. Bovin, 'Mirnoe sosushchestvovanie i mirovaia sistema sotsializma', *MEMO*, no. 7, 1988, pp. 5–15, at p. 15.

95. C. Gati, 'Gorbachev and Eastern Europe', *Foreign Affairs*, Summer 1987, pp. 958–75.

96. Budapest Home Service, 19 April 88, *BBC Monitoring Report, Eastern Europe*, 21 April 1988, p. B11.

97. M. Szürös, 'Hungary Europe and the World', *The New Hungarian Quarterly*, vol. 28, Autumn 1987, pp. 15–25, at p. 18.

98. *The Times*, 3 May 1988, p. 7.

99. *Pravda*, 22 April 1987.

100. V. V. Kusin, 'Gorbachev's Impact on Eastern Europe After Three Years', *RFER.RADBR*/47 (Eastern Europe), 17 March 1988, pp. 1–4, at p. 3.

101. B. Donovan, 'The GDR and Gorbachev's Reforms', *RFER.RADBR*/ 60 (Eastern Europe), 6 April 1988, pp. 1–5, at p. 1.

102. *Time* magazine, 18 April 1988, p. 13.

103. A. U. Gabay, 'Ceauşescu rejects Soviet style Reform', *RFER.RBR*, Romania Special Report/16 Feb. 1987, p. 3.

104. A. Maier, 'Ceauşescu criticises CMEA cooperation', *RFER.RBR*, Romania Special Report/1, Jan. 1986, pp. 3–6.

105. W. H. Luers, 'The U.S. and Eastern Europe', *Foreign Affairs*, Summer 1987, pp. 976–94, at p. 979.

106. O. V. Borisov, 'Soiuz novogo tipa', *VIKPSS*, no. 4, 1984, pp. 34–49, at p. 44.

107. Ionescu, 'A Geopolitical Aspect . . .', pp. 266–7.

108. G. Gerasimov in BBC interview, Dec. 1987, in Kusin, 'The "Yugoslavisation" of Soviet–East European Relations?', p. 4.

Select Bibliography

SOVIET SOURCES

Journals (with abbreviations in text)

Bol'shevik
International Affairs (Moscow) (IA(M))
Kommunist
Kommunist vooruzhennykh sil (KVS)
Mirovaia ekonomika i mezhdunarodnye otnosheniia (MEMO)
Mirovoe khoziaĭstvo i mirovaia politika (MKhMP)
Novoe vremia (NV)
Planovoe khoziaĭstvo (PKh)
Politicheskoe samoobrazovanie (PS)
Sovetskoe gosudarstvo (SG)
Sovetskoe gosudarstvo i pravo (SGP)
Sovetskiĭ ezhegodnik mezhdunarodnogo prava (SEMP)
Social Sciences (SS)
Voprosy ekonomiki (VE)
Voprosy filosofii (VF)
Voprosy istorii (VI)
Voprosy istorii KPSS (VIKPSS)
World Marxist Review (WMR)

Aleksandrov, G. F., 'Kosmopolitizm-ideologiia imperialisticheskoĭ bur-zhuazii', *VF*, no. 3, 1948, pp. 174–92.
Alekseev, A., 'Ekonomicheskoe sorevnovanie mezhdu sotsializmom i kapitalizmom', *MEMO*, no. 2, 1957, pp. 13–25.
Bolkhovitinov, N., 'Doktrina Monro: legendy i deĭstvitel'nost'', *MEMO*, no. 9, 1960, pp. 14–26.
Borisov, O. V., 'Soiuz novogo tipa', *VIKPSS*, no. 4, 1984, pp. 34–49.
Borko, Iu., 'O nekotorykh aspektakh izucheniia protsessov zapadnoevropeĭskoĭ integratsii', *MEMO*, no. 2, 1988, pp. 33–50.
Bovin, A., 'Mirnoe sosushchestvovanie i mirovaia sistema sotsializma', *MEMO*, no. 7, 1988, pp. 5–15.
——, 'New Thinking is the Imperative of the Nuclear Age', *SS*, no. 3, 1987, pp. 164–77.
Butenko, A. P., 'Protivorechiia razvitiia sotsializma kak obshchestvennogo stroia', *VF*, no. 10, 1982, pp. 16–29.
——, 'Eshche raz o protivorechiiakh sotsializma', *VF*, no. 2, 1984, pp. 124–9.
Bykov, O., 'SShA i real'nosti mezhdunarodnoĭ razriadki', *MEMO*, no. 8, 1976, pp. 28–38.
——, 'Novoe politicheskoe myshlenie v deĭstvii', *MEMO*, no. 2, 1988, pp. 8–20.
Chernichenko, S. V., 'Sub"ektivnye granitsy mezhdunarodnogo prava i

vnutrenniaia kompetentsiia gosudarstv', *SEMP*, 1985, pp. 101–24.

Dudinskiĭ, I., 'Ekonomicheskaia konsolidatsiia sotsialisticheskikh gosudarstv i evropeĭskaia "integratsiia"', *MEMO*, no. 6, 1960, pp. 3–16.

Farberov, N., 'Leninist Principles of Nation-State Organisation of the USSR', *SS*, no. 1, 1980, pp. 35–42.

Fedoseev, P., 'Razvitie proizvodstvennykh otnosheniĭ pri perekhode ot sotsializma k kommunizmu', *Kommunist*, no. 9, 1958, pp. 12–26.

——, 'Dialektika internatsional'nogo i natsional'nogo v sotsialisticheskom obraze zhizni', *VF*, no. 12, 1981, pp. 24–36.

Frantsev, Iu., 'Ideologiia burzhuaznogo natsionalizma na sluzhbe imperialisticheskoĭ reaktsii', *Bol'shevik*, no. 8, 1947, pp. 39–47.

Frolov, I. T., 'Filosofiia global'nykh problem', *VF*, no. 2, 1980, pp. 29–44.

Gantman, V., 'Imperialisticheskaia "integratsiia" i mezhdunarodnye otnosheniia', *Kommunist*, no. 16, 1962, pp. 96–107.

——, 'Detente and the System of International Relations', *SS*, no. 2, 1980, pp. 171–81.

Gubin, V. F., 'Kommunisticheskiĭ manifest i mezhdunarodnoe pravo', *SEMP*, 1973, pp. 43–62.

Gurvich, G. S., 'Narod, narodnyĭ suverenitet i narodnoe predstavitel'stvo v sovetskoĭ sistemye', *SGP*, no. 12, 1958, pp. 38–47.

Kornilov, F. D., 'Problema suvereniteta i natsional'nogo samoopredeleniia v svete Brest-Litovska i Versalia', *SG*, no. 2, 1929, pp. 3–35.

Inozemtsev, N., 'Mezhdunarodnye otnosheniia novogo tipa', *MEMO*, no. 4, 1957 pp. 72–85.

——, 'The Scientific and Technical Revolution and the Modern World', *SS*, no. 3, 1980, pp. 8–17.

——, 'Razvitie mirovogo sotsializma i novyĭ etap mezhdunarodnykh otnosheniĭ', *Kommunist*, no. 9, 1961, pp. 93–105.

Irinin, O. and F. Nikolaev, 'Sotsialisticheskiĭ internatsionalizm v deĭstvii', *SGP*, no. 12, 1968, pp. 3–9.

Ivanov, I., 'Transnational Corporations in the International Division of Labour', *SS*, no. 3, 1983, pp. 74–85.

——, 'Mezhdunarodnye korporatsii i burzhuaznoe gosudarstvo: al'iansy i konflikty', *MEMO*, no. 1, 1976, pp. 46–59.

Kapchenko, N., 'Foreign Policy and Ideological Struggle Today', *IA(M)*, no. 3, March, 1985, pp. 45–54.

Khachaturov, K., 'U.S. Ideological Aggression in Latin America', *IA(M)*, no. 1, 1986, pp. 64–71.

Khrushchev, N. S., 'Za novye pobedy mirovogo kommunisticheskogo dvizheniia', *Kommunist*, no. 1, 1961, pp. 3–37.

Kirshin, Iu. Ia., 'Problema voiny i mira i sovremennaia epokha', *VF*, no. 5, 1981, pp. 17–28.

Kiva, A., 'Sotsialisticheskaia orientatsiia: nekotorye problemy teorii i praktiki', *MEMO*, no. 10, 1976, pp. 19–32.

Konstantinov, F., 'Internationalism and the World Socialist System', *IA(M)*, no. 7, 1968, pp. 3–9.

——, 'Markistsko-Leninskaia filosofiia. Ee mesto i rol' v sovremennom mire', *VF*, no. 7, 1982, pp. 37–45.

Korolev, B., 'Ideologicheskaia bor'ba na mirovoĭ arene v sovremennykh usloviiakh', *PS*, no. 12, 1975, pp. 70–9.

Korovin, E., 'Mezhdunarodnoe pravo na sovremennom etape', *Bol'shevik*, no. 19, 1946, pp. 24–39.

——, 'Proletarskiĭ internationalizm i mezhdunarodnoe pravo', *SEMP*, 1958, pp. 50–73.

Kortunov, V., 'Novoe politicheskoe myshlenie-imperativ sovremennosti', *MEMO*, no. 10, 1986, pp. 16–25.

Kozhevnikov, F. I. and I. P. Blishchenko, 'Sotsializm i sovremennoe mezhdunarodnoe pravo', *SGP*, no. 4, 1970, pp. 88–104.

Krasin, Iu., 'Leninizm i mirovoĭ revoliutsionnyi protsess', *MEMO*, no. 4, 1969, pp. 3–14.

Ladygin, B., 'Socialist Internationalism', *IA(M)*, no. 6, 1973, pp. 3–10.

Lemin, J., 'K voprosy o protivorechiiakh mezhdu kapitalistichestimi stranami na sovremennom etape', *MEMO*, no. 8, 1960, pp. 25–40.

Leont'ev, A., 'Ekonomicheskie osnovy novoĭ demokratii', *PKh*, no. 4, 1947, pp. 63–79.

Lepeshkin, A. I., 'Suverenitet v sovetskom soiuznom gosudarstve i ego ukreplenie v period razvitogo sotsializma', *SGP*, no. 7, 1976, pp. 26–34.

——, 'Obshchenarodnoe gosudarstvo i ego osnovnye cherty', *SGP*, no. 9, 1962, pp. 3–15.

Levin, I. D., 'K voprosu o sushchnosti znachenii printsipa suvereniteta', *SGP*, no. 6, 1949, pp. 33–46.

Li, V. F., 'Politicheskaia nad stroika v obshchestvakh sotsialisticheska orientatsii', *VF*, no. 9, 1981, pp. 3–16.

Manelis, V. L., 'Edinstvo suvereniteta Soiuza SSR i suvereniteta soiuznykh respublik v period razvernitogo stroitel'stva kommunizma', *SGP*, no. 6, 1964, pp. 17–26.

Minayev, L., 'The International Significance of the Formation of the USSR', *IA(M)*, no. 6, 1982, pp. 8–18.

——, 'American Hegemonism and InterImperialist Contradictions', *IA(M)*, no. 8, 1983, pp. 49–57.

Mitin, M., 'Nerushimoe edinstvo sotsialisticheskikh stran', *Kommunist*, no. 2, 1961, pp. 11–22.

Morozov, Iu., 'Klassovyĭ kharakter sovetskoĭ vneshneĭ politiki', *KVS*, no. 19, Oct. 1975, pp. 9–17.

Osipov, M., 'V. I. Lenin o printsipe mirnogo sosushchestovania dvukh sistem', *MEMO*, no. 10, 1969, pp. 3–13.

Paromov, M., 'Formy i metody ekonomicheskogo sotrudnichestva SSSR i stran narodnoĭ demokratii', *VE*, no. 12, 1950, pp. 34–50.

Plimak, E. G., 'Novoe myshlenie i perspektivy sotsial'nogo obnovleniia mira', *VF*, no. 6, 1987, pp. 73–89.

Pomelov, I., 'Razvitie sotsializma i proletarskiĭ internatsionalizm', *Kommunist*, no. 1, 1957, pp. 15–31.

——, 'KPSS-velikaia progressivnaia sila sovremennosti', *Kommunist*, no. 13, 1962, pp. 11–20.

——, 'Splochenie sil sotsializma i nekotorye voprosy ideologicheskoĭ bor'by v Vengrii', *Kommunist*, no. 10, 1957, pp. 73–90.

Pozdniakov, E., 'Natsional'nye gosudarstvennye i klassovye interesy v mezhdunarodnykh otnoshenniakh', *MEMO*, no. 5, 1988, pp. 3–17.

Ponomarev, B., 'Osnovnye voprosy bor'by s revizioniznom na sovremennom etape', *Kommunist*, no. 8, 1958, pp. 115–31.
Primakov, E., 'Newly Free Countries: Common Features', *SS*, no. 4, 1981, pp. 21–36.
Rubinshteǐn, M., 'Kapitalisticheskie monopolii SShA podzhigateli novoǐ voiny', *PKh*, no. 3, 1949, pp. 66–83.
Rymalov, V. 'Imperializm bez imperii', *MEMO*, no. 10, 1968, pp. 29–51.
Sanakoyev, Sh., 'Foreign Policy of Socialism: Sources and Theory', *IA(M)*, no. 5, 1975, pp. 108–18.
Semenov, V. S., 'Problema protivorechiǐ v usloviiakh sotsializma', *VF*, no. 7, 1982, pp. 17–32.
Shakhnazarov, G., 'The "Great Power" Approach to International Politics', *WMR*, no. 5, 1972, pp. 34–6.
——, 'K probleme sootnosheniia sil v mire', *Kommunist*, no. 3, 1974, pp. 77–89.
——, 'Politika skvoz' prizmu nauki', *Kommunist*, no. 17, 1976, pp. 104–14.
——, 'Governability of the World', *IA(M)*, no. 3, 1988, pp. 17–24.
Shakhnazarov, G. and F. M. Burlatskiǐ, 'O razvitii Marksistko-Leninskoǐ politicheskoǐ nauki', *VF*, no. 12, 1980, pp. 10–23.
Sheinis, V., 'Socio-Economic Differentiation of the Developing Countries', *SS*, no. 2, 1980, pp. 140–50.
Shevtsov, V. S., 'Sovetskoe grazhdanstvo i gosudarstvennyǐ suverenitet', *SGP*, no. 6, 1970, pp. 39–47.
Shitarev, F., 'Edinstvo-istochnik nepobedimosti Marksistsko-Leninskoǐ partiǐ' *Kommunist*, no. 5, 1957, pp. 24–39.
Starushenko, G., 'Mirnoe sosushchestvovanie i revoliutsiia', *Kommunist*, no. 2, 1962, pp. 78–89.
Stepanov, A., 'Soviet Foreign Policy and the Restructuring of International Relations', *IA(M)*, no. 1, 1974, pp. 3–9.
Tadevosian, E. V., 'Internatsionalizm sovetskogo mnogonatsional'nogo gosudarstva', *VF*, no. 11, 1982, pp. 16–29.
Tarabin, Ye., 'Newly Free Countries and International Relations', *IA(M)*, no. 4, 1986, pp. 29–36.
Tikhomirov, M., 'Vneshniaia politika Sovetskogo Soiuza', *MKhMP*, no. 3, 1940, pp. 36–52.
Tolkunov, L., 'Novyǐ etap v razvitii mirovoǐ sistemy sotsializma', *Kommunist*, no. 3, 1961, pp. 14–27.
Tunkin, G. I., 'Sotsialisticheskiǐ internatsionalizm i mezhdunarodnoe pravo', *NV*, no. 51, 1957, pp. 10–11.
——, 'Sorok let sosuschchestvovaniia i mezhdunarodnoe pravo', *SEMP*, 1958, pp. 15–49.
——, 'Novyǐ tip mezhdunarodnykh otnosheniǐ i mezhdunarodnoe prava', *SGP*, no. 1, 1959, pp. 81–94.
Usenko, E. T., '25 let mezhdunarodnoǐ organisatsii novogo tipa', *SEMP*, 1974, pp. 11–38.
Varga, E. 'Demokratiia novogo tipa', *MKhMP*, no. 3, 1947, pp. 3–14.
Vasilenko, V. A., 'Gosudarstvennyǐ suverenitet i mezhdunarodnyǐ dogovor', *SEMP*, 1971, pp. 60–79.
Vereshchetin, V. S. and R. A. Miullerson, 'Novoe myshlenie i mezhdunar-

odnoe pravo', *SGP*, no. 3, 1988, pp. 3–9.
Volkov, M. 'The Imperialist Essence of Collective Neocolonialism', *IA(M)*, no. 4, 1986, pp. 64–71.
Vyshinskiĭ, A. Ia., 'Mezhdunarodnoe pravo i mezhdunarodnaia organizatsiia', *SGP*, no. 1, 1948, pp. 1–24.
Zagladin, V., 'World Balance of Forces and the Development of International Relations', *IA(M)*, no. 3, 1985, pp. 65–79.
——, 'Partiia-narod-sotsializm', *MEMO*, no. 5, 1987, pp. 3–16.

Books (all published in Moscow unless otherwise stated)

Aganbegyan, A., *The Challenge: Economics of Perestroika*, Hutchinson, London, 1988.
Aĭrapetian, M. E. and V. V. Suzhodeev, *Novyĭ tip mezhdunarodnykh otnosheniĭ*, Mysl, 1964.
Anghelov, S., (ed.), *Socialist Internationalism: Theory and Practice of International Relations of a New Type*, Progress Publishers, 1979.
Brutents, K. N., *Sovremennye natsional'no-osvoboditel'nye revoliutsii*, Izdatel'stvo politicheskoĭ literatury, 1974.
——, *National Liberation Revolutions Today*, pts 1 and 2, Progress Publishers, 1977.
Brutin, M., *et al.*, *Leninizm i bor'ba prostu burzhuaznoi ideologii i antikommunizma na sovremennom etape*, Izdatel'stvo nauka, 1970.
Butenko, A. P., *Sotsializm kak mirovaia sistema*, Politizdat, 1984.
——, A. P. (ed.), *Sotsializm i mezhdunarodnye otnosheniia*, Izdatel'stvo nauka, 1975.
Chubar'ian, A. O., *Mirnoe sosushchestvovanie: teoriia i praktika*, Politizdat, 1976.
Dorogin, V., *Suverenitet v sovetskom gosudarstvennom prave*, Akedemiia obshchestvennykh nauk, 1948.
Fedoseyev, P. N., *et al.*, *Lenin and The National Question*, Progress Publishers, 1977.
Fel'dman, P., *Sotsialisticheskie mezhdunarodnye otnosheniia*, Izdatel'stvo nauka, 1981.
Gantman, V. I., *Sistema, struktura i protsess razvitiia sovremennykh mezhdunarodnykh otnosheniĭ*, Izdatel'stvo nauka, 1984.
Gorbachev, M. S., *Perestroika. New Thinking For Our Country And The World*, Collins, London, 1987.
Gromyko, A. A. and B. N. Ponomarev, *Istoriia vneshneĭ politiki SSSR 1945–1980*, Izdatel'stvo nauka, 1981.
Iroshnikov, M., D. Kovalenko and V. Shiskin, *Genesis of the Soviet Federative State (1917–25)*, Progress Publishers, 1982.
Kashlev, Iu. B., *Razriadka v evrope-ot Khel'sinki k Madridu*, Politizdat, 1980.
Kirilin, I. A. (ed.), *Istoriia mezhdunarodnykh otnosheniĭ i vneshneĭ politiki SSSR*, IMO, 1967.
Klimenko, B. M. (ed.), *Slovar' mezhdunarodnogo prava*, Mezhdunarodnye otnosheniia, 1982.

Konstantinov, F. T., *et al.*, *Sotsialisticheskiĭ internatsionalizm v deĭstvii*, *IMO*, 1974.

Korolyov, B. I., *Real Socialism and Ideological Struggle*, Progress Publishers, 1985.

Korovin, E., *Sovremennoe mezhdunarodnoe publichnoe pravo*, Gosudarstvennoe izdatel'stvo, 1926.

——, *et al.*, *Mezhdunarodnoe pravo*, Akademiia nauk SSSR institut prava, 1957.

Kozhevnikov, F. I., (ed.), *Mezhdunarodnoe pravo*, Akademiia nauk SSSR institut prava, 1975.

Krasin, Iu., *The Contemporary Revolutionary Process: Theoretical Essays*, Progress Publishers, 1981.

Kuusinen, O., *O pretendakh na opeku nad narodami evropy*, Ogiz gospolitizdat, 1947.

Lebedev, N., *The USSR in World Politics*, Progress Publishers, 1982.

Leĭbzon, B. M., *Mezhdunarodnoe edinstvo kommunistov*, Politizdat, 1980.

Lenin, V. I., *Sochineniia*, Gosudarstvennoe izdatel'stvo politicheskoĭ literatury, (4th edition, 1941–67, in 45 vols).

Levin, D. B., *Aktual'nye problemy teorii mezhdunarodnogo prava*, Izdatel'stvo nauka, 1974

Levin, I. D., *Suverenitet*, Izdatel'stvo ministerstva iustitsii SSSR, 1948.

Lisovskiĭ, V. I. *Mezhdunarodnoe pravo*, Izdatel'stvo 'vysshaia shkola', 1970.

Luk, I., *Sotsializm i mezhdunarodnoe pravo*, IMO, 1977.

Menzhinskiĭ, V. I., *et al.*, *Mezhdunarodnye organizatsii sotsialisticheskikh stran*, IMO, 1971.

Mitin, M. B. (ed.), *Sotsialisticheskaia ekonomicheskia integratsiia*, Izdatel'stvo ekonomika, 1976.

Narochnitskiĭ, A. L., (ed.), *SSSR v bor'be za mir i bezopasnost' narodov istoricheskiĭ opyt*, Mezhdunarodnye otnosheniia, 1984.

Ostoia-Ovsianyĭ, I. D., *et al.*, *Diplomatiia sotsializma*, IMO, 1973.

Pashukanis, E., *Ocherki po mezhdunarodnomu pravu*, Izdatel'stvo Sovetskoe zakonodatel'stvo, 1935.

Shakhnazarov, G. Kh. (ed.), *Contemporary Political Science in the U.S.A. and Western Europe*, Progress Publishers, 1985.

Shevstov, V. S., *National Sovereignty and the Soviet State*, Progress Publishers, 1974.

Shvetsov, L. A., *Internatsional'naia rol' KPSS v mirovom revoliutsionnom dvizhennii*, Lenizdat, 1972.

Sorokin, A. I. (ed.), *Sovetskie vooruzhennye v usloviiakh razvitogo sotsializma*, Izdatel'stvo nauka, 1985.

Stalin, I. V., *Sochineniia*, Izdatel'stvo politicheskoĭ literatury, 1947–51, in 13 vols.

Stalin, I., *Voprosy Leninizma*, Gospolitizdat, 1952.

Suslov, M. A., *Marksizm-Leninizm i sovremennaia epokha*, Izdatel'stvo politicheskoĭ literatury, 1982.

Tarasov, F. S., *SShA i latinskaia amerika*, Izdatel'stvo politicheskoĭ literatury, 1972.

Tunkin, G. I., *Voprosy teorii mezhdunarodnogo prava*, Iuridicheskoĭ literatury, 1962.

Ul'ianovskiĭ, R. A., *Pobedy i trudnosti natsional'no-osvobitel'noi bor'by*, Politizdat, 1985.
Ushakov, N. A., *Suverenitet v sovremennom mezhdunarodnom prave*, IMO, 1963.
Valiuzhenich, A. V., *Vneshne-politicheskaia propaganda SShA*, IMO, 1973.
Zarodov, K., *Leninizm i sovremennye problemy perekhoda ot kapitalizma k sotsializmu*, Mysl, 1981.
Zuev, V. I., *Mirovaia sistema sotsializma: ekonomicheskie i politicheskie aspekty edinstva*, IMO, 1975.
Zhurkin, V. V. and E. M. Primakov, *Mezhdunarodnye konflikty*, IMO, 1972.

NON-SOVIET SOURCES

Journals

Achminov, H., 'Khrushchev's "Creative Development" of Marxism-Leninism', *Studies on the Soviet Union*, no. 3, 1962, pp. 5–17.
Aspaturian, V. V., 'Soviet Global Power and the Correlation of Forces', *Problems of Communism*, May–June, 1980, pp. 1–18.
Bell, D., 'Ideology and Soviet Politics', *Slavic Review*, Dec. 1965, pp. 591–603.
Comey, D. D., 'Marxist-Leninist Ideology and Soviet Policy', *Studies in Soviet Policy*, vol. ii, no. 4, 1962, pp. 301–19.
Davletshin, T., 'Limited Sovereignty: The Soviet Claim to Intervene in Defence of Socialism', *Bulletin of the Institute for the Study of the USSR*, vol. xvi, no. 8, 1969, pp. 3–9.
Dawisha, Karen and Jonathan Valdez, 'Socialist Internationalism in Eastern Europe', *Problems of Communism*, March–April 1987, pp. 1–14.
Evans Jr, Alfred B., 'The Polish Crisis in the 1980s and Adaptation in Soviet Ideology', *Journal of International Communist Studies*, vol. 2, no. 3, 1986, pp. 263–85.
——, 'Developed Socialism in Soviet Ideology', *Soviet Studies*, vol. xxix, no. 3, 1987, pp. 409–28.
Garthoff, Raymond L., 'The Concept of the Balance of Power in Soviet Policy Making', *World Politics*, vol 4, 1951–2, pp. 85–111.
Gati, Charles, 'Gorbachev and Eastern Europe', *Foreign Affairs*, Summer 1987, pp. 958–75.
Ginsburgs, G. 'A Case Study in the Soviet Use of International Law: Eastern Poland in 1939', *AJIL*, vol. 52, 1958, pp. 69–84.
——, 'Socialist Internationalism and State Sovereignty', *YBWA*, 1971, pp. 38–55.
Glazer, Stephen G., 'The Brezhnev Doctrine', *International Lawyer*, vol. 5, no. 1, 1969–70, pp. 168–79.
Griffith, William E., 'Superpower Problems in Europe: A Comparative Assessment', *Orbis*, vol. 29, no. 4, 1986, pp. 735–50.
Hazard, John N., 'Renewed Emphasis upon a Socialist International Law',

AJIL, vol. 65, no. 1, 1971, pp. 142–8.

Hofheinz, P., 'Piecing Together the Gorbachev Puzzle', *Jl. of Communist Studies*, vol. 3, no. 2, 1987, pp. 161–77.

Ionescu, Ghita, 'A Geopolitical Aspect of an Eminently Geopolitical Crisis', *Government and Opposition*, vol. 22, no. 3, 1987, pp. 259–69.

Korey, W., 'The Comintern and the Genealogy of the Brezhnev Doctrine', *Problems of Communism*, vol. 18, 1969, pp. 52–8.

Korowicz, Marek Stanislaw, 'Some Present Aspects of Sovereignty in International Law', *Recueil Des Cours, Académie De Droit International De La Haye*, no. 1, 1961, pp. 5–118.

Kux, E., 'Contradictions in Soviet Socialism', *Problems of Communism*, vol. 33, 1984, pp. 1–27.

Lendvai, P., 'How To Combine Detente With Soviet Hegemony', *Survey: American Journal of East European Studies*, vol. 77, Autumn 1970, pp. 75–92.

Lerner, Warren, 'Attempting a Revolution From Without', *Studies on the Soviet Union*, vol. xi, no. 4, 1971, pp. 94–106.

Luers, W. H., 'The U.S. and Eastern Europe', *Foreign Affairs*, Summer 1987, pp. 976–94.

Mitchell, R. Judson, 'The Revised "Two Camps" Doctrine in Soviet Foreign Policy', *Orbis*, vol. xvi, no. 1, 1972, pp. 21–34.

Mitchell, R. Judson and Alan T. Leonhard, 'Changing Soviet Attitudes Toward International Law: An Incorporative Approach', *Georgia Journal of International and Comparative Law*, vol. 6, 1976, pp. 227–44.

Schroeder, G. E., 'Gorbachev: Radically Implementing Brezhnev's Reforms', *Soviet Economy*, no. 2, 1986, pp. 289–301.

Schwarzenberger, G. 'The Forms of Sovereignty', *Current Legal Problems*, vol. 10, 1957, Stevens, London.

Service, R., 'Gorbachev's Political Reforms', *Jl. of Communist Studies*, vol. 3, no. 2, June 1987, pp. 276–85.

Sestanovich, S., 'Gorbachev's Foreign Policy: A Diplomacy of Decline', *Problems of Communism*, January–February 1988, pp. 1–15.

Shearman, Peter, 'Soviet Foreign Policy in Africa and Latin America: A Comparative Case Study', *Jl. of International Studies*, vol. 15, no. 3, 1986, pp. 339–66.

Shlapentokh, V., 'The XXVII Congress – A Case Study of the Shaping of a New Party Ideology', *Soviet Studies*, vol. xl, no. 1, 1986, pp. 1–20.

Soloveitchik, Samson, 'International Law as "Instrument of Politics"', *University of Kansas City Law Review*, vol. 21, 1953, pp. 169–83.

Svec, Milan, 'The Prague Spring: 20 Years Later', *Foreign Affairs*, vol. 66, no. 5, 1988, pp. 981–1001.

Urban, Pavel, 'The Nationality Question', *Studies on the Soviet Union*, no. 1, 1969, pp. 56–72.

Valenta, Jiri, 'From Prague to Kabul: The Soviet Style of Invasion', *International Security*, vol. 5, no. 2, 1980, pp. 114–41.

Vali, Ferenc A., 'Soviet Satellite Status and International Law', *JAG Journal*, Oct.–Nov. 1961, pp. 169–72.

Valkenier, E. K., 'Revolutionary Change in the Third World: Recent Soviet

Assessments', *World Politics*, no. 3, 1986, pp. 415–34.
Vishniak, Mark, 'Sovereignty in Soviet Law', *The Russian Review*, Jan. 1949, pp. 34–45.
——, 'Eurocommunism and Eastern Europe', *Problems of Communism*, March– April 1978, pp. 41–5.
Vernon, Graham D., 'Controlled Conflict: Soviet perceptions of Peaceful Coexistence', *Orbis*, no. 2, 1979, pp. 271–97.
Zimmerman, William, 'Hierarchical Regional Systems and the Politics of System Boundaries', *International Organisation*, Winter 1972, pp. 18–36.
——, 'Dependency Theory and the Soviet-East European Hierarchical Regional System: Initial Tests', *Slavic Review*, vol. xxxvii, 1978, pp. 604–21.
Zorgbibe, Charles, 'La doctrine soviétique de la "souveraineté limitée"', *Revue géneralé de droit international publique*, no. 4, 1970, pp. 872–905.

Books

Adelman, Jonathan R., *The Superpowers and Revolution*, Praeger, New York, 1986.
Avineri, S., *Varieties of Marxism*, Martinus Nijhoff, The Hague, 1977.
Bernier, Ivan, *International Legal Aspects of Federalism*, Longman, London, 1973.
Beyme, Klaus von, *The Soviet Union in World Politics*, Gower, Aldershot, Hants, 1987.
Borys, Jurij, *The Russian Communist Party and the Sovietisation of the Ukraine: A Study in the Communist Doctrine of the Self-Determination of Nations*, Norstedt, Stockholm, 1960.
Bradsher, Henry S., *Afghanistan and the Soviet Union*, Duke University Press, Durham, 1985.
Brzezinski, Z., *The Soviet Bloc: Unity and Conflict*, Harvard University Press, Cambridge, Mass. 1960.
——, *Ideology and Power in Soviet Politics*, Praeger, New York.
Claudin, F., *The Communist Movement from Comintern to Cominform*, Penguin, Harmondsworth, 1975.
Dallin, A. (ed.), *Soviet Conduct in World Affairs*, Greenwood Press, West Point, Conn., 1975.
Davis, Lynn Etheridge, *The Cold War Begins: Soviet-American Conflict Over Eastern Europe*, Princeton University Press, New Jersey, 1974.
Dawisha, Karen, *The Kremlin and The Prague Spring*, University of California Press, Berkeley, 1984.
Eran, O., *The Mezhdunarodniki: An Assessment of Professional Expertise in the Making of Soviet Foreign Policy*, Turtledove, Ramat Gan, Israel, 1979.
Franck, Thomas M. and Edward Weisband, *Word Politics: Verbal Strategy Among the Superpowers*, Oxford University Press, New York, 1971.
Gerner, Kristian, *The Soviet Union and Central Europe in the Post-War Era*, Gower, Aldershot, Hants., 1985.
Hutchings, Robert L. *Soviet-East European Relations: Consolidation and Conflict 1968–1980*, University of Wisconsin Press, Madison, 1983.

James, Alan, *Sovereign Statehood*, Allen and Unwin, London, 1986.
Kaufman, Edy, *The Superpowers and their Spheres of Influence*, Croom Helm, London, 1976.
Keal, P., *Unspoken Rules and Superpower Dominance*, St Martin's Press, New York, 1983.
Kelsen, Hans, *The Communist Theory of Law*, Stevens, London, 1955.
Kolakowski, Leszek, *Main Currents of Marxism* (3 volumes), Clarendon Press, Oxford, 1978.
Kubálková, V., and A. Cruickshank, *Marxism-Leninism and Theory of International Relations*, Routledge Kegan Paul, London, 1980.
Lewis, Paul G. (ed.), *Eastern Europe: Political Crisis and Legitimation*, Croom Helm, London, 1984.
Lider, Julian, *Correlation of Forces: An Analysis of Marxist-Leninist Concepts*, Gower, Aldershot, Hants., 1986.
Lynch, Allen, *The Soviet Study of International Relations*, Cambridge University Press, 1987.
Medvedev, Z., *Gorbachev*, Basil Blackwell, Oxford, 1986.
Mićunović, Veljko, *Moscow Diary*, Chatto and Windus, London, 1980.
Mitchell, R. Judson, *Ideology of a Superpower, Contemporary Soviet Doctrine on International Relations*, Hoover Press, Stanford, 1982.
Moreton, Edwina, *East Germany and the Warsaw Alliance: The Politics of Detente*, Westview Press, Boulder, Colo., 1978.
Nollau, Gunther, *International Communism and World Revolution*, Greenwood Press, Westport, Conn., 1961.
Pipes, R., *The Formation of the Soviet Union: Communism and Nationalism 1917–23*, Atheneum, New York, 1980.
Ramundo, B. A., *Peaceful Coexistence, International Law in the Building of Communism*, Johns Hopkins Press, Baltimore, 1967.
Rozman, M., *A Mirror For Socialism: Soviet Criticisms of China*, Princeton University Press, New Jersey, 1985.
Seliger, Martin, *The Marxist Conception of Ideology*, Cambridge University Press, 1977.
Seroka, J. and M. D. Simon (eds.), *Developed Socialism in the Soviet Bloc: Political Theory and Political Reality*, Westview Press, Boulder, Colo., 1982.
Shlapentokh, V., *Soviet Public Opinion and Ideology: Mythology and Pragmatism in Interaction*, Praeger, New York, 1986.
Szporluk, R. (ed.), *The Influence of Eastern Europe and the Soviet West on the USSR*, Praeger, New York, 1975.
Skilling, W. Gordon, *Czechoslovakia's Interrupted Revolution*, Princeton University Press, 1976.
Schmidt-Hauer, C., *Gorbachev: The Path To Power*, Pan, London, 1986.
Taras, R., *Ideology in a Socialist State: Poland 1956–1983*, Cambridge University Press, 1984.
Terry, Sarah M., *Soviet Policy in Eastern Europe*, Yale University Press, New Haven, 1984.
Uldricks, Teddy J., *Diplomacy and Ideology. The Origins of Soviet Foreign Relations 1917–1930*, Sage, Beverly Hills, 1979.

Unger, Aryeh L., *Constitutional Development in the USSR: A Guide to the Soviet Constitutions*, Methuen, London, 1981.
Wettig, Gerhard, *Community and Conflict in the Socialist Camp. The Soviet Union, East Germany and the German Problem 1965–72*, Hurst, London, 1975.
Zimmerman, William, *Soviet Perspectives on International Relations 1956–1967*, Princeton University Press, New Jersey, 1969.

Index